MACRO
economics
A N A L Y S I S
& P O L I C Y

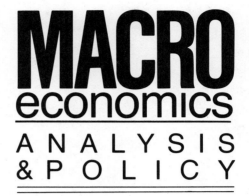

MACRO economics
ANALYSIS & POLICY

Lloyd G. Reynolds

Sterling Professor of Economics
Yale University

1985   Fifth Edition

RICHARD D. IRWIN, INC.
Homewood, Illinois   60430

ISBN 0–256–03218–1

Library of Congress Catalog Card No. 84–82026

Printed in the United States of America

1 2 3 4 5 6 7 8 9 0 V 2 1 0 9 8 7 6 5

for MARY

Preface

The past 20 years have brought great changes in macroeconomics. Inflation has emerged as a stubborn continuing problem. Monetary policy has come increasingly to center stage. Fine tuning, once taken for granted, has become controversial. The Phillips curve view of the world has dropped out of fashion. A vast amount of quantitative research has clarified structural relations in the economy.

A text correctly lags behind the frontier of the subject; but it should not lag too much. This edition, therefore, is not an ordinary revision. It is a major rethinking and reorganization of the subject.

Money has been moved up to a more prominent position, immediately after the simple Keynesian model and before the discussion of inflation. We know more about inflation than we did a decade ago, and I trust that students will find the rewritten chapter on that subject intellectually satisfying. I have made a clearer separation between analysis of how the economy operates (Chapters 4–10) and discussion of policy issues (Chapters 11–13). The policy discussion is more skeptical and I hope more judicious than it was before, reflecting the accumulated experience of the past 30 years.

I have made a strenuous effort to limit the discussion to central concepts, which belong at the principles level rather than at more advanced levels. And I have tried to write concisely, to present more ideas in fewer pages than most other books in the field. Some relatively technical material has been placed in chapter appendixes to remove possible stumbling blocks in the main text. In short, the book is written for the student rather than to impress the profession.

The policy chapters are not intended to "solve" our macroeconomic problems but rather to demonstrate how economics can help us think more effectively about them. The discussion is not meant to be exhaustive or to duplicate the large amount of supplementary material now available. I have tried to say just enough to provide an effective bridge to this material and to interest students in exploring it.

All this will help, I hope, in making economics an exciting subject for your students, as it deserves to be.

I am grateful to several colleagues at other places who reviewed the manuscript and made suggestions for improvement. Thanks also to Adrienne Cheasty, who assembled the statistical material; and special thanks to Roberta Milano-Ottenbriet for her speed and skill in typing draft chapters and compiling and checking the final manuscript.

LLOYD G. REYNOLDS

Contents

Introduction

Basic Economic Concepts

1

What Economics Is About

The theory of economics does not furnish a body of settled conclusions immediately applicable to policy. It is a method rather than a doctrine, an apparatus of the mind, a technique of thinking, which helps its possessor to draw correct conclusions.

—JOHN MAYNARD KEYNES

In a general way, we all know what economics is about. It is concerned with the production, distribution, and use of goods. It deals with the activities of the 5 million businesses, 110 million workers, and 60 million households that produced and consumed more than $3 trillion worth of output in the United States in 1984. As Adam Smith said, economics is "an inquiry into the nature and causes of the wealth of nations."

But how is economics concerned with these things? What is its "apparatus of the mind"? This chapter deals with several key aspects of economics.

The central fact of economic life is *scarcity* of goods and of resources to produce goods. This forces individuals and also the nation to choose what shall be produced and who shall get how much of what is produced.

Economics is a special way of thinking which uses simplified *models* to explore reality. The use of such models to analyze and explain economic events is called *positive economics*.

But economics is also a policy science with important applications in business and government. Decisions about proper government action involve what is called *normative economics*.

PRODUCTION AND THE CIRCULAR FLOW

Economics deals with the production, distribution, and use of *goods*, including material goods or *commodities* and nonmaterial goods or *services*.

3

A good is a *free good* if there is so much of it that people can have all they want at a zero price. Water in a mountain stream is an example. A good is *scarce* if there is not enough of it for everyone to have all they want at a zero price. Coffee on the supermarket shelf is an example. Economics deals only with scarce goods, since free goods present no problems of supply or distribution.

The American economy is usually called a *private enterprise economy,* or a *market economy.* Government produces some goods—police and fire protection, public education, streets and highways. But most goods are produced by *businesses.* We use this term in a broad sense. A farm is a business. So is the office of a doctor, lawyer, or other professional person. Instead of *business,* we could say *producing unit,* but the former term is simpler and more familiar.

In order to carry on production, a business needs *inputs,* also called *factors of production.* The most important inputs are *labor* and *capital,* which have a special meaning in economics. *Labor* means any kind of physical or mental effort exerted in production. It includes the work of the corporation executive, lawyer, or college teacher as well as that of the farmer, salesclerk, or plumber.

The term *capital* is especially confusing. In everyday speech it is often used to mean a sum of money representing the assets of a corporation or an individual. We say that a company has a capital of $2 billion or that a person is worth $200,000. Such sums of money are important; but when that is what we mean, we should be careful to say *financial capital.*

In economics, the term *capital* used alone means *physical capital,* or *instruments of production.* Machinery in an automobile assembly plant is capital. So is the building which houses the machinery. So is any building used for production—a department store, an office building, a hotel. Raw materials and semifinished goods in the hands of producers are also capital.

The factors of production are owned by individuals. In the case of a company, this may seem not to be true. Doesn't the Coca-Cola Company own the plants and machinery it operates? Yes, but who owns Coca-Cola? The company, and thus all of its assets, belongs to the many thousands of people who own common stock in the company.

The core of a private enterprise economy, then, consists of a twofold interchange between individuals and businesses, illustrated in Figure 1–1. Individuals supply labor and capital to businesses and receive money income in return. This exchange is shown in the lower half of the figure. Businesses use labor and capital to produce goods that are sold to individuals for money. This exchange appears in the upper half of the figure.

This diagram shows the circular flow of economic activity. It can easily be modified to include the activities of government, as shown in Figure 1–2. Government buys goods from businesses, and it also levies taxes

FIGURE 1-1
The circular flow of economic activity

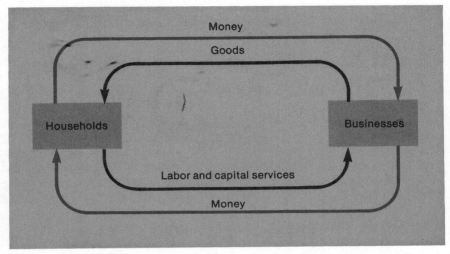

In the bottom half of the diagram, people sell labor and capital services to businesses for money. In the top half of the diagram, people spend this money on goods produced by businesses.

on businesses. These two flows appear on the right-hand side of the diagram. The goods purchased from business are combined with labor hired by government to produce *public goods*. On the left side of the diagram we see that government pays out income to individuals and collects taxes from individuals.

This network of activities can be viewed in two different ways, which are called *macroeconomics* and *microeconomics*. *Macroeconomics* looks at large totals for the economy as a whole. It asks questions like this: Why was the rate of national output at the end of 1983 almost 7 percent higher than at the end of 1982? Why did employment rise by 4 million over this period? Why, in spite of this, was 8.2 percent of the labor force still unemployed at the end of 1983?

Microeconomics, on the other hand, looks at the details of the economy. It holds a microscope over particular industries and occupations. It asks questions like this: In 1983, why did the United States produce 2,425 million bushels of wheat and 83 million tons of steel? Why did the wheat sell for $4 a bushel and the steel for $350 a ton? Why did plumbers earn, on the average, $20 per hour, steelworkers $15 per hour, secretaries $8 per hour?

Which approach to economics should come first in an elementary course? Macroeconomics is usually considered the liveliest branch of the subject. It deals with the big picture—prosperity, depression, changes

FIGURE 1-2
The circular flow with government added

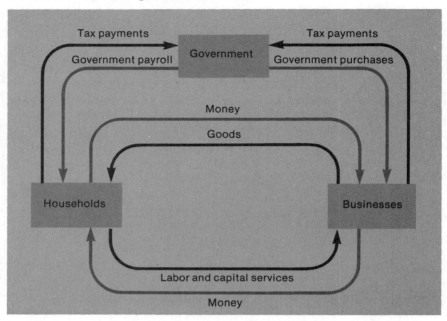

The flows between businesses and households are just the same as in the previous figure. Now in addition, businesses get money for goods sold to government and also make tax payments. People get money by working for government and also make tax payments.

in the general level of prices, output, employment—things which are in the newspapers every day. So teachers and texts often lead off with macroeconomic issues because of their popular appeal.

The difficulty is that it is hard to understand the whole without understanding the parts. If total output is rising, this must be because many businesses are deciding to increase their production. Why are they doing this? How does a business decide what to produce, how much to produce, what prices to charge, what wage rates to pay? These microeconomic questions are a necessary foundation for macroeconomics.

Since microeconomics is basic, we explain some of the main micro ideas right at the start, in Chapter 2. Having laid this foundation, we will then come back to macroeconomics in Chapter 3.

THE CENTRAL ECONOMIC PROBLEM: SCARCITY AND CHOICE

One fact of economic life stares you in the face: you don't have enough money to buy everything you want. Most other people are in the same position. On the surface, this looks like a shortage of money. But printing twice as much money would not solve the problem. The underlying fact is a scarcity of goods: No economy can produce nearly as many goods as people would like to consume. And behind this lies a scarcity of resources to produce goods. The United States has just so much labor, capital goods, land, and natural resources, and this limits the size of our national output.

Choice at the personal level

Scarcity forces a choice among alternatives. Everyone faces this problem at a personal level. Your income will not allow you to buy everything you would like to have, so you are forced to budget, to decide how much of each good to buy. Time is also scarce. There are only 24 hours in the day, so you must budget—or, as economists say, *allocate* your time among competing uses.

Choosing one thing involves giving up something else. For example, you have $10 with which you can buy a book or go to a football game. You buy the book. What did it cost you? You might say, ten dollars. But what it really cost you is the football game you might have enjoyed instead. Economists call this *opportunity cost*—the cost of foregone alternatives.

Use of time also involves a cost. If you spend three hours this evening studying economics, the opportunity cost of the knowledge you gain is the pleasure you might have gotten from spending those three hours visiting with friends or watching a movie.

What does it cost to spend a year in college? One cost is the goods which you (or your parents) might have bought with the money spent on tuition, books, and fees. The most important cost item, however, is the value of your time. Had you not been studying, you could have been working, which would have meant more income for you and more output for the nation. What you do *not* produce while studying is the main opportunity cost of education.

Choice at the national level

The opportunity cost principle applies also at the national level. What is the cost of requiring strip-mining companies to clean up after themselves and to restore the soil surface to its original condition? This will raise the money cost of mining coal and will eventually raise the price of coal to consumers. The underlying fact, however, is that the cleanup activities require economic resources—workers, supervisors, engineers, trucks, and bulldozers. If these resources were not being used for land restoration, they could be producing something else. What they do not produce is the real cost of the cleanup activities.

A useful way of viewing economic choice at the national level is illustrated in Figure 1–3. We imagine a simple economy producing only food and clothing. If all resources were devoted to food production, *OA* units could be produced. If all resources were put into clothing, an output of *OB* units would be possible. If resources are divided between the two products, the economy can produce various combinations of food and clothing, represented by points on the line *AB*. Point *E*, for example, shows that if the economy produces the amount of food shown by the distance from *E* to the horizontal axis, then it can produce only the amount of clothing shown by the distance from *E* to the vertical axis. *E, F,* and other points on *AB* show maximum feasible combinations of food and clothing which can be produced with the resources available.

FIGURE 1–3
The production possibilities curve

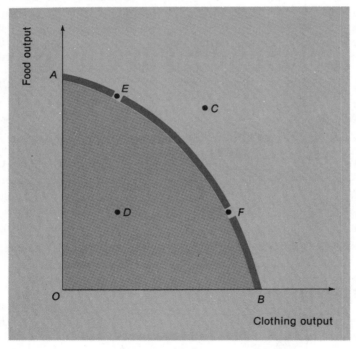

Any point on *AB* shows maximum feasible quantities of food and clothing which can be produced with the resources available. *E* and *F*, for example, represent feasible output combinations. *C*, which lies outside the production frontier, is not a feasible combination. *D*, which lies inside the frontier, is feasible but not desirable, since more could be produced with available resources.

AB is usually called a *production possibilities curve* or *production frontier*. It separates feasible output combinations (shown by the shaded area below AB) from combinations which are not possible (shown by the region above AB). Point C, for example, cannot be attained with the available resources.

An economy can never operate outside its production frontier; and it will not want to operate inside the frontier. Look, for example, at point D. This is a feasible output combination but not a desirable one. Why? Because by moving, say, to E the economy could produce as much clothing as at D but considerably more food. Alternatively, moving to F would mean considerably more clothing with no sacrifice of food. A point such as D means that the economy's resources are not being used most effectively.

But there are many points on the frontier, many bundles of goods which can be produced with the same resources. This is why there is always a problem of *choice*—the guns-versus-butter choice which a nation faces in wartime, the machinery-versus-housing choice faced by planners in the USSR, and so on.

Why is AB concave downward? What is the economic meaning of drawing it this way? Suppose we start moving up the curve from point B. At the beginning, we can get much more food by giving up only a small amount of clothing. But as we move up the curve, there is a steady increase in the amount of clothing we have to sacrifice *for the same increase in food production*. Finally, as we approach point A, we are giving up a large amount of clothing for only a small increase in food.

This is what the curve is telling us. But does what it tells us make sense? Yes, it does. The reason is that the economy's resources are not equally well adapted to producing the two goods. Some resources are relatively more suited for, and therefore more productive in, the clothing industry; while others are not very well suited to clothing but are better for food. So what happens as we start moving up from B by shifting resources from clothing to food? The first resources diverted to food will be those which are least productive in clothing and whose transfer produces only a small drop in clothing output. This is certainly what an all-wise economic planner would do; and it is also what would happen in a market economy like our own, for reasons which will become clearer as the course goes on.

But as more and more resources are transferred to food, we shall have to draw on resources which are better and better adapted to clothing production, and the sacrifice of clothing output will increase steadily. Finally, as we approach A, we are transferring resources whose relative productivity in clothing is greatest, and are sacrificing a large amount of clothing for a small amount of food.

Another important characteristic of the production possibilities curve is that it does not remain stationary. The output capacity of an economy normally is increasing. There are two reasons for this. The first is growth of the supply of productive resources. The labor force increases through population growth. The stock of buildings, machinery, and other capital goods increases through investment. Many countries even have a land frontier, and can bring new land into production as needed.

The second reason is improvement in technology, which enables us to get more output from the same quantities of resources. In fact, technical progress is *defined* as an increase in the quantity of output which can be produced from a given input of resources.

In Figure 1–4, we show an increase in output capacity by moving the production possibilities curve upward, or to the northeast. If the in-

FIGURE 1–4
An increase in production possibilities

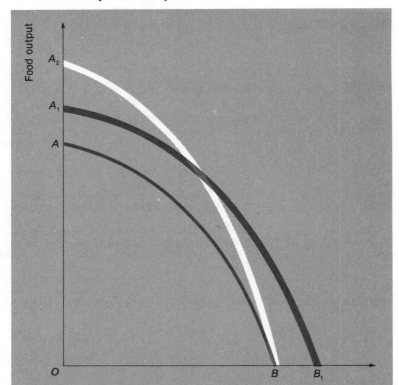

The production capacity of an economy normally grows over time through increase in resource supplies and improvement of technology. We show this graphically by moving the production possibilities curve northeast, from AB to A_1B_1. If the source of expansion is improved technology in food production, the new production possibilities curve would look like A_2B.

crease in capacity affects both kinds of output equally, the new production possibilities curve would look like A_1B_1. But this is not the only possibility. Suppose the increased capacity comes from a technical change affecting only food production—say, the discovery of hybrid corn. Then the new production possibilities curve will look like A_2B. The interesting point revealed by this illustration is that a technical improvement, even though it is limited to one product, enables us to have more of *both* products. Increased productivity in the food industry makes it possible to increase food output while at the same time *releasing* resources from that industry, which can then be employed to raise the output of clothing.

The production possibilities curve alone cannot tell us what combination of the two goods will actually be produced. This depends also on preferences, which are influenced by custom, climate, and other factors. In Uganda, where all seasons are warm and clothing needs are minimal, a point close to A may be preferred. But people in Iceland might choose a point closer to B.

THINK ABOUT THIS

1. Many people deny that scarcity is a serious problem in the American economy. The real problems, they argue, are:
   a. To make sure that our productive capacity is fully utilized—to achieve ''full employment.''
   b. To distribute our output equitably among the population so that no one lives in poverty.
   In view of these arguments, can we still maintain that scarcity is the central economic problem?
2. Consider the following facts:
   a. U.S. output is roughly double that of the USSR.
   b. The United States allocates about 20 percent of its resources to producing capital goods, while the USSR allocates 30 percent.
   How could you illustrate these facts on a production possibilities diagram?

THE BASIC DECISIONS: WHAT, HOW, AND FOR WHOM?

These questions sum up the key decisions in any national economy. *What* goods shall be produced? *How* shall they be produced, as regards production methods? *Who* shall get what share of the national output?

The first question is where to operate on the production possibilities curve. Why, in a particular year, does the economy turn out just so many machine tools, trucks, bushels of corn, boxes of cornflakes? A large part of microeconomics is devoted to answering this question. For private consumer goods, shoppers go to market, and how much they choose to buy is important in shaping the pattern of production. For government-produced goods, which are not marketed at a price, decisions are reached by legislators and administrators; and how these decisions are reached is an important subject for economic analysis. Output of capital goods depends heavily on whether business concerns think they can make a profit by buying and using such goods.

In addition to deciding what to produce, an economy must decide how to produce it. There are often several ways to produce a good, usually differing in degree of mechanization. In India, some cotton cloth is still produced by hand-loom weavers using very simple equipment. Similar cloth is produced by highly automated textile mills in South Carolina.

Where alternative methods are available, which should be used? The most highly mechanized method? Not necessarily. The economically correct method is that which yields lowest cost per unit of output. This *least-cost production method* depends on the cost of labor and capital, which in turn depends on their relative abundance in the economy. The correct choice for India, where labor is cheap and capital expensive, will not be the same as that for the United States, where things are just the opposite.

After deciding what to produce and how to produce it, we face the last decision: who shall get how much of each good? In a money-using economy, this depends on the distribution of money income. A family with an income of $30,000 a year can buy, and may choose to buy, more of everything than a family with $15,000 a year.

The distribution of money income is mainly determined by the quantity of resources—labor services or services of land and capital goods—which the family contributes to production and by the price which these services command in the market. But income distribution is also influenced by government. Income is subject to taxation, and there may be a considerable difference between the distribution of income before and after taxes. People also receive some income not earned in current production, such as old-age pensions, unemployment compensation, veterans benefits, or welfare payments. These types of income are called *transfer payments*. Since they go mainly to the lowest income brackets, they have a leveling effect on the distribution of income.

HOW ECONOMISTS THINK

The languages of economics

If you take a college course in history or chemistry, you are doing more of what you have already done in high school. You know what you are up against. But high schools rarely teach economics, so students approach it with a certain fear of the unknown. Economics has the reputation of being complicated and difficult. How much is there to this?

It would not be honest to say that you won't be called on for hard thinking later in this course. You will be, and if you aren't willing to stretch your mind, stop now. But some of your fears may be groundless, and a few reassuring words are in order.

Economics is a semisolid subject, not as precise as the natural sciences but more so than most nonscientific subjects. As J. M. Keynes remarked, "Economics is an easy subject in which few excel." The solidity comes from the fact that economics deals with relations among *quantities*, which are usually measurable; and quantitative relations lend themselves to mathematical expression.

"I'd like to study economics, but I can't do math." How often does one hear this despairing cry. The truth is that propositions in economics can be expressed in four ways: in English prose, in arithmetical tables, in geometry, and in algebra. These are simply different languages, which are translatable into each other. The choice among them is largely a matter of taste. My own preference is for prose, arithmetic, and geometry. If you have trouble reading an ordinary two-dimensional graph, some coaching and practice are in order. But the key ideas in each chapter are also explained in prose and illustrated by arithmetic.

"Splendid, my boy, splendid! You're really
putting two and two together, now."

From The Wall Street Journal, *with permission
of Cartoon Features Syndicate.*

The four alternative languages can be illustrated with the Principle of Demand.

1. Verbal expression.   A decrease in the price of a product, everything else in the economy remaining unchanged, will lead to an increase in the quantity purchased.

2. Arithmetical illustration.   Take a particular product, say gasoline. It seems probable that if the price of gasoline is higher, people will use less of it. But how much less? Unlike the scientist, we cannot experiment by shifting the price of gasoline up and down and observing what happens. But over past history the price has varied a good deal and so has the quantity consumed, and there are statistical methods by which we can estimate the relation between the two.

Suppose we find that the relation is as shown in Table 1–1. At a price of $2.60 a gallon, only 8 million gallons of gasoline would be bought per day. At lower prices, larger quantities would be purchased. If the price got as low as $1.00 a gallon, consumers would buy 16 million gallons a day. This schedule, showing how much would be bought at each of many alternative prices, is called a *demand schedule.*

TABLE 1–1
Demand schedule for gasoline

Price of Gasoline (dollars per gallon)	Quantity of Gasoline Purchased (millions of gallons per day)
2.60	8
2.40	9
2.20	10
2.00	11
1.80	12
1.60	13
1.40	14
1.20	15
1.00	16

3. Geometric equivalent.   It is easy enough to plot the information in Table 1–1 in graph form. It is customary to plot prices on the vertical axis and quantities on the horizontal axis. We know that at a price of $2.60, purchases are 8 million gallons a day. So we plot a point with coordinates (8,2.60), which is point 1 on the diagram. Going down to a price of $2.40, we see that sales are 9 million gallons, so we plot point 2 with coordinates (9,2.40). Similarly we derive each of the other points on the diagram. (See Figure 1–5.)

Since the price can be varied by as little as one tenth of a cent per gallon there are many other price-quantity points lying in between the

FIGURE 1–5
Demand schedule for gasoline

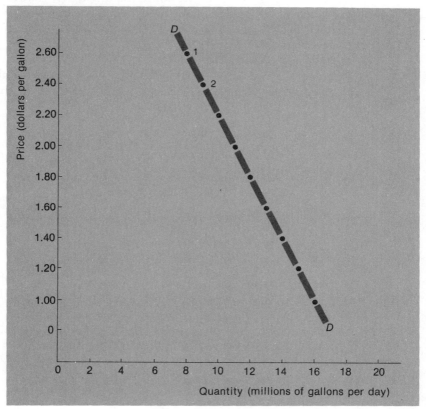

ones we have charted. This warrants our linking up points 1, 2, and so on by the solid line *DD*. This is the demand schedule in graphic form, usually called a *demand curve,* since it is not necessarily a straight line. Each point on *DD* shows the quantity which would be demanded at a particular price. *DD* slopes downward to the right because of the principle of demand.

Geometrical illustrations or graphs are very useful in discussing economics. It's often true that a picture is worth a thousand words. So ability to read a simple graph is the one skill you will need in later chapters. If you aren't used to reading graphs, study the explanation in the study guide or some other source and then practice drawing them yourself until you feel comfortable with them.

An economic graph is not something to be looked at and admired like a picture on the wall. It is a working tool like a saw or hammer.

So when you meet one of these graphs, attack it aggressively and master it. Sit down with a sketch pad and draw the graph for yourself. What is the graph saying? What do the different lines mean? What would it mean to draw these lines differently? The more of this you do, the more self-confident you will become.

4. Algebraic expression. While we won't be using this very much, it is another alternative language. What we were saying above is that the quantity of gasoline purchased *(Q_g)* is a *function* of the price of gasoline, a relation which can be written as

$$Q_g = F(P_g).$$

If we define Q_g as millions of gallons per day and P_g as the price in cents per gallon, the equation for Figure 1–5 is

$$Q_g = 21 - 0.05P_g.$$

Note that this equation expresses the principle of demand: An *increase* in price leads to a *decrease* in quantity sold.

THINK ABOUT THIS

There is a principle of supply corresponding to the principle of demand: An increase in the price of a good—everything else in the economy remaining unchanged—will lead to an increase in the quantity offered by sellers. How would you express this principle in the languages of arithmetic, geometry, and algebra?

Economic models and their uses

There is another characteristic which may make economics look more mysterious than it really is. Economists do not try to cope directly with economic events in their full complexity. Rather, we work with simplified pictures of reality, which we call *economic models.*

This is necessary because reality is extremely complicated. If a particular event depends on 15 causal factors, you can't think effectively about all of them at once, nor can you predict what will happen if all of them are changing at the same time. So we get rid of most of them for the time being by building a simplified economy with only a few variables. The advantage of this is that we can now *predict* what will happen if one of these variables changes. We can then compare our predictions with actual events. The test of a model is how close its predictions come to tracking events in the real world.

One of the oldest and most famous economic models is that of a purely competitive market. Briefly, this is a market that anyone is free to enter or leave and that has many buyers and sellers, where there is no collusion or price-rigging and no intervention by government. Suppose that there is a purely competitive market for mechanical engineers, whose key features are sketched in Figure 1–6. The horizontal axis shows the number of practicing mechanical engineers. The vertical axis shows the average annual salary of mechanical engineers. In analyzing this market, we assume that conditions in all other occupations in the economy remain unchanged. So a movement up the vertical axis in Figure 1–6 means an increase in mechanical engineers' salaries *relative to those in other occupations.*

The downward-sloping demand curve D, says that the number of mechanical engineers employers will hire depends partly on how much they cost. At higher salary levels, employers will manage to get along with fewer engineers. The upward-sloping supply curve, S, says that

FIGURE 1–6

A competitive market for mechanical engineers

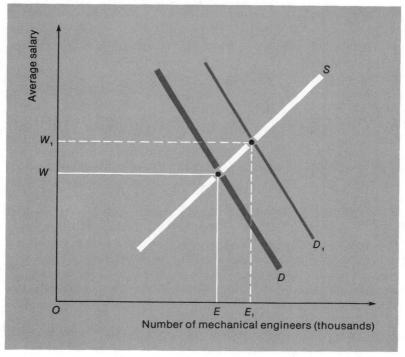

If D is the demand schedule for engineers and S is the supply schedule, then the average salary will be W and the number employed will be E. An increase in demand to D_1 will increase both the salary level and employment to W_1 and E_1.

the number of people who will choose to become engineers depends partly on salary levels. As salary levels for engineers rise relative to those in other occupations, more people will decide to become engineers.

We can now make some useful predictions:

1. The number of people wishing to become mechanical engineers and the number of mechanical engineers employers are willing to hire will be equal if, and only if, the salary level for engineers is at W. So this is the *equilibrium wage* in the market, the wage which just balances quantities demanded and supplied.

2. The model predicts further that if the actual wage at this movement is above or below W, it will tend to move *in the direction* of W. If the actual wage is above W, the number choosing to become mechanical engineers will exceed the number employers are willing to hire. There is then a surplus of engineers. Competition among unemployed engineers for jobs will bring down the relative wage for the profession.

Conversely, at a wage below W, the number of mechanical engineers employers wish to hire will exceed the number of people choosing this occupation. There is then a shortage of engineers. Employers who cannot get as many engineers as they want will bid up the wage rate, and it will rise toward W.

3. A change in demand or supply will change the equilibrium wage and the number employed. Suppose that demand *increases* from D to D_1. An increase in demand means that at any salary level we choose, the number of engineers demanded is greater than before. This could happen, for example, because of an expansion of metal and machinery industries requiring mechanical engineers. The demand shift, with no change in supply, will raise the equilibrium wage to W_1 and increase the number employed to E_1. (Figure out for yourself the effect of a decrease in demand for engineers or of an increase in supply of engineers, shown by moving the S curve to the right.)

4. The labor market illustrated in Figure 1–6 is a purely competitive market. But here is a point that may surprise you: We can use this same model to illustrate the effect of departures from competition. In Figure 1–7, the demand and supply curves for engineers are just as they were in the previous diagram. So under competition, the salary level would be W, and E engineers would be employed. But now suppose that the enrollment capacity of engineering schools is limited and that the number who can get into them is smaller than the number who would like to get in. For this reason the number of engineers is limited to E_1, and the salary level W_1 remains permanently above the market equilibrium. The policy moral would be that educational capacity should be expanded sufficiently to allow the number of engineers to rise toward E, with a decline in relative salaries.

Or suppose mechanical engineers form a union and bargain with em-

FIGURE 1-7
The effect of restrictions on competition

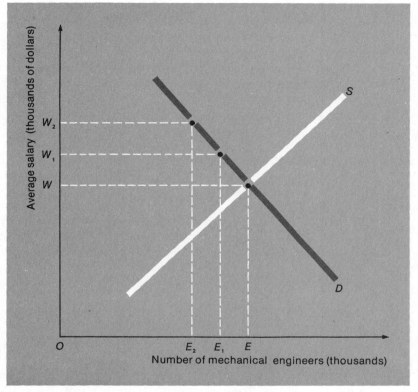

The competitive model can also be used to analyze departures from competition. Here the competitive wage, W, and the competitive employment, E, are the same as in Figure 1–6. But if only E_1 people can become engineers because of limited training capacity, the salary level will be higher, at W_1. Or if an engineers' union demands and enforces a salary level of W_2, only E_2 will be employed.

ployers for a wage of W_2 in Figure 1–7, leading employers to respond by hiring only E_2 engineers. Here, too, the wage can remain permanently above and employment permanently below the market equilibrium. This is not a common situation in the professions, which are largely nonunion. But there are many occupations in which the relative wages of unionized workers are higher than they would be in the absence of unionism.

A complicating feature of the market for engineers, as well as those for other professional occupations, is the length of the training period. The number of engineers graduating today depends on how many freshmen chose engineering courses four years ago, which depends on how attractive engineering salaries were four years ago. And even if salaries today are unattractive and freshmen enrollments drop off, this will not affect the flow of new graduates until four years from now. So we need a somewhat fancier model which takes time lags into account, and in such a model, wages and employment may circle around the equilibrium level without ever hitting it precisely.

Richard Freeman of Harvard University has constructed such models, not only for engineers but for other professions and for college graduates in general. These models do a good job of tracking actual employment and salary levels over the years.[1]

EXPLANATION, PREDICTION, AND POLICY

Explanation: Positive economics

Economists are often held responsible for economic events. If unemployment rises or food prices explode, people say that economists don't know what they're doing. All this is a misconception. The economist is an observer and an analyst, not a decision maker. Decisions are made by business executives and politicians, who may or may not seek economic advice.

The main job of the economist is to understand and explain past economic events. We do this by building and testing economic models, revising and refining them until their predictions come close to historical experience. This kind of work is called *positive economics.*

Economists don't worry much about whether their subject should be considered a science. They approach the problem of explanation in a scientific spirit, without preferring one result to another. They work mainly with statistical data. They frame propositions about economic behavior which can be tested against, and possibly refuted by, the data. Only propositions which pass such a test can survive as part of the body of economics.

But while the method and spirit is scientific, the results are not as precise as those of organic chemistry. The reason is that economists deal with more variables, which are related in more complicated ways. In addition, these relations do not remain constant over time. An atom will behave in the same way in 1990 as in 1910; but a business concern, a government agency, or a trade union is not likely to behave with the same consistency. The physicist Max Planck relates that he started out to become an economist but abandoned the subject as too difficult.

---

[1] See Richard Freeman, *The Market for College-Trained Manpower: A Study in the Economics of Career Choice* (Cambridge, Mass.: Harvard University Press, 1971); and Richard Freeman, ed., *The Over-Educated American* (New York: Academic Press, 1976).

Prediction: Economic forecasting

Another view of the economist is as a prophet, able to peer into the future and predict what is about to happen. When economists come up with different predictions or when a prediction turns out to be wrong, they are denounced as false prophets. What about such criticisms?

Ability to predict is a by-product of ability to explain. A model which gives a good explanation of past events does provide some ability to predict future events. But these predictions are always imprecise, and it is important to understand why this is so.

Suppose we've built a model to explain the price of wheat on the Chicago market. This price, the thing to be explained, is the *dependent* variable in the model. Next, by observation and armchair reasoning we select several explanatory or *independent* variables: the size of the U.S. wheat crop; the amount of wheat carried over from the previous year; U.S. national income (which affects consumer demand for grain products); the wheat crop in the USSR, which is a major wheat importer; and perhaps still others. We know the values of these variables for past years. So we test the model against data for the years 1960 through 1985 and refine it until the predicted price for each past year comes close to the actual price.

Now we want to predict the price of wheat in 1990. How well can we expect the model to perform? What are the possible sources of error?

First, no model can be complete enough to give fully accurate estimates *even for past years*. We must expect that future estimates will be at least as inaccurate as past estimates.

Second, to get an estimate at all, we must have a value of each of our independent variables: the current wheat crop, the wheat carryover, U.S. national income, and so on. We cannot know today what these values will be in 1990. We can assume certain values in order to get a 1990 price prediction. But to the extent that these assumptions turn out to be incorrect, our price prediction will be similarly incorrect.

Third, our model was based on behavior in the past. But can we expect similar behavior in the future? Only if there are no significant changes in the international wheat market. Suppose Argentina pulls itself together and once more becomes a large wheat exporter. Suppose China finds money to increase its wheat imports. Suppose the wheat exporting countries, taking a lesson from OPEC (Organization of Petroleum Exporting Countries), get together to fix the price of wheat. Such changes in the rules of the game can easily throw off predictions based on past experience.

Two other points about the accuracy of economic predictions should be made. First, predictions for next year are more accurate than predictions for 5 or 10 years ahead. The further ahead the prediction extends, the harder it is to assume accurate values for the independent variables and the more likely it is that there will be important changes in the rules of the game.

Accuracy depends also on the size and complexity of the model. A microeconomic model with a half-dozen variables designed to predict the average salary of engineers may do quite well. But macroeconomic models to predict national output, employment, and price levels are much more complex, often using several hundred variables. With modern computer technology, it is quite possible to build and manipulate these large models. But with so many variables, the sources of possible error are multiplied. So macroeconomic models, while better than guesswork, haven't yet achieved a high degree of accuracy.

Policy analysis

In modern times most government decisions are economic decisions. What can economists contribute to such decisions? Let's ask first, what can an economist contribute *while remaining within the bounds of positive economics?* Then we'll face the question whether the economist can prescribe what actually should be done.

Let us use a concrete illustration—the oil problem, which has been debated since 1973 and will probably still be debated in 1990! Many economists are working in this area for the Department of Energy, the Council of Economic Advisers to the President, the Congressional Budget Office, and various congressional committees. What can they contribute?

One basic task is to organize the facts of what has happened and where we now stand. What happened during the 1970s to sources and uses of crude oil in the United States, to prices and consumption of specific petroleum products, and to output and prices of alternative fuels? A useful selection and ordering of the facts implies models of the markets for crude oil and its products and of the markets for alternative fuels. On the basis of models of the past, what can we predict for fuel prices and use during the 1980s? Where would we be in 1990 if government did nothing?

Second, economists can clarify the nature of the oil problem. The fact that people are paying much more for gasoline, heating oil, and electricity than they used to pay is a problem for them. But in what sense, if at all, is there a national problem? Not everyone would agree on the answer. Let me suggest, tentatively, that the high price now being paid for crude oil imported from other countries does constitute a burden on Americans, since ultimately we must pay for these imports *in goods,* not just in paper money. The fact that we have to turn over a growing share of our annual output to other countries in exchange for oil reduces the amount we can consume ourselves. This is one reason why U.S. living standards have recently been rising more slowly. In the background is the possibility that foreign oil supplies might suddenly be cut off for political reasons, as they were for several months in the winter of 1973–74. This would quickly create a critical fuel shortage in the United States.

A reduction of crude oil imports, then, is in the national interest, and this requires a sustained reduction in crude oil use. What can government do about this? The economist can lay out a menu of policy alternatives, which might include such things as setting a ceiling on crude oil imports; encouraging discovery of new oil supplies in the United States; encouraging use of alternative fuels—coal, shale oil, nuclear power; eliminating price controls on petroleum products, which would lead to higher prices and reduced consumption; compulsory conservation measures, such as miles per gallon (mpg) targets for automobiles and requiring electric utilities to convert from oil to coal; modernization of railroad and local transit systems; and government funds for research into novel energy sources—gasohol, geothermal energy, solar energy.

These policies are not mutually exclusive. Several could be used together. Each line of policy is controversial. Each has benefits in terms of reducing crude oil use, but each also has costs. Each will injure some groups in the population and perhaps benefit others. Economists can try to spell out the direct and indirect effects of each policy, so that government officials who choose a particular policy can see clearly what they are buying.

What to do: Normative economics

Having laid out the alternatives, can the economist recommend what the actual policy should be? If he does, he is venturing into the area of *normative economics* or *welfare economics*.

To see the problem we run into, let's continue our discussion of energy policy. Consider the policy of letting fuel prices rise to discourage consumption. Lower-income people spend a larger percentage of their incomes on fuel than do higher-income people. So, a policy of letting prices rise takes a larger percentage bite out of the incomes of the poor than the rich. It increases the inequality of incomes.

Subsidizing local transit systems would have an opposite effect. These systems are used more heavily by the lower-income groups. So, improving service and holding down fares through subsidies will benefit mainly those groups. The cost, however, is spread over taxpayers generally, including higher-income people who never use the transit system. In this case there is an income transfer from rich to poor.

If you examine any other item on our policy list, you will find that the people who benefit are not identical with the people who pay. The distribution of income is affected. So, to say that a particular policy should be adopted means that its income effects are considered acceptable. This requires some standard of what is a desirable distribution of income.[2] How much inequality is acceptable? Can economics say anything about this, or is the question purely ethical and political?

The predominant view is that we cannot say anything about income distribution as economists. An economist, of course, is also a citizen. Like any other citizen, he or she is entitled to say: "In my scheme of values, income should be more equally (or less equally) distributed then it is at present." Having set up a standard, we can proceed to make policy judgments based on that standard. But these are personal rather than professional judgments.

THINK ABOUT THIS

Do you agree that what constitutes a desirable distribution of income is entirely an ethical and political question and that economic science can say nothing about it? Can you think of any counterarguments?

NEW CONCEPTS

good	normative economics
free good	dependent variable
commodity	independent variable
service	scarcity
business	allocation
factor of production	capital good
labor	production
capital	opportunity cost
macroeconomics	production possibilities curve
microeconomics	technology
positive economics	technical progress
economic model	transfer payments
economic prediction	private enterprise economy
policy analysis	market economy

---

[2] You may have thought of a possible way around this. Why not require those who gain from a policy action to pay off (compensate) those who lose? There is indeed a standard proposition in welfare economics: An action is desirable if the gainers can compensate the losers and still feel better off than before. But in fact the losers are hardly ever compensated. So the proposition, while correct in principle, has little practical usefulness.

input   circular flow
public good

SUMMARY

1. Production involves a circular flow of income among businesses, households, and government. Analysis of total income, output, or employment is called *macroeconomics.* Analysis of the detailed composition of output or employment is called *microeconomics.*

2. The central economic problem is that the economy cannot produce as many goods as people would like to consume. This forces us to choose among alternatives.

3. At a personal level, this problem appears as a scarcity of income, which forces people to *budget* or *allocate* their income among goods. The real cost of buying one good is the other goods which you might have bought with the same money. Economists call this *opportunity cost*—the cost of foregone alternatives.

4. There is a similar problem at the national level of choosing among alternative goods which might be produced with the same resources. A useful device for visualizing this problem is the *production possibilities curve* or *production frontier,* which shows alternative combinations of two goods which can be produced with a fixed amount of resources.

5. Other important economic choices include which production methods to use and how much of the national output to distribute to each person in the economy.

6. Most propositions in economics can be explained and illustrated by using words, arithmetic, geometry, or algebra. These are alternative languages, which are translatable into each other.

7. Economists usually reason about simplified *models* of an economy or some part of an economy. These models yield predictions about behavior which can be tested against statistical evidence. This process of explaining economic events by building and testing models is called *positive economics.*

8. A model which comes close to explaining past events can also be used to predict future events. But such predictions are always subject to error, which increases with the complexity of the model and the period of future time covered.

9. On issues of government policy, positive economics can contribute by analyzing the present situation, laying out a menu of policy alternatives, and exploring their probable consequences. *Normative economics* goes beyond this to prescribe some choice among alternatives, which usually involves a value judgment on the proper distribution of income.

TO LEARN MORE

Look at Richard B. McKenzie and Gordon Tullock, *The New World of Economics: Explorations into the Human Experience,* 3d ed. (Homewood, Ill.: Richard D. Irwin, 1981). You will be surprised and may be entertained to find that economic reasoning can be applied to decisions about going to college, studying, dating, marriage and divorce, criminal activity, tax evasion, driving and parking, and many other activities.

2

The Microeconomy: Markets and Prices

" 'Tis so," said the Duchess; "and the moral of it is 'Oh! 'tis love, 'tis love that makes the world go round!' "

"Somebody said," whispered Alice, "that it's done by everybody minding their own business!"

"Ah, well! It means much the same thing," said the Duchess.

—LEWIS CARROLL, ALICE'S ADVENTURES IN WONDERLAND

Once you have gone to market you have told the whole world.

—RUSSIAN PROVERB

This chapter explains the central ideas of microeconomics, a useful foundation for the discussion in later chapters. We will focus on four ideas.

A market economy like that of the United States is coordinated by an interlocking network of *markets* for goods and for factors of production. A central feature of each market is the market *price*.

The price is determined by *demand* from potential buyers and *supply* from potential sellers. We'll examine how demand and supply operate under competitive conditions.

Free market pricing serves important economic functions, and private or public intervention to regulate the price is generally undesirable.

Each market in the system is linked to many others, and a change in one market can have repercussions throughout the economy. We'll illustrate this by looking at the impact of increases in crude oil prices during the 70s.

MARKETS AND PRICES

Nobody in Washington decides how much of each good shall be produced. How, then, are the key economic decisions made? Russian leaders refer to capitalist economies as "unplanned," "chaotic." Yet these economies actually show a good deal of order and stability. What is it that produces order rather than chaos?

I go down to the supermarket on Saturday afternoon and lay hands on a market basket. No one has any notice of my coming. Yet the goods I want are usually there, and at about the prices I had expected to pay. The people who produced the goods may be thousands of miles away. Yet their activities are somehow coordinated with my desires.

What holds the economy together? A brief answer is that the system is coordinated through an interlocking network of *markets*. A key feature of each market is the *price* prevailing in the market. These two terms have a special meaning in economics and require a word of explanation.

Markets

The term *market* does not refer just to fishmarkets or fresh vegetable stalls or even to retail trade in general. Every good has a market in which supplies are bought and sold. There is a market for basic steel, electric power, textile machinery, cotton cloth, dry cleaning, barber services, and every other item produced in the economy. Moreover, a product may pass through a series of markets before reaching the ultimate user. For instance, a farmer sells wheat to a miller, who sells bran to a food manufacturer, who sells bran flakes to wholesale distributors, who resell to retail grocers, who supply consumers in the retail market.

There are also markets for the factors of production—for land, labor, and capital. In the "labor market," employees deal with employers, exchanging so many hours or weeks of labor for a certain wage.

A market is not necessarily, or even usually, a single place. Cournot, the distinguished French economist, defined a market as "the whole of any region in which buyers and sellers are in such free intercourse with one another, that the prices of the same goods tend to equality easily and quickly." Some markets are virtually worldwide. This is true of many basic raw materials and also of securities of the U.S. government and of leading U.S. business concerns. The requirements for a wide market are that the product be sufficiently standardized that it can safely be bought and sold without being seen and that its value be high relative to the cost of transporting it. Gold, precious stones, and gilt-edged securities, whose value is high and transport cost low, are the international commodities par excellence. But other staples such as copper, aluminum, rubber, coffee, cocoa, wool, and cotton also enjoy a world market.

Other markets are national in scope. Men's and women's clothing can be shipped anywhere in the United States at a cost which is small relative to the value of the merchandise. A clothing manufacturer in any part of the country, then, is in direct competition with makers of similar products in other regions. This is true also of other light manufactured goods. As one gets into heavier products with a low value per pound, shipment to distant points becomes less feasible, and the market shrinks to regional or local proportions. Each city has its own sand and gravel quarries, which do not compete with suppliers in other cities. Brick factories have a narrow market area because of the great weight and low value of their product.

Retail markets, particularly markets for groceries and other staple necessities, are centered in a single town or city. But the rise of the automobile has made retail markets larger than they used to be. An enterprising shopper will drive to an area shopping center miles from home, or even to the next town to take advantage of a difference in quality or price. The market area of each town thus interlocks with that of neighboring towns in an endless chain.

The size of the labor market depends on the level of labor in question. An outstanding business executive, scientist, actor, or surgeon enjoys a national market. He or she is known throughout the country, is well informed about opportunities in other areas, and will move to another location if it offers sufficient advantage. For most manual, clerical, and subprofessional jobs, however, one can take the locality as the relevant market area. A worker who is settled in a community and perhaps owns a home there is unlikely to know about, or to be much interested in, jobs in other cities. These local labor markets are linked, however, by the possibility that people *might* move if the wage level of City A rose much above that of City B. This possibility is sufficient to keep wage levels of nearby cities reasonably well in line with each other.

Prices

A *price* is the amount paid for a specified quantity and quality of any good or service. Bricklayers are paid, say, $15 an hour in Minneapolis. This is the price at which this kind of labor is sold by workers in the Minneapolis labor market. Thus a wage rate is a price. An interest rate is also a price—the price paid for use of a certain quantity of money for a stated period of time. Most frequently, price is used in its everyday meaning as the amount paid for a pair of shoes or a pound of butter. But when the term is used in a general way, when one speaks of "competitive pricing" or "the price mechanism," it should be taken to include wage rates, interest rates, rents, and other payments for productive services.

PRICE DETERMINATION UNDER COMPETITION

What is a competitive market? The main requirements are many buyers and sellers, freedom to enter or leave the market at will, no collusion among buyers or sellers to control the price, and no price-fixing by government. Under these conditions we can set up a model to predict what the market price will be and how much will be sold at that price.

This *demand-supply* model rests on the idea that two kinds of pressure are at work in a market. On one side is the willingness of purchasers to buy larger or smaller quantities of the product, depending on its price. On the other side is the willingness of sellers to produce and bring to market various amounts of the product, depending on the price that they expect to receive. Demand-supply analysis is a way of separating these forces, analyzing each in turn, and then bringing them together to explain price and output.

We will start with demand, go on to supply, and then explain how the two interact in the market.

Individual demand

How much of a particular good will Mr. A buy? This depends, first, on his personal preferences. Some people like spinach while others do not, and purchases will vary accordingly. Second, Mr. A's income will make a difference. The higher a person's income, the larger will be his or her purchases of most goods.

Third, the price of the good will have an effect. In general, the lower the price, the greater will be the quantity purchased. Finally, the prices of related goods will make a difference. Another good may be related either because it is a *substitute* for or because it is normally used along with (is *complementary* with) the good in which we are interested. Butter and margarine are substitutes. The *higher* the price of butter, the larger will be purchases of margarine. Gasoline and automobiles are complementary. The *lower* the price of automobiles, the larger will be purchases of gasoline.

A full explanation of consumer behavior would require exploration of all these dimensions. In this chapter, however, we focus on one aspect of demand: the relation between the quantity of a good purchased and the price of that good. When we do this, we are supposing that the buyers' incomes, their tastes, and the prices of all related products are given and constant.

Given all these things, what can we say about Mr. A's demand for a particular good, such as coffee? First of all, what is demand in this sense? How do we describe it?

Demand is a list (or schedule) of the quantities that will be bought at various prices. In economics, the term *demand always refers to a schedule.* **It is** *not a single quantity.* **If we want to focus on the quantity which will be bought at some particular price, we call it the** *quantity demanded.*

To describe Mr. A's demand for coffee, we must specify the quantity demanded at each of the various possible prices for coffee. For example, Mr. A's demand schedule might look as in Table 2–1. If the price is $2.50, he will get along with only 1 pound. At lower prices he will buy more until, if the price fell to 25 cents, he would buy 10 pounds a month.

The same information is shown graphically in Figure 2–1. Since coffee is usually bought in pound packages, its graph would consist of a series of disconnected points. For products where the quantity purchased can be increased by very small amounts, the demand schedule becomes a continuous line like the solid line in Figure 2–1. Such a line is called a *demand curve.* We shall be using demand curves very freely as we go along, so it is well to remember that a demand curve is simply a graphic picture of the demand schedule.

Why is it reasonable to think that demand curves slope downward from left to right; that is, that people will normally buy more of a good at a lower price? The traditional line of argument rests on the notion of satisfaction or *utility.* Why do I buy a product at all? Obviously, because it yields me some sort of satisfaction. But a second unit of the product will usually not yield as much satisfaction as the first, and a third will yield still less. As I go from being a one-car householder to a two-car or three-car householder, the utility yielded by additional cars will decline. This is called the *law of diminishing marginal (or additional) utility.* If this rule holds, then I will not be willing to pay as much for a second car as I would for the first; and to get me to buy a third car, the price would have to be still lower. My demand curve for cars slopes downward to the right.

TABLE 2–1

Price of Coffee (dollars per pound)	Quantity Bought (pounds per month)
2.50	1
2.25	2
2.00	3
1.75	4
1.50	5
1.25	6
1.00	7
0.75	8
0.50	9
0.25	10

FIGURE 2-1
At a lower price, larger quantities will be purchased

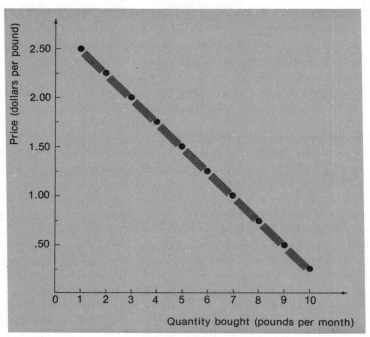

This is a graph of Mr. A's demand schedule for coffee. Each point means that if the price were as shown on the vertical axis, Mr. A would buy the number of pounds shown on the horizontal axis. If the price and quantity intervals were made very small, the graph would become a continuous line, termed a *demand curve*.

We seem, then, to be on safe ground in concluding that consumers will buy less of a product if its price rises, and more if its price falls. But the ground is more treacherous than it appears. Remember the qualifications that were laid down earlier:

1. Buyers' preferences must remain unchanged. If we allow Mr. A's preferences to jump about at the same time that the price of coffee is shifting, we can no longer be sure of the outcome.

2. The desirability of the good to consumers must be *independent* of the market price. Without this stipulation, a price cut might sometimes *reduce* the quantity sold. If the price of diamonds fell drastically, they might cease to be prestige symbols and engagement rings might contain emeralds instead.

3. Buyers' incomes must remain unchanged. If Mr. A's money income

rises at the same time that coffee prices rise, he may end up buying more coffee rather than less.[1]

4. Prices of other products must remain unchanged. This is especially important for closely related products, such as tea, cocoa, soft drinks, sugar, and cream. We must hold these prices constant if we wish to observe the pure effect of a change in coffee prices on coffee sales.

5. Prices must be expected to continue at about their present level. If coffee rises 10 cents a pound and consumers fear it will rise another 10 cents next month, they may rush out and buy heavily to beat the price rise. *Speculation on price changes* may mean that a price increase, at least for a while, will *raise* sales of the product instead of reducing them.

> **The principle of demand may now be restated in a stricter form: A consumer will purchase less of a product the price of which has risen, and more of a product the price of which has fallen, *provided* that his or her income and preference system remain unchanged, that the prices of all other products remain unchanged, and that present prices are expected to continue indefinitely in the future.**

MARKET DEMAND

Will *total* purchases of a product obey the same principle as purchases by an individual consumer? Will a decline in shoe prices, everything else in the economy remaining unchanged, lead to an increase in shoe purchases?

Yes, it will. The reason is that total national demand is simply the sum of the demands of individual households. A drop in shoe prices will cause at least some families to buy more shoes, and thus there will be more shoes bought in the country as a whole.

A hypothetical list of how many pairs of shoes might be bought at various price levels is shown in Table 2–2. This is termed a *market demand schedule.* As we go down the price column to lower and lower prices, we find larger and larger quantities appearing in the purchases column. The same information is shown graphically in Figure 2–2. *D* shows the amount which purchasers would be willing to buy at various alternative prices. This *demand curve* is drawn as a continuous line, indicating that

---

[1] Strictly speaking, if the price of one item in the consumers' budget falls and other prices remain the same, their real incomes *cannot* remain unchanged. They can now buy more than before, hence their real incomes must have risen. If the good in question is a small item in peoples' budgets, it is safe to ignore this complication, as is normally done in demand analysis. But if the item takes a large part of the budget, one may encounter the "Giffen paradox." Sir Francis Giffen, a 19th-century British economist, noted that, when Irish potato prices rose in bad years, many Irish families consumed *more* potatoes rather than less. Why? Because with high potato prices and no increase in their money incomes, they were now too poor to afford meat and other foodstuffs. How did they keep alive? By eating more potatoes.

TABLE 2-2
Market demand schedule for men's shoes

Price of Shoes (dollars per pair)	Quantity Bought (millions of pairs per year)
30	85
27	110
24	130
21	160
18	190
15	240
12	300
9	375
6	500

FIGURE 2-2
Market demand obeys the same principle as individual demand

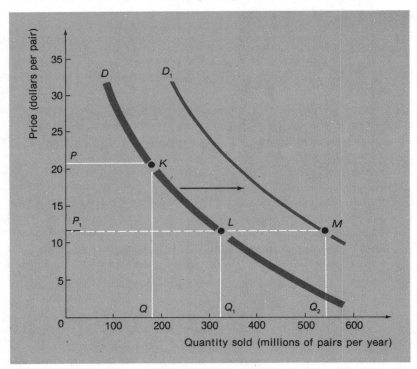

D is a demand curve. Each point on the curve shows how many pairs of shoes consumers would be prepared to buy at a specified price. D_1 indicates a change in demand to a higher level.

price can be varied by very small amounts and that sales will always respond.

Figure 2–2 looks deceptively simple. Since we shall be using demand curves frequently in later chapters, we had better pause to consider exactly what they do and do not mean. Three main points should be kept in mind:

1. A demand curve is not a historical chart showing the course of events over a period of time. The demand curve does not say that if price falls from P in 1980 to P_1 in 1985, then the quantity sold will increase from Q to Q_1. Over this period, preferences, incomes, and other prices will have changed, and thus the basis we laid down for constructing a demand schedule will have been swept away.

The demand curve is a timeless, not a historical, concept. All the points on the curve hold true *simultaneously* and at the same moment. They represent alternative possibilities, only one of which can actually be realized. If price were to be P, then quantity sold would be Q. If instead the price were to be P_1, then quantity sold would be Q_1. But only one of these possibilities can be realized in a particular market at a particular time.

2. The term *change in demand* is often used incorrectly. If price in Figure 2–2 rises from P_1 to P and sales consequently fall from Q_1 to Q, many people would say that "demand has fallen." *This is wrong.* Consumer preferences have not changed, and the demand curve is exactly where it was. There has simply been a *change in the quantity demanded* in response to a change in price.

Movement from one point to another *on the same demand curve*—in this case, from L to K—is not a change in demand. A change in demand occurs only when *the whole demand curve shifts to a new position*. Suppose D moves upward to the position D_1. This is truly an increase in demand, because whatever the price, it will now be possible to sell more than with the previous demand curve. At price P_1, for example, one can now sell Q_2 units of product instead of Q_1. The movement from L to M does represent a change in demand, while that from L to K does not.

Why might demand rise from D to D_1? Basically, because of a change in one or more of the things which we specified earlier as constant: people's preferences, their incomes, and the prices of other goods.

3. The figures for the table and for Figure 2–2 were pulled out of the air to illustrate the principle that demand curves slope downward to the right. But if we were dealing with a real product in the real world, we could not make up figures in this way. Any actual demand curve has a specific shape. Some products have a very steep demand curve, indicating that consumers will buy almost as much at a high price as a low price. In other cases, purchases may fall off sharply as the price rises, which would mean a flat demand curve.

Speaking of a demand curve as "steep" or "flat," however, can be quite misleading. The reason is that the visual appearance of a curve depends on the scales used on the two axes.

We need a precise measure of just how quantity demanded responds to a change in price. The measure used for this purpose is termed *price elasticity of demand.* We make a small change in price (ΔP) and observe the change in quantity sold (ΔQ). Price elasticity of demand is defined as:[2]

$$e = -\frac{\Delta Q}{Q} \div \frac{\Delta P}{P}$$

$$= -\frac{\text{Percentage change in quantity}}{\text{Percentage change in price}}.$$

Consider the effect of a 1 percent reduction in price. Then if quantity sold rises less than 1 percent, $e < 1$. If quantity sold rises by exactly 1 percent, $e = 1$. If it rises by more than 1 percent, $e > 1$. This leads to a definition:

If $e < 1$, demand is inelastic.
If $e = 1$, demand is of unit elasticity.
If $e > 1$, demand is elastic.

Price elasticity of supply is defined in exactly the same way.

Actually, one should not refer to an entire demand schedule as "elastic" or "inelastic." The fact is that price elasticity differs over different ranges of the same demand schedule. For the simplest kind of schedule—a linear demand curve with constant slope—elasticity declines continuously as we move down the curve (see Figure 2–3). Why is this? The explanation is that elasticity is based not on *absolute* changes in prices and quantities but on *percentage* changes. In the neighborhood of point A, a dollar cut in price is only a *small* percentage change, because we are starting from a high price level. A sales increase of 10 units, however, is a *big* percentage increase, because we are starting from a small sales volume. Hence the elasticity measure, percent change in Q/percent change in P, is large and demand is elastic. As we move down the curve toward C, however, each dollar reduction in price is a larger percentage change than before, while the percentage changes in quantity become steadily smaller. The shrinking numerator and the growing denominator cause the elasticity measure to fall.

---

[2] Why the negative sign in the formula? The reason is that price and quantity usually change in opposite directions—a negative P change means a positive Q change, and vice versa. Hence, when we divide one into the other, we come out with a negative number. Working with negative signs in the formula, we convert the result back to a positive number.

Example: $e = -(-0.6) = 0.6$.

FIGURE 2-3
Elasticity changes as we move down the demand curve

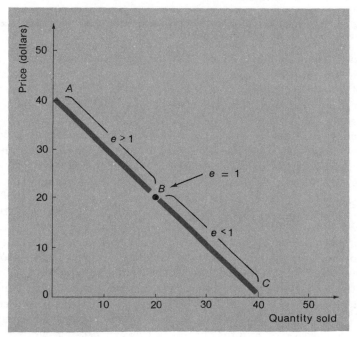

While the slope of the demand curve *AC* is constant, elasticity of demand falls steadily as we move from *A* toward *C*. Demand is elastic over the range *AB*, passes through a point of unit elasticity at *B*, and becomes increasingly inelastic as we move from *B* toward *C*.

THINK ABOUT THIS

1. You are a monopolist with complete control of the supply of widgets. You are considering whether it would pay you to raise the price of widgets by 10 percent. Would it help you to know the price elasticity of demand for widgets? Why?
2. In 1973–74 the OPEC (Organization of Petroleum Exporting Countries) countries decided that it would be to their advantage to raise the price of crude oil by 500 percent. What does this suggest about the demand schedule for crude oil?

MARKET SUPPLY

Demand is only one of two sets of forces influencing price. Buyers are only one side of the market. What about the sellers on the other side of the market? How does price influence the amount they will be willing to produce and sell?

Supply is a list (or schedule) of the quantities that will be offered on the market at various prices.

In the case of demand, we could say flatly that demand curves always slope downward to the right. Supply is more complicated. We can suggest the nature of the complications without exploring them in depth.

There are situations in which price has no effect on quantity supplied. There are just so many Cezannes, and there aren't going to be any more. The quantity of fresh fish on the Boston market this morning depends on how much the fishermen delivered last night. For today, supply is fixed. In such cases, the supply curve is a vertical line.

But consider next the supply situation for men's shirts. Here producers can vary their output, and price will influence their decisions. Other things equal, a price increase will make shirt production more profitable and will lead factories to increase production. Beyond some point, increases in output will raise production costs per shirt because of overtime work, overcrowding of plants, higher material costs, and so on. But producers will be willing to pay these higher costs "if the price is right."

In this case the supply curve slopes upward to the right: the higher the price, the larger the quantity offered in the market. Such a curve is termed a *short-run supply curve,* because we are looking at adjustments over a few weeks or months. It slopes upward because we are forcing out more output *from the same plants,* and because this eventually means higher production costs per shirt.

If we consider a period of several years, however, a price increase which makes shirt production unusually profitable will cause new shirt plants to be built. As additional output from these plants comes onto the market, the price of shirts will fall. So, if new producers can enter the industry at the same cost level as previous producers, output can be increased indefinitely *with no permanent increase in price.* Thus the *long-run supply curve,* which allows time for new plants to be built, is a horizontal line.

In this section, for illustrative purposes, we shall work with an upward-sloping supply curve. But the reader can work through the examples which follow using a horizontal rather than a sloped supply curve without changing the general drift of the results.

In Figure 2–4, *S* is a *supply schedule or supply curve.* Each point on it shows the amount per unit of time which sellers of the product will be willing to bring to market at the price in question. The fact that the curve slopes upward to the right says that producers will offer more goods at higher prices.

We must observe the same cautions about the supply curve that we noted earlier in the case of demand. Specifically:

1. The supply curve is not a historical curve linking prices and quanti-

FIGURE 2–4
The market supply schedule

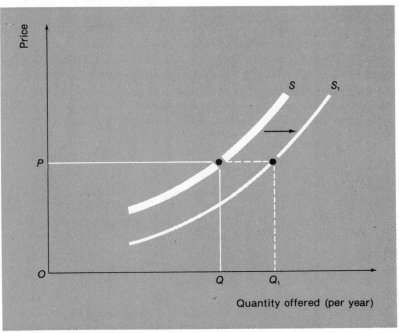

S is a supply curve. Each point on the curve shows how much of the product sellers will offer at a specified price. S_1 shows an increase in supply—more offered at each price than was true previously.

ties sold in different time periods. It shows alternative possibilities available ble *at a moment of time.* If price were at a certain level, then a certain quantity would be offered on the market. But only one of these possiblities will actually be realized at a particular time.

2. The supply curve for each good has a specific shape, depending on how easy or hard it is to expand production. The shape of the supply curve is of great importance to buyers. If the supply curve slopes up steeply, this means that an increased demand can be gratified only at substantially higher prices. Conversely, a gently sloped supply curve indicates that production can be expanded readily and that higher demand will not cause much increase in price.

3. In drawing the supply curve we suppose that everything except price remains constant. In the case of demand, we assumed that buyers' preferences, their incomes, and the prices of substitute products were known and constant. In the case of supply, the most important things we hold constant are the methods of production and the supply conditions of the materials, labor, and other things needed for production. If any of these things change, the supply curve also changes.

4. A movement from one point to another on S is not a change in supply. It is simply a change in the quantity offered in response to a change in price. A change in supply means *a shift of the entire curve to a new position,* such as S_1 in Figure 2–4. Note that at any price sellers will now offer more goods than before. At the price P they will now supply Q_1 units instead of Q. Thus a rightward shift of the supply curve indicates an increase in supply. This might happen because improved production methods have been developed, which make it possible to turn out the product at a lower cost and offer it at a lower price. In the converse case of a decrease in supply, S would move to the left.

THINK ABOUT THIS

Can you think of situations in which the supply curve would be *vertical;* that is, supply is completely unresponsive to price?

Can you define conditions under which the supply curve would be *horizontal;* that is, an indefinitely large supply can be made available at a constant price?

MARKET EQUILIBRIUM

We are now in a position to bring the demand and supply curves together on the same diagram, as is done in Figure 2–5. What is the point of this diagram and what does it tell us? The intersection of D and S defines a price P and a quantity sold Q, which have a special significance. We call these the *equilibrium price and quantity* in the market. This means:

1. The price P is a stable price. It is the only price which precisely "clears the market," the only price at which the amount consumers are willing to buy exactly equals the amount producers want to sell. This being so, there is no reason for the price to change until there is a shift in D or S.

2. If the market price starts out either above or below P, forces will operate to move it toward P. Suppose, for example, the market opens on a particular morning at price P_1. What will happen? At this price the amount sellers stand ready to offer (P_1K) is much larger than the amount buyers are willing to take (P_1L). As soon as this becomes apparent, some sellers will begin to offer the product at lower prices. The market price will fall, with no logical stopping point until it reaches point P.

Suppose, on the other hand, that the market starts off at P_2. At this low price, the amount buyers want (P_2M) is much larger than the amount producers are willing to supply (P_2N). Some of the eager buyers will

FIGURE 2-5
Demand, supply, and equilibrium price

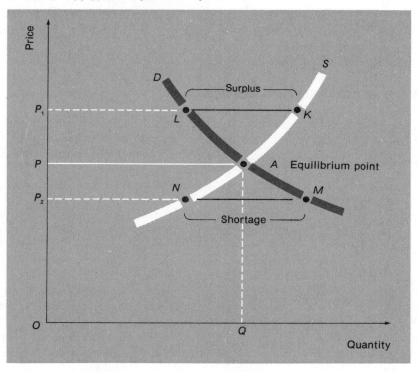

If demand and supply are in this position, the market price will be P and the quantity exchanged will be Q. Other prices, such as P_1 and P_2, will not be feasible. Explain why.

now begin to bid up the price, preferring to pay a bit more rather than go unsatisfied. As this process goes on, the market price will rise, and there is no reason for it to stop short of P. In short, P is the only price which is stable and which will maintain itself so long as the underlying demand and supply conditions continue unchanged.[3]

Does the demand-supply diagram explain price and output? Not in any ultimate sense. A full explanation requires that one know everything which lies behind the S and D curves. Behind the demand curve lies the whole array of consumer preferences. Behind the supply curve lie many things which we still have to examine—notably, costs of production. But these things affect price through their effect on the position of the demand and supply curves. Anything which affects the price of a product

[3] There are cases, however, usually considered exceptional in which price will move *away* from the equilibrium level rather than toward it.

must do so either by altering the willingness of consumers to buy *(D)* or the willingness of producers to bring various quantities to market *(S)*. The demand-supply apparatus thus gives us a basis for *classifying* the ultimate determinants of price and for reasoning about them in an orderly manner.

SHIFTS IN DEMAND AND SUPPLY

In defining the demand and supply schedules we were careful to hold everying constant *except* the price of the good in question. In the real world, however, these "other things" do not remain constant for long; and any change in them will shift the location of the schedules. Let's ask first *why* such shifts may occur, and then look at the effect on market equilibrium.

The main things which may shift the demand curve for a good are a change in buyers' *preferences,* or in their *incomes,* or in the price of a *related good.* If men's preferences shift from collar-and-tie outfits to sport shirts, the demand schedules for dress shirts and neckties will shift downward, while that for sport shirts will shift upward. An increase in consumers' incomes will enable them to buy more of what they were previously buying, and to add new items to their shopping list. Demand schedules for most consumer goods will shift upward.

The effect of a price change for a related good depends on whether this is a good that is an alternative to the one we are considering (a *substitute good*), or whether it is normally used along with that good (a *complementary good*). A familiar example of substitutes is butter and margarine. A rise in the price of butter will cause people to use more margarine, *raising* the margarine demand curve; and conversely automobiles, gasoline, and tires are complementary goods, since all are used in driving. A rise in the price of gasoline, which makes driving more expensive, will *lower* the demand schedules for automobiles and tires.

In the case of supply, the main things we held constant were the prices of inputs used in production and the method of production. An increase in wage rates, raw material prices, or any other input cost means that producers will want a higher price than before for the same quantity of output. The supply schedule shifts upward. Invention of an improved method of production which lowers production costs will have the opposite effect of shifting the supply schedule downward. In natural resource industries, new discoveries can be important. The great jump in oil prices in the 1970s gave a powerful stimulus to aid exploration. As new fields were discovered in the North Sea, the Alaskan slope, Mexico, and elsewhere, the supply schedule for crude oil has been shifting to the right.

Why are shifts in demand and supply schedules important? How do they affect price and quantity sold? Consider first a change in supply

FIGURE 2-6
A supply increase lowers price, raises quantity sold

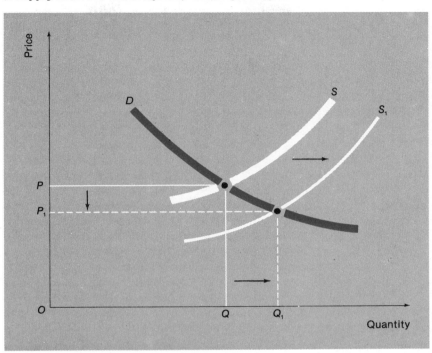

Supply increases from S to S_1, demand remaining unchanged. The new equilibrium is shown by the intersection of S_1 and D. Price falls from P to P_1, and quantity sold rises from Q to Q_1.

conditions. Figure 2–6 shows an increase in supply from S to S_1. This means that producers are now willing to offer a larger quantity of goods at the same price, or the same quantity at a lower price. This might happen, for example, because of invention of a new production method which reduces costs.

The new market equilibrium is shown by the intersection of D and S_1. The equilibrium price has fallen from P to P_1, while equilibrium quantity has increased to Q_1. A decrease in supply would have opposite results. Sketch in a new supply curve to the left of S. It is easy to see that market price will be higher than before the quantity sold lower.

Figure 2–7 shows a rise in demand from D to D_1. Buyers are now willing to buy more than before at each price level. This shift will raise the equilibrium price from P to P_1 and will raise the equilibrium quantity from Q to Q_1. (This short-run increase in price, however, will not necessarily persist. Producers will probably respond to it by increasing their

FIGURE 2-7
A demand increase raises quantity sold and price

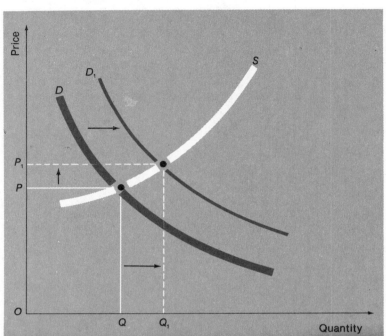

Demand rises from D to D_1, while the supply curve remains unchanged. Quantity
sold will increase, and price will also increase in the first instance.

plant capacity. Thus S will shift to the right, and price will tend to fall
again.)

The rules for market adjustment, then, are:

1. *A supply increase raises Q and lowers P.*
2. *A supply decrease lowers Q and raises P.*
3. *A demand increase raises Q and also raises P in the short run, but not
   necessarily over a longer period.*
4. *A demand decrease lowers Q and also lowers P in the short run, but not
   necessarily over a longer period.*

FREE PRICING AND REGULATED PRICING

While economists admire competitive pricing, the participants often
do not. Sellers usually regard the market price as too low, while buyers
denounce it as too high. Those who consider the market price unfair

often appeal to government to peg it at a higher or lower level. This is usually not a good idea. To explain why let us look at the functions which a freely fluctuating price performs and then at what happens when government intervenes.

The functions of price

To ask whether a price is fair or unfair is to ask the wrong question. Rather, we should view prices as the basic control mechanism in a market economy. Prices in the broad sense, including wage rates and interest rates, perform three main functions: They provide an *incentive to production,* a means of *rationing scarce supplies,* and a *signaling mechanism* indicating the need to transfer resources from one use to another.

The *incentive* function is obvious. People work to earn a wage or salary and save in order to get interest or dividends. Companies produce a product because its price is high enough to cover costs. No one has to be told what to do. Their response to the prices they see before them is sufficient to keep the economic machine in motion.

The *rationing* function requires a little more thought. There is only a certain amount of gasoline available this month for automobile drivers. Who is to get it, and how much shall each get? A government agency could issue ration tickets. Or people could simply line up at the pumps, and first come, first served. But there is another way: Set a market price high enough so that the amount consumers want to buy *at that price* just equals the available supply. In a purely competitive market, the price will settle at this equilibrium level, and it will ration supplies among consumers *automatically.* This is an enormous convenience in a world where people would like more of almost everything if goods could be had for free.

A final function of price, or more correctly of a *change* in price, is to serve as a *signaling mechanism,* indicating the need for resource transfers from one line of production to another. If the price of soybeans rises relative to the price of corn, this tells us that some farm acreage should be shifted to soybeans, and it will also induce farmers to make the shift. If the wage of oil-well drillers rises relative to other wages, this signals that more workers should be transferred to oil drilling, and the wage increase itself will lead more people to apply for this kind of work.

If resource transfers are not brought about through free movement of prices, they have to be made through administrative orders. This is the main method used in the Soviet Union and other centrally planned economies, but it is a clumsy method, subject to delay and error. A price-directed economy is quicker on its feet and leads to a faster adjustment of resource use to changing demands.

A practical implication is that we interfere with price movements at our peril. Preventing a price from changing in response to changing demand and supply conditions means that the signaling mechanism is blocked. The message does not get through, and the desirable resource transfers will not occur.

Price-fixing: Surpluses and shortages

What happens when government intervenes to fix a price above or below its equilibrium level? The effects can be seen by looking back at Figure 2–5. Under competitive conditions, the equilibrium price in this market will be P. But sellers would like to get more, and they mobilize political pressure on government to set a higher price, P_1. What will happen? The amount sellers would like to produce and sell at this price is larger than the amount buyers are willing to buy. There is a *surplus* of the good. Price can no longer serve its function of restraining quantity supplied to equal quantity demanded. What will happen to the surplus has to be decided in some other way.

Consider the opposite case in which buyers get the upper hand and persuade government to set a price below equilibrium, say at P_2. At this price the quantity buyers would like to get is larger than the quantity sellers are willing to supply. There is a *shortage* of the good. Price can no longer serve its function of restraining quantity demanded to equal quantity supplied. The question of who will get how much of the scarce supply must be decided in some other way.

The terms *surplus* and *shortage* are often used loosely in popular discussion. The only precise meaning of these terms is that shown in Figure 2–5. Surplus means a situation in which the price is being held above equilibrium. Shortage means the opposite situation in which price is being held below equilibrium. Let's look briefly at some illustrative cases.

1. Price supports and farm surpluses. For many years the federal government has guaranteed a minimum price—called a *support price*—for many farm products, including wheat, corn, cotton, sugar, tobacco, milk, butter, and cheese. The price is maintained by a government guarantee to buy any amount offered at the support price. So farmers regularly produce more than buyers are willing to take, and the surpluses piling up in government warehouses have sometimes reached embarrassing levels.

What to do? One way out would be to persuade farmers to grow less, and there have been efforts in this direction. Farmers have been paid to shift land out of surplus crops or to take it out of production altogether. Occasionally, government has gone further and limited how much wheat, say, a farmer could sell at the support price. This illustrates a general principle: Price regulation leads quite quickly to quantity regulation as well.

The other solution has been to get rid of surplus farm products abroad, partly through normal export sales, partly through cut-price sales, or even gifts of food to very poor countries with food shortages.

2. Minimum wages and labor surpluses. The Fair Labor Standards Act prohibits employment of workers in interstate commerce, which means the bulk of all workers, at wages below a specified hourly rate. The minimum wage has been raised gradually from 25 cents an hour in the late 30s to $3.35 an hour at present. This is below the market equilibrium for steel workers or truck drivers, so it has no effect on their wages. But in many communities it is above the market equilibrium for unskilled and inexperienced workers, particularly teenagers. So there is a surplus of such workers. This is not the only reason for high rates of unemployment among teenagers and unskilled adults, but it appears to be an important contributing factor.

In addition to government wage fixing, there is wage fixing by trade unions. Some unions are more successful than others in raising wages for their members. But on the average, it appears that union members earn about 20 percent more than nonunion members with the same education, work experience, and other personal characteristics. The result of a union wage above the market equilibrium is typically a surplus of labor in unionized occupations. More workers would like to be steelworkers, truck drivers, or construction workers than can find jobs in those fields. These surplus workers will not necessarily remain unemployed, but they will be forced to seek work in other occupations at lower wage rates.

3. Price ceiling and black markets. Instead of a price *floor,* as in the above cases, government may set a *price ceiling,* a maximum price which is *below* the market equilibrium. This was done on a large scale during World War II. The result, again illustrated in Figure 2–5, is that there is now a shortage of the good. At the ceiling price, consumers would like to buy more of the good than sellers are willing to supply.

Which lucky customers will get the limited quantity available? Unless some control system is installed, people may simply line up in front of the store. The early-comers at the head of the line will be served, while those at the end get nothing. Favoritism and bribery spring up. The storekeeper keeps a stock of the product under the counter for favored customers, or insists on tie-in sales. This means forcing the customer to take some slow-moving item which he doesn't want in order to get the scarce item he does want.

If one wants to achieve a fair distribution of the available supply, this can be done through *rationing.* Ration coupons can be issued to each family, entitling it to buy a specified quantity of the product. Storekeepers are forbidden to sell the product except to people holding ration coupons. If the system is well managed, the number of coupons issued should just add up to the supplies available (Q_1). Once more we have a managed equilibrium, in which price control is supported by quantity control.

Rationing was used on a large scale during World War II for gasoline, tires, fuel oil, meat, canned goods, dairy products, coffee, sugar, and other commodities. Supplies of these things were below what people would have liked to buy with their high wartime incomes. Rationing helped to distribute the scarce supplies in an equitable way. The system led, however, to difficult problems of evasion and enforcement. A buyer whose ration coupons had run out could often get supplies by offering more than the official ceiling price. This was illegal, but some sellers were willing to break the law for enough money. A new class of middlemen grew up who specialized in getting scarce goods from producer to consumer outside the rationing system and at premium prices. These deals were called *black market* transactions.

4. Rent ceilings and housing shortages. People who rent apartments in large cities often complain that the rent is too high. Especially if they are poor, they will argue that they can't afford the rents landlords are asking. Being numerous enough to have political leverage, they may persuade the city government to impose a rent ceiling, holding rents below the level which the market would establish. The rent controls imposed during World War II have now been phased out in most parts of the country, but they linger on in some cities, notably New York City. They usually apply, however, to only part of the housing supply— for example, to apartments but not to houses or to cheap apartments but not expensive ones.

The result, once more, is a shortage of rent-controlled apartments. Demand for them exceeds the quantity available. One result is considerable evasion of the system. The landlord may insist on "key money" or other side payments, which bring his rent up closer to the market level. But to the extent that the ceiling holds, some of those who can't get rent-controlled apartments will be forced into houses or apartments which aren't rent controlled, at considerably higher rents.

One consequence is injustice within the tenant population. Those who manage to get into the limited number of rent-controlled apartments get a break. But other families in the same circumstances are forced to pay substantially more for the same space. The most serious effect, however, is on the quantity and quality of housing available. Landlords faced with fixed rents and (probably) rising costs, will do as little maintenance as possible in an effort to maintain some return on their investment. Housing quality will deteriorate. Further, the fixed rent and the low return on apartments will make it unprofitable to build any more of them. So construction will stop, and as population grows, crowding will increase. Rent ceilings, in short, tend to create a permanent housing shortage. (The classic case is France, where rent ceilings imposed in World War I were not removed after the war. As a result, there was virtually no construction of rental housing in France from 1914 to 1945.)

But what about the argument that many people are too poor to pay the market price for housing? They are presumably too poor also to buy adequate amounts of food, clothing, and other goods. But does this mean that we should establish a two-price system for everything, with a low price for the poor and a high price for the prosperous? Such an approach seems unworkable and undesirable. So why apply it to housing? If the community decides that the situation of poor people should be improved, isn't the simple answer to give them more money? The real answer to low income is more income, rather than to distort the pricing system.

Any argument that a price or a wage is too high or too low and that government should rush in to correct it should drop a warning flag in your mind. Before agreeing that government action is needed, you should ask three questions: (1) What do we mean by too high or too low? Are there any objective standards, or are we hearing arguments that are merely emotional or self-interested? (2) Is the situation *permanent,* or will it tend to correct itself as resources move into or out of the occupation or industry? (3) If there is an inequity, can it be corrected by methods other than price-fixing? We do, after all, have a tax-and-transfer system. If low-income farmers are judged to be making too little, there are ways of getting cash to them without fixing the price of wheat or cotton. Thus inequities, where they exist, can be corrected without the harmful side effects of price controls.

INTERRELATION OF MARKETS: GENERAL EQUILIBRIUM ANALYSIS

When we focus on one market in isolation, we are assuming that events in this market do not have a significant impact on other markets in the economy and that there are no feedback effects from those markets to the one we are considering. This is called *partial equilibrium* analysis— partial because it deals with only one part of a larger system.

For many markets partial equilibrium analysis is quite satisfactory. What happens in the market for men's shoes in Decatur, Illinois, or in the fresh cabbage market in West Bend, Wisconsin, is not going to have much effect elsewhere in the economy. But a change in the price of steel or crude oil or labor is going to affect many markets throughout the economy. When we try to take explicit account of the interrelation of a large number of markets, we are engaged in *general equilibrium* analysis.

The interdependence of markets was illustrated dramatically in 1973–74 when the price of imported crude oil was suddenly increased fivefold, and again in 1979–80, when prices tripled. Oil flows, literally, into thousands of different uses. It is a raw material for plastics and petrochemicals, so costs and prices of these products have risen. It goes into fertilizer production, raising farmers' costs and thus making for higher food prices. It is used by truckers as well as automobile drivers, so transportation costs have risen for everything moving over the nation's highways. To offset higher fuel costs, cars have become smaller and miles per gallon (mpg) ratings have risen. Many electric power plants are oil-fired, so utility rates have been raised to cover the higher costs; and since almost everyone uses electricity, these rate increases penetrate into every corner of the economy.

But because of the possibilities of *economizing* on oil, what has hurt some industries has benefited others. Coal is now cheaper than oil for many uses, so coal mining has been stepped up. There has been a rush to drill new oil wells and to extract oil from shale deposits. Homeowners using fuel oil are insulating their houses and putting on storm windows to reduce their heating costs. Some people who used to go everywhere by car are going by train or bus or subway instead. So producers of coal, coal mining machinery, oil drilling equipment, insulating materials, train and subway cars, and many other goods have experienced an *increase* in demand.

Not only does the increased price of petroleum products affect many other markets, but events in these other markets have feedback effects on the petroleum industry. This industry is itself a large user of gasoline and diesel oil for everything from ocean tankers to the tankwagon trucks which deliver gasoline to filling stations. It is also a large user of electricity, the price of which is closely linked to the price of crude oil. So an increase in the price of petroleum products means an increase in the *cost of producing them,* which tends to raise the price still more.

Such feedback effects are common. A rise in the price of steel will eventually raise the price of machinery, some of which is bought by the steel industry. As the demand for labor rises during an economic upswing, wage rates rise, but as wage earners spend their increased earnings at the store, retailers' orders to manufacturers will increase, further raising the demand for labor.

It is now clearer why we are justified in speaking of an economic *system.* Markets throughout the system are linked by the existence of alternatives and the consequent possibility of choice. A shift in one market is transmitted through these linkages into markets which on the surface seem quite remote from the first. A market economy may be visualized as a kind of giant computer, constantly receiving information from all parts of the system and working out appropriate adjustments. A shift in one market starts lights flashing all through the machine, and many prices and outputs may have to change before the computer settles down. A major function of economics is to analyze and predict these indirect effects, which the public often overlooks.

THINK ABOUT THIS

To gain experience in thinking about the interrelation of markets, consider the following:

1. Imports of foreign oil are costing the United States a lot of money— about $80 billion in 1980. Reducing these imports has become an important policy objective. What actions, in what markets, might be useful in reducing imports?

2. Suppose that young people entering the labor force become less and less willing to work in meat-packing plants because of disagreeable working conditions. What would be the consequences in labor markets and product markets?

3. Slimness becomes fashionable and consumers' preferences shift away from potatoes and toward lettuce. What will happen next?

NEW CONCEPTS

demand	black market
quantity demanded	rationing
utility	shortage
marginal utility	surplus
change in demand	price elasticity of demand
supply	price elasticity of supply
quantity supplied	market
change in supply	price
price support	pure competiton
equilibrium price	equilibrium-analysis, partial
equilibrium quantity	equilibrium-analysis, general
price ceiling	equilibrium

SUMMARY

1. A consumer will normally buy more of a product at a lower price. Since total demand is the sum of individual demands, it behaves in the same way. A reduction in price leads to an increase in quantity sold. The responsiveness of quantity to price is measured by the *price elasticity of demand.*

2. Movement from one point to another on the same demand curve is not a change in demand. A change in demand means that the whole curve has shifted to a new position.

3. The supply curve shows the quantities, per unit of time, which

sellers will offer at alternative market prices. The price-quantity relation is normally positive—more will be offered at a higher price.

4. The intersection of the supply and demand curves defines an equilibrium price and quantity exchanged. This is a price which, once established, will be stable so long as demand and supply conditions remain unchanged.

5. A shift in the demand or supply schedule produces a new equilibrium price and quantity, and the market will move toward the new equilibrium. Review the four rules set out in the chapter and work them out by using graphs.

6. Market prices serve important economic functions. They provide an *incentive to production,* a means of *rationing* scarce supplies, and a *signaling mechanism* that indicates the need for resource transfers.

7. A continuing *surplus* in a market indicates that price is being held above the equilibrium level. A *shortage* indicates that price is being held below equilibrium. Shortages and surpluses tend to disappear when price is freed to perform its normal functions.

TO LEARN MORE

The classic defense of competitive markets is still Adam Smith, *The Wealth of Nations* (published in 1776, numerous modern editions in print). A modern book in the spirit of Smith is Milton Friedman, *Capitalism and Freedom* (Chicago: University of Chicago Press, 1962). A clear exposition of demand-supply analysis is H. D. Henderson, *Supply and Demand* (Chicago: University of Chicago Press, 1962). There are many casebooks illustrating the application of this analysis to specific products; for example, Donald S. Watson, *Price Theory in Action* (Boston: Houghton Mifflin, several editions).

The Macroeconomy: National Output and Income

Never ask of money spent
Where the spender thinks it went.
Nobody was ever meant
To remember or invent
What he did with every cent.

—ROBERT FROST

We turn now from the details of the economy to the big picture—total output, total spending, total employment. We want to learn what determines these totals and why they move upward or downward over the course of time. Economists call this branch of the subject *macroeconomics*.

The purpose of this chapter is to explain some key ideas which we'll be using again and again in later chapters.

The accepted measure of total output is *gross national product* (GNP). There are several statistical problems in adding up national output. We'll discuss these briefly, leaving a fuller explanation to the chapter appendix.

The goods produced each year can be divided into *consumer goods, capital goods, government-produced goods,* and *net exports* to foreign buyers. Demands for these types of goods behave differently, and these differences help to explain fluctuations in total demand and output.

For every dollar of output produced, a dollar of income is created. This income can be used for *consumer spending, tax payments, personal saving,* or *business saving.* All income is used in one of these ways.

In Chapter 2 we showed how to define *equilibrium* in a single market. In a similar way we can define equilibrium for the economy as a whole. The basic condition for equilibrium is that total demand for output must just equal the total value of output, so that businesses can sell what they are currently producing.

This concept of aggregate equilibrium is central to everything that follows. In this chapter we explain the idea in words. In Chapters 4 and 5 we will see how the same idea can be illustrated by simple geometry.

MEASURING NATIONAL OUTPUT

In reading about gross national product (GNP) you may have been puzzled by the word *gross*. Why is this word included, and what does it mean? There is a simple explanation: Suppose that total output this year is $3,000 billion. Does this mean that we have $3,000 billion of goods available for use this year? No, it does not. In the course of the year's production, some capital goods are used up—either worn out and scrapped or partially worn out so that their future life is shorter. Business accountants call this *depreciation*. National income accountants call it *capital consumption*.

Both terms mean the same thing: Part of this year's output must go to replace capital goods that have worn out during the year. If that were not done, the total capital stock, and hence the productive capacity of the economy, would decrease. We would be living on our capital from a national standpoint. So businesses count depreciation as a cost of production and deduct it from revenue in calculating net income. Similarly, national income accountants deduct capital consumption from the GNP figure. This yields a smaller total, *net national product* or NNP, which is the amount of output we can use this year while maintaining our capital stock intact.

Wherever you see the terms *gross* and *net,* this is the difference between them. Thus *gross capital formation,* or gross investment, is the total amount of new capital goods created during the year. When we deduct capital consumption during the year, we get a smaller figure of *net capital formation,* or net investment. The net figure tells us how much the nation's capital stock increased during the year.

Problems in adding up output

There are several problems involved in adding up national output: the problems of *double-counting,* of valuing *nonmarketed output,* and of *price-level change.* Here we'll say just enough about these so that you'll realize their existence. You'll find a fuller explanation in the appendix.

You should remember also that GNP is a measure of output, and so only sales of *newly produced goods* can affect the GNP total. If someone sells you a used car or a used house, the sale is not included in GNP.

The same is true of stock or bond sales and of other financial transactions. If you are in doubt about a particular transaction, recall the newly produced output rule and the difficulty should disappear.

Double-counting. This problem can be illustrated by a simple example: A farmer sells wheat to a milling company, which grinds it into flour which is sold to a bakery, which produces bread distributed to a grocery store, which sells the bread to consumers. How much has this chain of events added to GNP? If we total the sales receipts of each producer—the farmer, the miller, the baker, the grocer—we'll come out with too large a total. A little thought will show that if you do this, you are counting the value of the original wheat four times, the value added by the miller three times, and the value added by the baker twice.

Once the problem is recognized, it's perfectly easy to get around it. There are in fact two possible methods, which yield the same result. The most obvious and the method mainly used in practice is to count only the value of the bread in consumers' hands. This figure is correct because it already includes the output of all those at earlier stages of production. So, statisticians get a GNP figure by totaling the value of all *final output*—goods ready for use without further processing or distribution.

Nonmarketed output. The procedure just described works well for goods which are distributed through markets at a market price. But there are some goods for which this is not true. The most important category is government-produced output, or *public goods*. These are normally distributed to citizens without charge, their cost being covered by taxation.

Government buys labor services from households, as we showed in the government payroll arrow in Chapter 1. It also buys goods from business concerns. These purchased goods and hired labor are combined to produce a wide variety of public goods—public education, police and fire protection, national defense, and so on.

These goods are usually not sold in markets at a price. So what are they worth? On this point, GNP estimates follow a simple rule: A public good is worth what it costs to produce it. If the federal government this year spends $200 billion on national defense, then defense is worth that amount. Thus the total value of all public goods is equal to government purchases of goods and labor. There is no way to show that this rule is correct, but no one has yet come up with a better one.

An important kind of output not counted in GNP is that produced in the household. Until fairly recently homemakers in the United States did most of the baking, clothes making, laundry, and other household services. Since these things were done at home without pay, they didn't count as part of national output. Since 1900, more and more of this work has been shifted outside the home. We have prepackaged and precooked foods, commercial bakeries, garment factories, commercial laundries and dry-cleaning establishments, repair shops of every description. The output of these establishments is bought and sold, hence is counted in GNP. Thus even if people consumed no more food or clothing than before, it would look as though GNP had increased. In recent years, on the other hand, sales of home power tools, do-it-yourself kits, and so on suggest that there may have been a net increase in household production. Nor should one forget the vast amount of unpaid chauffeur service provided by car owners and their families.

Many people, particularly leaders of the women's movement, argue that household work should be given a value and included in GNP. This is worth thinking about. Would it be a reasonable thing to do? If so, how would one go about valuing household production?

Price-level change. We can add up outputs only in terms of dollars. But how much is a dollar worth? As the price level rises, the amount of goods which a dollar can buy declines. We find that we're working with a rubber yardstick.

For example, suppose that GNP this year is $3,300 billion, while last year it was $3,000 billion. Has physical output increased? Not necessarily. Suppose that prices, on the average, are 10 percent higher this year than last. A little arithmetic shows that real or physical output hasn't risen at all. All that's happened is that the same output, which at last year's prices had a value of $3,000 billion, has a value this year of $3,300 billion. The increase in value is due entirely to the higher price level.

Over any period of time, the prices of different goods change at different rates, so we need an average of these individual price movements. The most commonly used index is the consumer price index (CPI), but there are several others, whose meanings will be explained in the appendix.

Example. Suppose we wish to compare real GNP in 1982 with that in 1972. In 1972 GNP was $1,171 billion. In 1982 GNP was $3,073 billion— almost three times the 1972 figure. Real GNP did not increase that much, however, because prices were much higher in 1982. If we define the 1972 price level as 100, the 1982 price index was 206.9. So we deflate the 1982 GNP total by dividing it by the price index. We find that real GNP, measured in constant 1972 dollars, was only $3,073/206.9 = $1,485 billion. Instead of tripling, real GNP increased by only 27 percent between 1972 and 1982.

HOW OUTPUT AND PRICES BEHAVE

The behavior of output, employment, and prices over the course of time affects everyone in the economy. Our capacity to produce goods grows at a rather steady rate, shown by the potential GNP line in Figure 3–1. The reasons, examined more thoroughly in a later chapter, include growth of population and labor force, growth in our stock of capital

FIGURE 3-1
Actual and potential GNP, 1950-83 (billions of 1972 dollars)

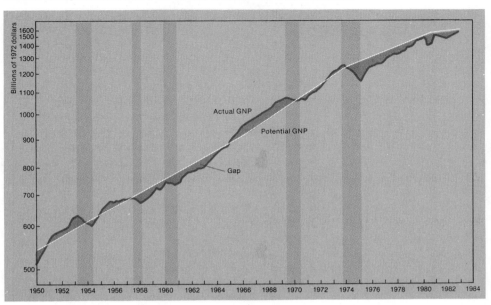

Source: *Economic Report of the President, 1984.*

goods, and improvement of production methods through technical progress.

Actual output also rises over the long run but not in a steady way.
After several years of rising GNP, the economy turns downward into a
recession. Real GNP falls, and the GNP gap between actual and potential
output, shown by the white area in Figure 3–1, becomes wider. Recession
periods, shown by the shaded bars in Figure 3–1, usually last only for
a year or so, after which GNP begins to rise again.

These fluctuations in GNP are illustrated from another standpoint
in Figure 3–2. The output line shows the percentage growth rate of GNP
year by year since 1953. Note that on the upswing GNP often rises by
5 percent or more per year. But when a recession occurs, the growth
rate falls below zero. The unemployment rate, as one would expect, moves
in the opposite direction to output. When output falls, unemployment
rises, and conversely.

These facts of life pose the problems we shall be examining throughout
this book. How can the gap between actual and potential output be held
to modest proportions? Could recessions be prevented by timely government action? If not prevented, can we take steps to ensure that they
will be short and shallow?

FIGURE 3-2
Growth rate of real GNP and the unemployment rate, 1950–83

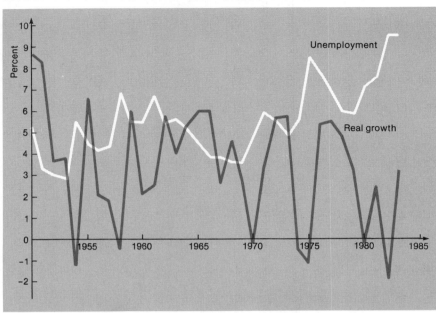

Source: *Economic Report of the President, 1984.*

Another set of questions involves price-level behavior. A stable price level is usually listed among the important economic objectives. But it is clear from Figure 3–3 that the actual price level has been notably unstable. With one exception, the price level has risen every year since 1940. Even in the years before 1965, the price level was typically rising at 2 or 3 percent a year. After 1965 the inflation rate accelerated, partly because of the output boom associated with the Vietnam War. During the 70s, the inflation rate has been much higher than in previous decades—usually in the range of 5 to 10 percent per year.

A continuing rise in the price level seems now to be a built-in feature of our economy, something which was not true before 1940. What are the reasons for this inflationary bias? Who gains and who loses from inflation? Does it do any economic damage overall? Can we restrain the advance of prices without interfering with normal growth of output and employment? These questions form part of the agenda for later chapters.

We noted earlier that because of the rapid rise of price levels, real GNP behaves quite differently from GNP in current dollars. This point is illustrated in Figure 3–4. Real GNP rises rather consistently at a modest rate, though a bit more slowly in the 70s than in the 60s. GNP in current

FIGURE 3-3
Annual percentage increase in GNP price index, 1950-83

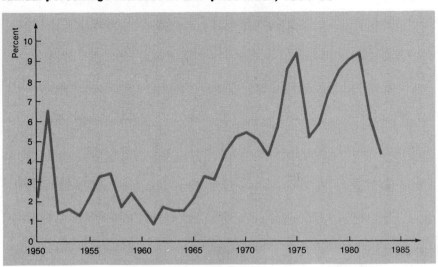

Source: *Economic Report of the President, 1984.*

dollars shoots upward much more rapidly, especially since about 1965, because of rapid price increases.

THE COMPOSITION OF OUTPUT: CONSUMPTION, INVESTMENT, GOVERNMENT, FOREIGN TRADE

We are usually interested not just in total national output but in the main kinds of output. It is especially useful to subdivide output in terms of who bought it. It may have been sold to consumers, to other businesses, to a government agency, or to foreign buyers. These groups buy goods for different reasons, and so their demands behave differently. This helps to explain the fluctuations in total demand for goods, which will be our main concern for several chapters to come.

You'll remember that back in Chapter 1 we drew a circular flow diagram outlining the main flows of money and goods in the economy. It will be useful to reproduce this here, as Figure 3-5, with a few alterations. Note that in addition to adding government at the top of the diagram, we have added foreign trade at the bottom. The solid lines are money flows in the direction of the arrows. But remember that each of these money flows is accompanied by a movement of goods of equal value in the opposite direction.

FIGURE 3–4
Real GNP may behave quite differently from money GNP

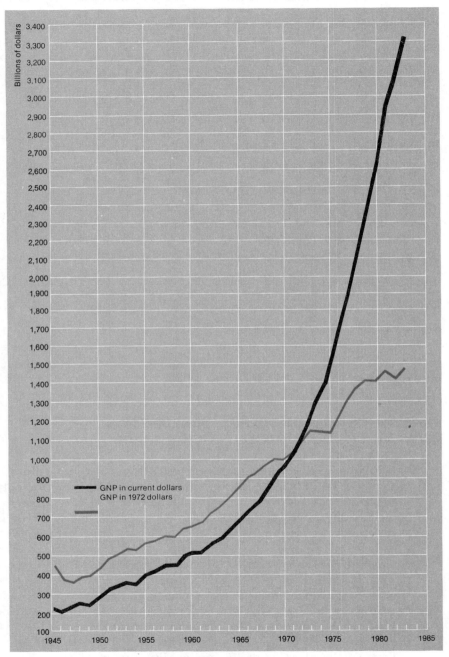

GNP in current dollars has risen considerably faster than GNP measured in dollars of constant (1972) purchasing power. The reason is that prices have risen in almost every year since 1945.

Source: *Economic Report of the President, 1984.*

FIGURE 3-5
The flow of income: Trade and government added

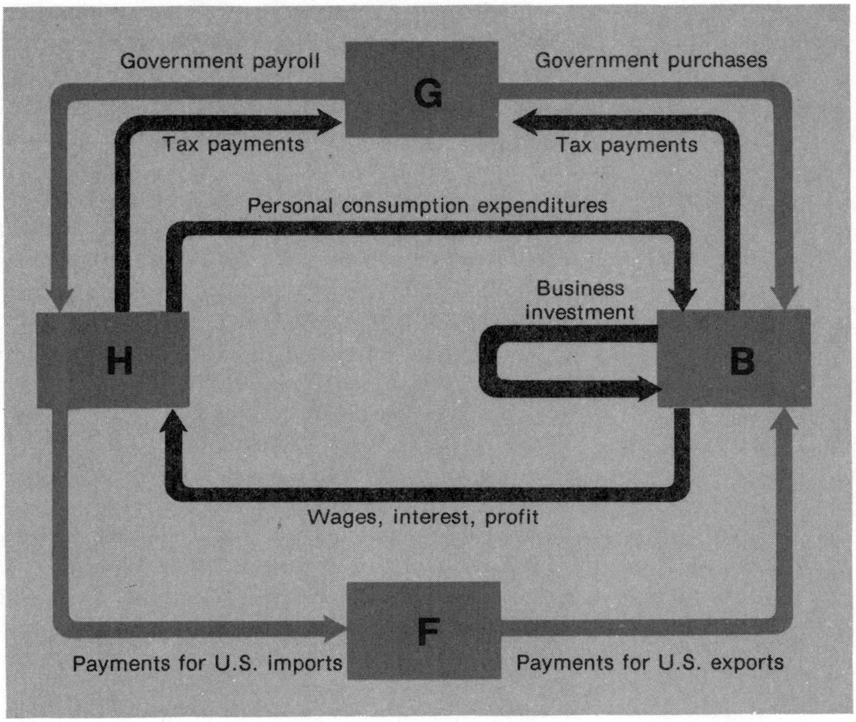

The boxes indicate households, government, businesses, and foreign trade. The solid lines are money flows moving in the direction of the arrows.

Consumer purchases

This includes all final output bought for consumer use except new housing construction, which is counted as part of investment. Consumer purchases are usually subdivided into (1) durable goods, such as automobiles, furniture, kitchen appliances; (2) nondurable goods, of which food and clothing are more important; and (3) services, such as travel, recreation, beauty care, hotels, and restaurants. The reason for this separation is that these components behave differently over time. Replacement of a durable good is often postponable—you can trade in your old car this year or next year. So purchases of durable goods, particularly automobiles, show larger fluctuations than purchases of nondurables. Over the years, purchases of services rise considerably faster than purchases of commodities.

Business purchases

In Figure 3–5 you will notice a line which starts out from the business sector and circles right back to it. These are sales by business *to* business. But this looks a bit odd. A few pages back we made a great point of *deducting* sales by one business to another in totaling GNP. This is certainly the right procedure for intermediate goods; that is, materials and services *to be used up in current production.* But the sales to business shown in Figure 3–5 consist of buildings, machinery, and other *capital goods* destined to last beyond the current year. These are final goods and stand on exactly the same basis as final goods for consumer use or government use. Like the latter, their production creates an equal amount of income, and our basic rule still applies.

In addition to commercial buildings, factories, and machinery, we count as part of business investment the *net change in business inventories.* This must be brought in because GNP is calculated for a period of time, say, January 1, 1985–December 31, 1985. The amount of goods produced in a 12-month period will not correspond exactly with the amount sold. Suppose the X Manufacturing Company, while producing $1.3 million worth of goods during 1979, had managed to sell only $1.2 million of goods. The extra $100,000 worth is sitting in the warehouse as increased inventory. This should certainly be counted as output, because $100,000 of income *was* created in the course of producing it. But it does not yet show up in sales to consumers, government, or foreign buyers. So we show it as part of business investment—a kind of sale by the X Company to *itself.* (The inventory change can be either positive or negative. If a company sells *more* than it produces in a certain year, this shows up as a *reduction* in business investment.)

Residential construction is also considered part of investment, even though houses are bought by households rather than businesses. The basis for this is that houses are very *durable,* more comparable to office and commercial buildings than to food, clothing, and other items of household consumption.

Investment includes output of capital goods, net change in business inventories, and residential construction.

Government purchases

Government makes two kinds of purchases. It buys labor services from households, shown by the government payroll arrow in Figure 3–5. It also buys goods from business concerns. These purchased goods and hired labor are combined to produce a wide variety of public goods— public education, police and fire protection, national defense, and so on. We noted earlier that these goods are valued at what it costs to produce them. So government purchases of goods and services = value of public output = government share of GNP.

The government share of GNP has risen substantially during this century. In 1900, and even as late as 1929, it was only a few percent of GNP. Today it is a bit over 20 percent. The private consumption share of GNP is typically 62–64 percent, while the investment share is 17–18 percent.

We commonly say that government purchases are stable, while purchases of investment goods and consumer durable goods are somewhat unstable. But caution is necessary here. State and local expenditures, and federal expenditures on civilian goods, are indeed stable, rising gradually and predictably over the course of time. But this is not true of the military expenditures which bulk large in the federal budget. These rose sharply in the early stages of the Korean and Vietnam wars and were cut back at the end of those wars, contributing some instability to total demand.

Foreign trade

This is a tricky area, because we must consider imports as well as exports, and we must look at both output produced and income created.

Consider exports first. If U.S. business concerns produce $200 billion worth of goods for export to foreign buyers, then $200 billion of income must have been created, and this is added to the wages-interest-profit stream within the United States. But this $200 billion of money flow does not have any "shadow" flow of goods moving in the opposite direction *within the United States*. The goods have vanished to foreign parts.

On the other hand, American consumers buy goods produced abroad. Here is a stream of goods going to the household sector, but without any corresponding flow of income created *within the United States*. The labor and capital which produced these goods are employed abroad, and the income derived from their selling price is distributed abroad. This is just the reverse of what happens in the case of exports.

If the flow of exports exactly equaled the flow of imports, they would cancel out, but there is no reason why they should be equal, and they usually are not. So we balance the books by counting as part of GNP *the value of exports minus imports*. If this is positive (exports > imports), then more income has been created within the United States in export industries than has been drawn off to pay for imports, and this extra income just equals the excess of exports over imports.

The American economy is very large and largely self-contained. Traditionally, exports and imports have formed only a few percent of our GNP. But this is no longer true as it was 10 or 20 years ago. The very large increase in crude oil prices since 1973 has greatly increased the number of dollars we must spend on imported oil. But many of these dollars come back in the form of increased demand for our exports. So both the export total and the import total have risen and are now running at more than 10 percent of our GNP. But while the totals are large, the difference between them is usually small. They come close to canceling out.

To sum up:

Total output = Consumer goods output + Capital goods output + Government output + (Exports − Imports).

If we use C for consumer goods, I for capital goods, G for government goods, X for exports, and M for imports, then

$$\text{Total output} \equiv C + I + G + (X - M).$$

The identity sign ($\equiv$) indicates a statement which must be true because of the definition of its terms.

"I have prepared this simple chart to show population increase, food scarcity, price spiral, sugar scarcity, growth of corruption, unemployment—all in one."

Laxman in The Times of India.

OUTPUT EQUALS INCOME

In circular flow diagrams such as Figure 3–5, money moves around the diagram in one direction, while goods and services move in the opposite direction. Moreover, *the two flows are exactly equal.* So, we can total the value of all the goods produced in the economy this month or this year. Or we can total all the money which businesses and government spent (and households received) in producing these goods. Whether we measure *output* or whether we measure *income,* we will get the same result.

The equality of output and income is a central principle, on which much of our later reasoning will depend. To convince ourselves that it is true, let us look at the operations of a particular business, the X Manufacturing Company, in 1985.

The right-hand side of Table 3–1 shows that the X Manufacturing Company in 1985 bought $5,000 million of raw materials and supplies from other companies. It processed these materials into finished goods worth $10,000 million. Its own output (value added), then, was $5,000 million.

This money had to go somewhere. The left-hand (income) side of Table 3–1 shows where it went. The company had to set aside some money to provide for depreciation of its plant and equipment, which is a cost of production. It had to pay wages and salaries to its employees. It had to pay interest to bondholders and other providers of capital, and it had to pay state and local taxes. What is left over after meeting these payments is its *profit* (net income) for the year.

Part of the profit is taxed away by the federal government through the corporate income tax. What is left after that belongs to the common stockholders, who are the owners of the corporation. But they don't usually get all of it. Company boards of directors determine what percentage of profit shall be paid out in dividends. Here we show them following a 50 percent rule, which is quite common in practice. The remaining $300 million, which stays in the business, is called *retained earnings.*

We have now accounted for the full $5,000 million of income generated by the X Manufacturing Company's $5,000 million of output. Not all of this income, to be sure, is paid out by the company. The company

TABLE 3–1
Output and income statement for the X Manufacturing Company, 1985 (millions of dollars)

Income (payments)			*Output (receipts)*	
Output		$5,000	Finished goods	
Minus depreciation	$ 500		produced	$10,000
Wages and salaries	3,000		Minus: raw materials,	
Interest, local taxes	500	4,000	etc., bought from	
Net income before taxes		1,000	other producers	5,000
Minus corporate income tax		400	Output (value	
Net income after taxes		600	added)	$ 5,000
Minus dividend payments		300		
Retained earnings		$ 300		

holds back for its own use the $500 million of depreciation allowances plus the $300 million of retained earnings. The sum of these two items is called *business saving*. These dollars are still around, available for spending, and in fact most of them are spent on expansion of the business.

   Example.   In 1983, total business investment was $346.5 billion. To help finance this expenditure there was $287.0 billion of business saving, of which $231.6 billion came from depreciation allowances and $45.4 billion from retained earnings. In this year, then, businesses were able to finance more than four fifths of their investment from internal sources.

THE USES OF INCOME

   Just as we divided total output into its main parts, we can divide total income (which has the same value) into its major uses. Most of the income generated in production is paid out to consumers, who can use it for consumption or for personal saving. Some of it goes into business saving, while some goes in tax payments to government by businesses and individuals. Thus we see that

Total income = Personal consumption expenditure + Personal saving + Business saving + Tax payments.

   If we use C for consumption, S_p for personal saving, S_b for business saving, and T for tax payments, then

$$\text{Total income} \equiv C + S_p + S_b + T.$$

As before, the identity sign ($\equiv$) indicates a statement which is true by definition.

THINK ABOUT THIS

1. Are you convinced that since every dollar of output creates a dollar of income, there is no *inevitable* "shortage of purchasing power"?
2. Suppose a commonsensical friend says to you, "Look, there must be a shortage of purchasing power. If all producers tried to operate at full capacity, they wouldn't be able to sell all their output. The proof is that they aren't operating at capacity." What would you say?

AGGREGATE EQUILIBRIUM AND DISEQUILIBRIUM

   Breaking down output and income into their components gives us a powerful set of tools. Let us put our basic identities together. Thinking in output terms,

$$\text{Total output} \equiv C + I + G + (X - M) \tag{1}$$

But in income terms, we know that

$$\text{Total income} \equiv C + S_p + S_b + T \tag{2}$$

We have also shown that every dollar's worth of output generates a dollar of income. Total output and total income are equal. Since things equal to the same thing are equal to each other, it follows that

$$C + I + G + (X - M) \equiv C + S_p + S_b + T. \tag{3}$$

But C means the same thing on both sides of the equation—total spending on consumer goods. So we can cancel out C, leaving

$$I + G + (X - M) \equiv S_p + S_b + T. \tag{4}$$

These are equal because they mean the same thing: that part of this year's output which was not purchased by U.S. consumers.

Looked at another way, the items on the left-hand side are *injections* into the income stream—sources of demand for goods in addition to consumer demand. The items on the right-hand side represent *leakages* from the income stream—income generated in the course of production which is not used to buy consumer goods.

Think of the level of national output as similar to the water level in a storage tank. Part of the income generated in production leaks out through a drainage pipe at the bottom of the tank in the form of personal saving, business saving, and tax payments. But at the top of the tank is a pump which is pouring in new income from business investment, government purchases, and net exports. If the inflows just equal the outflows, the water level in the tank will remain unchanged.

In Chapter 2 we showed that a single market is in equilibrium when the quantity demanded equals the quantity supplied. In just the same way we can define a condition of *aggregate equilibrium* in the economy as a whole. Equilibrium requires equality in the two sides of Equation 4, a situation in which total injections into the income stream equal total leakages from the stream. If this condition is met, total demand for goods just equals the value of goods being produced. If producers go on operating at the current rate, they will just be able to sell their output. Thus there is no reason for the output rate to change.

But this presents a puzzle. Haven't we just shown that the two sides of the equation *must* be equal by definition? How, then, can the system ever be out of equilibrium? The answer depends on whether we are looking *backward* over the past or *forward* toward the future. If we are talking about last year, or any other completed period, $I + G + (X - M)$ must equal $S_p + S_b + T$. This follows from the definition of our terms and from the equality of output and income.

But suppose instead that we are talking about the year ahead. Now we are no longer talking about facts but about *intentions* or *plans* for the future. We are talking about how much businesses plan to invest, how much government plans to spend, how much households and businesses plan to save. Decisions on these points are made by millions of households, businesses, and government units. There is no reason why the *planned* quantities on one side of the equation should add up to equality with those on the other side. This would be the sheerest accident, and as a practical matter, we cannot expect it to happen.

But unless plans on the two sides of the equation are equal, the system is in *aggregate disequilibrium.* Planned demand for goods in the period ahead will not equal planned supply. Something will have to give, and this something is the level of national output.

Suppose that the planned injections to income are greater than the planned leakages.

$$I + G + (X - M) > S_p + S_b + T$$

Then demand for output will be larger than the current rate of output, and as producers become aware of this, the rate of output will rise.

Suppose on the other hand that the planned injections fall short of the planned leakages from the income stream.

$$I + G + (X - M) < S_p + S_b + T$$

Then demand will be insufficient to buy the current rate of output, and as producers realize this, the output rate will drop.

These simple equations are useful in another way. Suppose we ask: What changes in the system are capable of producing a rise or a fall in the output rate? Our equations provide a complete checklist of such changes. Specifically,

C: An increase in consumer spending, which means a reduction in personal saving, will raise the rate of output; and conversely for a fall in spending.

I: Increased investment demand—for housing, business plant and equipment, or business inventories—will raise the rate of output; and conversely.

G: Increased government demand for goods and services will raise the rate of output; and conversely.

X: Increased demand for U.S. goods by foreign buyers will raise the rate of output: and conversely.

M: Increased demand by Americans for foreign goods will lower the rate of output; and conversely.

S_b: An increase in business saving will lower the rate of output; and conversely.

T: An increase in tax rates will lower the rate of output; and conversely.

Anything which affects the rate of output must operate through one of these channels.

Especially important in practice are variations in investment demand, particularly for housing and for additions to inventories. But consumer demand for automobiles and other durable goods is also somewhat unstable. And even government demand, usually stable, may vary because of changes in military expenditure such as occurred during and after the Korean War and the Vietnam War.

The idea of aggregate equilibrium and the possible sources of change in equilibrium is central to macroeconomics and should be thoroughly learned at this point. In Chapters 4 and 5 we shall demonstrate how this idea can be illustrated by simple geometry. But the central principles are exactly the same, and if you master them now you should have no trouble later on.

THINK ABOUT THIS

1. Wouldn't it be reasonable to count the value of household production as part of GNP? How would you go about estimating this value?
2. Between 1950 and 1980, U.S. GNP per head of population (measured in constant 1972 dollars, that is, adjusted for changes in the price level) rose from $3,510 to $6,160, or by about 75 percent. Does this mean that consumers in the United States were 75 percent better off in 1980?
3. If we compare the GNP accounts for the United States and Indonesia (converting the Indonesian figures from rupiahs into U.S. dollars), we find that GNP per capita in the United States is about 30 times that for Indonesia. Does this mean that Americans are 30 times as well off as Indonesians?

NEW CONCEPTS

aggregate equilibrium
aggregate disequilibrium
business saving
capital consumption
capital formation, gross
capital formation, net
consumer price index
deflation
depreciation
double-counting
final output
gross national product, constant dollars
gross national product, current dollars

injections into the income stream
inventory change
investment
leakages from the income stream
net national product
nonmarketed output
personal income
personal saving
price index
price-level change
real national output
retained corporate profits
value added

SUMMARY

1. In the course of producing this year's gross national product, we wear out some of the capital goods existing at the beginning of the year. We deduct this *capital consumption* from GNP to get *net national product*. Gross capital formation and net capital formation also differ by the amount of capital consumption.

2. There are several difficulties in adding up national output. We must avoid double-counting and must include some types of output which are not sold in the market, notably government output. We must also adjust for price-level changes by using a price index to estimate changes in *real output*.

3. For every dollar of output produced, a dollar of income is created. Those who receive the income, of course, may decide not to spend all of it, but there is no necessary shortage of purchasing power.

4. Total output consists of consumer purchases; investment, including residential construction; government purchases of goods and services; and net sales to foreigners (exports minus imports). This can be expressed as follows:

$$\text{Total output} \equiv C + I + G + (X - M).$$

5. The income created in producing GNP must go either into consumer spending, personal saving, business saving, or tax payments. Thus

$$\text{Total income} \equiv C + S_p + S_b + T.$$

6. Since total output and total income are equal, it follows that

$$C + I + G + (X - M) \equiv C + S_p + S_b + T,$$

and since C means the same thing on both sides, we can cancel it out, leaving

$$I + G + (X - M) \equiv S_p + S_b + T.$$

7. The items on the left-hand side of this equation are *injections* into the income stream, while those on the right-hand side are *leakages* from the income stream. If injections and leakages are equal, the economy is in *equilibrium*, and the rate of output will not change.

8. For any *past* period, the two sides of the equation must be equal by definition. But if we are talking about a *future* period, such as the coming year, there is no reason why output and spending plans should be equal.

9. If output and spending plans are unequal, the economy is not in equilibrium, and the rate of output will have to change. If spending plans are *larger* than production plans, the rate of output will *increase*. If spending plans are *smaller* than production plans, the rate of output will *decrease*.

10. The terms in our equation provide a complete checklist of things which will raise (or lower) the rate of national output.

TO LEARN MORE

To keep up with what is happening in the economy, you should be familiar with the main statistical publications of the U.S. government. *The Economic Report of the President,* prepared by the Council of Economic Advisers and issued each year around February 1, contains basic data on GNP and its components, prices, employment and unemployment, and many other variables. For the latest current information, see the monthly publication *Economic Indicators,* also prepared by the CEA and available from the Government Printing Office, Washington, D.C. You should also look at the *Federal Reserve Bulletin,* the *Survey of Current Business,* and the *Monthly Labor Review,* which contain statistical information in their respective fields.

Appendix: The U.S. national income accounts

The official national income estimates for the United States are prepared by the U.S. Department of Commerce. They are published initially in the *Survey of Current Business* and are reprinted in the annual *Economic Report of the President,* the monthly bulletin *Economic Indicators,* and numerous other sources.

The estimates for 1983, with a little rearrangement, are shown in Table 3–2. The right-hand side of the table shows national output divided among the four types of purchasers. The total of this side is

$$C + I + G + (X - M) = GNP.$$

On the left-hand side of Table 3–2, we look

at income created rather than output produced, but as emphasized earlier, we must come out with the same total. Wages, rents, interest, and profit require no explanation. But note that sizable item for *income of unincorporated enterprises.* This includes the incomes of millions of farmers, storekeepers, and other small producers whose businesses are not set up as companies. A farmer, for example, pays for purchased materials, pays property taxes, and perhaps pays some interest to the local banker. What's left over is the net income for the year. We may say, if we like, that part of this income is wages for labor, part is interest on land and farm machinery, and part may be profit. But it is all in-

TABLE 3–2
U.S. national product and income, 1983 (billions of dollars)

Income		*Output*	
Wages and salaries	$1,990.1	Personal consumption expenditures	$2,158.6
Rent and interest	302.0	Gross private domestic investment	471.3
Corporate profits	226.3	Government purchases of goods	
Income of unincorporated		and services	690.2
enterprises	128.6	Exports minus imports	−10.6
Capital consumption	377.4		
Indirect business taxes	285.8		
Minor adjustments	−0.7		
Gross national product	$3,309.5	Gross national product	$3,309.5

Source: *Economic Report of the President, 1984.*

come and is hard to subdivide. The same is true for grocery store operators, professional practitioners, and other individual proprietors. All such people are lumped together as unincorporated enterprises.

When we total these income items, we are still a good deal below the output total on the right-hand side of the table. This looks disconcerting. But there is a straightforward explanation. While it is true that for every dollar of output there is a dollar of income created, not all of this income really belongs to the factors of production. First, a business concern must provide for wearing out of its capital equipment during the year. *Capital consumption,* which means the same thing as *depreciation,* is an estimate of this wearing out, covering both corporations and unincorporated businesses.

Second, businesses must pay sales taxes, excise taxes, property taxes, and various other fees and licenses. These are termed *indirect business taxes.* Along with depreciation, these taxes must be deducted from the value of sales. Only the amount remaining is available to the factors of production.[1] Or putting the point in reverse, we must *add* these two items to the total of factor incomes in order to get the sales value of output; that is, gross national product.

The grand total and some smaller totals

1. *Gross national product* measures all the productive activity in a country during a certain period of time. It is the best single answer to the question, "What did we turn out in the United States in 1980?" It gives a thermometer reading of the state of the economy, useful in following the ups and downs of the business cycle. Several other totals, however, are interesting for various purposes. the actual values in 1983 are shown in Table 3–3.

The word *gross* in gross national product means that in calculating the output of each producing unit we did not deduct anything for the wearing out of capital goods during the year, for *capital consumption.* But if a company wants to keep operating at the same rate year after year, it cannot pay out its full income to factor suppliers. Something must be set aside to replace the worn-out capital goods. Only after pro-

TABLE 3–3
GNP and subtotals, 1983

		Billions of Dollars
Gross national product		3,309.5
Minus:	Capital consumption allowances	377.4
Equals net national product		2,932.1
Minus:	Indirect business taxes	301.4
Plus:	Other minor items	16.3
Equals national income		2,646.9
Minus:	Corporate profits*	226.3
	Net interest	247.2
	Social security contributions	272.3
Plus:	Government transfers to persons†	387.9
	Personal interest income	366.3
	Personal divided income	70.5
	Business transfer payments	15.5
Equals personal income		2,741.9
Minus:	Personal tax payments	406.3
Equals disposable income		2,335.6
Consumption		2,222.5
Personal savings		113.1

* Includes inventory valuation and capital consumption adjustments.

† Includes interest payments.

Source: *Economic Report of the President, 1984.*

viding for replacement can we tell how much of the 1983 output was available for use without eating into capital.

2. This remainder is *net national product* (NNP), which equals gross national product minus capital consumption. The terms *gross* and *net* have a similar meaning as regards investment. Thus *gross investment* is the total of new capital goods built during the year, without allowing for wear and tear on existing capital. By deducting capital consumption from gross investment we get *net investment,* the true increase in the nation's stock of capital goods.

NNP is also sometimes called *national income at market prices.* It is the total sales value of output after deducting capital consumption. But even this smaller total is not fully available for the factors of production. Indirect business taxes must be paid. By deducting both capital consumption and indirect business taxes, we discover how much the suppliers of labor and capital have earned during the year.

---

[1] Why do we not also deduct taxes on business profits? Because they are logically different. They do not affect the amount of profit earned by business owners, as shown in Table 3–2. They do affect *what happens* to profit after it has been earned, but that is a different matter.

3. The result is termed *national income at factor cost,* usually shortened to national income. This is the amount which belongs, in priciple, to the factors of production. It is the figure to use if one is interested in tracing the changing importance of labor income relative to property income.

4. If, on the other hand, we want to know how much income households actually receive, the pertinent measure is *personal income.* Not all the income which belongs to the factors of production actually reaches them. This is notably true of profit income. The government takes close to half through the corporate income tax, and boards of directors vote to hold back part of the remainder. Thus the stockholders may end up getting a quarter or less of "their" profits. There are also deductions from labor income. The amount which workers pay into social security and private pension funds, as well as what the employer contributes on their behalf, is counted as belonging to them, but they never see it.

On the positive side, people receive some income which has not been earned in the course of current production. Veterans receive various cash benefits, farmers receive government checks for land taken out of production, workers receive unemployment compensation payments and old-age pensions, welfare clients receive checks from the city, and so on. All these government *transfer payments* are counted as part of personal income. There is also a small volume of business transfer payments through pensions and other private welfare plans.

Personal income, then, is income actually received from every source, including transfer payments, before payment of personal income taxes.

5. *Disposable income* is simply personal income *after* payment of income taxes. It is how much money people finally have left to spend or to save. It is an interesting figure for retailers and consumer goods manufacturers, since it indicates the size of the consumer market. If disposable income is rising, most businesses can expect to find their sales rising as well.

6. Finally, the last two items in the table show what people do with their disposable income. The great bulk of it is spend on consumer goods, but a small portion—typically 5 or 6 percent—goes into personal saving. A small shift in this percentage can make a big difference

to consumer demand, since consumer spending forms close to two thirds of all spending in the economy.

Measurement problems: Double-counting and nonmarketed output

The problems involved in adding up output were discussed briefly in the chapter, but it may be useful to say a bit more about them.

The double-counting problem can be illustrated by a little arithmetic and a simple graph. A farmer produces $100 worth of wheat, which is sold to a flour miller. The milling company, by adding labor and capital inputs to this raw material, produces flour which it sells for $150. A baking company uses this flour to produce $225 worth of food. Finally a grocery store sells this bread to consumers for $300. These transactions are shown in Table 3–4 and Figure 3–6.

How much has the milling company produced? Not its sales revenue of $150, since $100 of this was really produced by the farmer. The milling company's output is the sales value of its product minus its purchases from the preceding stage of production. We call this the value added at the milling stage, which in this example is $50.

Now, what is the total output at all stages of production? Simply adding the sales receipts of the farmer, the miller, the baker, and the retailer would give a total of $775. This is clearly too large. It counts the value of the original wheat four times, the value of flour three times, and the value of bread twice.

There are two ways of arriving at the correct value of output, both of which lead to the same result. The first is called the value-added method. Value added, as explained earlier, is the amount each producer contributes to the retail price of the final product. It is the difference between the

TABLE 3–4
Measuring output without double-counting

Stage of Production	Values of Sales	Purchases from Preceding Stage	Value Added
Farm	100	0	100
Flour mill	150	100	50
Baker	225	150	75
Retailer	300	225	75
	775	475	300

FIGURE 3–6
Adding up output

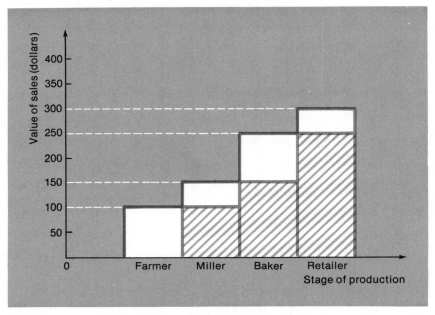

The white areas show value added at each stage of production. Total output can be measured by adding these areas or by taking the value of final sales by retailers. Both method yield the same figure of $300.

value of the goods the producer sells and costs of the materials the producer buys. The value added by each producer in our bread example is shown by the final column of Table 3–4 and by the shaded areas in Figure 3–6.

There is another, simpler approach which involves only the value of final output at the point of sale. In our bread example, it's the value of bread sold by retailers. If we use this method, we can forget about the farmer, the miller, and the baker. Why? Because the value of their output is already included in the retail price of bread. This method yields $300, the same output figure as the other method, but it is much easier and so is the method actually used by government statisticians in estimating GNP.

As regards nonmarketed output, we noted in the chapter that government output is included in GNP and is valued at its cost of production. We noted also that production within the household is not included in GNP, and that this can

have odd results. Transfer of some activity—laundering, baking, clothes making, or whatever—from the household to commercial production will increase the apparent size of GNP, while a transfer in the opposite direction will reduce GNP.

While, in general, home-produced output is not counted, there are two important exceptions. Food produced and consumed on a farm is counted as part of GNP. Further, a homeowner is regarded as renting his house from himself; and the "imputed rent" which he would have to pay as a tenant is counted in GNP. This makes sense, because otherwise the mere shift of a house from owner occupancy to tenancy or vice versa would change the GNP total.

Measurement problems: Adjustment for price change

Finally, we should say more about the problems introduced by price-level changes, partly because there is no fully satisfactory way of coping with these changes.

We would like to use GNP figures for historical analysis of how a country's output has changed over long periods of time. Has U.S. national output risen steadily or intermittently? At what rate, on the average? Are we growing by 2 percent a year or 5 percent?

The first difficulty in tackling these questions is that we are working with a rubber yardstick. All our figures of output and income are expressed in dollars. But a dollar sometimes measures a larger quantity of physical goods and sometimes a smaller quantity, depending on changes in prices. When prices rise, our yardstick shrinks—a dollar equals fewer goods than before, and if prices fall, the yardstick expands again.

Over any period of time the prices of different goods are changing at different rates. To judge what is happening we need an *average* of these individual price movements. Such an average is called a *price index*. Actually, there are several different price indexes in common use. They differ from one another with respect to the commodities included and also with respect to the relative importance attached to the various commodities. Three of the most commonly used price indexes in the United States are the consumer price index (CPI), the producer price index (PPI), and the GNP price index, usually called the GNP deflator.

The consumer price index is often called the "cost-of-living index," but this is an erroneous title, for the index does not measure "what it costs to live."[2] What it does measure is the relative cost at different points in time of a certain market basket of goods which is representative of the purchasing pattern of the "average" urban consumer.

Some years ago the Bureau of Labor Statistics of the U.S. Department of Labor, the agency which is responsible for the index, conducted a study of the spending patterns of urban consumers and came up with a representative market basket of goods. The agency collects data once a month on prices of each item in the basket and is thus able to calculate changes in the relative dollar cost of the basket in different years.

To get a better idea of how the CPI is constructed, suppose that the typical consumer bought only three commodities in 1970:

> 20 pounds of fresh lettuce.
> 10 gallons of regular gasoline.
> 2 haircuts.

Suppose also that the average prices of these commodities in 1970 were:

> $0.20 per pound of fresh lettuce.
> $0.30 per gallon of regular gasoline.
> $2.50 per haircut.

Thus the 1970 market basket cost:

$0.20 \times 20 + $0.30 \times 10 + $2.50 \times 2 = $12.00.

Now suppose that in 1980 the average prices of these commodities were:

> $0.30 per pound of fresh lettuce.
> $1.20 per gallon of regular gasoline.
> $5.00 per haircut.

so the cost of the 1980 basket was:

$0.30 \times 20 + $1.20 \times 10 + $5.00 \times 2 = $28.00

The cost of the market basket in 1980 relative to its cost in 1970 is:

$$\frac{\$28.00}{\$12.00} = 2.333 \text{ (approximately)}.$$

If we assign the index number 100.0 to 1970, the index number for 1980 is 233.3, indicating that the market basket cost more than twice as much in 1980 as in 1970.

The producer price index measures price changes in primary markets. Commodities covered by it include pig iron, winter wheat of a certain grade, sulfuric acid, and so on. Just as in the case of the CPI, the Bureau of Labor Statistics (which is also responsible for this index) started by making a study of the relative importance of various commodities in primary markets and came up with a representative market basket of primary commodities. Then, by getting the price of each commodity each month, it can construct an index of the relative cost of the market

---

[2] The coverage of the consumer price index is *not* limited to the necessities of life. It includes food, clothing, automobiles, house furnishings, household supplies, fuel, drugs, recreational supplies, fees to doctors, fees to lawyers, beauty shops, rent, repair costs, transportation fares, public utility rates, and so on. It deals with prices actually charged to consumers, including sales and excise taxes. It also includes real estate taxes on owned homes, but it does not include income or personal property taxes.

basket at different points in time. The PPI does not move precisely in step with the CPI, since its coverage is different. But if one sees the PPI rising, it is safe to predict a rise in the CPI within a few months, as the primary products covered by the PPI are processed into finished goods distributed to retail markets.

The GNP price index or, by its official name, the GNP implicit price deflator is constructed somewhat differently from the consumer and wholesale indexes, but it is meant to convey the same kind of information—namely, the relative dollar cost of a certain group of commodities at different points in time. The GNP price index is more comprehensive than either the CPI or the PPI, for it covers all goods and services produced in the U.S. economy. Unlike the consumer price index, its coverage is not limited to goods purchased by urban consumers, and unlike the producer price index, it does not just cover commodities which are traded in primary markets.

Now that we have seen how a price index is constructed, let us look at how it is used. The technique of adjusting for price changes by use of a price index is called *deflation*. It amounts to holding the yardstick constant so that instead of a GNP measured in current dollars of varying value, we get a GNP measured in constant dollars. This later figure is called *real GNP,* because it is the best estimate we can make of *physical changes* in quantity produced.

Example. We wish to compare real GNP in 1980 with that in 1972 (which happens to be the base presently used for the GNP price deflator). In 1972 GNP (measured at prices prevailing in that year) was $1,171 billion. In 1980, GNP at 1980 prices was $2,627 billion—an increase of 125 percent in current dollars. Real GNP did not increase that much, however, because prices were much higher in 1980. If we define the 1972 price level as 100, the GNP deflator in 1980 was 177. So we "deflate" the 1980 GNP total by dividing it by the 1980 price index, as in Table 3–5. We find that real GNP in 1980,

measured in constant 1972 dollars, was only $1,480 billion, an increase of only 26 percent instead of 125 percent.

Even after the price experts have done their best, we are far from being out of the woods. Here are a few brain teasers:

1. The deflation procedure assumes that we are dealing with unchanging products. Prices may vary up and down, but the products being priced are supposed to remain constant. But in practice product quality is always changing, usually for the better. The 1982 Ford is not the 1950 Ford. Today's drip-dry shirt is not the same as the older cotton broadcloth shirt. Quality can sometimes be measured. If a tire costs twice as much today as in 1950, but if it will also run twice as many miles, there has been no increase in the price per thousand miles of use. But in many cases no such measurement is possible.

Quality improvements, whether measureable or not, are certainly important. To the extent that they are not allowed for in our price indexes, the rise in price levels is overstated, and the rise in real GNP is consequently understated.

2. This difficulty becomes even more serious if some goods disappear completely from the shopping list and new articles take their place. How does one compare the price of a horse and carriage in 1890 with the price of a horseless carriage in 1940? Or the cost of traveling 1,000 miles by Pullman car in 1910 with first-class jet air fare for the same distance in 1980? What about products which don't replace anything, because nothing like them existed before? Television sets, vitamin pills, sulfa drugs, electronic computers, isotopes, and many other things now included in our national market basket are recent developments. They had no price in 1930 because they didn't exist.

Price indexes and GNP totals are not well adapted to covering drastic changes in the items going into national output. Over short periods during which people's way of life stays much the same, our measurements work reasonably

TABLE 3–5
Deflation of money GNP to get real GNP

Year	Money GNP (billions of current dollars)	Price Index	Real GNP (billions of 1972 dollars)
1972	1,171	100	$(1,171/100) \times 100 = 1,171$
1980	2,627	177	$(2,627/177) \times 100 = 1,480$

well. But as we stretch out the period covered, we run into increasing difficulty. How much does it mean to calculate that the average American lives four times as well today as in 1890? The truth is that we live very *differently*. By present standards, we seem to be living much better. But it is a bold person who would attach an exact percentage figure to the improvement.

There is a similar difficulty when we try to make comparisons between countries with very different ways of life. Does an average American family live twice as well as an average Russian family? Three times as well? Certainly the *pattern* of life is very different. How much more one can say is open to question.

Part One

Aggregate Demand, Output, and Prices

MODERN MACROECONOMICS: A HISTORICAL PRELUDE

If you compared this text with one written 50 years ago, you would find striking differences. Before 1930, the following propositions were widely accepted:

1. There cannot be an insufficiency of total demand for goods. Production of X dollars' worth of good A creates X dollars of income, which is available for spending on goods B, C, D, and so on; and production of these other goods provides income which can be spent on good A. This principle that "supply creates its own demand" was usually called "Say's Law" after Jean Baptiste Say, a 19th-century French economist.

2. The economy tends naturally to operate at full capacity. At any lower rate of output, the economy is not in equilibrium, and there are corrective mechanisms which will tend to restore capacity operation.

3. One such mechanism is the rate of interest. Suppose people decide to save more, thereby reducing demand for consumer goods. This will increase the supply of loanable funds in the money market, which will reduce the market price (the rate of interest), which will lead businesses to borrow more and spend more on investment. Thus resources not demanded to produce consumer goods will be used instead to produce capital goods, and full employment can be maintained.

4. A second corrective mechanism is the wage level. If workers are unemployed, it must be because their market price is too high. Lower the wage rate, and employers will find it profitable to employ more workers. The demand curve for labor slopes downward to the right, like any other demand curve.

5. Since the economy tends naturally to operate at capacity, there is no need for government intervention. Regulating total output and employment is not a proper function of government.

6. One exception was admitted: control of the money supply. Money was recognized as a possible destabilizing influence in the economy, but variations in money supply were regarded as affecting mainly the *price level* rather than the level of *output and employment.* The "quantity theory of money," in simplest form, held that there was a direct, proportional relation between changes in money supply and changes in the price level.

While economic thinking develops partly through its own intellectual momentum, it is also influenced by economic events. Never was this more evident than during the 1930s. The severity and length of the Great Depression caused a basic reexamination of accepted ideas. A prime mover in this reexamination was John Maynard Keynes.

Keynes was born in Cambridge, England, in 1883. His father, John Neville Keynes, was an economist whose works are still worth reading. The son studied economics and mathematics at Kings College, under the influence of the great Cambridge economist, Alfred Marshall. Keynes was associated intermittently with Kings College throughout his life, as teacher of economics and later as bursar (treasurer) of the college. Unlike many economists, he was a very successful investor and made a lot of money both for himself and for Kings. The handsome new quadrangle at Kings, which he helped to finance, has appropriately been named Keynes Court.

Keynes also had periods of government service, which included attending the Versailles Peace Conference after World War I, working in the Treasury on the financing of World War II, and leading the British delegation to the Bretton Woods Conference of 1944 which created the International Monetary Fund. Along with these mundane activities, he was active in the Bloomsbury Group of writers and artists, married a Russian ballerina, and founded the Cambridge Arts Theatre. He was one of the most literate and cultured of 20th-century economists, as well as the most influential. He died in 1946.

Keynes wrote many books, couched in an unusually fluent and persuasive style. His two-volume *Treatise on Money,* published in 1930, is still the best summary of the older ideas from which he was already struggling to free himself. Several years of additional effort produced the *General Theory of Employment, Interest, and Money,* published in 1935. This book propounded a highly original framework for thinking about macroeconomics, won rapid acceptance in university and government circles, and led to what has been called "the Keynesian Revolution."

Keynes attacked the pillars of classical doctrine as partly or entirely untrue, and proposed to substitute the following principles:

1. It is quite possible for the economy to be in equilibrium at less than full employment. The equilibrium rate of output depends on aggregate demand, which is the sum of demands by consumers, businesses (for capital goods), government, and foreign buyers (exports). These demands may be large enough to use the full capacity of the economy, but they need not be this large. If aggregate demand is below output capacity, the economy can be in equilibrium with unemployed workers and idle plants.

To demonstrate that there is no natural tendency for the economy to return to full employment, Keynes had to demonstrate the weakness of the classical correctives. He set about this task as follows:

2. Reducing the rate of interest will not necessarily stimulate business investment sufficiently to ensure full employment. While recognizing the importance of interest, Keynes thought that investment plans were much influenced by expectations of the future. During a depression, business leaders may be so pessimistic that they will not borrow or invest much even at low rates of interest.

3. Neither are money wage cuts an adequate corrective for unemployment. First, this remedy is not feasible because workers resist wage cuts so strongly that the wage level can be reduced only slowly and with much social strife. But even if wage cuts were feasible, they would reduce consumer income and consumer demand, which would offset the favorable effect of the cuts. Employers might end up hiring fewer workers rather than more. It is quicker and more effective, Keynes argued, to leave the wage level alone and to raise output through measures to raise aggregate demand.

   4. Money is important in determining output and employment.   In the Keynesian system, demand for and supply of money determine the rate of interest. The interest rate influences the amount of business investment, which in turn influences aggregate demand, which affects the level of output and employment. Other things equal, increasing the money supply will reduce the interest rate, increase investment, and raise output and employment. As output rises toward capacity, the price level will also tend to rise, but Keynes did not regard this side effect as very important.

   In short, Keynes created an *integrated theory* of money, output, employment, and prices. Contrast this with the classical "two-worlds" system, in which real output and employment are determined by the wage rate and the interest rate, while money supply determines only the price level.

   5. The government budget is also an important instrument for regulating aggregate demand.   If the system is below full employment, aggregate demand can be raised by increasing government expenditure or reducing tax rates. In severe depression, indeed, monetary policy acting through interest rates may be so ineffective that demand can be raised rapidly *only* through fiscal action.

   6. Government has a responsibility to regulate aggregate demand so as to hold the economy close to full employment.   "Business cycles" should not be regarded as a fact of nature, like droughts or tornadoes. They arise from defects in our economic institutions which can be corrected by deliberate action.

   With the perspective of 50 years, it appears that Keynes's attack was three quarters successful. He undermined the idea that unemployment could simply be left to cure itself and established the principle of government responsibility for aggregate demand. His demonstration that the government budget can be used to influence aggregate demand won general acceptance. The way in which we approach macroeconomics issues today owes more to Keynes than to any other single source.

   But no one can foresee everything. Written during the deepest depression in history, the *General Theory* was preoccupied with the problem of getting out of depression. It accordingly exalted fiscal policy and played down monetary policy to an extent which would not be accepted today. It failed signally to recognize the possibility of inflation at high employment. Keynes wrote as though a sustained expansion of output and employment need not raise the wage level, and while he recognized that prices might rise, he expected the increase to be moderate.

In fact, wage and price levels have proven very flexible on the upswing and very sticky on the downswing. So the reduced severity of business cycles since 1945, as compared with the century before that time, has been accompanied by a sharp uptrend of the price level.

Hardly any idea in economics is ever completely dead! Some ideas which seemed buried as of 1940 have reemerged and won modern supporters. These include the idea that the economy is inherently more stable than Keynes believed, that control of money supply is the most important policy instrument, and that the behavior of the price level is closely linked to money supply. This is simply to say that economics is a living subject, which has assimilated Keynes's work but at the same time moved beyond him. The fact that important intellectual issues continue in dispute and that pressing policy problems remain unsolved lends continuing fascination to the study of economics. In the chapters which follow we hope to convey something of this frontier spirit of intellectual inquiry.

INTRODUCTION TO PART ONE

In Part One, we explore what determines the level of real output and the general level of prices. To tackle this complicated problem we must approach it in stages.

We begin by focusing on output, leaving the price level for later on. As we saw in Chapter 3, the level of output depends on the level of *aggregate demand*—on total spending by consumers, businesses, government, and foreign buyers. A change in the spending plans of any of these groups will change the equilibrium level of output. In Chapters 4 and 5, we examine the components of aggregate demand and how the level of output responds to a change in aggregate demand. At this stage, we assume that an increase of, say, 5 percent in total spending will produce an increase of 5 percent in real output, *with no change in the price level.* This is a drastic simplification, justified only by the need to tackle one problem at a time.

When we discuss spending in Chapters 4 and 5, we don't worry about what it is that people are spending. But what they are spending, of course, is *money;* and money is a key actor on the economic stage. In Chapter 6, we ask what money is, how the supply of money can change, and how the Federal Reserve System tries to control money supply. In Chapter 7, we go on to examine the demand for money, and how demand and supply interact in the money market to determine the *rate of interest.*

How do monetary changes affect the economy? There are two main ways of approaching this question. One approach, which used to be called "the quantity theory of money," but is now usually called "monetarism," pictures a direct linkage of money supply to spending and national income. The other, often called "Keynesian," pictures a roundabout impact operating mainly through the rate of interest. In Chapter 8 we describe the two approaches without professing to choose between them. The fact that both are alive and well, with good economists holding different points of view, makes economics an interesting and growing subject.

Now at long last, the *price level*. In Chapter 9, we recognize that a change in spending will normally affect *both* output and prices. If spending rises by 5 percent, the effect will be *divided* between a rise in output and a rise in the price level. But what determines the division? It makes a big difference whether output rises 4 percent and prices only 1 percent, or whether there is a 1 percent output rise and a 4 percent price rise. There is no tidy body of theory on this point, but we shall outline the present stage of thinking about it.

Finally, in Chapter 10 we look at changes in government revenue, expenditure, and the government debt. In recent decades, there has almost always been a deficit in the federal budget, and in the early 1980s, the deficit struck many as alarmingly large. Is there reason for alarm? Does the deficit matter, and if so, why? This will complete our picture of the mechanics of the macroeconomy and lay a foundation for the discussion of policy in Part Two.

National Output in a Simplified Economy

We first survey the plot, then draw the model;
Then must we rate the cost of the erection;
Which if we find outweighs ability
What do we then but draw anew the model.

—WILLIAM SHAKESPEARE, *KING HENRY IV (PART II)*

We saw in Chapter 3 that the productive capacity of the American economy rises over the course of time. But output is usually below capacity and rises at an irregular rate. It may rise for several years (a business cycle upswing) but then turn downward for a year or so (a business cycle downswing or recession). As output falls during a recession, the unemployment rate rises. When an upswing sets in, the unemployment rate falls.

What explains this zigzag behavior of the economy? What determines the rate of output at a particular time? Why does the economy operate close to capacity in some years and a good deal below capacity in others?

It is a challenging task to explain the great tidal movements of the economy. But it is a very complicated task. The only way to untangle the complexities is to use a step-by-step approach. We start out in this chapter with a highly simplified economy, several steps away from reality. The main simplifications are as follows:

1. The economy consists only of businesses and households. There is no government and no foreign trade. Moreover, all saving is done by households, and business saving does not exist.

2. Consumers spend money on consumer goods, and businesses spend on capital goods, or investment. We take the amount businesses intend to spend on investment in a particular year as given, without attempting to explain it.

3. An increase in total spending by businesses and consumers leads to a proportionate increase in physical production *with no increase in the price level*. We "freeze" or disregard the price level by taking it as constant. While we measure spending and output in dollars, these are *dollars of constant purchasing power*.

These ground rules should be kept clearly in mind, and the simplified conclusions reached in this chapter should not be taken as a close approximation in reality. The complications which we set aside here will be reintroduced in an orderly way in later chapters. But it would be confusing to grapple with all of them at once.

AGGREGATE DEMAND: CONSUMPTION PLUS INVESTMENT

The circular flow once more

In our simple economy, businesses pay out all their receipts to consumers as disposable income. We know that consumers don't spend all of their income. Part of it is saved. So why isn't there a shortage of aggregate demand? Why isn't GNP continually falling?

The reason is that the demand for consumer goods is not the only component of demand for output. We saw in Chapter 3 that part of the output of the economy is new capital or investment goods. By implication, then, part of the demand for the output of the economy is the demand by business firms for new capital goods. If this demand just equals the rate of saving out of current income, then aggregate demand will just equal the rate of output.

Figure 4–1 shows the circular flow of income and expenditure for this simple economy. The boxes labeled H and B stand for households and businesses. Household savings at the left of the diagram are a leakage from the income stream. But the demand of businesses for new capital goods, which is an addition to consumer demand for consumer goods, appears as an injection at the right of the diagram. If leakages and injections are equal, the rate of output will remain unchanged.

Spending on consumption

So far so good. We have seen what is required if the rate of output and the flow of income are to remain unchanged. But unchanged at what rate? If businesses plan to produce goods at a rate of $3,000 billion a year, will there be enough demand to buy this amount? Or will there be too much or too little? This depends on spending plans, so we must look more thoroughly into what determines the aggregate demand for the output of the economy.

FIGURE 4–1
Saving and investment in the circular flow

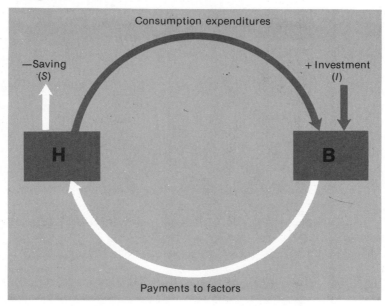

Household saving is a leakage from the income flow, while business investment is an addition.

Remember the ground rules for our simplified economy, which will be followed throughout this chapter.

1. The economy consists only of households and businesses—no government and no foreign trade.
2. Capital goods never wear out or become obsolete—there are no capital consumption allowances.
3. Businesses pay out all of their profits to households, so that saving is done only by households.
4. Since there are no taxes, all household income is available for spending or saving.

In this simple system:

GNP = Disposable personal income = Consumption + Savings

or

$$Y = Y_d = C + S$$

where the symbol Y stands for GNP, Y_d for disposable income, C for consumption, and S for saving.

How much will consumers choose to save out of disposable income?

The central fact about consumer spending is this: *As disposable income rises, consumer spending rises, but by a smaller amount.* Conversely, a decline in income brings about a smaller decline in consumer spending.

Both logic and observation suggest that when a household receives additional income, *it will spend a part but not all of that income.* Some of the additional income will be saved. This tendency was first emphasized by J. M. Keynes, who made it a key feature of this theoretical system and coined a new term, *the marginal propensity to consumer (MPC).* If a family, upon receiving an additional $100 of income, increases its spending by $75, its marginal propensity to consume is 75/100 or 0.75. There is a twin concept, *the marginal propensity to save (MPS),* which in this case would be 25/100 or 0.25. Since all of the family's disposable income must be either saved or spent, the two propensities must add up to 1.

> **The marginal propensity to consume (MPC) is the proportion of a small increase in disposable income which is spent on consumption. The marginal propensity to save (MPS) is the proportion which is saved. Since additional disposable income must be either spent or saved, MPC + MPS = 1.**

The household consumption schedule

The household consumption schedule for the hypothetical Jewkes family is presented graphically in Figure 4–2. Alternative rates of annual disposable income or Y_d are measured along the horizontal axis. Annual rates of consumption expenditures or C are measured along the vertical axis. The $C = Y_d$ line (drawn at an angle of 45 degrees from the horizontal axis) is for use as a reference. As its label suggests, at each point on this line, consumption would equal disposable income. The line labeled C shows the *actual* behavioral relationship between disposable income and consumption for the Jewkes family. It tells us what the family's annual consumption would be for alternative rates of annual family income. For example, it indicates that consumption would be $4,000 if income were $3,000; consumption would be $6,000 if income were $6,000; consumption would be $8,000 if income were $9,000; and so on. Note that for income rates less than $6,000 per year, the family spends *more* than its income or *dissaves.* "Dissaving" is another word for borrowing or running up unpaid bills. Of course, if income were to stay below $6,000 for a long time, the family could not *continue* to run up debts. This suggests a difference between the long run and the short run that we shall pursue later.

The consumption schedule for this family was drawn with a marginal propensity to consume of two thirds. Each increase of $1,000 in income brings increased spending for consumption goods of approximately $667 and increased saving (or reduced dissaving) of approximately $333. *Geo-*

FIGURE 4–2
Consumption schedule for the Jewkes family

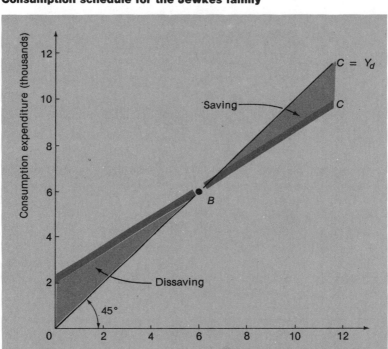

The Jewkes's consumption schedule, *C*, shows how much the family would spend at various levels of annual income. To the left of *B*, that is, below $6,000 a year, they spend more than they receive. To the right of *B*, spending is below income, and there is positive saving.

metrically, *the MPC is the slope of the C line.*[1] We have assumed that MPC is constant for all levels of income, so *C* is a straight line. This would not necessarily be true in reality, but it is a useful first approximation.

Columns (1) and (2) of Table 4–1 present the consumption schedule of the Jewkes family numerically. Column (1) contains a list of alternative rates of family disposable income, and column (2) shows the corresponding rate of family consumption expenditures. The relationship between disposable income and consumption which is indicated by columns (1)

---

[1] The slope of any line is defined as the rise (or vertical increase) divided by the run (or horizontal increase). In the case of the *C* line, this is the change in consumption divided by the change in income or

$$\frac{(\text{Change in } C)}{(\text{Change in } Y)} = \frac{MPC \times (\text{Change in } Y)}{(\text{Change in } Y)} = MPC$$

"What do you mean we can't go on living
beyond our means? We've always lived
beyond our means!"

From The Wall Street Journal, *with permission of Cartoon
Features Syndicate.*

TABLE 4-1
Consumption schedule of the Jewkes family (dollars per year)

(1) Disposable Income	(2) Consumption Expenditure	(3) Marginal Propensity to Consume (MPC)	(4) Average Propensity to Consume (APC)	(5) Net Saving	(6) Marginal Propensity to Save (MPS)	(7) Average Propensity to Save (APS)
0	2,000			−2,000		
		0.667			0.333	
1,000	2,667		2.67	−1,667		−1.67
		0.667			0.333	
2,000	3,333		1.67	−1,333		−0.67
		0.667			0.333	
3,000	4,000		1.33	−1,000		−0.33
		0.667			0.333	
4,000	4,667		1.17	− 667		−0.17
		0.667			0.333	
5,000	5,333		1.07	− 333		−0.07
		0.667			0.333	
6,000	6,000		1.00	0		0.00
		0.667			0.333	
7,000	6,667		0.95	333		0.05
		0.667			0.333	
8,000	7,333		0.92	667		0.08
		0.667			0.333	
9,000	8,000		0.89	1,000		0.11
		0.667			0.333	
10,000	8,667		0.87	1,333		0.13

and (2) is the same as that depicted by the C line in Figure 4–2—consumption is $2,000 when income is $0, and consumption increases by approximately $667 for every $1,000 increment in income.

We can now define an additional term, the *average propensity to consume* (APC). This is consumption expenditures as a fraction of income and is shown in column (4) of Table 4–1. Similarly, the *average propensity to save* (APS) is the fraction of income saved and appears in column (7). Note that as income rises, the *average* propensity to consume falls steadily, even though the *marginal* propensity to consume remains constant at two thirds. The average propensity to consume is greater than 1 for income less than $6,000 (reflecting the fact that consumption expenditures are greater than income for income rates below $6,000). It is equal to 1 when Y_d = $6,000 and is less than 1 for income rates above $6,000. When Y_d = $10,000, the APC is 8,667/10,000 = 0.87. Had we extended the schedule to an income rate of $50,000 (and the MPC continued unchanged), we should find that the APC had fallen to about 0.7.[2]

> The average propensity to consume (APC) is the proportion of disposable income which is spent for consumption goods, while the average propensity to save (APS) is the proportion which is saved. For any income rate, APC + APS = 1. As income increases, APC falls and APS rises.

The consumption schedule is logically similar to a demand schedule. It shows alternative possibilities (only one of which will be realized) for a short period of time. It says that *if* during this time period the income rate of the Jewkes family were $6,000 per year, the family's rate of consumption expenditures would be $6,000 per year. If, on the other hand, the income rate of the family were $8,000 per year, its consumption and saving would be approximately $7,333 and $667 per year, respectively.

The national consumption schedule

For overall analysis of the economy, we are interested not in the spending of the Jewkes family but in total consumer spending. A national consumption schedule is illustrated in Figure 4–3. The rate of aggregate consumption expenditures is measured along the vertical axis, while alternative rates of aggregate disposable income (which in this case equals GNP) are measured along the horizontal axis. The schedule resembles

---

[2] This follows from the equation of the consumption schedule C, which is

$$C = a + b\,Y_d$$

where C is consumption, Y_d is disposable income, a is the intercept on the vertical axis, and b is the slope of the C line. The average propensity to consume is

$$\frac{C}{Y_d} = \frac{a + b\,Y_d}{Y_d} = \frac{a}{Y_d} + b$$

Since a and b are constants, the value of this expression declines as Y_d increases.

FIGURE 4–3
The national consumption schedule

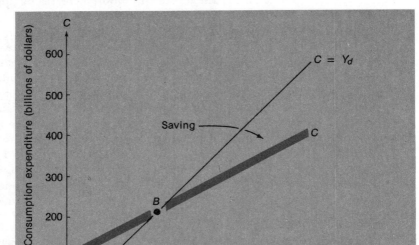

The national consumption schedule, C, shows how much all households in the country would plan to spend at each level of disposable income. As in the case of the Jewkes family schedule, there is negative saving to the left of B, positive saving to the right of B.

the Jewkes family schedule, except that we are now dealing with billions instead of thousands of dollars of income and consumption.

The rate of total saving is negative for rates of Y_d to the left of B, zero at B, and positive for rates of Y_d to the right of B. The region to the left of B is of little practical importance. The only modern instance of negative household saving occurred at the bottom of the Great Depression in 1932–33.

Long-run behavior: Shifts in the consumption schedule

The consumption schedule shows spending intentions *for a short period of time.* It says that if for this short time span the rate of aggregate disposable income were so-and-so many billions, consumers would plan to spend at a certain rate.

The C schedule of Figure 4–3 is definitely not a historical chart showing what happens to spending as income grows over the course of time. To take it in this way would be quite misleading. It would look from Figure 4–3 as though when the economy is growing and income is rising, the consumption proportion will fall steadily while the savings percentage will rise.

But what actually happens is quite different. Since World War II in the United States, consumer expenditures as a proportion of disposable income (the national APC) has been *virtually constant,* fluctuating only in a narrow range between 0.92 and 0.94. So APC does not seem to fall as income rises. Indeed, studies by Simon Kuznets indicate that this has been true over a much longer period. Kuznets found that the proportion

FIGURE 4–4
The consumption schedule shifts upward over time

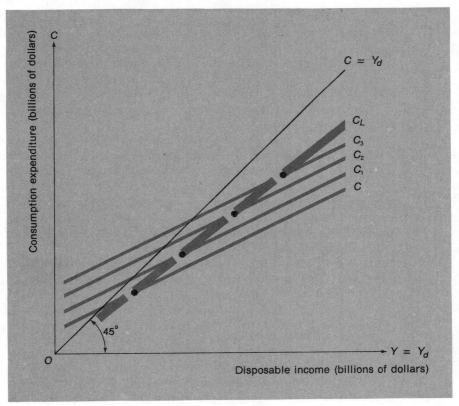

C shows short-run consumption reactions at a particular time. C_1 shows the same reactions 10 years later when people are habituated to higher living standards, and so on. Because of continued upward shifting of the short-run schedule, consumption over the long run follows the path shown by C_L.

of per capita income saved has not changed significantly since 1870, though real income per capita has risen severalfold since then.

How can we explain this result? The explanation is that the C curve in Figure 4–3 is a short-run schedule, and that in the short run, consumption habits are firmly fixed.

Given a longer period of adjustment, however, people are quite capable of finding ways to use additional income. Former luxuries come to be regarded as necessities, and creation of new products stimulates consumer demand. This gradual increase of living standards in response to rising incomes may be viewed as an *upward shift* in the short-run consumption schedule (Figure 4–4). The schedule rises from C to C_1, then to C_2, and so on into the future. The heavy dots may be regarded as representing the normal level of income at periods 10 years apart, so that C_3 carries a date 30 years later than C. When these are linked up, they form the long-run consumption schedule C_L.

Why should C shift upward over the course of time? One hypothesis is that a family's spending depends not on its *absolute* income but on its income *relative* to that of other families within its horizon. If the income of every family rises by 20 percent so that they keep the same standing relative to each other, there is no reason why any family should change the relative distribution of its income between saving and consumption. This competitive aspect of consumption was stressed long ago by Thorstein Veblen. In recent years, it has been emphasized by James Duesenberry and others.

Another idea is the *life-cycle hypothesis* of consumer saving, advanced by Franco Modigliani and Albert Ando. Most saving is done for specific purposes, such as home building, purchase of furniture and other consumer durables, education of children, or retirement income. The amount saved will be related to the family's expected future income and future responsibilities. It may be that saving is a nearly constant *proportion* of expected income and that as everyone's expectations increase in a growing economy, this proportion does not change.[3]

Another possible explanation, suggested by Milton Friedman, is the *permanent income* hypothesis. He argues that one should distinguish between permanent income, which is expected to continue indefinitely in the future, and temporary additions to or subtractions from this income. A change which is expected to be temporary will have little or no effect on consumption decisions. A temporary windfall will go mainly into in-

---

[3] There is a large literature on saving and consumption in the United States. Key references include: James S. Duesenberry, *Income Saving, and the Theory of Consumer Behavior* (Cambridge, Mass.: Harvard University Press, 1952); Milton Friedman, *A Theory of the Consumption Function* (Princeton, N.J.: Princeton University Press, 1957); Albert Ando and Franco Modigliani, "The 'Life Cycle' Hypothesis of Saving: Aggregate Implications and Tests," *American Economic Review*, March 1963, pp. 55–83; and Daniel B. Suits, "The Determinants of Consumer Expenditures: A Review of Present Knowledge," in *Impacts of Monetary Policy* [*Research Studies Prepared for the Commission on Money and Credit* (Englewood Cliffs, N.J.: Prentice-Hall, 1963)], pp. 1–57.

creased saving, while a temporary drop in income will be met by reducing saving.

Consumption decisions depend on permanent income. For most people this is rising over the years, and as it rises, spending on consumption will also rise. To Friedman, the evidence suggests that the average propensity to consume out of permanent income is virtually a constant. This would produce a long-run schedule like C_L in Figure 4–4, with the ratio of consumption to income constant over the years and decades.

> **THINK ABOUT THIS**
>
> In recession years, when GNP is falling and unemployment is rising, the federal government often proposes a temporary tax cut or cash bonus to consumers. It is argued that this will raise consumers' disposable income which will raise consumer spending, which will lead businesses to produce more.
>
> If the permanent income hypothesis is correct, would such a program do much to raise GNP? How would you test statistically whether this view is correct?

THE EQUILIBRIUM RATE OF OUTPUT

We explored consumption demand in detail, partly because it is the largest component of aggregate demand. The other source of demand in our simple model is business demand for new capital goods and inventories. For present purposes, we assume that investment demand is simply a fixed amount, regardless of the rate of GNP. We do not try at this point to explain *why* investment demand is what it is. This is a complicated question, which involves money and interest rates, so we leave it until Chapter 7.

Aggregate demand at any rate of GNP, then, is consumer demand at that rate, as shown by the consumption schedule, plus a fixed amount of investment demand. This aggregate demand schedule, together with the aggregate supply schedule, defines an *equilibrium rate of national output.* What does this mean? The economy is in equilibrium if, at the current rate of output, aggregate demand just equals that rate. All that is being produced can be sold. There is then no reason for the rate of output to change.

The idea of equilibrium output can be illustrated with either an arithmetic or geometric example, and we shall use both. We begin with the arithmetic example, presented in Table 4–2.

Columns (1) and (2) of Table 4–2 constitute an aggregate consumption schedule. Column (1) contains a list of alternative rates of GNP, and

TABLE 4–2

Determination of equilibrium income and output (billions of dollars per year)

(1)	(2)	(3) = (1) − (2)	(4)	(5) = (2) + (4)	
GNP and Disposable Income	Consumption Demand	Saving	Investment Demand	Aggregate Demand	Resulting Movement of Income and Output
300	250	50	100	350	Expansion
350	275	75	100	375	Expansion
400	300	100	100	400	Equilibrium
450	325	125	100	425	Contraction
500	350	150	100	450	Contraction
550	375	175	100	475	Contraction
600	400	200	100	500	Contraction

Note: The equilibrium rate of GNP is $400 billion per year. If GNP were less than this, there would be an excess of aggregate demand. If GNP were greater than $400 billion per year, there would be a deficiency of aggregate demand.

column (2) shows the consumption demand which would be forthcoming at each rate. Note, for example, that if the rate of GNP were $350 billion, the rate of consumption demand would be $275 billion. The remainder of disposable income, $350 − $275 = $75 billion, would be the rate of household saving, and this is presented in column (3). Thus, columns (2) and (3) show how households would allocate alternative rates of disposable income between spending for consumption goods and saving. Since disposable income can only be saved or spent for consumption goods, the sum of column (2) (consumption demand) and column (3) (saving) must equal column (1) (disposable income or GNP). In constructing Table 4–2, we have assumed a MPC of 0.5, which means that for every $50 billion increment in the rate of disposable income, consumption demand rises by $25 billion and household saving also rises by $25 billion.

Column (4) shows business investment demand, which we assume to be a fixed amount of $100 billion per year. The total or aggregate demand for the output of this economy at alternative rates of GNP is presented in column (5). Since the total demand in this economy is simply the sum of consumption and investment demand, column (5) is the sum of columns (2) and (4).

The crucial question is whether, if businesses produce a certain amount, there will be enough demand to buy all that is produced. If not, businesses will find unsold goods piling up and will reduce their rate of production. Suppose, for example, that production is at the rate of $500 billion per year. We see from column (5) that total demand will be only $450 billion per year. Producers cannot find a market for all that they are producing, and they will contract output.

On the other hand, suppose production were at a rate of only $300 billion. At this income rate, aggregate demand is $350 billion. Goods will move off the shelves briskly, inventories will run down, retailers will place larger orders, and producers will raise their output plans for the future.

If output were $400 billion, however, the rate of aggregate demand would just equal the rate of output. This is, consequently, *the equilibrium rate of GNP*. Note that, at this rate of national output, the rate of household saving is $100 per year and is exactly equal to the rate of investment demand. Stated differently, at this rate of national output, the deficiency in aggregate demand which results from saving is just offset by the $100 billion per year added to demand by investment.

The information contained in Table 4–2 is charted in Figure 4–5. Look first at the upper half of this figure. The $C + I = Y$ line slopes upward at an angle of 45 degrees. Thus at any point on this line, the distances to the two axes are equal. At any point on the line, demand for output just equals the rate of output, so that all that is being produced can be sold. We know, then, that any equilibrium position for the economy must lie somewhere on this line. But where this will be depends on the level of aggregate demand.

We next chart the two components of aggregate demand. The C line shows the demand for consumer goods at alternative rates of GNP. To the C line we add the $100 billion of investment demand to get the $C + I$ line, which is the aggregate demand schedule. Since investment demand is the same at all alternative rates of GNP, the $C + I$ line runs parallel to the C line at a vertical distance of $100 billion. This *aggregate demand schedule shows the total demand for output, at a particular moment in time, at different alternative rates of national output.*

We are now able to determine the equilibrium rate of GNP. The equilibrium rate of GNP is that rate at which the aggregate demand schedule intersects the aggregate supply schedule. In Figure 4–5, the $C + I$ line intersects the 45-degree line at point N. Looking down to the horizontal axis, we see that this corresponds to a GNP of $400 billion per year.

The fact that $400 billion is the equilibrium rate of GNP can be demonstrated by supposing that GNP were at some other rate and asking what would happen. Suppose output were running at only $300 billion per year. Looking up to point N_1 and across to the expenditure axis, we see that aggregate demand at this income rate would be $350 billion, well above the rate of current production. This excess demand would give businesses an incentive to expand production, and the rate of GNP would rise.

Suppose, on the other hand, that production somehow reached the rate of $500 billion per year. Could this level be sustained? No, it could not. Looking up to point N_2 and across to the expenditure axis, we see that total demand would be only $450 billion. There would be a deficiency

FIGURE 4-5
Consumption, investment, and equilibrium income

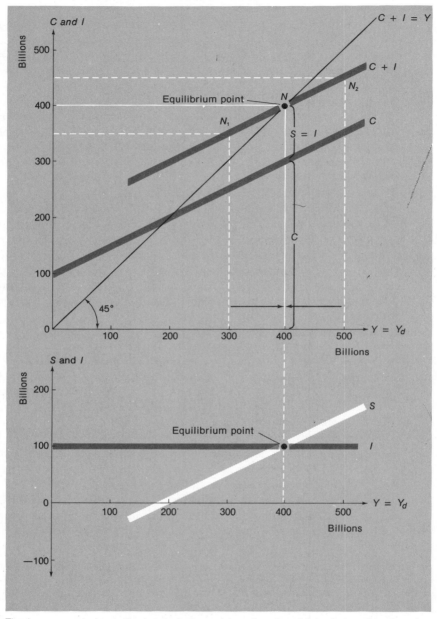

The lower panel shows the level of planned investment and intended saving at various levels of income. The economy can be in equilibrium only when these two quantities are equal, that is, at $400 billion. In the upper panel we add planned investment to consumption to get the total expenditure schedule, $C + I$. The intersection of $C + I$ with $C + I = Y$ at N defines the equilibrium level of income, which must of course be the same as that derived by the other method.

of demand, unsold goods would pile up, and businesses would cut production.

The arrows on the horizontal axis of this graph indicate that if actual output is anywhere below the equilibrium level of $400 billion, output will tend to rise. Conversely, if output is above the equilibrium level, it will tend to fall.

The same information is shown from a different point of view in the lower panel of Figure 4–5. Instead of the consumption schedule, we draw here its inverse, the saving schedule, labeled S. Note that the point of zero saving in the lower panel lies directly below the point where consumption demand is as large as GNP or Y_d in the upper panel. To the left of this point, saving is negative, and to the right, it is positive.

Now draw in the investment schedule I, showing investment demand at each rate of GNP. The I and S lines intersect, meaning that the rate of saving equals the demand for investment goods, at GNP = $400 billion per year. At output rates below $400 billion, investment demand exceeds the rate of saving, and at output rates above $400 billion, investment demand falls short of the rate of saving. Thus the equilibrium rate of GNP is $400 billion, for only at this rate does the demand for new capital goods just make up the deficiency in aggregate demand caused by the act of saving. This is the same result reached in the upper panel, as it should be, since the two diagrams rest on the same basic data.

THINK ABOUT THIS

If you follow the statistics month by month, you will note that the rate of GNP rarely remains constant. It is rising most of the time, but falling some of the time. In view of this, does the concept of an *equilibrium* rate of GNP make any sense?

THE AUTONOMOUS SPENDING MULTIPLIER

As we saw in Chapter 2, defining equilibrium is not an end in itself. The point is that we can then explore the impact of *changes* in the system. Suppose there is an increase in consumption or investment demand. What will this do to the rate of GNP?

It is important here to distinguish between two kinds of change in spending. Suppose my income rises by $1,000 a year, and as a result, I spend $500 more on consumption. This is an *induced* change—induced by a prior change in income. Suppose, on the other hand, that my income stays the same, but I just decide to increase my spending by $500 and reduce my saving by the same amount. This is an *autonomous* change, because it does not depend on a prior change in income.

An autonomous change in spending is a change which does not result
from a change in income.

What might cause an autonomous change in the consumption or investment schedules? Consumer spending plans are influenced by expectations about the future. A war scare, leading to an expectation that prices
will rise sharply, may cause consumers to rush to the stores to "beat
the price rise." The consumption schedule shifts upward. A business
downswing, with many people laid off and others fearing layoff, may
lead to expectations of falling income in the future and to efforts to
provide for the rainy day by increased saving. The consumption schedule
shifts downward.

The position of the investment schedule is also heavily influenced
by expectations or, in Keynes's language, by "the animal spirits of busi-
nessmen." If many business executives conclude that sales and profits
will be higher next year than this, they will be inclined to increase investment, including inventory investment. The investment schedule shifts
upward, and it may obviously shift downward if executives turn pessimistic. An autonomous increase in investment may occur also because of
the invention of a new product—the automobile, the computer, atomic
energy, television broadcasting—which generates a new demand and requires investment in plant and equipment to meet this demand.

The important, and at first glance puzzling, thing is that an autonomous
increase (or decrease) of $1 in spending produces an increase (or decrease)
of *more than* $1 in GNP. The ratio between the change in spending and
the consequent change in GNP is called *the multiplier.*

The autonomous spending multiplier is defined as

$$\frac{\text{Change in equilibrium rate of GNP}}{\text{Autonomous change in spending}}$$

This section will explain why there is a multiplier and what determines
its size.

Let's start from Table 4–2, where the equilibrium rate of GNP was
$400 billion. Now suppose there is an autonomous increase of $50 billion
per year in investment demand, from $100 billion per year to $150 billion
per year (at all rates of GNP). What effect will this $50 billion increase
in the rate of investment demand have upon the equilibrium rate of
GNP? Clearly, the equilibrium rate of GNP will rise. But by how much?
How large will the *new* equilibrium rate of GNP be as compared with
the *old* rate of $400 billion per year?

We can find out the new equilibrium rate of GNP by modifying Table
4–2 and Figure 4–5 to take into account the $50 billion larger rate of
investment demand. In Table 4–3, the data differ from those of Table
4–2 in only one respect: investment demand and, consequently, aggregate
demand at each of the alternative rates of GNP are $50 billion larger.
The equilibrium rate of GNP in Table 4–3 is $500 billion per year, the

TABLE 4–3
The autonomous spending multiplier (billions of dollars per year)

(1) GNP and Disposable Income	(2) Con-sumption Demand	(3) = (1) − (2) Saving	(4) Invest-ment Demand	(5) = (2) + (4) Aggregate Demand	Resulting Movement of Income and Output
300	250	50	150	400	Expansion
350	275	75	150	425	Expansion
400	300	100	150	450	Expansion
450	325	125	150	475	Expansion
500	350	150	150	500	Equilibrium
550	375	175	150	525	Contraction
600	400	200	150	550	Contraction

Note: A $50 billion increase in investment demand causes equilibrium GNP to rise by $100 billion.

only rate at which aggregate demand equals the rate of national output.

Figure 4–6 is the modified version of Figure 4–5. The C line in the upper panel and the S line in the lower panel are identical to those shown in Figure 4–5. However, the C + I line and the I line are each drawn $50 billion higher in Figure 4–6, reflecting our assumption of a $50 billion increase in the rate of investment demand. Note that both the upper and lower panels of Figure 4–6 indicate that the new equilibrium rate of GNP is $500 billion per year.

Thus, in answer to our question, the effect of a $50 billion increase in the rate of investment demand is to raise the equilibrium rate of GNP by $100 billion, from $400 billion to $500 billion per year. The change in equilibrium GNP is greater than the change in investment demand. In fact, it is twice as large. This may seem puzzling, but it is easily explained. How can the rate of investment increase from $100 billion to $150 billion per year? This can only happen by hiring workers to produce more capital goods. These workers receive wages, and part of what they get they will spend on consumption. So there is *an induced increase in consumption.* But the increase in GNP is simply the (autonomous) increase in investment plus the (induced) increase in consumption, and this has to be larger than the investment increase alone. If you compare Table 4–3 with Table 4–2, you will see that consumption has risen by $50 billion in the new equilibrium.

The movement from the old to the new equilibrium may be easier to visualize if we consider it as operating, as it actually does, over the *course of time.* What happens when investment demand rises by $50 billion? This stimulates firms producing capital goods to expand their rate of production from $100 billion to $150 billion per year. This directly causes a $50 billion rise in GNP and also, of course, in the flow of house-

FIGURE 4–6
Multiplier effect of an increase in aggregate demand

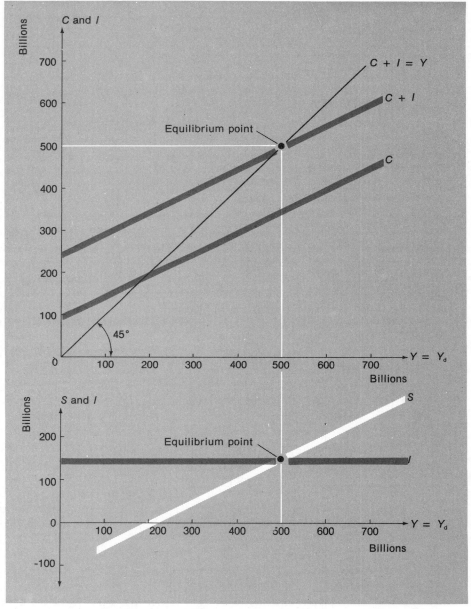

Investment here is $50 billion higher than in Figure 4–5. But the equilibrium rate of GNP is $100 billion higher. This is called the multiplier effect.

hold income. This is obviously not the end of the story, for on our assumption that the marginal propensity to consume is one half, the extra $50 billion of household income will cause the demand for consumption goods to rise by $25 billion. And even this isn't the end of the story, because the $25 billion of additional consumption demand will cause the producers of such goods to increase output, raising GNP and the rate of household income by an additional $25 billion. This further rise in household income will cause an additional $12.5 billion increase in consumption demand, GNP, and household income. And so the story continues. Each successive rise in GNP causes a rise in consumption demand of half that amount. The rise in consumption demand then causes a rise in GNP and, hence, brings about a further rise in consumption demand of half that amount, and so on and on.

How much increase in equilibrium GNP will finally result from the $50 billion increase in investment demand? The amount in billions is

$$\$50 + \$25 + \$12.5 + \$6.25 + \$3.12. \ldots$$

or

$$\$50 \times (1 + 0.5 + 0.5^2 + 0.5^3 + 0.5^4 \ldots).$$

By the formula for an infinite geometric progression, this sums up to:

$$\$50 \times \left[\frac{1}{1 - 0.5}\right] = \$50 \times \left[\frac{1}{0.5}\right] = \$50 \times 2 = \$100.$$

The multiplier in this case is 2, and its value clearly depends on the size of the marginal prospensity to consume. Suppose, for example, that we substitute a marginal propensity to consume of 0.8 in the above example. Then the increase in the equilibrium rate of GNP equals

$$\$50 \times (1 + 0.8 + 0.8^2 + 0.8^3 + 0.8^4 + \ldots).$$

This adds up to

$$\$50 \times \left[\frac{1}{1 - 0.8}\right] = \$50 \times \left[\frac{1}{0.2}\right] = \$50 \times 5 = \$250.$$

The multiplier in this case is 5.

We can now see that there is a general principle determining the size of the multiplier.

The autonomous spending multiplier $= \dfrac{1}{1 - MPC} = \dfrac{1}{MPS}.$

In this simple model, personal saving is the only leakage from the income stream. So what the formula tells us is that the *larger* the leakage on each round of spending, the *smaller* will be the multiplier effect of

an autonomous change in spending. Conversely, the *smaller* the leakage
on each round, the *larger* the multiplier effect. This makes good common
sense. To take extreme cases: Suppose that MPS were 1, meaning that
all of any increase in income is saved. Then the multiplier effect would
be zero. At the other pole, suppose that MPS were zero, meaning that
no income is ever saved. Then an autonomous spending increase of a
billion dollars would keep raising income by a full billion on each round,
forever and ever. The multiplier would be infinite.

The multiplier formula is perfectly general. It works for an autonomous
decrease in demand as well as for an increase. You can see this by going
back to Table 4–2 and *reducing* investment demand by $50 billion, from
$100 billion to $50 billion. The new equilibrium GNP will be $300 billion,
or $100 billion *lower* than before, which is what our formula predicts.
The formula works also if the autonomous change is in consumption
rather than investment. Again, you can see this by changing consumption
demand in column (2) of Table 4–2 and seeing what this will do to the
equilibrium rate of GNP.

APPLICATIONS OF THE EQUILIBRIUM CONCEPT

Good and bad equilibrium points

We have shown that there is always an equilibrium rate of output
toward which the economy is tending. But this output rate may or may
not be desirable. Suppose we want the economy to operate at point F
in Figure 4–7. If this is the objective, then aggregate demand can clearly
be too high or too low. If the demand schedule were $(C + I)_1$, leading
to equilibrium output of Y_1, the economy is underemployed. The policy
moral would be that steps should be taken to *increase* aggregate demand
and reduce underemployment.

Suppose, on the other hand, that the demand schedule were $(C + I)_2$, corresponding to equilibrium output of Y_2. Since the economy cannot
produce this much, the result will be a rise in the price level which will
continue as long as excess demand continues. The policy moral would
be that steps should be taken to *reduce* aggregate demand, so as to achieve
full employment without inflation.

If by some lucky chance the aggregate demand schedule were $(C + I)_3$, with an equilibrium output just equal to full employment output,
then all is well and policymakers can relax so long as this situation contin-
ues.

Government efforts to move the aggregate demand schedule upward
or downward, so as to keep it close to $(C + I)_3$, are known popularly
as "fine tuning." The methods available for this purpose and the difficulties
involved in using them will be examined in detail later on.

FIGURE 4–7
The concept of full employment

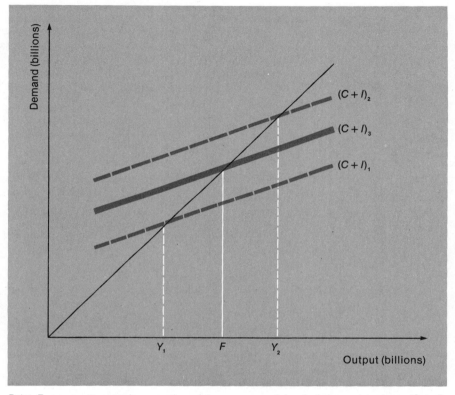

Point *F* represents capacity operation of the economy. A level of demand such as *(C + I)*₁ involves underemployment, since the equilibrium output *Y*₁ is below *F*. A level of demand such as *(C + I)*₂ involves inflation, since the output *Y*₂ cannot be produced with the resources available.

The paradox of thrift

Thriftiness is usually regarded as a virtue. It is also considered a public benefit because if people consume less, then more resources can be devoted to producing capital goods which raise the productive capacity of the economy. There is an important element of truth in this view. But it is also true that an increased desire to save, unaccompanied by any other change in the economy, can have awkward consequences.

Suppose the American public suddenly becomes more thrifty and decides to save more out of any given level of income. This means a *downward* shift of the *C* schedule, and hence of the *C + I* schedule, and an

FIGURE 4–8
The paradox of thrift

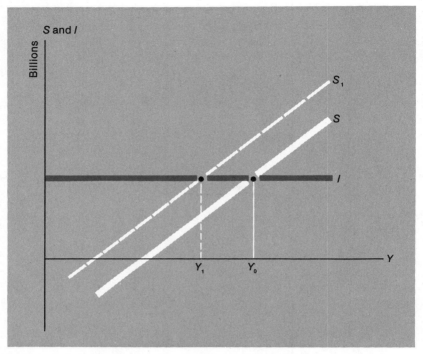

An increased desire to save, shown by the upward shift from S to S_1, will, if the investment schedule has remained unchanged, lead to a lower equilibrium output and no change in the amount saved.

upward shift of the S schedule in Figure 4–7. The result can be seen by looking at the lower half of that figure, reproduced here as Figure 4–8.

We start with a saving schedule S and an investment schedule I. Equilibrium output is Y, where S and I are equal. Now, because of increased thriftiness, the saving schedule shifts upward to S_1. The result, if the investment schedule has not changed, will be a *decline* in equilibrium output to Y_1.

Note that in the new equilibrium the amount actually being saved is just the same as before. People's desire for increased saving has been frustrated. This result is usually called the *paradox of thrift*.

While this result may seem odd, a moment's reflection will reveal why it occurs. In equilibrium, the flow of saving must equal the rate of investment demand. Now investment demand has not changed, and so the amount of realized saving cannot change. When households try to save a larger proportion of their disposable income, this causes the equilibrium rate of GNP to fall by just enough so that the flow of savings is the same as before.

Saving and investment: Planned and realized

We saw in Chapter 3 that GNP can be viewed as either total *output* or total *income* and that these amount to the same thing. In the simple model of this chapter, all output must go into consumption or investment. Hence we see that

$$Y \equiv C + I.$$

Turn now to the income side. All the income generated in the course of production must be either saved or spend on consumption. So from this standpoint,

$$T \equiv C + S.$$

But since things which are equal to the same thing are equal to one another,

$$C + I \equiv C + S$$

or by canceling,

$$S \equiv I.$$

Realized saving must equal realized investment. They are in fact the same thing: the unconsumed part of current output.

But suppose that instead of the past we are looking forward to the future. Here we stand on January 1, 1986, considering the movement of the economy over the year ahead. Now instead of *realized* saving and investment we are interested in *planned* or *intended* saving and investment. The former quantities are often called *ex post* (looking backward) values, while the latter are called *ex ante* (looking forward) values.

Can we now maintain that (planned) $S = I$? By no means. Consider that saving decisions are made by some 50 million households, with no central coordination. Investment plans are made separately by many thousands of large businesses and millions of smaller ones. These decisions could conceivably add up in such a way that total saving would equal total investment. But this would be no more than an accident and is in fact very unlikely.

But now we have a puzzle. How can things which are certain to be unequal at the beginning of a year be brought into necessary equality at the end of the year? What kind of trick are we playing here? The trick involves inventories of unsold goods and can be explained by looking at Table 4–4. Suppose that for one reason or another the current rate of GNP happens to be $800 billion per year, $40 billion above the equilib-

TABLE 4–4
**Aggregate demand and output
(billions of dollars per year)**

(1) $Y = Y_d$	(2) C	(3) S	(4) I	(5) C + I
600	550	50	90	640
640	580	60	90	670
680	610	70	90	700
720	640	80	90	730
760	670	90	90	760
800	700	100	90	790
840	730	110	90	820

rium rate. At this rate of output, the sum of consumption and investment demand is $700 + $90 = $790 billion per year, $10 billion per year *less* than the current rate of GNP. Therefore, businesses will find a ready market for only $790 billion of their $800 billion of output per year. What happens to the remaining $10 billion per year of output? It will go into business inventories. This will be the rate of *undesired accumulation of business inventories.*

Recall that the rate of change of business inventories is a component of gross private domestic investment, so this undesired change in business inventories is a part of investment. But it is a part of the rate of investment which is actually *realized* rather than that which was desired or demanded.

Thus, when the economy of Table 4–4 is operating at the disequilibrium GNP rate of $800 billion per year,

Consumption demand = Realized consumption = $700 billion per year.
Desired saving = Realized saving   = 100 billion per year.
Desired investment   =   90 billion per year.
Realized investment   = 100 billion per year.

The sum of realized consumption and realized investment is $700 + $100 = $800 billion per year and equals the actual rate of GNP. Furthermore, realized saving = realized investment = $100 billion per year.

Now let us consider the situation when the economy is operating at a rate of GNP which is below the equilibrium rate. Specifically, suppose that the economy of Table 4–4 is operating with a current rate of GNP which is $720 billion per year, $40 billion per year below the equilibrium rate. At this rate of output, the sum of consumption and investment demand is $640 + $90 = $730 billion per year, $10 billion per year *greater* than the current rate of output.

So what will happen? The extra $10 billion worth of goods—the amount by which the rate of demand exceeds the output rate—will have to come out of business inventories. Instead of the undesired inventory *accumulation* in the previous example, there will be an undesired inventory *decumulation.* The reduction of $10 billion in business inventories is an (undesired) reduction in investment. Thus, realized investment will turn out to be $80 billion rather than the $90 billion which was intended and will exactly equal the $80 billion of intended (and realized) saving.

In short, the books are brought into balance at the end of the year by an unintended increase or decrease of business inventories, which alters the total of (realized) investment.

THINK ABOUT THIS

In discussing the market economy in Chapter 2, it looked as though people's willingness to save determined the feasible level of capital formation (investment). But now in Chapter 4, it looks as though how much businesses decide to invest determines the level of saving, since for any past period the two must be equal. So what is going on here? Does saving determine investment, or vice versa? Or is there an element of truth in both views?

NEW CONCEPTS

equilibrium output
aggregate demand schedule
investment schedule
consumption schedule, household
consumption schedule, national
consumption schedule, long-run
marginal propensity to consume
marginal propensity to save
average propensity to consume
average propensity to save
autonomous change in spending
induced change in spending

autonomous spending multiplier
relative income hypothesis
permanent income hypothesis
life-cycle hypothesis
full employment
paradox of thrift
saving, desired
saving, realized
investment, desired
investment, realized
ex ante quantities
ex post quantities

SUMMARY

1. We consider a simple economy consisting only of households and businesses and in which all the income generated in production is passed on to households as disposable income. There is no business saving.

2. We assume also that the price level does not change as the rate of output varies.

3. *Aggregate demand* is the sum of consumption demand and investment demand. The key feature of consumption is that as income rises, consumer spending rises, but by a smaller amount. Review the definitions of the MPC, MPS, APC, and APS.

4. The (short-run) consumption schedule shows APC decreasing as income rises. Yet when we look at statistics over long periods, we find that the percentage of income consumed has remained roughly constant. The short-run consumption schedule keeps shifting upward over the course of time.

5. We assume a fixed amount of investment demand at any moment. Thus the aggregate demand *(C + I)* schedule runs parallel to the *C* schedule.

6. The intersection of the aggregate demand schedule and the 45-degree guideline defines an *equilibrium rate of output*. If actual output is above or below this rate at a particular time, it will tend to move toward equilibrium.

7. An *autonomous* change in consumption or investment demand is a change which does not depend on a prior change in income. An *induced* change is one which does result from a change in income.

8. An autonomous change in spending will cause the equilibrium rate of output to change by a larger amount. This is called the *multiplier effect*. Its size depends on the marginal propensity to consume, according to the formula.

$$\text{Multiplier} = \frac{1}{1 - MPC} = \frac{1}{MPS}.$$

9. Government efforts to shift aggregate demand to a level which will achieve full employment without inflation are called *fine tuning*. The feasibility of fine tuning is an important subject for later chapters.

10. An increase in consumers' desire to save will, if there is no change in investment demand, lead to a lower equilibrium rate of output with no change in actual saving. This is called the *paradox of thrift*.

11. Planned or *ex ante* investment at the beginning of any time period is very unlikely to equal planned saving. Yet at the end of the period, realized or *ex post S* and *I* must be equal by definition. The books are brought into balance by an *unintended* increase or decrease in business inventories, which count as part of investment.

TO LEARN MORE

You can dig deeper into macroeconomics by reading chapters of a good, modern text, such as Rudiger Dornbusch and Stanley Fischer, *Macroeconomics* (Boston: Little, Brown, 1978); or Paul Wonnacott, *Macroeconomics,* rev. ed. (Homewood, Ill.: Richard D. Irwin, 1978). You should of course use the most recent edition, since such texts are revised every few years.

Appendix: Algebraic derivation of the multiplier

The arithmetical illustration in the chapter contains the essence of the story. But let us work through the problem in simple algebra, for those who prefer that form of expression.

We know that in equilibrium, the rate of GNP must equal aggregate demand. It follows that, in order for equilibrium GNP to change, there must be a corresponding change in aggregate demand, which is the sum of consumption demand and investment demand. This can be expressed symbolically as

$$\Delta Y = \Delta C + \Delta I$$

where the Δ symbol (the Greek capital letter *delta*) indicates a change in the variable in question so that:

ΔY is the change in equilibrium GNP.
ΔC is the change in consumption demand.
ΔI is the change in investment demand.

Now think back to the nature of consumption demand. It depends upon the rate of GNP. More specifically, if the rate of GNP changes, consumption demand changes by a fraction of that amount—the fraction being the marginal propensity to consume. We can express the relationship between changes in the rate of GNP and changes in consumption demand as:

$$\Delta C = c_y \, \Delta Y$$

where c_y is the marginal propensity to consume. If this relationship is substituted into the above in place of ΔC, we obtain

$$\Delta Y = c_y \, \Delta Y + \Delta I.$$

Hence, the reason the equilibrium rate of GNP changes by more than the change in investment demand is that any change in GNP induces a change in consumption demand. *The change in the equilibrium rate of GNP must be such that it is equal to the sum of the induced change in consumption demand plus the change in investment demand.*

To see precisely what the change in equilibrium GNP must be in response to a change in investment demand, subtract $c_y \Delta Y$ from both sides of the relationship immediately above,

$$\Delta Y(1 - c_y) = \Delta I,$$

and then divide by $(1 - c_y)$ to obtain

$$\Delta Y = \frac{1}{(1 - c_y)} \Delta I.$$

Thus, we come out with the same formula as before. The multiplier is

$$\frac{1}{1 - c_y}.$$

5

National Output in a More Complex Economy

All theory, dear friend, is grey; but the golden tree of life springs ever green.

GOETHE, FAUST

In the simple model of Chapter 4, there is only *one* leakage from the income stream through personal saving (S_p) and only *one* injection into the income stream through business investment (I). In this chapter, we will look at an economy which is closer to the real world. There is a government which makes expenditures and levies taxes, businesses save as well as households, and there are exports to and imports from other countries.

In this economy, there are *three* injections to the income stream: investment (I), government expenditure (G), and net exports $(X - M)$; and there are also *three* leakages from the income stream: personal saving (S_p), business saving (S_b), and net tax payments (T_n).

But in this more complete model, everything still works exactly the same as in Chapter 4. There is an equilibrium rate of output, determined by the location of the aggregate demand schedule. When the economy is in equilibrium, total injections and total leakages must be equal. But instead of the simple condition that

$$S = I,$$

we now have the condition that

$$S_p + S_b + T_n = I + G + (X - M).$$

The autonomous spending multiplier also works as before, but with two differences: (1) An autonomous change in spending can now come from government or from exports, as well as from investment or consumption, (2) leakages from the income stream are larger, because part of the income generated in production leaks away into taxes and business saving and never reaches the consumer. Because the leakages are larger, the multiplier is smaller. The economy is *more stable,* upward and downward.

One ground rule laid down in Chapter 4 continues in force: We assume a constant price level, so that any change in GNP is a change in *real* GNP. We will not be able to get rid of this assumption until we have examined the monetary system.

FEATURES OF THE EXPANDED ECONOMY

We must first outline the features of this economy and the meaning of some key terms.

Government activities

Government produces a wide variety of public goods—national defense, roads and highways, public education, police and fire protection. To do this it must hire workers and buy supplies from business concerns. The sum of government payrolls and purchases, which is the cost of government output, is defined as *government expenditure (G).*

On the tax side, government pulls money out of the economy through personal and corporate income taxes, payroll taxes, sales taxes, property taxes, and so on. But it also puts money back into people's pockets by old-age pensions, unemployment compensation, veterans benefits, welfare payments, and other *transfer payments.*

A transfer payment is a payment from government, usually to an individual or family but occasionally to a business, which is not for services rendered in current production. While government tax receipts reduce disposable income, government transfer payments increase disposable income. For this reason, we regard these payments as *negative taxes,* and we deduct them from positive taxes in calculating the *net tax receipts* (T_n) of government.

Net tax receipts are total tax receipts less that portion which is returned to the private sector in the form of transfer payments.

These definitions are not the same as those used in government accounting. If you look at a summary of the federal budget for 1986, you will find on one side positive tax receipts only, listed as government revenue. On the other side, transfer payments are added to government purchases of good and services, and the total is called government expenditure. But this does not make much economic sense. A social security payment to a retired individual is not the same kind of thing as purchase of a bomber by the Defense Department. So it is important to remember the economic definitions of G and T_n and to use these terms consistently.

Business saving

In the simple model of Chapter 4, businesses paid out the full value of their output to individuals as wages, salaries, interest, and dividends. But we know that in fact this does not happen. Part of the value of output remains in the business. This retained income consists of two parts.

1. Capital consumption allowances.   Part of the cost of producing GNP is the wear and tear on the existing stock of capital goods. To compensate for this wear and tear, business firms set aside a portion of their gross sales receipts as depreciation allowances.

2. Retained corporate profits.   After a company has met its production expenses and paid its corporate income tax, it usually has some profit left over. What is left over belongs to the owners of the company, the common stockholders, and all of it *could* be distributed to them as dividends. But in practice only part is paid out, and the rest is plowed back into the business to finance purchases of new capital goods. In a young, rapidly growing company with large investment needs, 80 percent or more of profits may be retained and reinvested. In a mature company which is growing slowly, the proportion may be only 20 percent or so.

The sum of capital consumption allowances and retained corporate profits is called gross business savings (S_b).

Exports and imports

Goods exported to other countries have traditionally been only 5 percent or so of our GNP. But recently the proportion has been rising, partly because of high foreign demand for U.S. food and partly because we have been paying out more and more dollars for imported oil, and some of these dollars come back to us as demand for American goods. Recently exports have been about 10 percent of GNP, and imports have been running at about the same rate. This is large enough to have a significant impact on the American economy.

Export demand counts as part of total demand for U.S. goods. But this demand comes from other countries, so its size depends on conditions in those countries rather than in the United States. If Western Europe, Japan, and Canada, which are our major customers, go into an economic recession, demand for U.S. exports will be reduced. Recovery in those countries will raise our exports. If countries which are large buyers of American grain—the Soviet Union, China, and India—have a bad harvest year, our grain exports will shoot up. If crops are good abroad, our grain exports will fall.

What about imports? To the extent that Americans buy imported good, this reduces their demand for American goods. This doesn't mean, of course, that imports are bad, but they are different. They generate production and income in other countries rather than in the United States. So, to see whether foreign trade is making a net addition to demand for U.S. goods, we must deduct the import total from the export total. Only *net* exports *(X — M)* add to demand. This figure, unlike *G* and *I*, can be either positive or negative since imports sometimes exceed exports.

THE NEW CONSUMPTION SCHEDULE

The meaning of the consumption schedule is the same as in Chapter 4. This schedule tells us the amount of demand for consumer goods at different alternative rates of GNP. Suppose that the rate of GNP were to increase by $1 billion. How much would this raise consumer demand?

In the model of Chapter 4, the answer is simple. The full billion dollar increase in output is paid out to consumers as disposable income, which they divide between spending and saving. We assume that the MPC, and hence the MPS, are constant for all rates of GNP. Then if GNP rises by $1 billion, the increase in consumer spending will be $1 billion $\times$ *MPC*.

But in our new model, things are more complicated. The reason is that we have introduced two new leakages into the income stream— the drain into net tax payments and the drain into business saving. We will make the same assumption about these leakages that we made earlier for personal saving: Each is *a constant percentage of any increase in GNP*. This is reasonably realistic. Tax collections, business profits, and business saving do tend to rise at somewhat the same rate as GNP. Let's us t_y to indicate the *marginal net tax rate,* the percentage of any increase in GNP which goes into net taxes, and b_y to indicate the *marginal business saving rate,* the percentage of any increase in GNP which goes into business saving.

Now let's look again at what happens if the rate of GNP rises by $1 billion. Consumers no longer receive the whole billion as disposable income. Part leaks away into business saving and net tax payments. The increase in disposable income will be only $1 billion $\times (1 - t_y - b_y)$. Consumers then decide how to divide this increase in disposable income between spending and saving. Thus, the increase in consumer spending will be only $1 billion $\times$ *MPC* $\times$ increase in disposable income equals

$$\text{\$1 billion} \times \text{MPC} \, (1 - t_y - b_y).$$

Example. Suppose that the MPC is 0.80. In our Chapter 4 model, a $1 billion increase in GNP would increase disposable income by $1 billion. Consumer spending would rise by $1 billion $\times$ 0.80. = $800 million.

But in the model of this chapter, suppose that t_y is 0.20 and b_y is 0.05. Of each dollar increase in GNP, 20 cents goes to net taxes and 5 cents to business saving. Now, if GNP rises by $1 billion, disposable income will rise by considerably less than this. It will rise by only $1 billion $\times (1 - 0.20 - 0.05) = \$1$ billion $\times 0.75 = \$750$ million.

If we assume the same MPC of 0.80, then consumer spending will rise by $0.80 \times$ increase in disposable income $= 0.80 \times \$750$ million $= \$600$ million. The difference between the $800 million increase in consumer spending in the early model and the $600 increase in this model results from the two new leakages in the system.

The additional leakages *reduce the slope* of the consumption schedule. This slope, remember, shows us the ratio between a *change* in GNP and the corresponding change in consumer spending. Now, because of the t_y and b_y drains, the same dollar increase in GNP produces a smaller increase in consumer spending than before. In our example, the slope is reduced from 0.8 to 0.6.

This effect is illustrated in Figure 5–1. C_1 is the consumption schedule

FIGURE 5–1

Leakages and the consumption schedule

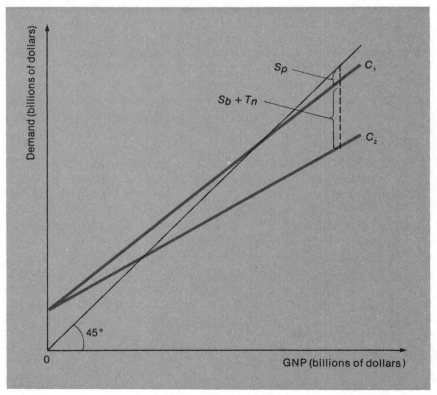

C_1 is the consumption schedule of Chapter 4, in which the only leakage is personal saving. The new leakages into business saving and net taxes introduced in this chapter shift the consumption schedule to C_2, lower than before and with a reduced slope.

in the simple model where all income is divided between consumption and personal saving. C_2 is the revised consumption schedule, which takes account of the additional leakages into business saving and net taxes. If you check with a ruler you will find that the slope of C_1 is four fifths, or 0.8, while the slope of C_2 is three fifths, or 0.6.

AGGREGATE DEMAND AND EQUILIBRIUM OUTPUT

In addition to a revised consumption schedule, we have two new sources of demand—government expenditure and net exports. We make the same assumption about these types of spending that we made earlier about investment spending: At any moment of time, their size is fixed and is independent of the rate of GNP. In the case of government spending, we can justify this by noting that government budgets actually are fixed for a year at a time. In the case of net exports, we note that demand for our exports depends on income levels and spending plans in other countries rather than in the United States. These, too, can be taken as given for short periods of time.[1]

On this assumption, we can chart the three nonconsumption components of demand as horizontal lines (Figure 5–2). The relative levels shown in the figure are realistic. Government expenditure is the largest of the three, though gross investment is not far behind. Net exports are much smaller and this figure, unlike the others, can be negative.

We now have everything we need to construct an aggregate demand schedule, from which we can determine an equilibrium rate of output for the economy. The procedure is illustrated in Table 5–1, which is charted in Figure 5–3. The assumptions behind Table 5–1, used just for illustration, are as follows: t_y is 0.20, b_y is 0.05, MPC is 0.80, and MPS is 0.20. Out of each $100 billion increase in GNP, therefore, disposable income rises by $75 billion, and this is split between a $60 billion increase in consumption and a $15 billion increase in personal saving. The nonconsumption components of demand—G, I, and X—add up to the same $600 billion at each and every rate of GNP. In the last column of the table, we get aggregate demand by adding consumption to these other components.

We know that the economy is in equilibrium only if total demand for output equals the current value of output. We see from Table 5–1 that this will be true if, and only if, the current rate of output is $1,400 billion per year. If instead producers were producing at a rate of $1,200 billion per year, total demand would be above this, at $1,280 billion; so

---

[1] We should note, however, that while export demand is not affected by U.S. GNP, import demand is affected. A higher rate of GNP in the United States will mean a higher demand for imports—consumers will buy more Datsuns as well as more Fords. Since net exports is exports minus imports, it is not correct to say that net exports is entirely independent of GNP. But this complication is best left to our later discussion of international trade and payments.

FIGURE 5–2
Nonconsumption components of demand

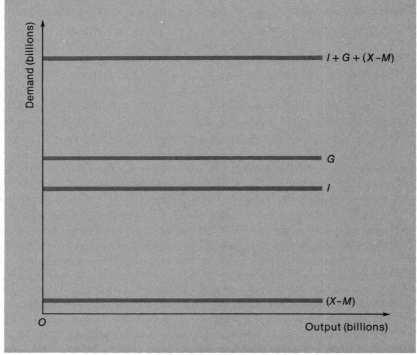

We assume that government expenditure *(G)*, gross private investment *(I)*, and exports minus imports *(X − M)* are constant at all rates of GNP. On this assumption, total nonconsumption demand, *G + I + (X − M)*, is also constant.

Table 5–1
The determination of equilibrium output (billions of dollars per year)

Y	T_n	S_b	Y_d	C	S_p	I	G	$X - M$	$C + I + G + (X - M)$
1,000	200	100	700	560	140	225	350	25	1,160
1,100	220	105	775	620	155	225	350	25	1,220
1,200	240	110	850	680	170	225	350	25	1,280
1,300	260	115	925	740	185	225	350	25	1,340
1,400	280	120	1,000	800	200	225	350	25	1,400
1,500	300	125	1,075	860	215	225	350	25	1,460
1,600	320	130	1,150	920	225	225	350	25	1,520
1,700	340	135	1,225	980	240	225	350	25	1,580

the rate of output would rise in response to this higher demand. Conversely, if producers were turning out $1,600 billion of goods per year, the aggregate demand of $1,520 would be insufficient to buy this amount, and production schedules would be revised downward. Only an output rate of $1,400 billion will be stable.

The same information is shown graphically in Figure 5–3. In the upper panel of the figure, we add nonconsumption demand on top of the consumption schedule. Since the nonconsumption components are taken as fixed, the aggregate demand schedule, $C + I + G + (X - M)$, runs parallel to the C schedule at a constant vertical distance. The intersection of the aggregate demand and supply schedules defines the equilibrium output rate of $1,400 billion per year.

The lower panel of Figure 5–3 reaches the same conclusion by a different route. Here we chart total leakages from the system, $S_p + S_b + T_n$, and total injections, $I + G + X - M$. Equilibrium output is defined by the condition that, in equilibrium, injections and leakages must be equal. This equilibrium rate of output must clearly be the same as that shown in the upper panel, since both depend on the same data.

APPLICATION OF THE EQUILIBRIUM CONCEPT

Figure 5–3 and the logic behind it are so similar to the equilibrium diagrams in Chapter 4 that the changes may appear trivial. Why, the reader may ask, add these extra pages to make essentially the same points? So we must emphasize that, while the geometry looks similar, the changes made in this model are important.

A new and smaller multiplier

In the Chapter 4 model, the size of the multiplier depends solely on the size of MPC and MPS. The multiplier formula is

$$\text{Multiplier} = \frac{1}{1 - MPC} = \frac{1}{MPS}.$$

Since saving is the only leakage in this model, we could call MPS the *marginal leakage ratio:* the larger this ratio, the smaller the multiplier.

In the expanded model, however, there are leakages into net taxes and business saving as well as into personal saving. Out of a dollar increase in GNP, the increase in consumer spending will be only $MPC\,(1 - t_y - b_y)$, which has to be smaller than MPC itself. The new multiplier formula is

$$\text{Multiplier} = \frac{1}{1 - MPC(1 - t_y - b_y)}.$$

FIGURE 5–3

Equilibrium output in a more complex economy

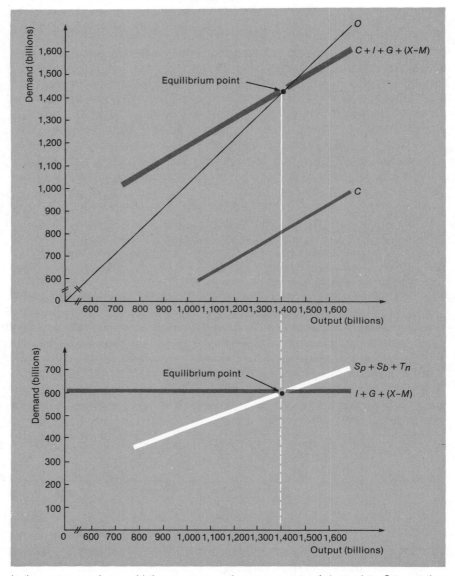

In the *upper* panel, we add the nonconsumption components of demand to *C* to get the aggregate demand schedule, $C + I + G + (X - M)$. The intersection of this schedule with the 45-degree line defines the equilibrium rate of output, which is $1,400 billion. The *lower* panel shows total injections to the income stream, $I + G + (X - M)$, and total leakages from the stream, $S_p + S_b + T_n$. The point at which these two are equal defines the equilibrium rate of output, which must of course be the same as that in the upper panel.

Just as before, we can call the denominator the *marginal leakage ratio.* Because of the two new terms, t_y and b_y, this must come out larger than before, and so the multiplier must be smaller.

   Example.   Let us go back to our earlier illustration in which MPC is 0.80, t_y is 0.20, and b_y is 0.05. Then in the simple model,

$$\text{Multiplier} = \frac{1}{1 - MPC}$$

$$= \frac{1}{1 - 0.80}$$

$$= \frac{1}{0.20}$$

$$= 5.$$

In the model of this chapter, however, the multiplier is

$$\text{Multiplier} = \frac{1}{1 - MPC(1 - t_y - b_y)}$$

$$= \frac{1}{1 - 0.80(0.75)}$$

$$= \frac{1}{0.40}$$

$$= 2.5.$$

   The reduction in the size of the multiplier makes the economy more stable. An autonomous shift in demand will have a smaller impact on the equilibrium rate of GNP. This result arises mainly from the large tax drain. The fact that t_y is considerably larger today than it was before 1940 helps to account for the greater stability of the economy in recent decades, an effect sometimes called the *built-in stabilizer.*

   The actual size of the multiplier is not easy to estimate, because instead of a single clear-cut change in autonomous spending whose effects can be traced out, we typically have numerous changes going on month by month. Thus statistical estimates differ, though most fall in the range of 2 to 3.

   An accurate estimate is clearly of practical importance. Suppose that at a particular time, the rate of output is $100 billion below what is judged to be desirable. How much of an increase in demand is needed to lift output by $100 billion? An untrained person might say, "$100 billion." But this would be wrong. Remember the multiplier. If it is 2, then an autonomous increase of $50 billion in demand would be enough to do the job, given a bit of time. But if the multiplier were 3, then an increase of only $33.3 billion in demand would be needed. So estimating the size of the multiplier is not just an academic exercise.

New sources of autonomous change

In the model of Chapter 4, there were only two types of autonomous change in spending: (1) businesses might revise their investment plans upward or downward, thus shifting the I schedule, and (2) consumers might decide for some reason to spend more or less out of a given income, thus shifting the C schedule. We saw that any such change will shift the aggregate demand schedule, and because of the multiplier effect, there will be an even larger change in the equilibrium rate of GNP.

In the expanded model, we have two new major sources of autonomous change: (1) a change in planned government spending and (2) a change in tax rates. Changes in government expenditure are usually gradual, but they can also be quite sharp. During the Korean and Vietnam wars, for example, military expenditures were stepped up substantially in the early stages of the war, then cut back substantially as military activity tapered off. A change in G has the same multiplier effect as any other autonomous change in spending. Suppose that G increases by $20 billion, raising the aggregate demand schedule by that amount, and suppose that the multiplier is 2.5. Then the change in G will raise the equilibrium rate of GNP by $20 billion $\times$ 2.5 = $50 billion. By the same reasoning, a drop in G—say, because of a cutback in military spending—would produce a larger drop in the equilibrium rate of output.

Autonomous changes in tax rate (T_n), like autonomous changes in G, are not uncommon in practice. T_n rose in 1951–52 and in 1968–69 because of income tax surcharges to offset costs of the Korean and Vietnam wars. T_n rose again in 1980 and 1981 because of large increases in social security payroll taxes to offset the rapid increase in pension payments to retired workers. During recessions, on the other hand, tax rates are sometimes reduced to raise consumer demand and promote recovery from the recession.

Tax changes affect the economy by *shifting the consumption schedule.* Suppose T_n is increased by $20 billion. This means that consumers' disposable income is reduced by $20 billion. Consumers will respond to this by reducing both their spending and their saving, the proportions depending on their marginal propensity to consume. If the short-run *MPC* were 0.8, consumption would drop by $16 billion. The C schedule, in other words, would be $16 billion lower than before, and the aggregate demand schedule would shift down by the same amount. Then, assuming the same multiplier of 2.5, the equilibrium rate of output would drop by $40 billion.

This illustration can be reversed for a reduction in T_n. A cut of $20 billion in T_n would (if the *MPC* is 0.8) *raise* the C schedule and the aggregate demand schedule by $16 billion, and this would lead, via the multiplier, to a rise of $40 billion in the equilibrium rate of output.

So, G changes and T_n changes work in opposite directions. An *increase* in G or a *decrease* in T_n will *raise* the equilibrium rate of GNP. Conversely, a *decrease* in G or an *increase* in T_n will *lower* the equilibrium rate of GNP.

But it is clear from our illustration that the size of the two effects is different. The $20 billion change in G produced a change of $50 billion in the equilibrium rate of output. The same dollar change of $20 billion in T_n altered the equilibrium rate of output by only $40 billion. Dollar for dollar, a G change delivers "more bang for a buck." Why is this?

The explanation is that a change in T_n causes a *smaller* shift in the aggregate demand schedule than does an equal change in G. If government purchases are cut by $20 billion, the aggregate demand schedule falls by the full $20 billion. But if net taxes are raised by $20 billion, the C schedule and the aggregate demand schedule fall by *less* than this amount. Part of the increased tax payment comes out of saving, so consumption demand (and hence aggregate demand) falls less, and the effect on output is reduced.

In practice, the impact of a change in T_n seems to depend partly on how it is made and particularly whether it is regarded as temporary or permanent. A permanent change in, say, personal income tax rates will cause consumers to revise both their spending and saving plans, as the permanent income hypothesis would suggest. But a purely temporary change may be regarded as a windfall and go mainly into savings or be taken out of savings, with little effect on consumption. A classic case is the 1968 income tax surcharge imposed at the height of the Vietnam War to restrain aggregate demand and reduce inflation. The tax was schedules to expire in 18 months, so consumers apparently responded by cutting their saving enough to pay the tax and continued to spend as before. The C schedule was little affected, and the objective of restraining inflation was not achieved.

THINK ABOUT THIS

The economy is operating below capacity, and the government wants to raise the equilibrium rate of output. It is considering whether to lower taxes or increase expenditures. This section of the chapter says that, dollar for dollar, an increase in expenditures will have greater impact.
a. Can you explain why this is?
b. Would you necessarily conclude that government should use the expenditure lever rather than the tax lever? Explain.

Still another possible source of autonomous change is an increase or decrease in foreign demand for American exports. A rise in X will raise aggregate demand and, through the multiplier, have an even larger effect on equilibrium output. A fall in X will have the opposite effect.

We noted earlier that foreign demand for U.S. goods depends mainly on aggregate demand in the other countries with which we trade, notably Canada, Japan, and Western Europe. If all these countries were suffering a recession at the same time, X demand might fall rather sharply. Fortunately, business cycles in different countries are not perfectly synchronized. While GNP in Canada is falling, that in West Germany may be rising. So in practice, shifts in X are not as large and significant as those in other components of aggregate demand.

The equilibrium condition once more

As we concluded in Chapter 3, GNP can be viewed either as total *output* or total *income*. Thinking in output terms, output may go for consumption, investment, government purchases, or net exports. Thus,

$$Y \equiv C + I + G + (X - M).$$

Thinking in income terms, income may go into consumption, personal saving, business saving, or net tax receipts. Thus,

$$Y \equiv C + S_p + S_b + T_n.$$

It follows directly that

$$S_p + S_b + T_n \equiv I + G + (X - M).$$

This will always be true when we look at the national accounts for any past period. The reason is that both groups of items mean the same thing—that part of output (income) which did not go into current consumption.

Looking toward the future, however, there is no reason why *planned* nonconsumption uses of income should precisely equal planned nonconsumption demand. If they are unequal, this will produce an upward or downward movement of GNP.

Specifically,

if $S_p + S_b + T_n > I + G + (X - M)$, the rate of GNP will fall;
if $S_p + S_b + T_n < I + G + (X - M)$, the rate of GNP will rise.

These conclusions have important practical applications. Suppose that GNP is declining—the economy is sliding into recession. Or suppose that GNP is stationary, but at an undesirably low level, with 7 percent or 8 percent of the labor force unemployed. In either case, one would like action to raise the rate of GNP.

What to do? What is needed is an autonomous increase in (planned) spending, which will raise the equilibrium rate of output. The items in the equation provide a complete checklist of the ways in which this could come about. Spending could rise because of:

1. An increase in one or more components of investment—residences, commercial buildings, plant and equipment, inventory accumulation.
2. An increase in government expenditure.
3. An increase in foreign demand for U.S. goods, leading to a rise in exports.
4. A reduction in net taxes, which will shift the consumption schedule upward.
5. A reduction in personal saving plans, which will also raise the consumption schedule.
6. A reduction in business saving, say through a decision to pay out a higher percentage of profits to stockholders.

Any of these changes would either pump more income into, or reduce the leakages from, the circular flow, and hence raise the equilibrium rate of GNP. In practice, government can influence items 1, 2, and 4 most directly, though it has indirect influence on the others as well.

The problem is not always too little aggregate demand. Occasionally in the United States, and more frequently in some other countries, there has been a problem of too much spending, leading to price inflation. In this case, government should try to raise the items on the left-hand side of the equation and/or reduce the items on the right-hand side.

THINK ABOUT THIS

1. It is often said that American economy is more stable today than it was before 1940. This would have to mean either that autonomous changes in spending are less violent, or that the multiplier is smaller, or both. What reasons can you think of why the multiplier might be smaller today than it used to be?
2. Suppose that you are on the Council of Economic Advisers to the president in a period when output is falling and unemployment is rising. What kinds of autonomous changes might serve to *raise* the equilibrium rate of GNP? Which of these would you advise?

NEW CONCEPTS

government expenditure
transfer payments
net tax receipts
business saving, gross
net export schedule

marginal net tax rate
marginal business saving rate
marginal leakage ratio
built-in stabilizer

SUMMARY

1. In this chapter, we expand the simple model of Chapter 4 in several directions: there is a government, which makes expenditures and levies taxes; businesses save as well as households; and there are exports to and imports from other countries.

2. In this economy, there are *three* injections to the income stream: investment *(I)*, government expenditure *(G)*, and net imports $(X - M)$. There are also *three* leakages from the income stream: personal saving (S_p), business saving (S_b), and net tax payments (T_n).

3. The consumption schedule in this model is *lower* than in the Chapter 4 model, and the *slope* of the schedule is reduced. The reason is that, out of the additional income generated by an increase in GNP, a sizable share is drained off into business saving and net tax payments and never reaches consumers as disposable income.

4. We assume that, at any moment, investment, government expenditure, and net exports are fixed amounts. So by adding these amounts to the consumption schedule, we get an *aggregate demand schedule*, which runs parallel to the *C* schedule at a higher level.

5. The intersection of the aggregate demand and aggregate supply schedules defines an *equilibrium rate of GNP*. We can define this rate also by noting that it is the rate at which total leakages from the income stream equal total injections.

6. In this model, the multiplier, whose size depends on the marginal leakage ratio, is smaller than in the Chapter 4 model. Because the multiplier is smaller, there will be a smaller change in GNP in response to any autonomous change in demand. The economy is more *stable,* upward and downward.

7. There are also, in this model, more possible sources of autonomous change in demand: a change in government expenditure, a change in tax rates, a change in business saving plans, and a change in foreign demand for U.S. goods. This can be viewed as providing more sources of instability or, alternatively, as providing more levers which government can manipulate to achieve a desirable rate of aggregate demand and output.

8. For any past period, it is necessarily true that

$$S_p + S_b + T_b \equiv I + G + (X - M).$$

9. Looking toward the future, however, there is no reason why plans on the two sides should be exactly equal. But

if $S_p + S_b + T_n > I + G + (X - M)$, the rate of GNP will fall;
if $S_p + S_b + T_b < I + G + (X - M)$, the rate of GNP will rise.

6

The Supply of Money

*Money is indeed the most important thing in the world;
and all sound and successful personal and national
morality should have this fact for its base.*

—George Bernard Shaw

Gross national product and national income are measured in dollars, and it is these dollars which circle around the economy from buyers to sellers. So you may have asked yourself occasionally, "Where do these dollars come from? Will the supply of money keep rising as GNP rises? What determines the rate of increase in money?"

This chapter will try to answer these questions. Specifically, we will make the following points:

Present-day money supply consists mainly of checking accounts, also called *demand deposits,* in commercial banks.

The banking system can increase money supply by making loans or buying securities, either of which will produce an increase in demand deposits.

The size of a bank's demand deposits is limited, however, by the need to hold some *reserves* against these deposits. Banks which are members of the Federal Reserve (the Fed) are required to hold a certain proportion (normally in the range of 10 to 20 percent) of their demand deposits as reserves, either in cash or in deposits (checking accounts) at the Fed.

The Fed can alter the quantity of bank reserves by purchase or sale of government securities in the open market, called *open-market operations.* An increase in reserve makes possible an increase of several times that amount in demand deposits, that is, in money supply. Conversely, if reserves decrease, money supply must also decrease. This is the leash by which the Fed tries to regulate the growth of money supply.

THE FUNCTIONS OF MONEY

Money serves several functions in the economy. First: It is a *medium of exchange*. It is what you use to buy weekly groceries, pay the monthly rent, make the down payment on the car. It is also the medium for paying wages or for engaging in a loan transaction.

Second: it is a *measure of value*. If we ask what any good or service is worth, the answer is "so many dollars." This is not logically necessary. Some other commodity, say, wheat could be used instead. Then the answer to the question "What is a shirt worth?" might be "five bushels of wheat." But because we use money for shopping, it is convenient to quote the price of everything in terms of money.

Third: Money can be used as a *store of value*. You can put it away in order to spend it at some later time. You can put away other things as well, but money has the advantage of immediate availability and general acceptability by others. It is not, however, a completely dependable store. If the price level is rising, your money stock will be shrinking *in terms of its real purchasing power over other goods*. For this reason, and because cash on hand yields no interest, people usually prefer to hold part of their wealth in other forms—savings accounts, stocks, bonds, and so on. These preferences have an important effect on the operation of the economy.

What is money?

Money is as money does. Anything which members of a community are willing to accept in payment for goods or debts is money. Large round stones serve the purpose on the island of Yap. They can't be carried around in one's pocket. Indeed, the happy inhabitants of this island don't have pockets. For the most part, the stones remain immovable on hillsides throughout the island, but each stone has an owner, and ownership changes as payments are made. One large stone fell out of a boat years ago and lies in deep water some distance offshore. It is still wealth to its current owner, however, and counts as part of the island's money supply.

Among the Bantu tribes of East Africa, animals serve as a means of payment. A prospective bridegroom must pay the father of the bride so many cattle, sheep, or goats as a "bride's price." Monetary systems have been based on cowrie shells, wampum, cloth, and beads. A prisoner-of-war camp during World War II developed an elaborate system of exchange in which cigarettes were used as money.

Gold and other metals have always exercised a special fascination. They are durable, they can be fashioned into personal ornaments and art objects, and this commercial value reinforces their value as money.

From Greek times until quite recently, money in the Western world meant metal coins which circulated partly by order of the sovereign but also by virtue of their metallic content.

The next stage in the development of modern monetary systems came with the rise of banking institutions in Europe during the 15th and 16th centuries. Banks gradually learned that they could issue paper notes which would be generally accepted as a means of payment. A bank note meant originally that the banker had an equivalent amount of gold in his vaults which he promised to pay to the holder of the note on demand. But so long as people had faith in the bank's soundness, there was no reason for them to demand payment. The notes passed freely from hand to hand because of the general belief that they were "as good as gold." After a time, most payments came to be made in this way, and coins were reduced to serving as small change.

Still more recent is the practice of making payments by check. Most businesses and individuals now hold ready cash in the form of a checking account. One occasionally reads of a hermit with a passion for keeping bundles of bank notes in brown paper bags, but these stories make the headlines only because they are so unusual. Most people regard a checking account as perfectly safe, and so it is. In the unlikely event that your bank should fail, deposits up to $100,000 per account are guaranteed through the Federal Deposit Insurance Corporation.[1] Bankers refer to checking accounts as *demand deposits,* because the owner is entitled to withdraw them at any time on demand, without advance notice.

It may seem odd to regard checking accounts as money, but they meet the test of general acceptability. Checks written by a business concern, government agency, or other institution are normally accepted without question. So are personal checks, with at most a quick glance at your driver's license. In addition, purchases are made increasingly on credit. When bills roll in at the end of the month, how are they paid? By check, of course. This is much more convenient than going to the bank for paper money, and it also provides a record of what you have spent.

In early 1984, there was about $150 billion of coins and paper currency in circulation. Checking accounts owned by the public totaled about $390 billion. Thus, checking accounts constitute about three fourths of the total money supply in the United States. Moreover, check money circulates faster than other kinds of money. More than 90 percent of all payments in the United States are made by check. So when we ask what determines the amount of money in existence, the main problem is what determines the amount of demand deposits.

We count checking accounts as money. Why do we not also count

---

[1] A very small minority of banks in the United States are not insured by the Federal Deposit Insurance Corporation, but they have only about 1 percent of the total demand deposits.

savings accounts? These are called *time deposits* because the holder can be required to give a certain period of notice before withdrawing them. In normal times, most banks overlook this requirement, and savings accounts can be withdrawn as freely as checking accounts. In early 1984, savings accounts and other time deposits totaled about $1,100 billion.

For that matter, why do we not count holdings of short-term government securities, which can be turned into cash without notice and with little risk? These resemble money in certain respects. They provide a safe way of holding reserve funds and are counted as part of the liquid assets of business and individuals who own them. Savings accounts and short-term government securities are often lumped together as *near-money*.

But they are still not *quite* money. They are not directly and universally transferable. You can't go to the store and spend a savings account or a U.S. treasury security. They must first be converted into currency or a demand deposit, which is then used as a means of payment. In the case of securities, the terms on which conversion can be affected are typically uncertain. A company knows that it can always sell its holdings of U.S. treasury securities for cash, but the price varies from day to day, and the outcome is uncertain until they are sold. Thus, if I put $1,000 into securities, I cannot know how many dollars I will be able to realize in a year's time (unless, of course, the securities which I bought happen to reach maturity within the year). The same $1,000 put into a checking account will always be worth $1,000. The difference is important. This is what one means by saying that money possesses *complete liquidity*.

The money supply of the United States is usually defined as the sum of currency and checking accounts owned by the "public." The public includes individuals, ordinary businesses, and state and local governments. It does not include the U.S. government or commercial banks.

The definition and measurement of money supply has been complicated recently by the growth of new types of accounts due partly to the high interest rates which have prevailed since the early 70s. Banks, eager to profit from these high rates, have competed for depositors' money by developing new types of interest-bearing accounts. At the same time, government regulations covering permissible types of accounts and maximum rates of interest have gradually been relaxed.

In the old days there was a clear distinction between a demand deposit, which allowed checking but paid no interest, and a time or savings deposit, which did not allow checking but did pay interest. But today, if I want to make a deposit in my bank, I have a choice among (1) an old-fashioned checking account, which pays no interest and requires no minimum balance; (2) a NOW (negotiated order of withdrawal) account, which permits unlimited checking and pays interest somewhat above 5 percent, but requires that I keep a minimum balance of $1,000; (3) a "money market account," which limits me to three checks a month, pays a higher rate of interest (currently about 8.5 percent), but requires a minimum balance of $2,500; (4) a "certificate of deposit," which in effect guarantees that I will leave the money in the bank for anywhere from 3 months to 3 years, with the interest rate rising as the period is lengthened. So people with sizable cash balances now have a nice problem of deciding how much to hold in each form.

These different types of accounts have different degrees of "money-ness," that is, immediate availability for making payments. Typically, as the degree of money-ness decreases, the rate of interest you can earn increases to compensate for the loss of convenience. But it is no longer very clear where the line should be drawn between what is truly money and what is not quite money. The old definition included only currency and ordinary noninterest checking accounts. But the $M1$ totals which you see in the newspapers also include NOW and money market accounts at banks and thrift institutions. This is the measure which conforms most closely to the function of money as a medium of exchange. Adding savings and other time deposits (exclusive of very large certificates of deposit held mainly by businesses) produces a larger total, $M2$. There is even an $M3$, which includes large time deposits and a few other items.

These totals are now affected somewhat by institutional changes. Thus, when the banks were allowed in 1982 to offer money market checking accounts, this put them in close competition with the "money market funds" operated by brokerage concerns. Many billions of dollars were transferred out of money market funds and into the new bank accounts, which pay slightly lower interest but have the checking convenience and are also covered by federal deposit insurance. Since the new accounts were included in $M1$ while money market funds were not, this raised $M1$ and made changes in it harder to interpret.

As of early 1984, $M1$ was running at about $520 billion, and $M2$ at $2,200 billion; these figures normally move upward over the course of time. The long-run trend from 1950–80 is shown in Figure 6–1. Note that money supply rose faster in the 60s than in the 50s, and still faster in the 70s. The rate of price increase—the inflation rate—has accelerated in a similar way. The price curve and the money supply curve parallel each other rather closely. The two are obviously related, but the relation is complex, as we'll see in the next two chapters. Years since 1980 are not shown, because the changes in definition noted earlier make comparability difficult. All the curves continue upward, however, in rough parallel with each other.

People sometimes ask, "*Why* are dollar bills regarded as money? What is the backing for them?" Before 1933, one could go into a bank with dollar bills and ask for gold coins in return. Not many people did this, but our currency was at least loosely linked to a metallic base. Today this is no longer so. The bills in your wallet are money simply because the government says they are. They are what is usually called *fiat money*.

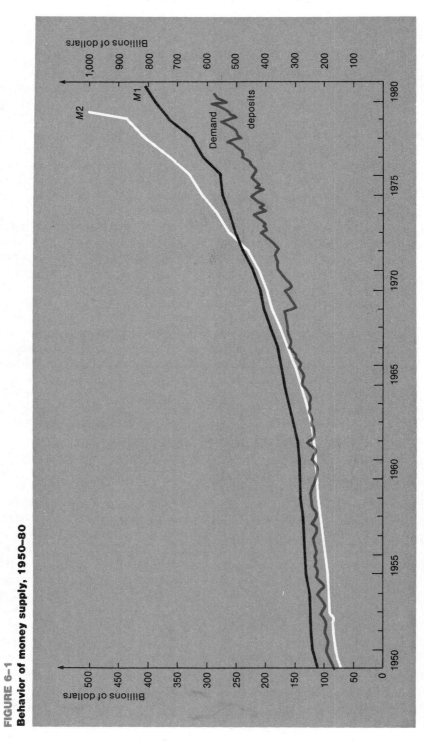

FIGURE 6–1
Behavior of money supply, 1950–80

Source: Survey of Current Business and Federal Reserve Bulletin.

THE BUSINESS OF BANKING

The banks whose operations mainly influence the money supply are called *commercial banks,* because in the early days, most bank borrowers were engaged in commerce rather than manufacturing. These banks perform a variety of service functions. My bank receives my paycheck every month, allows me to draw checks on the account, and sends me a statement at the end of the month. But this is an unexciting and not very profitable operation. The lifeblood of commercial banking is lending—sizing up would-be borrowers and advancing them money at a price.

What happens when a bank makes a loan? A company applies for a loan of $1 million, and the bank agrees. The company gives the bank a piece of paper promising to repay the loan after, say, six months. The bank gives the company an addition of $1 million to its checking account. Money supply increases. When the time for payment comes round, unless the loan is renewed, repayment is made by deducting $1 million from the company's checking account. The central principle is simple: Making a loan creates money, while repaying a loan extinguishes money.

This looks very easy and profitable—the bank just creates money by a stroke of the pen. So why not create as much money as possible? The difficulty with this idea is that when people and companies have checking accounts, they are likely to use them. In addition to writing checks, they may want to draw out part of their deposit in cash. So a bank must have some cash in the vault, and a place where it can go for more cash if necessary. In short, a bank must have *reserves.*

What, concretely, are reserves? They consist partly of currency (bills and coins) held in the bank to meet day-to-day requirements. Most reserves, however, take the form of deposits (checking accounts) with the Federal Reserve System. All national banks must be members of the system, and the Fed requires them to carry reserves equal to a specified percentage of their deposits. In addition, under the Monetary Control Act of 1980, all banks and savings institutions, whether members or nonmembers, must carry a certain percentage of their deposits as reserves and must report on this regularly to the Fed.

HOW DEMAND DEPOSITS EXPAND AND CONTRACT

When I write a check for $100, this is an order to my bank to deduct $100 from my account and transfer it to the recipient of the check. She then deposits it in her bank and gets the amount added to her account. If we both have checking accounts in the same bank, the transaction is simple. The bank deducts $100 from my account and adds $100 to hers. The bank's total deposits remain unchanged.

But suppose a check drawn on bank A is deposited in bank B. Bank

A then owes bank B that much money, and a transfer between the two banks is necessary. It is likely, however, that at the same time some checks drawn on bank B will have been deposited in bank A, so that the two debts will partially cancel each other. These cancellations are carried out through a central clearinghouse in each city. Each morning every bank sends to the clearinghouse all the checks which it has received on other banks in the city. The totals are added up. A bank which has sent in more dollars worth of checks on other banks than others have sent in against it receives a payment of that amount. A bank which has an adverse balance must pay in that amount to the clearinghouse. How does a bank "pay up" in such a case? By writing a check on its account with the Federal Reserve bank of its district or by paying out some of its currency holdings. Thus a bank which has more checks drawn against it than are being deposited with it suffers a loss of reserves. Similarly, a bank which has had more checks deposited than drawn against it has its reserves increased.

If a check drawn in one city is deposited in another, the clearance procedure is more elaborate but not basically different. Again, the important thing to the individual bank is whether the total checks drawn against it are greater or less than the checks drawn on other banks which it has received.

The term *demand deposits* is confusing. It suggests that to get a checking account I must deposit something in the bank. This idea seems so reasonable that it is hard to dislodge from one's mind. There is even an element of truth in the idea, for this is certainly one way to acquire a checking account. I can go into the First National Bank of Illyria and open a checking account by depositing either a check which I have received or a bundle of paper money. But note that this does not alter *the amount of money in the economy*. If I deposit a check, the increase in my checking account is exactly offset by a reduction in someone else's checking account. Total demand deposits remain unchanged. If I deposit currency, I merely exchange money of one form for money of another form. The demand deposit component of the money supply goes up, but the currency component goes down by the same amount, so the total money supply remains unchanged.

How, then, can there ever be an increase or decrease in the supply of money? The answer is that demand deposits can be created, and also eliminated, by the banking system. A bank can create (or eliminate) demand deposits in two ways:

1. By making a loan (or accepting repayment of a loan).
2. By buying securities from (or selling securities to) an individual or business.

Let us look first at how demand deposits can increase.

    1. Suppose I am a manufacturer with a growing business which re-

quires more working capital. I ask my bank for a loan of $100,000, and after looking into the soundness of the business, it approves the loan. What does the bank give me? Not a bale of $100 bills. It simply adds $100,000 to my checking account. In return, I give the bank a piece of paper promising to repay the money by a specified date. The transaction affects the bank's balance sheet as follows:

Assets	Liabilities
Loans +$100,000	Demand deposits +$100,000

Here is an increase in demand deposits. My need for a loan has increased the money supply by $100,000.

Actually, what has happened is that the bank and I have exchanged IOUs. I gave the bank a promise to pay at a certain date in exchange for its promise to pay on demand. My IOU is just an ordinary IOU, but the bank's IOU is an extraordinary IOU in that it is generally accepted as a means of payment. *The bank's IOU is money.*

2. Now for the seond way in which demand deposits can come into being. Suppose I own some marketable government bonds which are currently worth $50,000.[2] If I sell them to a bank, it will pay for them by giving me its IOU. The bank will either credit my checking account with a $50,000 deposit or, alternatively, it will give me a check drawn on itself for $50,000 which I can deposit in the bank of my choice. Either way, I will end up with $50,000 more money and $50,000 less government securities than I had initially. The bank will have paid for the government securities by increasing demand deposits and therefore the money supply by $50,000.

Whenever the commercial banks expand their loans or security holdings by creating demand deposits, the money supply of the country expands by that amount.

Now consider how the money supply can contract.

1. When a loan is repaid, total demand deposits decrease by that amount. Does this sound confusing? What happens when a loan is repaid? A wholesaler has borrowed $50,000 from a bank on a three-month promissory note. At the end of three months, unless the loan is extended or renewed, the bank *deducts* $50,000 from the wholesaler's checking account. *Repayment of loans extinguishes demand deposits.* If the banks stopped making new loans completely, acquired no additional securities, and simply waited for old loans to be paid off, demand deposits would fall quite fast.

---

[2] Marketable U.S. government bonds can be traded just like any other security. The unmarketable U.S. government savings bonds constitute only about 25 percent of the privately held federal debt. The remaining 75 percent is in the form of marketable securities.

2. Similarly, suppose that a bank sells $50,000 of marketable government securities to an individual or to an ordinary business firm. The buyer will pay for the securities by writing a check on his or her account for $50,000 and turning it over to the bank which is selling the securities. As a direct result, the "public" will end up owning $50,000 more government securities and $50,000 less demand deposits than before the transaction.

Whenever the commercial banks decrease their loans or security holdings by extinguishing demand deposits, the money supply of the country contracts by that amount.

BANK RESERVES, THE RESERVE REQUIREMENT, AND DEMAND DEPOSITS

Why don't banks keep making loans and buying government securities while all the time increasing demand deposits? What keeps the money supply from growing by leaps and bounds?

There is a limit to how much demand deposit liabilities the banks can create. The limit is determined by the amount of reserves which the banks possess in combination with the minimum legal reserves-to-demand-deposits ratio, usually called the *reserve requirement*. If the volume of demand deposits is already so large that the banks have just enough reserves to satisfy the reserve requirement, they can acquire no more certificates of indebtedness by creating additional demand deposits, for to do so would cause the reserves-to-demand-deposits ratio to fall below the minimum legal level. On the other hand, if the banks have more than enough reserves to meet the reserve requirement, they can expand their loans and investments by creating additional demand deposits.

To pin down the importance of bank reserves and the reserve requirement as factors limiting the money supply, suppose that the banks have $100 billion of demand deposit liabilities and the reserve requirement is 0.2. This means that the banks must hold 0.2 × $100 billion = $20 billion of reserves. But suppose that they actually hold $25 billion of reserves, $5 billion more than they are legally required to hold. Then, they are free to create more demand deposits by purchasing additional certificates of indebtedness.

How much additional demand deposits can they create? Let's reason it out:

1. With a minimum legal reserves-to-demand-deposits ratio of 0.2, the banks must hold $0.2 of reserves for every $1 of demand deposit liabilities. Or, they must hold $1 of reserves for every $5 of demand deposit liabilities.
2. This means that, with a reserve requirement of 0.2, $1 of reserves (in a sense) can support five times as much demand deposits.

3. Hence, since the banks have $5 billion of excess reserves, they can legally create 5 × $5 billion = $25 billion of additional demand deposits.

But once the banks have expanded their demand deposit liabilities to $125 billion, they can go no further. Without an increase in their reserves or a reduction in the reserve requirement, they cannot expand their loans and investments or create additional demand deposits. This is because $25 billion of bank reserves, when the reserve requirement is 0.2, can support a maximum amount of demand deposits of five times as much, or $125 billion.

Had the reserve requirement been 0.25 rather than 0.2, the banks would *not* have been able to expand their demand deposit liabilities beyond $100 billion. This is because, with a 0.25 reserve requirement, each dollar of reserves can support only 1/0.25 = 4 times as much demand deposits. So with $25 billion in reserves, the banks can have a maximum of only $100 billion of demand deposits.

On the other hand, had the reserve requirement been 0.1, then the $25 billion of bank reserves would have made it legally possible for the banks to expand their demand deposit liabilities to 1/0.1 = 10 times as much or to $250 billion.

For a given amount of bank reserves, the lower the reserve requirement, the more demand deposit liabilities the banks can have. The maximum amount of demand deposit liabilities which they can have is given by one divided by the reserve requirement times the amount of bank reserves, or $1/r \times R$, where r is the minimum legal reserves-to-demand-deposits ratio and R is the amount of bank reserves.

DEMAND DEPOSIT EXPANSION IN A STEP-BY-STEP PROCESS

Let's now see how an expansion of the money supply might take place in a simplified, step-by-step process.

We assume the existence of a small economy with a banking system like that of the United States. At this particular point in time, the money supply of this economy is $150,000, of which $100,000 is demand deposits and $50,000 is currency.

The banks in this economy are required to hold reserves equal to 20 percent of their demand deposit liabilities. At the present time, all the banks just hold the required amount of reserves, so they are currently unable to make any additional loans or investments. This means that the total reserves of the banking system equal

$$0.2 \times \$100,000 = \$20,000.$$

Step 1.   Now suppose that a Mr. Alan Arrow (who happens to own at least $1,000 of the public's supply of currency) decides to deposit

$1,000 of currency in his checking account with bank A. The immediate effect of this transaction upon bank A's balance sheet is as follows:

Step 1

BANK A			
Assets		Liabilities	
Required reserves	+200	Arrow's demand deposit	+1,000
Excess reserves	+800		
Total	+1,000	Total	+1,000

Arrow has merely exchanged money of one form (currency) for money of another form (demand deposits). Thus, the immediate effect of this transaction between Arrow and bank A upon the money supply is to leave it unchanged. The currency component of the money supply has gone down by $1,000, but the demand deposit component has gone up by $1,000.

Notice, however, that bank A now holds more reserves than it is legally required to hold. When Arrow deposited the $1,000 in currency, the bank's reserves went up by $1,000. But only $200 of this was a required increase in reserves (to accommodate the additional $1,000 of demand deposits at the minimum legal reserves-to-demand-deposits ratio of 1 to 5 or 0.2). Bank A now has $800 of excess reserves.

Step 2. Suppose that a Ms. Susan Martin goes into bank A and asks to borrow $800 to buy a used car. We assume that Martin has a good credit rating, and since the bank has excess reserves, the request is granted. How is the loan made? Martin and bank A exchange IOUs. Martin gives the bank a written statement to the effect that she promises to repay the loan on a specific date, and the bank gives Martin a promise to pay $800 on demand or it adds $800 to her checking account balance.

Bank A's balance sheet now looks like this (including Step 1):

Steps 1 and 2

BANK A			
Assets		Liabilities	
Required reserves	+360	Arrow's demand deposit	+1,000
Excess reserves	+640	Martin's demand deposit	+800
Martin's loan	+800		
Total	+1,800	Total	+1,800

In making the loan to Martin, Bank A has increased its demand deposit liabilities by an additional $800. It has also increased its assets (Martin's IOU) by $800. Furthermore, the bank now has less excess reserves than before. This is because, in creating the additional $800 of demand deposits for Martin, the bank's required reserves went up by 0.2 × $800 = $160, and its excess reserves went down by the same amount.

When Martin walks out of the bank, she has $800 more in money than when she walked in. No other member of the public has any less money on account of the loan transaction between Martin and bank A, so the money supply has risen by $800.

Note that bank A still has $640 of excess reserves. This suggests that it might make some additional loans (and in the process create some additional demand deposits) to further reduce its excess reserves. However, Martin arranged the loan for the specific purpose of buying a used car, and the bank knows that very soon Martin is going to spend the $800 for the car. Most likely, whoever she buys the car from will not be a customer of bank A, so the bank anticipates that it will soon have to honor an $800 check collection. Consequently, it is unlikely to want to make any additional loans, at least not until it sees what is the end result of the loan extension to Martin so far as its balance sheet is concerned.

Step 3. Suppose that Martin buys an $800 used car from Best Buy Motors. She pays for the car by writing out a check to Best Buy on her account with bank A. Best Buy deposits the check with its bank, bank B; and bank B collects on the check from bank A through the mechanism of the local clearinghouse. After the car-sale transaction between Martin and Best Buy and the subsequent check collection, the balance sheet of bank A is as follows (including Steps 1 and 2):

Steps 1, 2, and 3

		BANK A	
Assets		*Liabilities*	
Required reserves	+200	Arrow's demand deposit	+1,000
Martin's loan	+800		
Total	+1,000	Total	+1,000

And the effect upon the balance sheet of bank B is:

		BANK B	
Assets		*Liabilities*	
Required reserves	+160	Best Buy's demand deposit	+800
Excess reserves	+640		
Total	+800	Total	+800

Note that bank A now has $800 less in demand deposit liabilities and $800 less in reserves than it had at the end of Step 2. This is because

Martin's purchase of the car reduced her account back down to where it was before she arranged the loan and because bank A lost $800 in reserves in the check collection process. On the other hand, bank B now has $800 of additional demand deposit liabilities and $800 of additional reserves, of which $160 are required and $640 are excess reserves.

The car-sale transaction between Martin and Best Buy has not brought about any change in the money supply. Martin has $800 less money than before the transaction, but Best Buy had $800 more money. So on balance there has been no change in the public's holdings of money.

Step 4. Suppose that Mr. Ned Nelson has some marketable government securities that he would like to sell. The current market value of these securities is $640. Since bank B has this much excess reserves, it decides to buy the securities. Nelson gives bank B the securities in exchange for a $640 increase in his demand deposit with the bank. Bank B's balance sheet now looks like this (including Step 3):

Steps 1, 2, 3, and 4

BANK B			
Assets		*Liabilities*	
Required reserves	+288	Best Buy's demand deposit	+800
Excess reserves	+512	Nelson's demand deposit	+640
Securities	+640		
Total	+1,440	Total	+1,440

In buying the securities from Nelson, bank B has increased its demand deposit liabilities by $640. It has also increased its assets by $640 because it now owns this much additional government securities. Moreover, the bank now has less excess reserves. In crediting Nelson's account with a $640 deposit, it increased its required reserves by 0.2 × $640 = $128 and reduced its excess reserves by the same amount.

The security-sale transaction between Nelson and bank B has caused the money supply to go up by $640. Bank B bought the securities by giving Nelson a $640 IOU. It is just that the IOU was a demand deposit or money.

Let us stop the progress of the example here, take stock of what has happened thus far, and draw some conclusions:

1. There was an initial infusion of $1,000, of reserves into the banking system. This occurred in Step 1.

2. In Step 1 and in *some* of the subsequent steps, the demand deposit liabilities of the banks rose and so did their required reserves. Specifically, we had:

Summary

	Change in Demand Deposit Liabilities	Change in Required Reserves
Step 1	+$1,000	+$200
Step 2	+ 800	+$160
Step 3	0	0
Step 4	+$ 640	+$128
Total	+$2,440	+$488

Hence, thus far $488 of the initial infusion of $1,000 of reserves into the banking system have found their way into required reserves. This is because of the

$$\frac{1}{0.2} \times \$488 = 5 \times \$488 = \$2,440$$

increase in demand deposit liabilities of the banking system.

3. At the end of Step 4, the banking system (bank B, in particular) still held $512 of excess reserves. Therefore, the example could continue in this step-by-step fashion. Eventually, all of the $1,000 infusion of reserves would become required reserves. At that time, the demand deposit liabilities of the banking system would be

$$\frac{1}{0.2} \times \$1,000 = 5 \times \$1,000 = \$5,000$$

greater than they were at the beginning of the example or they would be $105,000 in total. Furthermore, the money supply of our economy would then be

$$\$49,000 + \$105,000 = \$154,000.$$

$$\uparrow \qquad \qquad \uparrow$$

Currency   Demand deposit
component   component

Demand deposit expansion and contraction in a more realistic context

The step-by-step case just examined is remote from real life. Actually, every working day in the United States, hundreds of millions of dollars of bank loans are repaid and bank investments reach maturity. Even the smallest banks experience thousands of dollars of repayments on a typical day. This means that nearly every bank is making new loans and new investments almost continuously, even when the total volume of bank assets and liabilities remains constant.

It is also unlikely that an increase in reserves would go entirely to one bank and that the other banks would have to sit idly by while the new reserves were gradually redistributed among them through successive rounds of depositing and lending or investing. The forces which increase or decrease bank reserves are examined in the next section. They include not only the deposit and withdrawal of currency by the public but, more importantly, policy actions of the Federal Reserve authorities. These forces are likely to hit many banks at about the same time and in the same direction, so an expansion or contraction of total bank loans and investments and total demand deposits is likely to involve large numbers of banks almost simultaneously.

Most of our illustrations have involved *increases* in bank reserves and demand deposits because, realistically, the money supply is expanding most of the time. Everything which has been said about expansion, however, applies equally to contraction. If the banking system is all loaned up (i.e., has no excess reserves), and if it then *loses* reserves (or the reserve requirement is *raised*), the banks will be obliged to reduce demand deposits by several times as much. How is this done as a practical matter?

The banks might sell some of their holdings of government securities to the public and thus reduce demand deposits by that amount. But if the loss of reserves is not too severe (or the increase in the reserve requirement is not too large), the banks will simply stop making new loans and investments as rapidly as the old loans and investments reach maturity. By merely holding back, so that repayments run ahead of new loans and investments, they can gradually reduce demand deposits to any desired level.

THINK ABOUT THIS

If you encountered a banker and told him that he has the power to create money, he would probably say: "Why, that's just wrong. I can't make additional loans unless someone first comes in and deposits some money with me." Is this statement *always* true? Is it *sometimes* true?

Suppose you persist and argue that the banking system *as a whole* can create money. How would you explain this to your banker acquaintance?

THE FEDERAL RESERVE SYSTEM

The Federal Reserve System was created by act of Congress in 1913 to serve limited and practical needs: to provide a rapid and effective system of national check clearance; to set up a single fiscal agent for the federal government; to enforce rules of sound lending procedure on individual banks through periodic reports and visits by bank examiners; to make available a readily expansible supply of currency; and to ward off "financial panics" (which had occurred with disastrous effect in 1873, 1884, 1893, and 1907) by creating a "lender of last resort" to which commercial banks could turn in an emergency.

In the course of providing for these needs, however, the authors of the Federal Reserve Act of 1913 gave the Federal Reserve power to influence the level of bank reserves. Its powers were enlarged by a major revision of the act in 1935, following the banking collapse of 1933. As the Fed has gained experience in using its powers, and with increasing confidence that fluctuations in economic activity can be moderated by deliberate action, the emphasis of the System's operation has shifted toward overall monetary control. The original service functions remain important but are now generally taken for granted.

Most countries have a single central bank located in the national capital. Some of the European central banks are much older than our own. The Bank of Sweden dates from 1656, the Bank of England from 1694, and the Bank of France from 1800.

Because of the geographic diversity of the United States and the influence of sectional interests in Congress, it was decided to create 12 Federal Reserve banks with headquarters in commercial centers throughout the country. These banks are located in Boston, New York, Philadelphia, Richmond, Atlanta, Cleveland, Chicago, Minneapolis, St. Louis, Kansas City, Dallas, and San Francisco. Each bank has jurisdiction over a "Federal Reserve District," comprised of states and parts of states in its trading area.

All commercial banks with national charters must be members of the Federal Reserve System, and state banks may become members by meeting certain qualifications. Some 8,000 state banks either have not been able to qualify or have been unwilling to accept the controls and obligations of Federal Reserve membership.

The 5,700 or so banks which are members, however, have about 80 percent of the demand deposits in the country. Furthermore, under the Monetary Control Act of 1980, nonmember banks may borrow from the Fed and must observe reserve requirements set by the Fed. So, for the most part, the policy decisions of the Federal Reserve authorities affect the whole commercial banking community, not just those banks which are members of the System.

The 12 Federal Reserve banks are *central banks* or *bankers' banks*. This is true in a double sense. First, each of them is owned by the member banks in its district. Second, Federal Reserve dealings are almost entirely with the commercial banks and the U.S. Treasury.

Despite their private ownership, they are in a real sense *public banks*. Their main function is to influence the volume and cost of money in a way which will promote stable prosperity. They are not primarily profit-making institutions. After the member banks have received a guaranteed annual 6 percent return on their capital subscriptions, all remaining Federal Reserve profits are turned over to the U.S. Treasury.

The System is directed by a seven-member Board of Governors, located in Washington, D.C., and appointed by the president of the United States with the advice and consent of the Senate. (When we speak of "the Board," "the Fed," or "the monetary authorities," it is this group that we have in mind.) Members of the board are appointed for 14-year terms, one expiring every 2 years. This protects the composition of the board against domination by a particular presidential administration and to some extent immunizes it against pressure from Congress. This vaunted independence of the Fed presents difficulties as well as advantages and has given rise to considerable controversy.

The Board of Governors appoints three of the nine directors of each Federal Reserve bank. (Of the remaining members, three are expected to be commercial bankers, and three are chosen to represent industry, commerce, and agriculture. All six are elected by member banks of the district.) The chief officers of each bank, the president and first vice president, must be approved by the Board of Governors. In addition, the Board of Governors dominates the strategic Federal Open Market Committee, which decides on Federal Reserve purchases and sales of government securities. Thus, despite the separation into 12 regional banks, the System approaches the centralization of authority found in the central banks of other countries.

The most important feature of the Federal Reserve System is its power to influence the size of bank reserves and the legal reserve requirement. The principal tools of Federal Reserve monetary control are:

1. Open-market operations.   The System can buy and sell federal government securities on the open market. The transactions have a direct impact upon commercial bank reserves and are the main instrument of day-to-day monetary control.

2. Discounts and advances.   The System can lend reserves to member banks. This lending is called *discounting* or *advancing*. The rate of interest at which reserves are lent is called the *discount rate*. The rate is altered from time to time, reflecting Federal Reserve objectives and changing conditions in the money market.

3. Reserve requirements.   The System can alter within specified limits the percentage reserve which member banks must carry against their deposits. But this is done only rarely and is not important for short-run policy.

FEDERAL RESERVE MONETARY CONTROL: OBJECTIVES AND TECHNIQUES

If Federal Reserve policy were the only force acting on commercial bank reserves, the control problem would be considerably simplified. But this is not the case. Reserves are changing all the time because of currency movements into and out of the banks, changes in U.S. government demand deposit balances, and other factors. Thus, even if the Federal Reserve does nothing at all, commercial bank reserves will still fluctuate from day to day. A sizable research staff, mainly in the Federal Reserve Bank of New York, is engaged in keeping track of these movements and trying to predict them for the near future. These estimates are checked by higher officials in New York and Washington in the light of their experience and "feel" of the money market.

Suppose Federal Reserve officials conclude that, as things are going, commercial bank reserves will shrink over the next week by $200 million. This will reduce the banks' lending ability and make for a tightening of the money supply. What should the Federal Reserve do? If Federal Reserve officials feel that monetary restriction is in order, they may simply abstain and allow the prospective shrinkage of reserves to occur. Inaction does not necessarily indicate neutrality or indifference to monetary developments. It can be a matter of deliberate policy.

Suppose, however, that the Fed considers that commercial bank reserves are now at about the right level. In this event, it will act to raise commercial bank reserves by $200 million to offset the decline which would otherwise occur. Such action to offset an undesired movement of reserves is usually termed *defensive policy*. If the policy is successful, the statistical charts will show bank reserves moving along on an even level week after week. This does not mean that the Federal Reserve has been inactive, as might appear at first glance. On the contrary, it means that its action has been deft enough to offset fluctuations which would otherwise have occurred.

Finally, Federal Reserve officials may feel that monetary expansion is in order and that member bank reserves should be increased by, say, $300 million. In this case, they will have to raise reserves by $500 million to offset the prospective decline of $200 million and still come out with the desired increase. These are the main permutations of Federal Reserve policy: abstaining and letting nature take its course; a defensive policy to offset undesirable changes; and an active policy aimed at reversing the prospective course of events.

Once the Fed has decided what to do, how does it go about doing it? The main day-to-day tool is open-market operations, that is, purchase and sale of federal government securities.

Open-market operations

Decisions on this front are made by the Federal Open Market Committee, consisting of the seven members of the Board of Governors, the president of the Federal Reserve Bank of New York, and four other presidents of Reserve banks. The committee meets on the third Tuesday of every month. In addition, its members and key staff officials normally confer every morning over a telephone hookup and arrive at decisions for the day. Actual trading is carried out through a trading desk in the Federal Reserve Bank of New York, since New York is the center for dealers specializing in government securities.

The impact of these operations is rapid and direct. When the System buys $100 million of securities, it pays by check on the Federal Reserve Bank of New York. If the seller is an individual or a nonbank corporation, it deposits the check in a commercial bank, which presents it to the Federal Reserve and receives credit. The balance sheet effect in this case is as follows:

System buys from a nonbank seller

COMMERCIAL BANKS			
Assets		*Liabilities*	
Reserves	+100	Demand deposits	+100

FEDERAL RESERVE BANKS			
Assets		*Liabilities*	
U.S. securities	+100	Member bank deposits	+100

If a commercial bank itself sells $100 million of securities to the Federal Reserve System, this gives it an immediate addition to its reserve balance. The balance sheet effect is as follows:

System buys from a commercial bank

COMMERCIAL BANKS			
Assets		*Liabilities*	
Reserves	+100	Demand deposits	0
U.S. Securities	−100		

FEDERAL RESERVE BANKS			
Assets		*Liabilities*	
U.S. Securities	+100	Member bank deposits	+100

When the System sells securities, opposite effects occur. A nonbank buyer gives the Federal Reserve a check drawn on his or her commercial bank. The Fed deducts this amount from the bank's reserve balance. If a commercial bank is the buyer, the amount of the purchase is deducted directly from its reserves.

The principle involved is simple: Federal Reserve purchases of securities *raise* bank reserves, while Federal Reserve sales of securities *lower* reserves. The effect on bank reserves is almost instantaneous, and its size is certain. This plus the fact that the size of security operations can be adjusted precisely to the supposed need makes them a natural choice for day-to-day use.

Member bank borrowing and the discount rate

A major complaint against the pre-1913 banking system was its inelasticity under pressure. There was no central reservoir of funds to which banks could resort in time of need. The authors of the Federal Reserve Act were at pains, therefore, to provide ways by which any solvent member bank could draw on the virtually unlimited resources of the System to meet temporary emergencies.

A member bank can secure Federal Reserve funds and increase its reserve balance in either of two ways:

1. It may sell commercial paper (i.e., short-term business certificates of indebtedness) to the Federal Reserve bank of its district. This is known as *discounting.*

Example. A bank brings to the Federal Reserve a promissory note from one of its customers for $100,000, due in three months' time. The discount rate at the time is 10 percent. The Federal Reserve discounts the note by deducting from its face value interest at 10 percent for three months, or $2,500. The remaining $97,500 is added to the member bank's reserve balance.

2. Since about 1933, however, the main technique has been a direct loan from the Federal Reserve to the member bank. The bank usually puts up U.S. securities as collateral for the loan. The Federal Reserve charges interest on the loan at a rate which is equivalent to the discount rate.

The borrowing privilege provides a safety valve which permits the other Federal Reserve powers to be used with greater assurance. Open-market operations and changes in reserve requirements are general instruments whose impact cannot be tailored to the situation of particular banks. Federal Reserve sale of securities reduces bank reserves in general, but it is impossible to say in advance which banks will be hit and how hard. Banks with sizable excess reserves may be little affected, while banks with little excess reserves may suddenly find themselves in a deficit position. The Federal Reserve is nevertheless free to push open-market operations as vigorously as it wishes, for if the policy leaves a particular bank short of reserves, it can always cover itself temporarily by borrowing.

As an alternative to borrowing from the Fed, a bank can borrow reserves from another bank which has excess reserves at the moment. There is an active "federal funds market" for such loans. The interest rate on these loans is called the "federal funds rate," and it is a sensitive indicator of money market conditions. A rise in the rate indicates that more banks are running out of reserves and that the money market is tightening, and conversely for a fall in the rate. Federal Reserve officials watch this rate carefully as an indicator of whether they are achieving their current objectives.

If a bank is short of reserves for only a few days, it will probably borrow in the federal funds market. If it needs help over a longer period, it may borrow from the Fed. The Fed, however, regards borrowing as a privilege rather than a right. It does not view it with favor, nor does a bank like to remain indebted to the Fed for very long. Instead, it will try to work its way back to a safe reserve position by going slow on loans or by selling some of its holdings of government securities.

Each of the 12 Federal Reserve banks sets its own discount rate. The rates are usually the same, however, and policy for the whole System is coordinated through the Board of Governors. The discount rate is normally raised gradually during a business upswing, keeping more or less in step with the rise of other short-term interest rates. In a recession, the discount rate is usually cut substantially.

An increase in the discount rate has two effects. Since it increases the cost of borrowing from the Federal Reserve, it strengthens the member banks' unwillingness to remain in debt. More important, it serves as a signal to the banking community of the direction in which Federal Reserve policy is moving. A discount rate increase indicates that the Federal Reserve authorities feel that expansion of loans should be slowed down and that it intends to exert pressure toward that end. This usually encourages member banks to raise their own lending rates—a step which is bound to be unpopular with borrowers, but which can now be defended on the ground that "this is what the Fed wants us to do." Similarly, a lowering of interest rates is a signal for more liberal lending policies and lower interest rates.

The behavior of the discount rate since 1970 is shown in Figure 6–2. Note the cyclical movement of the rate—falling during the recession of 1970, rising to a peak in 1974, falling during the recession of 1975, rising sharply again in 1979–80, falling once more during the recession of 1982. Note also the marked parallelism between the Fed's discount rate and the "prime rate" for commercial bank loans—the rate charged to (usually large) businesses with high credit standing. The movement is parallel because both rates are indicators of Federal Reserve policy. At the same time that it is raising the discount rate, it will also have been forcing up bank lending rates by tighter control of member bank reserves, and conversely on the downswing of the cycle.

The legal reserve requirement

The Fed can vary the percentage reserve which banks must carry against their deposits, within upper and lower limits specified by Congress.

FIGURE 6-2
Federal Reserve discount rate and commercial banks' prime lending rate, 1970–83

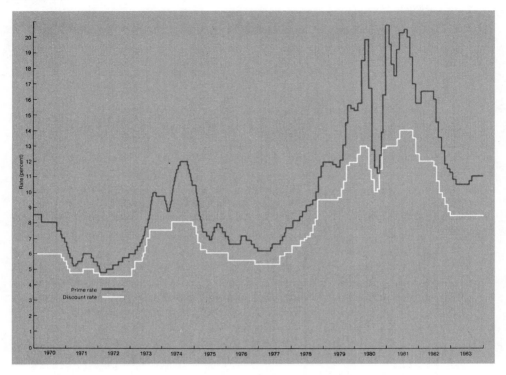

In practice, this power is used only rarely, since the same result can be achieved by operating directly on bank reserves through open-market operations.

Until recently, the legal reserve requirement applied only to banks which were members of the Federal Reserve System, and this had awkward consequences. A bank which holds its reserves as a deposit at the Fed earns no interest on those deposits. By dropping out of the System—which typically meant taking out a state charter rather than a national charter—a bank could hold more of its reserves in some interest-bearing form. There was thus a financial incentive to withdraw from the System, and during the 70s, withdrawals increased substantially. This was part of the reason for the Monetary Control Act of 1980, which extended the reserve requirement to all commercial banks, whether members or nonmembers, and also to thrift institutions. The burden on small banks was lessened, however, by setting a lower reserve ratio for the first $25 million of deposits.

The new reserve requirements are as follows:

Normal Reserves	Range within which Fed Can Vary Requirement (percent)
Demand deposits	
Less than $25 million	3
$25 million and over	8–14
Time deposits	
Personal	0
Business	0–9
Supplementary reserves*	0–4

* Imposition requires affirmative vote of five governors.

A bank may, of course, choose to hold reserves above the legal minimum. The difference between actual and legally required reserves is called *escess reserves*. Excess reserves may be held deliberately as a precaution or because, when a bank finds itself with increased reserves, it takes time to find appropriate loans or investments. There is an obvious financial incentive to put reserves to work earning interest, so excess reserves are small—typically less than 1 percent of deposits.

The original rationale of the legal reserve requirement was to protect against the possibility of bank failure. This consideration is less important today than it was 50 years ago because of the existence of the Federal Deposit Insurance Corporation. The banks pay premiums to FDIC, which in return insures bank deposits up to a limit of $100,000 per account. Small depositors are thus fully protected. Banks do still fail on occasion, in which case the FDIC usually arranges for the failing bank to be merged with one in sound financial condition.

THE MONEY SUPPLY PROCESS

We now have all the facts needed to explain how the supply of money is determined. The process involves decisions by the Fed, by the public, and by the banks. And we need to introduce two new concepts: the *monetary base* and the *money multiplier*.

The monetary base consists of bank reserves plus currency in the hands of the public. Currency held by a bank is part of its reserves. Thus, a flow of currency into the banks from the public immediately raises bank reserves by that amount. Conversely, a flow of currency out of banks to the public reduces bank reserves.[3]

The monetary base is often called "high-powered money." Why? Be-

---

[3] Currency is printed and distributed by the Federal Reserve System. A bank which finds itself short of vault cash can request more from the Fed, which supplies the cash and deducts the amount from the bank's deposit with the Fed. Conversely, a bank with more cash than it needs can deposit it at the Fed and receive credit.

cause a change in the base leads to a larger change in money supply. The amount of high-powered money in existence is decided by the Federal Reserve, which can raise or lower bank reserves at will through open market operations.

Suppose the Fed decides to add $1 billion to the monetary base. How much will this increase the money supply? The answer depends on the size of the money multiplier. If we call money supply M, the amount of high-powered money H, and the money multiplier m, then $M = mH$.

What determines the size of m? This depends on the behavior of the public and the behavior of the banking system. As regards the public, the key fact is how much currency they prefer to hold, as a percentage of their demand deposits. Let's call this currency–deposit ratio cu. If H increases and the banks respond by increasing demand deposits, the public will want to draw out part of these deposits in cash, to keep cu at its customary level. But this drains reserves from the banks, partly offsetting the original increase in reserves and braking the expansion of deposits. Thus the *larger* is cu, the *smaller* will be the money multiplier.

As regards the banks, the key fact is how much reserves they prefer to hold against a given amount of demand deposits. They must hold the minimum amount required by law. But they will usually prefer to hold somewhat more than this, to avoid running short and having to borrow either from other banks or from the Fed, with a consequent interest cost. Let's call their preferred reserve–deposit ratio r. Again, it is easy to see that if r is *larger*, m will be *smaller*. If it were 0.4 instead of 0.2, then a given increase in reserves would support only half as large an increase in demand deposits.[4]

The money multiplier, of course, is a quite different creature from the autonomous spending multiplier discussed in Chapters 4 and 5. The two should not be confused.

In popular discussion, it is often said that the Fed "controls the money supply." While it is true that the Fed *influences* the money supply, it cannot control it precisely. What the Fed controls is the *monetary base*. Then the money multiplier operates to determine the increase in money supply. And the multiplier is not entirely stable. It fluctuates somewhat in the short run and has shown a downward trend in the long run. In the 1950s, it ranged between 3.6 and 3.2, but by 1980 it had fallen to about 2.5. The main reason was a marked uptrend in cu, which rose by about one quarter during the 70s. The public now prefers to hold considerably more currency relative to deposits than it used to do, though the reasons for this are unclear.

The money supply depends on the amount of high-powered money and on the money multiplier. The amount of high-powered money is

---

[4] The formula for m, which you can accept without worrying about the derivation, is $m = \left(\dfrac{1 + cu}{cu + r}\right)$. Note that an increase in either cu or r raises the denominator relative to the numerator, thus reducing m.

decided by the Federal Reserve System. The monetary multiplier depends on the currency–deposit ratio, decided by the public, and the reserve–deposit ratio, decided by the banks.

NEW CONCEPTS

demand deposit	liquidity
time deposit	deposit expansion
money, M1	deposit contraction
money, M2	open-market operations
near-money	discount rate
bank, savings	federal funds market
bank, commercial	federal funds rate
bank, central	monetary base
reserves, bank	high-powered money
reserves, required	money multiplier
reserves, excess	

SUMMARY

1. Money serves as a *medium of exchange,* a *measure of value,* and a *store of value.*

2. The money supply of the United States is usually defined as the *sum of currency and demand deposits owned by the "public."* The *public* includes individuals, ordinary business, and state and local governments. It does not include the U.S. federal government or commercial banks.

3. The main business of a commercial bank is to make short-term loans to businesses and households. Commercial banks are also large holders of federal as well as state and local government securities. *When a bank makes a loan or acquires a security, it creates a demand deposit.* Conversely, when a loan is repaid or a bank disposes of a security, demand deposits decrease.

4. A commercial bank must hold minimum reserves equal to a specific percentage of its deposits. If a bank's actual reserve percentage is just equal to the percentage required by law, it is said to be *loaned up.* It cannot increase its loans and investments without an addition to its reserves.

5. A bank with excess reserves cannot lend or invest more than the amount of the excess. It must assume that the loans or investments will be respent rapidly, leading to the deposits of checks in other banks and a consequent transfer of reserves from the first bank to others.

6. *For the banking system as a whole,* however, any infusion of reserves can lead to an expansion of demand deposits (through loans and investment) of that amount times the reciprocal of the reserve requirement.

7. *Open-market operations* are the principal tool of Federal Reserve monetary control. When the Fed *buys* government securities from the public and from commercial banks, this causes bank reserves to *rise.* When the Fed *sells* government securities, bank reserves *decline.* The Fed uses open-market operations to control bank reserves from day to day.

8. The *discount rate* is the rate of interest at which Federal Reserve banks lend reserves to member banks. An increase in the discount rate tends to discourage member banks from borrowing reserves from the System, while a decrease in the discount rate does just the opposite. Changes in the discount rate also serve as a signal to the commercial banking community of changes in the direction of Federal Reserve policy.

9. The Federal Reserve has the power to change member bank *reserve requirements* (within specified limits). An *increase* in reserve requirements has the same impact upon the money supply as a *decrease* in bank reserves, and a *decrease* in reserve requirements is like an *increase* in reserves. The Fed does not change reserve requirements very often.

10. The money supply depends on the monetary base, which is controlled by the Federal Reserve System, and on the money multiplier, *m.* The size of *m* depends on the currency-deposit ratio, *cu,* and on the reserve-deposit ratio, *r.* The larger *cu* and *r* are, the smaller *m* is. The size of *m* changes over the course of time.

TO LEARN MORE

The standard source for statistics and current developments in the monetary area is the monthly *Federal Reserve Bulletin.* Summary statistics appear also in *Economic Indicators.*

The macroeconomics texts mentioned at the end of Chapter 4 contain several chapters on the monetary system. See also any standard text on money and banking, such as Lester V. Chandler, *The Economics of Money and Banking* (New York: Harper & Row); and Albert G. Hart and Peter Kenen, *Money, Debt, and Economic Activity* (Englewood Cliffs, N.J.: Prentice-Hall), most recent editions.

7

Demand for Money and
the Rate of Interest

*Money knows nobody; money has no ears; money has
no heart.*

—HONORÉ DE BALZAC

It seems obvious that the supply of money must affect spending plans
and hence aggregate demand and the equilibrium rate of output. But
just what is the relation? How do changes in money supply work their
way through the economy?

Economists have developed two ways of thinking about the influence
of money supply. The first, usually called the *quantity theory of money,*
was developed around 1900 by Alfred Marshall in England and Irving
Fisher in the United States. It regards money supply as operating directly
on spending plans. Give people more money, and aggregate demand will
rise. If we assume that the economy is producing near capacity—an important proviso—the main impact will be on the price level. Crudely, double
the quantity of money, and you will double the level of prices.

Another set of ideas, sometimes called Keynesian, but actually going-
back well before Keynes, regards money as affecting the economy through
the *rate of interest.* The supply of money, together with the demand for
money, determines the market rate of interest. The interest rate, in turn,
affects business decisions about investment, including housing. It also
affects consumer spending on automobiles and other goods bought partly
on credit. And it even affects government spending, especially state and
local spending on large projects financed by borrowing. Thus, a change
in interest rates shifts the *C, I,* and *G* schedules and, hence, the level
of aggregate demand. The causal chain is

Money supply → Interest rate → Aggregate demand → Equilibrium
output.

An *increase* in interest rates tends to *lower* the C, I, and G schedules and, hence, to lower the equilibrium rate of output. A *decrease* in interest rates tends to *raise* the C, I, and G schedules and to raise the equilibrium rate of output.

The rate of interest is a price and, like any price, is determined by the twin forces of supply and demand. In Chapter 6, we explained how the supply of money is determined. Now we must look at the demand for money and how it interacts with supply to determine the interest rate.

THE DEMAND FOR MONEY

You may find it odd to speak of a "demand for money." Doesn't everyone want more than they have? Isn't the demand for money unlimited?

This is to confuse *money* with *income* or *wealth*. The demand for wealth may indeed by unlimited. But money—currency and checking accounts—is only one of many ways to hold wealth. People hold part of their wealth in the form of money, but they usually hold wealth in other forms as well. Some common nonmoney forms of household wealth include time deposits, savings and loan shares, government securities, corporate stocks and bonds, and physical items such as houses and automobiles, or even gold bars and impressionist paintings. Similarly, all business concerns hold some money, but they also hold other kinds of assets, such as government and corporate securities, buildings, equipment, and inventories.

What determines how much of total private wealth will be held in the form of money? Stated differently, what determines *the demand for money?*

There are two main components of the demand for money: the *transactions demand,* and the *asset or investment demand.* Let's look briefly at each of these.

Transactions demand

People and businesses need to have cash on hand to cover day-to-day expenditures. Suppose a person receives a monthly salary check of $2,000. The normal thing might be to deposit this in the bank on the first of the month. Then, if expenditures are spread evenly over the month, the balance will fall gradually to zero at the end. In this case, the average amount of money held during the month would be $1,000.

This example illustrates two points. First, the transactions demand for money is positively related to *size of income.* If the monthly salary were $4,000 instead of $2,000, the average money holding during the month would be larger. Second, the transactions demand is influenced by payment practices. Whether income is received once a week or once a month or once every six months will make a difference to money holdings. So, too, does the timing of expenditures—for example, whether purchases are made on credit and paid for only at the end of the month. We usually assume that customary payment practices don't change much in the short run and, hence, that they do not cause shifts in the demand for money.

Still another factor influencing money demand is the rate of interest. To see the importance of this, consider that I don't *have* to put my monthly paycheck into a checking account. Instead, I could put it into a savings account, or a money market fund, or Treasury bills. Then next week, when I need to make a payment, I could draw out part of the savings account or sell some Treasury bills. Running to the savings bank several times a month, of course, would involve some shoe-leather cost, and buying and selling securities usually involves a brokerage cost. But I might be willing to bear these costs if the reward for holding nonmoney assets were sufficiently great. This reward, of course, is the interest that can be earned on time deposits or short-term securities. The higher the rate of interest, the more people will try to hold down their cash holdings in order to earn interest. We conclude, then, that the *transactions demand for money is inversely related to the rate of interest.*

For people with small monthly incomes, interest rates would probably have to be very high to induce them to scrimp on cash balances in this way. But people with larger incomes will make a more careful calculation. And this is certainly an important consideration for business concerns.

Over the course of a month, a fair-sized business might take in $100 million or so in receipts. Its monthly expenditures are likely to be clustered about particular dates—around the first of the month for wage and salary payments and around the 10th of the month when bills for materials fall due. If the firm merely deposits receipts in its checking account as they come in and then draws checks on the account as expenditure needs arise, there may be periods when its account has a balance of $10 million or more. The firm is using money as a temporary store of purchasing power. But this is an expensive way of storing purchasing power, for the firm is foregoing the interest income which it could receive if it held, say, government securities rather than money. Suppose that if the firm were always careful to minimize its money holdings by shifting into short-term government securities at every opportunity, its average temporary holdings of government securities would amount to $2 million. Then, if the interest rate on these securities were 10 percent per year, the firm would earn an extra $200,000 per year.

This additional income might very well compensate the firm for the extra trouble and inconvenience of reducing its use of money as a temporary store of purchasing power. On the other hand, if the interest rate on government securities were only 5 percent, the firm might not reduce its use of money to the same extent. It probably would not devote as much effort to avoiding the use of money as a temporary store of purchasing power as when the interest rate is 10 percent. And if the interest rate were as low as 1 percent, the firm might feel that holding government securities rather than money is just not worth the extra trouble.

There is a further reason for holding cash balances. Future events are somewhat uncertain. The check you are expecting may not arrive just when you expect it. Or some large unexpected expense may come up: a breakdown of the old car which means buying a new one, a health emergency requiring medical care, an unexpected business trip. Businesses face similar uncertainties about future sales volume, prices, and costs. So in addition to the money held for transactions purposes, people and businesses will want to hold a nest egg or contingency fund against emergency needs. Failure to do this can mean an awkward shortage of funds or being forced to borrow and pay interest.

How large will these contingency holdings be? This depends on the same factors which influence transactions balances—the size of income and the rate of interest. Holding a contingency fund amounts to buying security for the future. As a person's income rises, he or she can buy more of everything, including security. So, the demand for contingency funds is positively related to income.

But the nest egg can be held in a variety of forms—money, time deposits, short-term government securities, money market funds—and is frequently spread among all of these. Money is convenient because it is available immediately. But the drawback of holding money is that it pays no interest or, at least since the invention of new forms of checking accounts, pays *less* interest than nonmoney assets. So, the higher the rate of interest on such assets, the less money will be held for contingency purposes.

Asset demand

Up to this point, we have been looking at money as a means of payment. But money is also an asset, a way of holding part of one's wealth. Wealth can be held in a variety of forms, including bonds, stocks, and other securities. So people and businesses have to decide how much to hold in cash and how much in these other forms.

A word about securities. Corporate or government bonds pay the owner a fixed dollar income per year. Therefore, if the market price of a bond rises, its market yield declines. Consider a long-term U.S. government bond with a face value of $1,000 and a 10 percent coupon, which thus guarantees the owner $100 of interest income per year. If the market price of this bond is $1,000, then its market yield is $100/$1,000 = 10 percent per year. But if the market price is $1,250, then the yield is only $400/$1,250 = 8 percent. The higher the price, the lower the yield, and vice versa.

A corporate stock pays a dividend decided on by the company rather than a guaranteed amount, but the same principle applies. Suppose that IBM stock currently pays a dividend of $6 per share. Then if you can buy the stock for $100, the yield is $6/$100 = 6 percent. But if the price goes to $150, the yield is only $6/$150 = 4 percent.

The higher the market price of a security, the lower the yield or market interest rate on that security, and vice versa.

Thus, to say that security prices have *risen* is equivalent to saying that their rate of interest has *fallen*. Conversely, a *fall* in security prices amounts to a *rise* in their rate of interest.

Now back to our investor trying to decide how much wealth to hold in cash and how much in securities. Money has the advantage of being a riskless asset—a dollar is always worth a dollar—but it has the disadvantage of usually paying no interest. A security does pay interest but involves a risk of loss through a fall in price. Different people will judge these risks differently at a particular time. Further, some will be more willing to bear risk than others—there are always conservative investors and "plungers." But most investors will decide to hold down the risk in their total portfolio by keeping a certain amount of cash.

The decision on how much cash to hold will be influenced by the rate of interest. A higher rate of interest increases the advantage of holding securities and will cause some reduction in money holdings. Thinking in stock market terms, as interest rates rise (securities prices fall), more and more people will conclude that securities have become cheap and that now is the time to buy.

Thus, once more we see that money demand moves inversely to the rate of interest. Asset demand for money will decline as interest rates rise (securities prices fall) and will rise as interest rates fall (securities prices rise).

Since this is true of both transactions demand and asset demand, we conclude that:

The quantity of money demanded varies positively with the level of income and negatively with the rate of interest.

This principle is illustrated in Figure 7–1. The curve Y_1 is drawn for a particular rate of GNP. It shows the quantity of money demanded (measured along the horizontal axis) at alternative rates of interest (measured along the vertical axis). Note that the lower the rate of interest, the larger the quantity of money demanded, and vice versa. The curve labeled Y_2 is for a different and higher rate of GNP. For each rate of interest, the quantity of money demanded is larger along Y_2 than along

FIGURE 7–1
Demand for money depends on interest and income

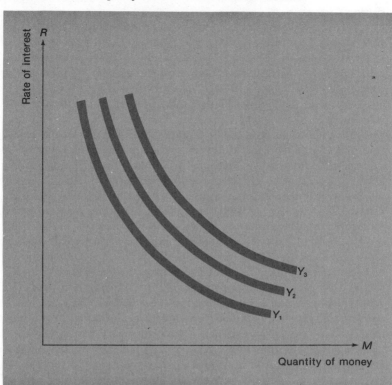

The curve Y_1 is drawn for a particular rate of GNP. It shows the relationship between the rate of interest and the demand for money, given that rate of GNP. The curve Y_2 is for a higher rate of GNP, and Y_3 is for a still higher rate of GNP.

Y_1, since we have seen that higher incomes mean greater money demand. The same is true for Y_3, which is drawn for a still higher rate of GNP.

Evidence on the demand for money

In addition to knowing that GNP and the interest rate affect the demand for money, it would be useful to know the size of these effects. Stephen Goldfeld made a comprehensive study[1] of the evidence on money demand up to 1973. His main findings were:

1. The long-run elasticity of demand for money with respect to a

---

[1] Stephen Goldfeld, "The Demand for Money Revisited," *Brookings Papers on Economic Activity,* 1973, pp. 577–646.

change in real GNP was 0.68. This means that a 10 percent increase in real GNP eventually leads to an increase of a bit under 7 percent in demand for money.

2. The long-run elasticity of demand for money with respect to the two short-term interest rates used by Goldfeld was 0.23. This means that a 20-percent increase in these interest rates—say, from 10 percent to 12 percent—would eventually reduce money demand by about 4½ percent.

3. The demand for money adjusts to changes in income and interest rates only with a *lag*. When the level of income or interest rates changes, there is at first only a small change in the demand for money. Then the effect builds up gradually over the course of time. Only about one quarter of the impact is felt within the first three months. After a year, about 70 percent of the eventual response has occurred, and after two years about 90 percent. The importance of this is that a monetary change initiated by the Federal Reserve System has little effect immediately and works out its full effect only over a couple of years.

4. Goldfeld also investigated the effect of price level changes on money demand. Suppose prices and money GNP rise by 10 percent, with *no change in real GNP.* Goldfeld found that in this event, the demand for money will also rise by 10 percent. For the same level of *real GNP,* people will want the same level of *real money balances.* They are not fooled by the price change or, in fancier language, do not suffer from "money illusion."

An important question relates to the *stability* of the money demand function. Can Goldfeld's results for past years be counted on to prevail in the future? Apparently not entirely. Economists who used the Goldfeld equations to predict money demand in the 70s found that by 1979 they were *over predicting* by about 15 percent. The demand curve had apparently shifted downward so that for any level of GNP and interest rates, the public was holding considerably less money than before 1973. The explanation for this is unclear.[2] One possibility is that the very high interest rates in the 70s led the public, and especially businesses, to work harder on holding down their cash balances and holding interest-bearing assets instead. Once learned, these new methods of cash management continued to be used in later years.

The question is important for monetary policy. Suppose next year that the Fed increases bank reserves, and through the money multiplier, money supply rises by 8 percent. How will this affect the rate of interest? We can predict this only if we know the money demand curve. If the curve is shifting over time, this weakens our ability to predict the impact of monetary changes.

---

[2] For an exploration of the problem, see John P. Judd and John L. Scadding, "The Search for a Stable Money Demand Function," *Journal of Economic Literature,* September 1982, pp. 993–1023.

THE SUPPLY OF MONEY AND THE RATE OF INTEREST

We must now see how the quantity of money demanded and the amount of money available determine the rate of interest. Suppose that the money demand curve at the current rate of GNP is shown by Y_1 in Figure 7–2. And suppose that the quantity of money—controlled approximately by the Federal Reserve System—is M_1. Then the equilibrium rate of interest, defined by the intersection of the demand and supply schedules, will be R_1. At this rate, and only at this rate, will people be willing to hold exactly the amount of money in existence.

We can use this diagram also to illustrate the effect of a change in demand conditions. Suppose that because of an increase in GNP, the money demand schedule shifts upward to Y_2. If the money supply remains unchanged, the rate of interest will have to rise to R_2. But the Fed may not want this to happen because of the adverse effect on investment

FIGURE 7–2
Demand and supply of money determine the rate of interest

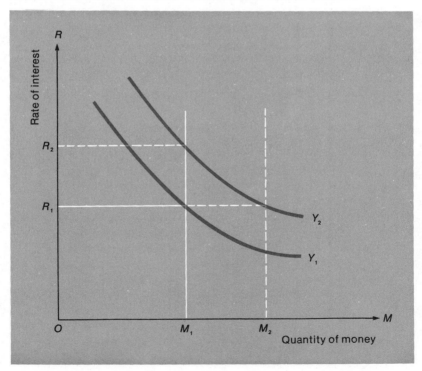

If the money demand curve is Y_1 and the money supply is M_1, the interest rate will be R_1. An increase in money demand to Y_2, with money supply unchanged, will raise the interest rate to R_2. But if money supply is increased to M_2, the interest rate R_1 will remain unchanged.

and other types of spending. If it wants, say, to hold the interest rate at the old level R_1, it will have to increase money supply to M_2. At this point, the increase in quantity of money available will just balance the increase in quantity demanded.

We can draw another important conclusion from Figure 7–2. The Fed cannot determine *both* the interest rate and the supply of money. If it pegs one of these rates at a certain level, it loses control of the other. Suppose the Fed decides to hold interest rates steady at R_1 to promote business confidence. It then loses control over the money supply. It will have to increase M at a rate determined by how rapidly the money demand curve shifts to the right as GNP rises.

Alternatively, if the Fed tries to maintain a fixed growth rate of money supply, it loses control over interest rates. If the demand for money is rising faster than the fixed increase in supply, interest rates will rise; and if demand is rising more slowly than supply, they will fall.

Now consider the effect of a change in money supply, illustrated in Figure 7–3. With no change in money demand, the Fed decides to lower

FIGURE 7–3
A change in money supply will alter the rate of interest

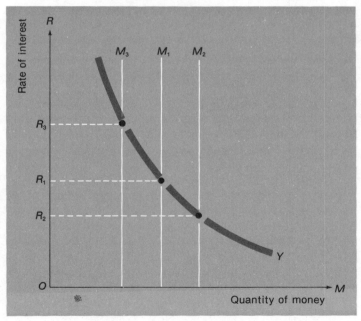

The curve labeled Y shows the relationship between the rate of interest and the demand for money, given a particular rate of GNP. The lines labeled M_1, M_2, and M_3 indicate different money supplies. The larger the supply of money, the lower must be the rate of interest in order for there to be equilibrium between the demand and the supply of money.

the rate of interest to stimulate aggregate demand, so it increases the money supply from M_1 to M_2. The demand curve Y tells us that the interest rate must fall to R_2. Only at this lower rate of interest will the public be willing to hold M_2 of money. But you may feel that there is a sleight-of-hand air about this explanation. Just how does the economy move from the old equilibrium position to the new one?

If the Fed wants to increase the money supply, it will do this through open-market purchases of federal securities. The increase in demand for such securities will tend to raise their price. But we saw earlier that when the price of a security rises, its *yield* must fall. So the yield of federal securities, which is an important interest rate, will decline.

The Federal Reserve purchases, as we saw in Chapter 6, will also increase the reserves of the commercial banks. They will want to put these reserves to work by increasing their loans or their holdings of securities. To increase their loans, they will probably need to reduce their charge for loans, another key interest rate in the system. To the extent that they buy securities, this will tend to raise security prices and lower their yields.

The increase in bank loans and security purchases means an increase in demand deposits (i.e., in money supply). Thus, money supply rises gradually toward M_2, while the interest rate sinks gradually toward R_2. When it reaches it, the system is once more in equilibrium, because *at that interest rate,* individuals and businesses are just willing to hold the increased supply of money. Why are they willing to hold more money than they were at the outset? Because security prices are now so high, and their rate of return so low, that they are less attractive (compared with money) as a component of asset portfolios.

The picture shown by Figure 7–3, in which the demand curve sits unchanged while the system adjusts to a larger money supply, is of course an oversimplification of reality. We'll see in Chapter 8 that the monetary expansion will produce an increase in GNP, so that the demand curve Y will shift upward. Part of the increase in money supply will thus be absorbed in larger transactions and contingency balances corresponding to the higher income level. The upward shift of Y means that the rate of interest will not have to fall as much as figure 7–3 suggests. In fact, during a business cycle upswing, when Y is shifting upward month by month, the effect of monetary expansion may be simply to slow down or prevent the *rise* of interest rates rather than to produce an actual *reduction,* which normally occurs only during recession.

Everything we have said about monetary expansion can be reversed for monetary contraction. Federal Reserve action to reduce the money supply, say from M_2 to M_1, would set off an opposite chain of events: open-market sale of securities, causing their price to fall and their yield to rise; a decline in commercial bank loans, leading them to reduce loans by raising their lending rate; and an effort by households and businesses

"Bless you, sir, and may the prime rate never go up."

Copyright, Saturday Review, 1975. Drawing by Al Ross.

to exchange interest-earning assets for money. This will cause the price of these assets to decline and their market interest rate to rise. When the interest rate has risen to R_1, the system is once more in equilibrium.

One rarely sees a monetary contraction in modern times. As the economy grows over the course of time, bank reserves, money supply, and money demand are normally moving upward. The Fed does occasionally apply the monetary brakes to check an overrapid expansion. But this normally takes the form not of a reduction in bank reserves, but of a reduction in the rate of increase of reserves.

The complex of interest rates

Our discussion of "the rate of interest" may have struck you as strange. *What* rates? A look at the financial pages reveals that there are dozens of different interest rates. It is time now to describe the more important of these and to explain why, despite their variety, the concept of "the rate of interest" still makes sense. Some of the important rates in the system are:

1. Federal funds rate. This is the rate at which a bank that is short of reserves can borrow from a bank with excess reserves for a very short time, often only overnight. A rise in this rate indicates that more banks are running short of reserves, while a fall indicates the opposite. This rate also indicates whether the Fed is feeding reserves into the system as rapidly as banks would like. A rise in the federal funds rate signals a more restrictive policy by the Fed, while a decline indicates a loosening of policy.

2. Prime rate. This is the rate charged by commercial banks to their most credit-worthy business customers. Businesses with lower credit standing are charged more. Thus, a company may have a standing arrangement with its bank allowing it to borrow at "2 percent over prime." The prime rate is thus a bellweather rate. If it is raised, the whole complex of actual rates moves upward together, and conversely for a decline.

3. Consumer loan rate. Americans are in the habit of borrowing to pay for automobiles, furniture, and household appliances, and even travel, restaurant meals, and clothing. The total amount of consumer credit outstanding in late 1983 was about $370 billion. Interest rates vary somewhat with the customer, length of loan, and type of loan. They are considerably higher than the rates charged to business customers, because small loans involve more administrative expense per dollar, but they normally move up or down with business rates.

4. Mortage rate. This is charged by savings and loan associations and other thrift institutions to home buyers. Most of the cost of a house is usually borrowed and repaid in monthly installments over 20 or 30 years. The home buyer, indeed, judges the "cost" of the house by the size of these monthly installments. A jump in mortage rates raises monthly payments, makes people less able and willing to buy houses, and has a depressing effect on new house construction.

5. Treasury bill rate. There are many short-term federal securities, issued for periods ranging from a month to 2 years. Of these, the Treasury bill, usually maturing in three or six months, is best known. The T bill is the mainstay of money market funds and money market deposit accounts in commercial banks. The money you put into such funds is reinvested by the bank or the broker in T bills and other short-term governments, and the interest rate you receive floats upward or downward with the T bill rate.

6. Rate on long-term bonds. Here again there are a variety of rates, depending on the length of the bond and who issued it. 30-year bonds pay a higher rate than 10-year bonds because their price fluctuates more with changes in the level of interest rates, and so they involve a greater risk of capital loss. U.S. government bonds pay somewhat less than corporate bonds because repayment is certain. Corporate bonds are rated for safety by Moody and Standard and Poor, the ratings falling by fine degrees from AAA to BB. The lower the rating, the higher the risk, and so the higher the interest rate that must be offered to induce potential buyers to take the risk.

7. Yield on corporate stocks. The yield of a stock is its dividend rate divided by its purchase price. A rise in price means a fall in yield,

FIGURE 7-4

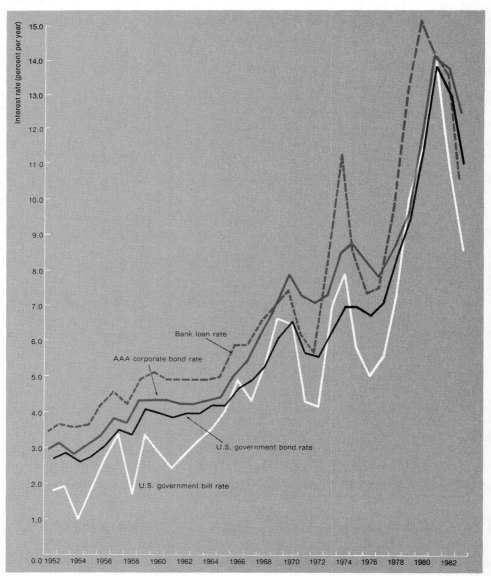

The U.S. government bill rate is the average market rate of interest on the shortest term government securities (90 days). The bank loan rate is the average interest rate charged by commercial banks on short-term loans to businesses. The AAA corporate bond rate is the average market rate of interest on the least risky class of corporate bonds. The U.S. government bond rate is the average market rate of interest on long-term government bonds. All figures are annual averages.

Source: *Economic Report of the President, 1981.*

and vice versa. You may be surprised in looking at the financial pages to see that the yields of various stocks vary from 0 to 10 percent. A rapidly-growing company may pay little or no dividend, putting most of its profits back into plant expansion. Yet investors will buy these "growth stocks" because their price is expected to rise with the growth of the company. A mature company, on the other hand, will reinvest less of its profit, pay higher dividends, and offer higher yield but less chance of capital gain.

The movement of several typical rates since 1955 is charted in Figure 7–4. Note that the general level of rates drifted upward during the 50s and 60s, and then rose even more sharply in the 70s. Rates fluctuate a good deal from year to year and even month to month. This is true especially of short-term rates such as the T bill rate and the bank loan rate, but since 1970, it has been true even of bond rates and securities yields.

The most striking conclusion from Figure 7–4 is that all interest rates tend to move in the same direction at the same time. The basic reason is that investors have a choice among different types of assets and will shift toward any security which offers an appreciably higher yield (for the same degree of risk). Banks, brokerage houses, and other professional investors devote a great deal of research time to seeking out such differences, and this holds yields in close alignment with each other.

This is our justification for simplifying the picture and speaking of the *rate of interest,* by which we mean essentially an average of the many rates prevailing in the market at a particular time.

THINK ABOUT THIS

1. Do you understand why an *increase* in the price of a stock or bond is equivalent to a *decline* in its yield? Check in the *Federal Reserve Bulletin, Economic Indicators,* or some other source to verify the existence of this inverse relation.
2. Check in the same source to verify the movement of key interest rates over the past year. Have they moved in the same direction at roughly the same time? Why is it reasonable to expect them to behave in this way?

NEW CONCEPTS

money, demand for
transactions demand
asset demand
interest rate

yield (of a security)
prime rate
federal funds rate

SUMMARY

1. There are two reasons for holding money: *(a)* the *transactions* motive—the need for cash to pay for current purchases; *(b)* the *asset motive*—holding cash as part of one's asset portfolio.

2. Total demand for money is related *directly* to the level of income. An increase in money income due to a rise in the price level will increase the demand for money proportionately. An increase in real income, after adjustment for price changes, will also increase the demand for money but, in this case, less than proportionately.

3. Total demand for money is related *inversely* to the rate of interest. The higher the rate of interest, the smaller the quantity of money demanded. A demand curve relating interest and money slopes downward to the right in the usual way.

4. The demand curve for money and the amount of money available determine the *rate of interest*. When demand and supply are both rising, as is usually the case, the behavior of the interest rate depends on which is rising faster.

5. The Fed cannot achieve both a money supply target and an interest rate target at the same time. If it aims at steady growth of money supply, the interest rate will fluctuate with changes in money demand. If it aims at a stable rate of interest, it must gear changes in money supply to shifts in demand.

6. There are, in fact, many different interest rates in the money market. But they are linked by the *substitutability* of different securities in investors' portfolios, and so tend to move in the same direction at the same time. Thus, it is legitimate to speak as though there were a simple rate of interest.

TO LEARN MORE

See the macroeconomics texts and money and banking texts listed at the end of Chapter 4.

Money, Interest, and Output

Everyone agrees that changes in money supply and interest rates affect demand for goods, and thus the level of output and employment. But just how does this operate? What is the *transmission mechanism* linking money and output?

Here there are two main approaches, reflecting different opinions about what is the most useful *model* of the economy. A majority of economists prefer to use the aggregate demand model discussed in Chapters 4 and 5, in which the *C, I, G,* and *(X − M)* schedules are added to obtain total demand for goods. As total demand for goods moves up and down, so do output and employment. This view was developed in J. M. Keynes' *General Theory of Employment, Interest, and Money* (1936) and so is usually called "Keynesian." But this does not mean that economics has stood still for a half-century. There has been a vast amount of research on the behavior of the various expenditure schedules; and the models in use today, while they may be in the spirit of Keynes, look decidedly different from his original structure.

In this view, money supply works its effects through the rate of interest. If money supply is increasing relative to demand, this tends to lower the rate of interest, which raises both investment spending (the *I* schedule) and consumer spending (the *C* schedule). This increase in aggregate demand raises output and employment. Conversely, a more restrictive monetary policy which *raises* the rate of interest will *lower* the *C* and *I* schedules and thus tend to reduce output and employment.

The alternative view, termed "monetarism," is held by only a minority of economists but has been growing in influence since the 1950s. It uses a model usually called "the quantity theory of money," which has a long history in economic thought. Monetarists regard money supply as the dominant influence, some would say the only important influence, on output and prices. They regard the Keynesian model as overelaborate and in some ways misleading. The quantity theory offers a simpler model, in which money supply operates directly on spending plans. Give people more money, and they will spend more—aggregate demand will rise.

This does not mean that economists are split into two completely different and opposing camps. While one can find "strong Keynesians" and "strong monetarists," most people occupy some intermediate position. There is considerable agreement on detailed questions of fact; moderate Keynesians and moderate monetarists often don't look very different from each other.

Our strategy here is to expound the monetarist view first. We'll look at the quantity theory, the monetarist view of the transmission mechanism, and some other propositions which most monetarists accept. After that, we'll return to the Keynesian approach and trace the impact of interest rate changes on aggregate demand.

THE QUANTITY THEORY OF MONEY

The quantity theory comes in two different versions, both developed around 1900 by Alfred Marshall at Cambridge and Irving Fisher at Yale. The Marshall version focuses on what the late Dennis Robertson called "money sitting"—the *stock* of money in existence at any time. The Fisher version focuses on what Robertson called "money on the wing"—the *flow* of money in making purchases.

Marshall started from the idea that people want to hold a certain proportion of their income in ready cash. Let's define national income as *PQ*, the amount of real output *(Q)* multiplied by the price level *(P)*. Let's call the stock of money *M*, and the ratio of money to income *k*. Then:

$$M \equiv k \times PQ$$

The identity sign means that the statement is true by the definition of its terms.

Now suppose we assume that *k* is a constant, that people (and businesses) always insist on holding the *same* proportion of their income as money. We can then draw some useful conclusions. Suppose a lot of money falls from heaven, and the quantity of money doubles. Income has not changed, so people find themselves holding more money than they want to hold.

What will happen? People will adjust to this extra money and restore their cash holdings to the old ratio. Spending will increase. This must mean an increase in output, or the price level, or both. Economists of Marshall's era tended to assume that the economy normally operates close to capacity. If the economy is already producing at capacity, the whole impact will be on prices. P must double. The end result is that M and P have doubled, Q is unchanged, and k is back to its old level.

The Fisher version runs in terms of money *flows*, money on the wing. Fisher argued that the rate of spending on goods and services can be thought of as the amount of money in existence, M, multiplied by the average number of times each dollar is spent per year. This second quantity, usually called V, is termed the *income velocity of money*. Total spending per year, then, is $M \times V$, or MV.

Now total spending must equal the value of goods sold. They are simply different ways of looking at the same thing, one from the standpoint of the buyers and the other from that of the sellers. The value of goods sold is the unit quantities Q, times the price of each unit P, which can be summed up as PQ. It follows, then, that

$$MV \equiv PQ.$$

The Fisher equation, like the Marshall equation, is simply an identity, true by definition. It does not say anything about causal relations in the economy.

But suppose we take the further step of assuming that V is constant, month after month and year after year. This is enough to turn the *quantity equation* into a *quantity theory*. The theory tells us that if the money supply is increased, then PQ ($=$ GNP) must increase proportionately. On the other hand, if M declines, GNP will fall.

When M rises and PQ rises in consequence, the equation does not tell us how much of the increase will be in output and how much in prices. But as we noted earlier, the pre-1930 or "old quantity theorists" tended to assume that the economy operates naturally at full capacity. So they regarded Q as a constant along with V. The message of the quantity theory then becomes very simple. An increase in M will cause a proportionate increase in P. Double the quantity of money, and you double the price level.

The Great Depression, during which the output of the U.S. economy dropped dramatically below capacity and remained below capacity for more than a decade, helped to discredit this older monetary reasoning. So did the rise and widespread acceptance of the alternative Keynesian model. Further, during World War II, there was no possibility of an independent monetary policy. The Fed was instructed to finance the large wartime deficits in the federal budget and to finance them at a low and stable rate of interest. The Fed complied, and the federal budget became the dominant factor in the expansion of money supply.

In 1951, however, the Fed was liberated from this restraint and could once more follow a semiindependent course. Thus, monetary policy and monetary theory began to resume their traditional importance. The leader in this revival was Milton Friedman of the University of Chicago, who attracted a growing number of followers over the years.

Today's monetarists are sometimes called "new quantity theorists": They are "new" because their models are more complex and sophisticated than the Marshall or Fisher models. They recognize that:

1. The demand for money does not depend solely on income. The interest rate also has an effect. But since, as we saw earlier, the interest elasticity is quite low (money demand curves are steep), they regard this as only a minor qualification.

2. The income velocity of money, V, is by no means constant. It has shown a strong uptrend over the years. Between 1950 and 1980 the GNP/$M1$ ratio rose from about 2.5 to about 6.5. Moreover, velocity is variable in the short run. It tends to rise during an economic upswing and to fall in recession. Between the last quarter of 1977 and the first quarter of 1979, it jumped from 5.8 to 6.5, giving an extra push to what was already a strong upswing. Then during the recession of 1981–82, it fell sharply, partly offsetting the continued growth of money supply.

Thus, the old proposition that V and k are *constant* has now been replaced by the proposition that they are *predictable*. The determinants of V and k are known and stable. If this is true, we can predict the effect of changes in money supply.

3. The economy does not necessarily operate at full capacity. If the economy is well below capacity, the initial impact of an increase in M will be mainly on the rate of output rather than on the price level (as, for example, in 1983 and 1984). But monetarists are more interested in the long run than in the short run. Over a period of years, they believe that there is a close relation between the rate of increase in money supply and the rate of increase in prices. The reasoning is as follows: Suppose the output capacity of the economy (Q) grows, on the average, at 4 percent per year. We want to utilize this growing capacity, but we also want the price level (P) to remain stable. The quantity equation tells us that this can happen *only if* M *also grows on the average at 4 percent per year* (perhaps adjusted for predictable changes in velocity).

If M grows faster than Q, inflation is inevitable. Monetarists would say that the basic reason for the persistent inflation since 1945 is an unduly high rate of increase in money supply, and they blame this partly on undue permissiveness by the Federal Reserve System.

Some monetarist propositions

While modern monetarism is thus more complex than pre-1930 reasoning, it retains much of the same spirit and policy outlook. It will be useful to summarize some of the things on which most monetarists agree.

The first three of these involve economic analysis, while the last three involve policy outlook.

1. Changes in the money supply are the dominant force behind changes in GNP. If you want to predict the economic future, the best thing you can do is to keep your eye fixed on the money supply figures.

2. The transmission process is simple and direct. An increase in money supply (or more correctly, a rate of increase greater than the rate of increase in money demand) means that people and businesses are holding more money than they wish to hold. They will try to spend the excess amount. Total spending will rise, which will raise the money value of GNP. This will go on until money income has risen enough to reduce the money stock/income ratio to its normal level of k. Now people are willing to hold the increased amount of money, and the system is back in equilibrium.

While the rate of interest is somewhat incidental in this story, it is not entirely out of the picture. The public, with excess money on hand, will spend part of it on goods; but part will be spent on securities. This will tend to raise securities prices, which amounts to lowering the rate of interest. A lower interest rate will stimulate both consumer and investment spending and, thus, reinforce the movement toward higher GNP and a new equilibrium.

3. Monetarists regard the private economy as rather stable and departures from capacity operation as self-correcting. They believe it would be even more stable if government's monetary and fiscal policies followed a steady and predictable course. Frequent shifts in policy, often called "fine-tuning," which Keynesians tend to advocate as a way of stabilizing the economy, are in fact a destabilizing influence.

4. As regards policy outlook, monetarists are more concerned with the behavior of the economy over a period of years than with short-run fluctuations. They are less concerned with unemployment, which they tend to regard as self-correcting, then with inflation, which they view as a serious and chronic disease.

5. Most (though not all) monetarists favor a policy under which the Fed would increase money supply at a steady rate year after year. This is usually called the "constant money growth rule" (CMGR). They believe one could estimate a rate which would keep the price level roughly constant. In any event, the main point is the steadiness of the rate, rather than hitting exactly the right level.

6. Tax and expenditure changes by government to influence the GNP level—"fiscal policy"—are regarded as weak instruments with undesirable side effects. Further, fiscal policy can be effective only through its effect on money supply and is thus not an independent tool.

These points are interconnected rather than independent. In Milton Friedman's writings, and probably in the view of most other monetarists, they are related to a political outlook best characterized as "19th-century liberalism," now usually called conservatism. This view, which dominated economics before 1930 and is now undergoing a revival, holds that the private economy works pretty well and that detailed government intervention in the economy is usually undesirable. To the extent that government does intervene, this should be mainly through monetary policy which, being general in its application, has the virtue of neutrality toward private economic activities.

We have now wandered farther than we should have into policy discussion. Macroeconomic policy is the business of Part Two rather than Part One. In Chapter 12, we'll examine monetarist and nonmonetarist policy proposals in greater detail.

INVESTMENT AND THE RATE OF INTEREST

We return now to the alternative view that monetary policy produces its effect through the rate of interest. Changes in the rate of interest raise or lower the C, I, and G schedules and thus the level of aggregate demand.

The most important effect is usually thought to be on investment. Let's look first at business investment in plants, machinery, nonresidential buildings, and other capital goods. These items appear in the national income accounts as "plant and equipment" and "nonresidential construction." What determines the amount of such investments at a particular time?

A business buys capital goods for one of three reasons: *to replace worn-out capital goods, to increase production capacity, or to reduce production costs,* perhaps by substituting machinery for labor or more productive machines for less productive ones. These objectives are not mutually exclusive. A new piece of equipment may reduce production costs as well as replace worn-out equipment and perhaps add to productive capacity.

The company must be satisfied that the new equipment will be profitable. It must bring in more than it costs. What kind of calculation is required here?

Determining the return on investment

A machine or other capital good is bought because it produces something. So the first step is to take the value of this product and deduct from it all the necessary additional costs which accompany the use of the machine: the extra labor, materials, power, maintenance, and other costs.

Whatever is left over after deducting all accompanying costs is the net product of the machine. This product continues year after year until the machine is worn out. A capital good, then, yields its owner a *stream of future income.*

If we know the cost of the capital good and the size of the future income, we can convert the income into a percentage yield on the initial cost. Then, by comparing the yield with the rate of interest, we can tell whether purchase of the machine is worthwhile.

Alternatively, if we know the size of the future income stream, and if we know the rate of interest, we can calculate *how much the machine itself is worth* to its user. This process of deriving the value of an asset from its future yield is known as *capitalization.* It applies to any physical asset—a machine, a farm, an apartment house. It can be applied also to a college education.

Take a piece of equipment which will yield a net income of $1,000 next year, another $1,000 the year following, and so on. How do I work back from this future income stream to the present value of the machine? Concentrate first on the $1,000 I expect to receive next year. This is not worth the same to me as $1,000 today. If the market rate of interest is 5 percent, and if I lend $950 at interest today, this will grow to approximately $1,000 a year from now. Thus next year's $1,000 yield from my machine is equivalent to only about $950 today. To be precise, it is worth $1,000/1.05 = $952.38. The present value of an income due one year hence is obtained by *discounting that income by the rate of interest.*

The $1,000 which the machine will yield two years from now must be discounted more heavily, since it is further away. And we apply the same principle. If the rate of interest is 5 percent, $1 put out at interest today will in two years be worth $1 \times (1.05)^2$ To get the present value of income two years hence, we throw this into reverse. The $1,000 two years away is worth today $1,000/(1.05)^2 = \$907.03$.

If the machine will last 20 years, and will fall apart at the end of that time, then the present value of all the future income it will yield is:

$$\frac{\$1,000}{1.05} + \frac{\$1,000}{(1.05)^2} + \frac{\$1,000}{(1.05)^3} + \ldots + \frac{\$1,000}{(1.05)^{20}}.$$

This amounts to $12,462.21. To the prospective buyer, *the present value of the machine equals the present value of the future income stream which it yields.* So this machine is worth $12,462.21. Why? Because if the machine is bought at that price, and if the future yields work out as expected, the buyer will have earned the market rate of interest on his or her investment. Or, put another way, if the buyer borrows money to buy the machine, the loan can be paid off from the machine's earnings.

Suppose that the market price of the machine is only $10,000. Then it is clearly profitable to buy it, and the prospective buyer will proceed to do so. But if the machine cost $13,000, its purchase would not be profitable.

Let us now shift over to the other approach, which brings us to the same conclusion by a different route. Put the question this way: If the prospective purchaser buys this machine for $10,000, and if it brings in a net income of $1,000 a year for 20 years, *what rate of return is being earned on the investment?* This is the same as asking: At what rate of interest will the present value of the future income stream just equal the cost of the machine?

> **The rate of return on an investment is the rate of interest at which the present value of the income stream yielded by the investment is equal to its cost.**

Call the rate of return in this case r. Then, using our previous formula for present value, r, must satisfy the condition that:

$$\$10,000 = \frac{\$1,000}{(1+r)} + \frac{\$1,000}{(1+r)^2} + \frac{\$1,000}{(1+r)^3} + \ldots + \frac{\$1,000}{(1+r)^{20}}.$$

Solving for the value of r, which can be done with a compound interest table, we find that the machine yields a bit over 7.5 percent per year.[1] So if the company can borrow money at anything less than this, it will pay to make the investment. If the market rate of interest is 5 percent, as we supposed earlier, the investment will pay.

The marginal efficiency of investment

There are millions of businesses in the economy, and at any time they will be considering millions of possible investment projects. Suppose we had in front of us engineering estimates of every last one of these, giving the cost of new capital and the expected rate of return; and suppose we then ranked the projects from those with the highest returns to those with the lowest. There would undoubtedly be some investment opportunities with yields of, say, 50 percent or better, and these would absorb a few billion dollars of investment expenditure. If we lower the yardstick to a 40 percent return or better, some more projects would pay off, and feasible investment expenditures would be larger. The amount of investment with an expected yield of 30 percent would be still larger, and so on.

In this way, we can trace out the marginal efficiency of investment *(MEI)* schedule in Figure 8–1. This shows, for any level of investment expenditure we select, the expected yield on the last dollar—hence *marginal* efficiency. For example, if $80 billion were spent on new capital

---

[1] This rate is usually called the *internal rate of return.* We should note, however, that its calculation depends on the assumption that each item in the future income stream is *positive.* If one or more of these items is negative, it may not be possible to calculate a unique, positive, internal rate of return. For this reason, the alternative approach using the market rate of interest is regarded as preferable.

FIGURE 8-1

Expected returns fall as more investment is undertaken

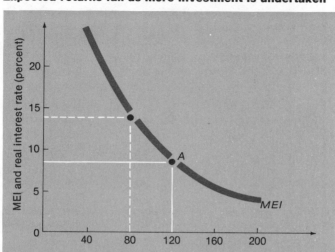

This is the marginal efficiency of investment *(MEI)* schedule for the nation. Point *A* shows that if $120 billion of new investment projects were undertaken next year, the least profitable of these projects would yield an expected return of 8 percent. Any other point on *MEI* has the same significance.

goods this year, the marginal efficiency of investment would be 13 percent. As the amount of expenditure increases, the marginal efficiency falls, because we are adding projects with lower and lower rates of return.

Given this roster of investment opportunities, how much investment will actually be undertaken this year? This will depend on the market rate of interest. A business will carry out an investment project only if the expected return is at least equal to the interest rate. Thus, if the interest rate is 8 percent, it will pay to undertake only projects whose expected rate of return is 8 percent or higher. We can read off from Figure 8-1 that this will mean an investment expenditure of about $120 billion per year.

The downward slope of the *MEI* schedule tells us that:

The lower the rate of interest, the higher the rate of investment demand, and vice versa.

Other factors influencing business investment demand

This is not to say that the rate of interest is the only factor influencing business investment decisions. Many other things also influence these decisions: how much funds the firm has available for investment from accumulated capital consumption allowances and retained profits, how close to capacity the existing plant is now operating, the business outlook for the near future, the riskiness of projects contemplated, and so on. The more important of these deserve brief description.

Risk. It is no accident that the word *expected* recurred frequently in our discussion of investment plans. The return from a prospective investment is always an estimate, not a certainty. It depends upon a whole series of subestimates about sales prospects, product prices, input prices, and production efficiency. So a 20 percent return calculated this way will not be valued as highly as a 20 percent *guaranteed* return on a sure thing. Depending upon the confidence which management feels in the estimates and depending upon whether they are temperamentally inclined toward taking risks or prefer to avoid them, they may rate a 20 percent expected rate of return as equivalent to only 10 percent on a sure thing, or 8 percent, or even 5 percent.[2] Thus, a risk-avoiding business executive may turn thumbs down on an investment project with a 20 percent expected rate of return when the interest rate is only 8 percent.

The risk element explains why businesses often seem to be demanding exorbitant returns on proposed investments. They often talk in terms of the "pay-out period," that is, the number of years required for the net income from an investment to equal its original cost. A company may have a rule of thumb that new machines must pay for themselves in three years or that a new plant must pay out in five years. At first glance, these rates of return seem high. But when we adjust them for the risk that the expected return may not materialize, they are a good deal lower.

Internal funds. Most of the funds needed for business investment are generated within the company. In Chapter 5, we discussed *capital consumption allowances* and *retained earnings,* which together constitute *gross business saving.* In 1983, capital consumption allowances and retained earnings totaled about $287 billion. This provided most of the $347 billion spent on private corporate investment.

Companies normally prefer internal to external funds. To secure external funds, the company must either borrow, in which case it is faced with future fixed interest charges, or it must sell new common stock, which usually brings in additional stockholders and may conceivably risk loss of control of the company.

The aversion to external financing has two consequences. First, many

---

[2] The estimation of risk is a highly technical subject, the complexities of which can only be hinted at here. It normally involves, not a single expected rate of return but a range of possibilities. Suppose there is a 50–50 chance that project A will yield either a 60 percent return or a zero return. Then by a kind of averaging we can say that the estimated return is 30 percent. Suppose project B promises a 1-in-4 chance of a 20 percent return, a 2-in-4 chance of a 30 percent return, and a 1-in-4 chance of a 40 percent return. Here, too, the simple average of expected returns is 30 percent. But the two situations are obviously not equivalent. An investor with an aversion to risk will probably choose project B, since the *worst* he or she can do here is 20 percent, while in the A case the return could be zero.

firms rely almost exclusively upon internal funds to finance investment projects. The amount of these funds determines, or at least limits, the amount of investment undertaken.

Second, while companies perhaps should take the market interest rate into account in deciding how to use their internal funds, there is little evidence that they actually do so. The interest rate, therefore, mainly affects investors who lack internal funds and must resort to the market. This includes small businesses just getting started, companies in expanding industries which have unusually large investment needs, and public utilities whose earnings are regulated by government.

The state of the economy and the outlook for the future. Business investment spending is much influenced by the state of the economy and the outlook for the future. If the economy is in a recession, many firms are operating at less than full capacity, profits are falling, and the business outlook is uncertain if not pessimistic. Each of these is conducive to low business investment spending. When there is already excess plant capacity, capacity-expanding investment projects will appear unnecessary and unprofitable (at least for the near future). When corporate profits are depressed, firms which rely upon internal financing will postpone major investment expenditures until the profit picture improves. And an uncertain or pessimistic business outlook will be reflected in the calculated rate of return for investment projects, so there will be fewer projects with an expected yield of, say, 10 percent or greater.

All this amounts to saying that the *MEI* schedule shifts to the left during a business recession (for example, from MEI_A to MEI_B in Figure 8–2), so that the rate of investment demand is less at each rate of interest than before.

On the other hand, during a rapid economic expansion, the *MEI* schedule shifts to the right (from MEI_B to MEI_A in Figure 8–2). This is because rising sales in the recent past tend to be projected into the future, generating an optimistic outlook for future sales. Then too, rapidly rising sales are usually accompanied by rapidly rising corporate profits and retained earnings, and we have just seen that these internal funds are a major source of finance for new investment. Finally, as the expansion continues, many firms will approach capacity output, leading to consideration of capacity-expanding investment projects.

Keynes argued, and many economists continue to think, that the MEI schedule shifts about quite violently in the short run because of changes in the business outlook and that the fluctuations in business investment spending which we actually observe are mainly due to *shifts* of the schedule rather than *movements along* the schedule.

It is important to remember that the interest rate on the vertical axes of Figure 8–1 and 8–2 is defined as the *real* rate, that is, the market rate corrected for price-level changes. For example, if the market rate of interest is 10 percent but prices are rising at 5 percent per year, the

FIGURE 8-2

The *MEI* schedule shifts during economic upswings and downswings

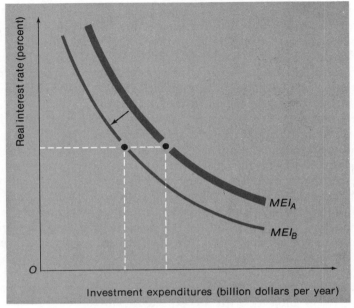

When the *MEI* schedule shifts to the left (from *MEI*$_A$ TO *MEI*$_B$), a smaller rate of business investment demand is forthcoming at each rate of interest.

real interest rate is only 5 percent. (To see this, consider a person who borrows $100 at 10 percent for one year and puts the money immediately into some physical asset. At the end of the year, said person must pay back $10 more than was borrowed. But against this the borrower has a capital gain of $5 because the asset has risen 5 percent in price. So the *net* cost of the loan to the individual is $10 − $5 = $5.)

This helps to explain some facts which might otherwise be puzzling. During the upswing of 1976–79, market interest rates rose sharply. The banks' prime lending rate rose from about 7 percent in 1976 to 12½ percent in 1979. But gross investment also increased from $119 billion in 1976 to $149 billion in 1979 (measured in constant 1972 dollars). This seems to contradict what the *MEI* schedule tells us, but it really does not. The reason is that the consumer price index (which rose only 4.8 percent in 1976) rose 13.3 percent in 1979. So the real rate of interest—the market rate corrected for price changes—was falling. Indeed, the real rate of interest in 1979 was slightly below zero. No wonder people were eager to borrow and invest. But why were lenders willing to lend? The only reasonable explanation is that they underestimated the rate of inflation and so expected a positive return which failed to materialize.

Business investment: Some evidence on behavior

The question of how businesses make their investment decisions is so important that much research has been done on it.[3] Some of the main findings which emerge are:

1. The dominant influence over the long run is the company's expected level of sales compared with its present production capacity. Studies suggest that the elasticity coefficient is close to 1.0; that is, if a company's expected level of sales rises by 10 percent, its desired capital stock will also rise by about 10 percent. Then, if its actual capital stock is below the desired level, it will take steps to close the gap.

The moral is that the *MEI* does shift but that such shifts are unlikely to be violent because they are geared to *long-run* expectations. Even if sales drop 20 percent during a recession, this will be discounted as temporary. The company will "look across the valley," as the saying goes, and try to estimate what it can expect to sell on the next upswing.

2. The rate of interest also has a significant influence on investment plans. Most studies estimate the elasticity coefficient in the range of 0.25 to 0.35 percent, that is, a 10 percent rise in interest cost will *reduce* investment spending by 2½ to 3½ percent. The *MEI* schedule is rather steep.

3. Even after an investment decision has been reached, carrying out the decision takes considerable time—an average of about a year in the case of machinery and about two years for buildings and other physical structures. For buildings, it takes about 7 months from the drawing of initial plans to the start of construction, and an additional 15 months for construction to be completed. Thus the effect of an interest rate change on actual spending is spread out over a considerable period of time.

OTHER EFFECTS OF THE RATE OF INTEREST

We have discussed at length the effect of interest rates on business investment in plant and equipment because this is a large item in the

---

[3] For a good summary and analysis, see S. J. Nickell, *The Investment Decisions of Firms,* Cambridge Economic Handbooks Series (Cambridge University Press, 1978).

national accounts and because it fluctuates considerably over the business cycle. In the 9181–82 recession, for example, nonresidential fixed investment fell from an annual rate of $368 billion in late 1981 to $332 billion at the bottom of the recession.

But we should not overlook important effects on other types of spending, which in the aggregate are at least equally important. These include investment in inventories, investment in housing, consumer spending, and government spending.

Inventory investment

Manufacturing plants need inventories of raw materials and work in process to avoid shortages which could interrupt production. Wholesalers and retailers carry substantial stocks of finished goods to be sure of having what buyers want when they want it.

How large should a company's inventories be? The answer depends, as usual, on a balancing of costs and benefits. Larger inventories increase the company's safety margin, but this benefit decreases as inventories rise. On the other hand, inventories tie up money. Part of this is usually borrowed from banks, which involves an interest cost. An even if the company is using its own money, there is an implicit interest cost, since the money could be used in other ways.

The inventory decision, then, involves a weighing of interest costs against gains in security and convenience. A rise in the rate of interest will shift the balance, causing businesses to want smaller inventories than before, while a drop in the interest rate will incline them to carry larger inventories. The inventory decision is also strongly influenced by whether company sales are rising or falling and by the expected trend of sales in the future, as we'll explain in our discussion of business cycles in Chapter 11. But the interest rate remains an important influence.

Inventory changes over the cycle are large. In the third quarter of 1981, which was a cycle peak, businesses were adding to inventories at an annual rate of $24 billion. But at the bottom of the recession, in the fourth quarter of 1982, they *reduced* inventories at an annual rate of $54 billion. This turnaround in inventory investment was a major factor in the recession.

Housing investment

Housing construction is strongly influenced by the level of interest rates. The reason is that most home buying is financed mainly by mortgage borrowing, and the higher interest rates are, the higher are monthly mortgage payments. For example, consider a $20,000 mortgage to be paid off over 25 years. If the interest rate is 6 percent, the payments will be

$128.87 per month. But if the interest rate is 7 percent, the payments will be $141.36 per month; and if the interest rate is 8 percent, the payments will be $154.37 per month. Each one-point rise in the interest rate raises the monthly payment by about 9 percent.

As mortgage rates rise, then, some potential home buyers will be priced out of the market or will have to settle for smaller and cheaper homes. On the other hand, when mortgage rates fall, buying a house becomes feasible for more and more families, and it becomes possible to buy a larger and more expensive house without an increase in the monthly payment. Residential construction activity tends to fall sharply during periods of rising interest rates and to rise sharply when interest rates fall.

Again, we can illustrate from the 1981–82 recession. Housing investment fell from an annual rate of $97 billion in the third quarter of 1981 to $83 billion in the third quarter of 1982. Then, as the recession brought mortgage rates down from their peak of about 16 percent to an average of about 12.5 percent in mid-1983, housing rebounded sharply and by late 1983 was up to an annual rate of $155 billion.

Consumer spending

While early Keynesian reasoning emphasized the effect of interest rates on the I schedule, it is now recognized that there is also an important effect on the C schedule. And since C is close to two thirds of GNP, even a small percentage change in this item means a large change in dollar terms.

The interest rate has two effects, one on consumer spending in general, and the other on spending on durable consumer goods. Studies of consumption indicate that a family's propensity to consume, while related mainly to expected income, is also influenced by its *wealth.* An increase in wealth increases the family's sense of security, reduces the urgency of additional saving, and thus raises the propensity to consume. Most of the wealth of high-income families is in the form of securities. We saw in Chapter 7 that the value of these securities varies inversely with the rate of interest: When interest rates fall, security prices rise. Many people are better off, or at least feel better off, which is what matters. This has a favorable effect on consumer spending.

The more specific effect arises from the fact that purchases of some consumer goods are financed partly by borrowing. The classic case is automobiles, where to most buyers the monthly payment is the most significant figure. A rise in the interest rate raises the monthly payment and reduces willingness to buy, and vice versa. There were several reasons for the 1983 recovery of the U.S. auto industry after three lean years, but a substantial reduction in borrowing costs was certainly important.

While this is the most conspicuous case, purchases of furniture, household appliances, clothing, even travel and recreation are financed partly on credit. The total amount of consumer credit outstanding in 1983 was about $370 billion, and it keeps growing year by year. But while American consumers seem devoted to the credit system, this devotion is not entirely blind. A higher rate of interest means larger monthly payments which must be fitted into the family budget. So, as the interest rate rises, consumers will restrain their borrowing, which will tend to lower the C schedule. Conversely, a drop in interest rates will tend to encourage borrowing and raise the C schedule.

Government spending

As regards the G schedule, the rate of interest has little effect on federal expenditure. The federal government, with its unlimited credit, simply borrows what it needs to and pays the going rate. We should note, however, that there is a built-in conflict of objectives between the U.S. Treasury Department and the Federal Reserve System. The Treasury, like any borrower, prefers a lower interest rate to a higher one. It is apt to be especially unhappy if the Fed is forcing down securities prices (that is, forcing up the interest rates) just when the Treasury needs to sell a large new bond issue. At such times, there is likely to be discussion of the need for Federal Reserve "cooperation" with the Treasury. The implication is that the Fed should abandon its effort at monetary control for the time being and help out the Treasury by keeping interest rates low.

A direct impact of interest rates on government spending occurs mainly at the state and local level. These governments usually finance large construction projects—highways and turnpikes, water supply systems, urban housing, school or college expansion—by selling bonds to private investors. Interest on these bonds must be met out of future tax revenues, so the size of the interest payments has a major effect on the cost of a project. If the interest rate rises to a level which seems abnormally high, states and localities will put some projects on the shelf for the time being. The G schedule falls. If and when interest rates come down, these projects will be revived and the necessary bonds issued. Thus, variations in the interest rate have a substantial effect on the *timing* of government construction projects.

CONSEQUENCES OF ADDING MONEY TO THE MODEL

Over the last several chapters, we have been following the strategy laid down at the beginning of Chapter 4: building up by stages from the simplest possible model of the macroeconomy to increasingly complex (and realistic) models. Throughout Chapters 4 and 5, we ignored the existence of a monetary system, a rate of interest, and monetary influences on the C, I and G schedules. Then, in Chapters 6–8, we brought money and interest to the center of the stage. What difference does this make? How does a model with a monetary system differ from one without money?

The first major difference is that we now have *two* equilibrium conditions rather than one. There must be equilibrium in the *market for goods*—total demand for output must equal the current value of output. The condition for this, laid down at the end of Chapter 5, remains unchanged.

$$I + G + (X - M) = S_p + S_b + T_n.$$

But now, in addition, we must also have equilibrium in the *money market*. The amount of money the public wishes to hold must just equal the amount of money in existence. If we call the amount of money demanded L (for liquidity) and the quantity of money M, the equilibrium condition is simply

$$L = M.$$

If these two conditions are met simultaneously, the economy is in *full equilibrium* and the rate of GNP will continue unchanged. This proposition is illustrated in the appendix by some simple geometry, which will repay careful study.

Second, including money in the economy gives us a new feedback mechanism which increases the stability of the system. Suppose we start from a situation in which both the equilibrium conditions are being met. Now there occurs an autonomous increase in, say, federal government spending. This throws the goods market out of equilibrium and starts an expansion of output through the multiplier process discussed in Chapters 4–5. The size of the multiplier, as we saw there, depends on the size of the leakages into savings and net payments. These leakages have a *braking effect* on any expansion or contraction of output. The larger they are, the smaller is the multiplier, and the stabler the economy.

But the autonomous increase in spending will also throw the money market out of equilibrium. As output and income rise, the amount of money demanded will also rise, and if the quantity of money remains unchanged (or rises more slowly than demand), the rate of interest will rise. But the rise in the rate of interest will tend to lower the C, I, and G schedules, or at least to retard their rate of increase. Thus, money and interest provide a second *braking mechanism*, which will tend to slow down the expansion of output.

How strongly the brakes take hold, of course, depends on the behavior of money supply, which in turn depends on policies of the Federal Reserve System.

So, the third main difference in our new model is that we have an

additional policy lever—control of money supply and interest rates—
which can be used to influence the behavior of output and prices. The
problems involved in using monetary policy will be discussed more fully
in Chapter 12. But one preliminary question should be raised here. We
saw earlier that the Fed cannot determine both the growth rate of money
supply and the level of interest rates. So which should be chosen as
the target for monetary policy? Should the Fed look at the growth rate
of money supply and try to hold this steady, allowing interest rates to
fluctuate? Or should it try to hold interest rates steady, allowing money
supply to fluctuate?

There is no agreed-upon answer at present, and the Fed's practice
has varied over the years.[4] There is also a third alternative: To keep an
eye on both M and r and to follow an activist policy of steering them
so as to raise or lower aggregate demand as required. This leads into
the issue of fixed rules versus activism which we will explore in Chapter
12.

NEW CONCEPTS

monetarist
quantity equation
quantity theory
income velocity of money
constant monetary growth rule
capitalization

rate of return (on a capital good)
marginal efficiency of investment
equilibrium, goods market
equilibrium, money market
equilibrium, full

SUMMARY

1. The *quantity equation* (Fisher version) says that the amount of
money spent in a given time period *(M × V)* must equal the value of
goods purchased *(P × Q)*.

2. If V is assumed to be constant, we have a *quantity theory,* which
says that an increase in the quantity of money will cause a proportionate
increase in money GNP by raising output or prices or both. If the economy
is already producing at capacity, the whole effect will be on the price
level.

3. Monetarists believe that changes in money supply are the dominant
force behind changes in GNP. They believe also that the transmission

---

[4] The answer seems to depend partly on where instability in the economy is coming from. If demand
for commodities is fluctuating while demand for money is stable, a policy of steady monetary growth
will lead to smaller output fluctuations than a policy of stable interest rates. But if it is demand for
money that is unstable, while commodity demand is stable, the reverse is true. See on this point Robert
J. Gordon, *Macroeconomics* (Boston: Little, Brown, 1978), pp. 420–22.

mechanism is simple and direct—an increase in money supply relative to demand leads directly to an increase in spending.

4. Nonmonetarists also consider money supply important, but they think its effects operate mainly through changes in the rate of interest. A decline in the rate of interest raises both consumer and investment demand, and conversely.

5. Investment is undertaken because a capital good is expected to yield a *stream of future income*. This future income must be *discounted* to determine its *present value*.

6. Purchase of a capital good is profitable if: (1) the present value of the future income stream, discounted at the market rate of interest, exceeds the price of the capital good; or (2) the rate of return which the capital good yields is greater than the market rate of interest. These mean the same thing.

7. The *marginal efficiency of investment schedule (MEI)* shows, for each level of investment expenditure which might be undertaken in the next period, the expected rate of return on the last dollar of investment. If the rate of interest is r, planned investment will be that amount at which $MEI = r$.

8. Thus, by affecting the interest rate, the Fed can influence the rate of investment demand and (through the autonomous spending multiplier) the rate of aggregate demand. The rate of interest also affects consumer spending on durable goods and state and local government construction projects.

9. In a model which includes a monetary system, there are *two* equilibrium conditions rather than the one stated in Chapter 5. The new condition is that the amount of money the public wishes to hold must equal the amount of money in existence, or $L = M$.

10. A model with money also has *two* braking mechanisms rather than the one resulting from leakages from the income stream. An upswing of GNP tends to raise the interest rate, which has a braking effect on the upswing and similarly for a downswing of GNP.

Appendix: The synthesis of money and income

Where do we stand in our analysis of national income and output? In Chapters 4 and 5, we explained the determination of equilibrium GNP by the equality of saving and investment.

Now we have introduced some new elements into the analysis. We have shown that by altering the supply of money we can change the rate of interest and that this in turn will affect investment demand, aggregate demand, and the equilibrium rate of GNP.

The problem is that, having introduced money and interest, we have two equilibrium conditions to satisfy instead of one. These are:

1. *Equilibrium in the product markets.* Aggregate demand must equal the rate of GNP. We saw in Chapter 5 that this condition is satisfied when

$$S_p + S_b + T_n = I + G + (X - M).$$

For simplicity, call this the $S = I$ condition.

2. Equilibrium in the money market. This requires that the demand for money must equal the amount of money in existence. If we designate the former as *L,* and the latter as *M,* the condition is

$$L = M.$$

Suppose we know the quantity of money in existence. The problem is then to find the rate of GNP *(Y)* and the rate of interest *(i)* which will satisfy *both* of the equilibrium conditions simultaneously. If we can do this, we shall have a general equilibrium for the economy, in which the money supply, interest rate, aggregate demand, and GNP will be mutually consistent.

Is it a solvable problem? Yes, it is. The solution can be shown in several ways. The one chosen here requires careful study, but it ties up a lot of things in a neat package.

Since we are now trying to determine *Y* and *i* simultaneously, our diagrams from here on will show *Y* on the horizontal axis and *i* on the verti-

cal axis. The eventual solution, then, will be a *point* on this sort of diagram.

Product market equilibrium

Start with the first condition of equilibrium, *S = I,* and look at Figure 8–3. Choose any rate of interest, say, i_1. Now, for this rate of interest there must be some level of GNP which will make *S* equal *I.* The rate of interest determines a certain amount of investment, so we must find a rate of income at which there is just this amount of saving. Suppose this turns out to be Y_1. Then point *A* on the diagram, with coordinates i_1, Y_1, is one point at which the *S = I* condition is fulfilled.

But there are obviously many more such points. Choose a lower rate of interest, i_2. With the lower interest, there will be a larger volume of investment. If the saving-investment equality is to hold, there must be more saving, and this will only happen at a higher rate of GNP. The

FIGURE 8–3
Product market equilibrium

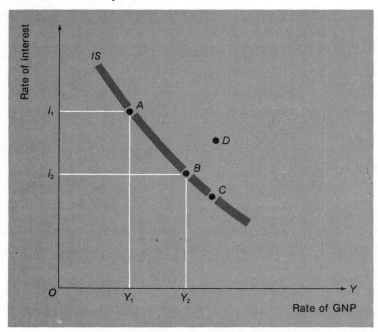

IS contains all combinations of GNP rate *(Y)* and interest rate *(i)* which satisfy the conditions *S = I.* Thus, *A, B,* and *C* are possible equilibrium positions for the economy, while *D* is not.

required level of income turns out to be Y_2. This gives us another point, B, which meets the $I = S$ condition. By repeating the same process we discover a third point, C, and so on.

By linking together all such points, we derive the curve IS. This is the *set of all combinations of i and Y which satisfy the S = I condition.* Wherever the economy may settle, then, it must be at some point along this curve. Point D, for example, cannot be an equilibrium point because it does not satisfy this condition.

The IS curve slopes downward to the right. Why? Because a lower interest rate means a higher rate of investment, which means a higher equilibrium GNP. There are two steps here: the size of the investment response to a change in the interest rate and the size of the GNP response to a change in investment, which depends upon the multiplier. The shape of IS, then, depends on the size of the multiplier and on the responsiveness of investment to a change in the interest rate.

Money market equilibrium

Turn now to the second condition, $L = M$, and look at Figure 8–4. We proceed as before. Choose any rate of interest, i_1. Given this rate, the amount of money people wish to hold depends solely on the rate of GNP. But the supply of money is fixed. Thus, we can find some rate of GNP at which the aggregate of households and businesses are just willing to hold this fixed quantity of money. Suppose this turns out to be Y_1. Then point E gives us one combination of i and Y which satisfies the $L = M$ condition.

Choose another interest rate, i_2. At this rate, it will take a different income level, Y_2, to equate L and M. This gives us a second point, F. By discovering more and more such points and joining them up, we obtain the LM curve in Figure 8–4. This is the set of all combinations of i and Y which satisfy the $L = M$ condition.

Why does the LM curve slope upward to the right? As we move to the right, we are moving

FIGURE 8–4
Money market equilibrium

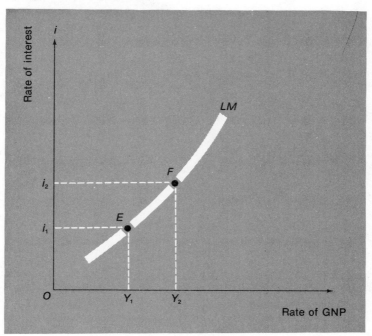

LM contains all combinations of Y and i which satisfy the condition $L = M$. Only points on this line are possible equilibrium positions for the economy.

to higher and higher rates of GNP. This tends to cause the demand for money to rise, so in order to hold the demand for money equal to the fixed supply of money, the interest rate must rise. Only in this way can the $L = M$ condition continue to be satisfied for a fixed supply of money.

General equilibrium

Once the construction of the *IS* and *LM* curves has been grasped, the solution to the problem becomes simple. Look at Figure 8–5, where the two are brought together. Each curve shows a basic condition of equilibrium. For the economy to be in general equilibrium, *both* conditions must be satisfied simultaneously. The equilibrium combination of interest rate and GNP *must* lie on both the *I* and *LM* curves. But this can happen only where the two curves intersect.

The intersection at *P*, then, defines the general equilibrium of the system. The equilibrium interest rate will be *i* and the equilibrium rate of GNP will be *Y*.

Changes in the rate of GNP

In practice, the underlying conditions often change. The usefulness of the *IS–LM* diagram is in exploring what will happen if one of the basic conditions does change. Let us consider first the impact of shifts in the aggregate demand schedule, then the consequences of a change in the money supply.

A shift in the IS curve

We start with the IS_1 and LM_1 curves of Figure 8–6, with interest rate i_1 and output Y_1. Now suppose government purchases are in-

FIGURE 8–5
General equilibrium: Simultaneous determination of interest rate and national income

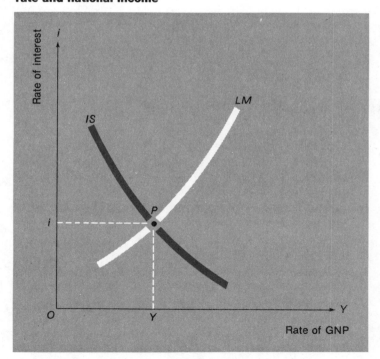

Any equilibrium position for the economy must lie on both *IS* and *LM*. The only point for which this is true is the intersection point *P*. Hence, the equilibrium rate of GNP will be *Y* and the equilibrium interest rate *i*.

creased, net tax rates are cut, or the *MEI* sched-ule shifts to the right. Any one of these events will cause the *IS* curve to shift rightward, say, to *IS*$_2$. If the interest rate *could* remain at the level *i*$_1$, then equilibrium GNP would rise all the way out to *Y*$_3$. But the interest rate cannot remain at *i*$_1$. It must rise. Why? Because of our assump-tion that the supply of money, and hence the position of the *LM* curve, has remained un-changed. (A rise in GNP must be accompanied by a rise in the interest rate in order for the *L* = *M* condition to continue to hold when the money supply is fixed.)

This necessary rise in the interest rate, then, reduces investment demand some, *partially* off-setting the effect upon equilibrium GNP of the rightward shift of the *IS* curve. We end up with a new equilibrium involving national output *Y*$_2$ and interest rate *i*$_2$. The rightward shift of the *IS* curve raises both GNP and the interest rate.

Consider now a leftward shift of the *IS* curve. This could be caused by a cut in government purchases, an increase in net tax receipts, or a leftward shift of the *MEI* schedule, and it will result in a decline in equilibrium GNP. But the interest rate must also fall (with a fixed supply of money), and its decline will stimulate invest-ment demand, *partially* offsetting the effect of the leftward shift in the *IS* curve upon equilibrium GNP. This can be seen if we begin with *IS*$_2$ in Figure 8–6 and then shift to *IS*$_1$. The new equilib-rium will involve *both* a lower GNP and a lower interest rate.

A change in the money supply

Suppose that the Federal Reserve causes the money supply to increase. This shifts the *LM* curve to the right from, say, *LM*$_1$ to *LM*$_2$ in Figure 8–7. What does this mean? Looking hori-zontally, the new position *LM*$_2$ says that at a given rate of interest, GNP can be larger than before because of the expansion of the money supply. Looking vertically, we see that at any rate of GNP, the interest rate can be lower than

FIGURE 8–6
A change in the expenditure schedule

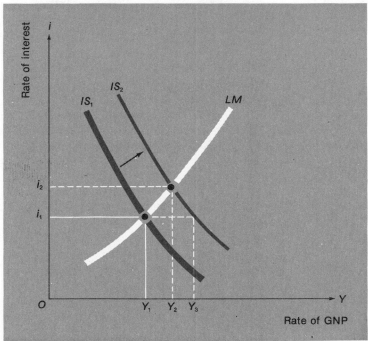

A shift from *IS*$_1$ to *IS*$_2$ causes a rise in both GNP and the interest rate.

FIGURE 8-7
A change in the supply of money

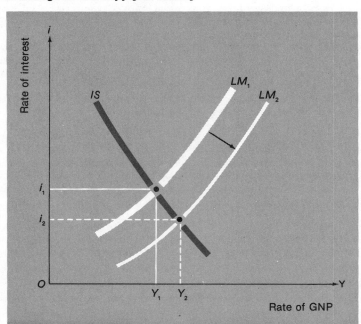

An increase in the supply of money shifts *LM* rightward, say, from *LM*₁ to *LM*₂. This causes a rise in GNP and a decline in the interest rate.

before because of this same monetary expansion.

The *IS* curve intersects the new *LM*₂ curve further to the right so that there is a new equilibrium level of interest rate and GNP. But note that these change in opposite directions. Output

rises from Y_1 to Y_2. The rate of interest falls from i_1 to i_2.

A decrease in the money supply brings about just the opposite results. The *LM* curve shifts to the left, causing the equilibrium interest rate to rise and equilibrium GNP to fall.

TO LEARN MORE

See the macroeconomics texts and money and banking tests listed at the end of Chapter 4.

Inflation

Bell, book, and candle shall not drive me back,
When gold and silver becks me to come on.

—William Shakespeare, King John

Introduction

In Chapter 8, we discussed two ways of explaining changes in aggregate demand. One of these works directly through the effect of a change in money supply on total spending, through the MV formula in the quantity equation. The other works indirectly through the effect of money supply on the rate of interest, which in turn shifts the C, I, and G schedules. Whichever model one chooses, an increase in aggregate demand leads to an increase in the money value of GNP, usually called *nominal GNP*.

But how much of the change will be in the quantity of *output* and how much in the general level of *prices?* How will the impact be *divided* between P and Q? This is a central issue, which we'll be exploring throughout this chapter.

Keynesian theory tended to assume stability of wage and price levels and to emphasize the variability of output and employment. An early Keynesian, faced with the above question, would probably have answered: The output effect will be 100 percent, the price effect will be zero.

A newer school of thought—often called "the new classical macroeconomics" (NCM)—gives an exactly opposite answer. In NCM theory, wages and prices are perfectly flexible, and markets are always in equilibrium. An NCM theorist, then, would answer: The price effect will be 100 percent, the output effect will be zero.

This is not just an argument among theorists. It has practical implications. Suppose the price level is presently rising at 8 percent per year. Policymakers want to reduce the inflation rate to 3 percent by restricting aggregate demand. What will happen? An NCM theorist would say: Prices will respond promptly, with little change in output. Thus the cost of reducing the inflation rate is low. A Keynesian would say: There will be a sharp drop in output and employment, with little immediate effect on the inflation rate. The cost of reducing the inflation rate is quite high.

Studies of the actual behavior of the American economy suggest that it comes closer to the Keynesian model. In the short run, something like 80 percent of the impact of a change in aggregate demand falls on output, and only the remaining 20 percent is transmitted to prices.[1] Thus, reducing the inflation rate is a slow and costly process.

Another way of putting the matter is to say that wage and price levels are quite sluggish or show marked *inertia*. An increase or decrease in aggregate demand has only a limited price impact in the first two or three calendar quarters, and the full effect builds up gradually over several years. In the long run, to be sure, there is a remarkable similarity between the rate of monetary expansion and the rate of price increase. During the 50s, for example, M1 rose at an average rate of 2.20 percent per year. The price level (GNP deflator) rose at 2.24 percent per year. In the 70s, on the other hand, M1 rose at 4.13 percent per year and the GNP deflator at 3.92 percent.[2] But the reader should be warned: This fact of life does not warrant any quick conclusion either about cause and effect or about proper monetary policy. These are complicated matters which will occupy us for many pages to come.

We have been using the word "inflation" without defining it. *Inflation* is an increase in the general level of prices, as measured by some comprehensive index. As we saw in Chapter 3, there are several commonly used indexes in the United States: the Consumer Price Index, the Producer Price Index, and the GNP Price Deflator. We shall generally refer to the GNP index, which is the most comprehensive. A general decrease in the price level, rare in modern times, would be a *deflation*. The term *disinflation* has come into use recently to describe a decrease in the inflation rate to a lower (but still positive) level.

What we would like to know is *why* the inflation rate this year was 5 percent rather than something else. What might cause it to rise to 8 percent or fall to 3 percent? Why does it never seem to fall to zero?

We do not at present have a tidy theory which answers these questions satisfactorily and is widely accepted by economists. But we do have some useful ideas about inflation which may add up to pieces of a theory. In this chapter, we'll make the following points:

---

[1] This is only an average. The division is affected by how close the economy is to capacity operation. If output is far below capacity, an increase in aggregate demand may go almost entirely into increased output. The closer the economy comes to capacity output, the more of a further increase in aggregate demand will go into price changes rather than output changes.

Relevant research studies include Charles Schultz, "Some Macro Foundations for Micro Theory," *Brookings Papers on Economic Activity*, no. 2 (1981), pp. 521–576; Robert J. Gordon, "Price Inertia and Policy Ineffectiveness in the United States, 1890–1980," *Journal of Political Economy* 90 (December 1982), pp. 1087–1117; and Robert J. Gordon, "A Century of Evidence on Wage and Price Stickiness in the United States, the United Kingdom, and Japan," in *Macroeconomics: Prices and Quantities*, ed. James Tobin (Washington: Brookings Institution, 1983), pp. 85–133.

[2] James Tobin, "The Monetarist Counter-Revolution Today: An Appraisal," *Economic Journal*, March 1981, pp. 29–42.

1. It is still true, as it always has been, that a drop in aggregate demand will reduce the inflation rate. Before 1940, this often meant an actual drop in prices, a negative inflation rate. Since 1940, on the other hand, it has typically meant only a *drop in the rate of increase* of prices. In only two years since 1940 (1949 and 1955) has there been even a slight drop in the price level. Prices rise less rapidly in recession, but they still rise. The economy thus seems to have a marked inflationary bias. What are the sources of this bias?

2. The sluggishness of the price level is sometimes expressed by saying, "The best explanation of this year's inflation is last year's inflation." Once inflation is underway, it tends to perpetuate itself from year to year. This built-in tendency is described by such terms as "the underlying rate of inflation." What does this mean?

3. This underlying rate gets disturbed in two main ways. The first is changes in aggregate demand. As aggregate demand rises during an economic upswing, the inflation rate eventually accelerates. Why is this? And why does inflation decelerate so slowly on the downswing?

4. The inflation rate may be disturbed also by a *supply shock,* such as the sharp increases in grain and oil prices in 1973–74 and the second round of oil price increases in 1979. How different is this kind of inflation from traditional demand inflation?

5. Most people don't like inflation. But does it do any economic harm? If so, just how and to whom? This has a bearing on public policy. Thus far, the only sure way of reducing inflation seems to be to cut aggregate demand. This is costly in terms of unemployment and lost output. Are the costs of inflation serious enough to warrant bearing these other costs?

SOURCES OF INFLATIONARY BIAS

We've noted that since World War II, prices seem to move only in one direction—upward. The year-to-year change in the consumer price index since 1950 is shown in Table 9–1. Apart from an insignificant drop in 1955, there are no minus signs in the table. Note also that the inflation rate was much higher in the 1970s than in earlier decades.

While everyone hopes that the inflation rate will be lower in the 80s than the 70s, hardly anyone believes that it can be reduced to zero. Continuing inflation, at higher or lower rates, seems now to be a built-in characteristic of the system.

This inflationary bias arises partly from characteristics of labor markets. In the competitive markets discussed in Chapter 2, any shortage or surplus tends to be eliminated by a price adjustment. If there is a surplus, the price will tend to fall until the surplus is absorbed.

But labor markets, even nonunion labor markets, do not operate in this way. An excess supply (unemployment) does not bring down the

TABLE 9–1
Percentage change in the consumer price index from previous year, 1950–83

Year	Percent Change	Year	Percent Change	Year	Percent Change
1950	1.0	1961	1.0	1972	3.4
1951	7.9	1962	1.1	1973	8.8
1952	2.2	1963	1.2	1974	12.2
1953	0.8	1964	1.3	1975	7.0
1954	0.5	1965	1.7	1976	4.8
1955	−0.4	1966	2.9	1977	6.8
1956	1.5	1967	2.9	1978	9.0
1957	3.6	1968	4.2	1979	13.3
1958	2.7	1969	5.4	1980	12.2
1959	0.8	1970	5.9	1981	8.9
1960	1.6	1971	3.4	1982	3.9
				1983	3.8

Source: *Economic Report of the President, 1984.*

market price. On the contrary, during a recession, wage *increases* continue even though there are plenty of unemployed workers around. It would seem that an employer could save money by laying off the present work force and hiring unemployed workers at a lower wage. Yet employers don't actually do this. Why?

One consideration is that employment is a *continuing* relation, and employers thus find it in their interest to take a long-range view. It costs something to recruit, screen, and hire a new employee. It takes additional expense and time to train the new employee for a specific job in the company. The employer thus has an investment in the worker, which would be lost if he or she were to leave. Considerations of personal relations and worker morale are also important. A company which tried always to pay the lowest possible wage, and which made a practice of replacing present high-wage employees with new lower wage employees, would be shunned by the better workers and would find its production operations hampered by low morale and low efficiency.

So wage cuts are out. On the contrary, workers feel entitled to an annual increase of respectable size. In only 5 of the last 30 years has the increase in employees' hourly compensation been less than 4 percent, and during the 70s, it settled into a range of 6 to 8 percent. Against this, there is typically an increase in labor productivity, which in the 50s and 60s was about 3 percent a year but recently has averaged less than 2 percent. To the extent that the rate of wage increase exceeds the rate of productivity increase, there is an increase in labor cost per unit of output, which eventually gets reflected in prices.

Another reason why the wage system has an upward bias is the heterogeneity of the labor force. Instead of a single labor market, we have thousands of submarkets. Some of these will at any time have an excess of unemployed workers over vacant jobs, while others will have an excess of vacancies over unemployed. Suppose that overall, total vacancies and total unemployed are exactly equal. One might think that with labor supply and demand apparently in balance, the money wage level will remain unchanged. But it will not. In the markets with excess demand for labor, wages will certainly rise. But in the markets with excess supply, wages will not fall. Thus we come out with an increase in the average wage level.

This leads to a broader point. The *average* level of wages is a statistical fiction, obtained by averaging thousands of rates for specific jobs. These specific rates are always changing *relative* to each other, often for good economic reasons. If a particular kind of labor is in abnormally high demand, or if the job is changing so as to require more skill or effort or education and training, it may be reasonable for its wage to rise 5 percent relative to another job which has undergone no change.

This adjustment in *relative* wages could come about in two ways. The wage for the job which has risen in value could go up by 2.5 percent, while that for the other job could go down by 2.5 percent, leaving the average wage level unchanged. But this is not feasible because of the convention against wage cuts. So in practice, the wage for the job whose relative value has risen will go up 5 percent, the wage for the other job will remain unchanged, and the average wage level will rise 2.5 percent.

A parallel argument can be made about changes in relative prices. Such changes are normal and are going on all the time, reflecting differing rates of change in demand and production costs. But suppose there is a strong tradition against reducing prices. Then changes in relative prices can come about *only* through price increases for goods whose relative value has risen. The result is an upward drift of the average price level.

The convention against reducing prices and wages is strengthened by the fact that business and labor leaders no longer fear depression. They believe that government will move quickly to offset any drop in aggregate demand, so that any recession will be short and shallow. Experience since 1945 proves them right in this belief. If businesses did fear a serious drop in demand, they might hesitate to push up prices for fear of losing sales and would also put up stronger resistance to wage increases. But instead, they ride through the (typically short) recession periods without qualms, continuing to raise wages and prices in the confident expectation that government will bail them out.

This leads to our final point: Government policy itself has an inflationary bias. Public opinion polls to the contrary, more voters are more seriously concerned about unemployment than about inflation. So government leans in the direction of fighting unemployment, especially as election time approaches. In addition, government is besieged by interest groups demanding more money: higher minimum wages, higher farm price supports, higher prices for military supplies, and import duties which enable U.S. producers to raise prices. Thus, the specific acts of government, as well as its broader macroeconomic policies, are biased in an inflationary direction.

INFLATIONARY MOMENTUM: THE WAGE-PRICE-WAGE SPIRAL

We said earlier that the best explanation of this year's inflation is last year's inflation. Once an inflationary movement is underway, there is a strong tendency for it to continue at about the same rate. This is the meaning of such phrases as "inflationary momentum," "the underlying rate of inflation," the "wage-price-wage spiral." What is this spiral, and why is it so hard to break?

Suppose that this year, for reasons rooted in the past, the CPI rises by 6 percent. Suppose also that labor productivity (output per worker hour) is rising at 2 percent a year. What will workers expect in the way of wage increases? A bare minimum would be 6 percent, sufficient to offset the rise in living costs and keep real wages unchanged. But if productivity is rising, workers will reason that they are entitled to an increase in *real wages* at least equal to the productivity increase. To provide an increase of 2 percent in real wages, money wages would have to rise by 2 percent more than living costs, that is, by 8 percent.

So let's suppose that workers obtain hourly wage increases of 8 percent to maintain their customary rate of improvement in living standards. The wage increase will raise employers' costs of production, which are mainly labor costs.[3] Costs will not rise by the full 8 percent, since we have assumed that output per worker hour is also rising 2 percent a year. Thus labor cost per unit of output will rise by 8 percent minus 2 percent, or 6 percent.

These higher production costs will soon be reflected in product prices. Just how this happens depends on the nature of competition in the product market. In a purely competitive industry with many producers, each producer simply looks at the market price, looks at the production costs, and decides how much it pays him or her to produce. If costs rise, it will take a higher price to get the producer *to produce as much as before.* Thus the market supply curve shifts upward to the left, and if demand has not changed, the market price will rise.

Where competition is restricted, the process is more visible and dramatic. Consider the common case in which prices are set by tacit cooperation among a small group of producers, usually called *oligopoly.* By one

---

[3] For the private economy as a whole, compensation of employees constitutes about 80 percent of the value of output.

member of the group serving as accepted "price leader," or by informal "signaling" of intentions back and forth through press releases, it is possible to maintain effective control of the product price without openly violating the antitrust laws. The price is an *administered price* rather than a freely fluctuating market price.

How does an oligopolist go about calculating the "right" price at a particular time? The first step is usually to estimate unit cost of production at a "normal" or average rate of plant operation. The company realizes that the actual rate of operation will fluctuate and so will actual production cost, but it does not want to recalculate prices every day. It wants to set a price which will be satisfactory on the average over a period of months. So it works with "standard costs." It then adds a percentage markup to cover general administrative expenses, selling costs, and profit. The size of this markup varies from one industry to another. But in a particular industry at a particular time, one will find companies using similar formulas.

So, under either oligopoly or competition, prices will move up as unit costs rise. If we chart unit labor costs of production against the price level, as is done in Figure 9–1, we see a striking parallel movement of the two series.[4] It could scarcely be otherwise.

In our illustration, then, the 6 percent increase in unit production costs will mean a 6 percent increase in the price level. But this increase in prices will feed back into the next round of wage increases. Since prices have been rising at 6 percent a year and are expected to continue at that rate in the year ahead, workers will expect wage increases large enough to "stay ahead of the cost of living." (Research studies indicate that people's expectations of future inflation are closely related to actual inflation in the recent past.) Once more, they will demand an 8 percent increase in money wages in the hope of achieving a 2 percent gain in real wages. If they get this 8 percent, then unit labor costs and product prices will rise at the expected 6 percent. The expectation is self-fulfilling. This circular reaction is often called the wage-price-wage spiral. And the 6 percent rate of price increase assumed in our illustration is called the underlying rate of inflation. This rate is built into the system in the sense that there is no reason for it to change without some shock to the system from the demand or supply side. How such shocks will affect the underlying rate we'll see in a moment.

The spiraling process is normally accompanied by much bickering over who is to blame for inflation. Workers accuse companies of marking up prices unreasonably, while companies accuse workers of excessive wage demands. This doesn't make much sense. No one is really to blame, or perhaps everyone is equally to blame. This is just the way the system operates.

_____

[4] Data for Figure 9–4 are from the *Economic Report of the President, 1984.*

FIGURE 9–1
Parallelism of unit labor costs and product prices

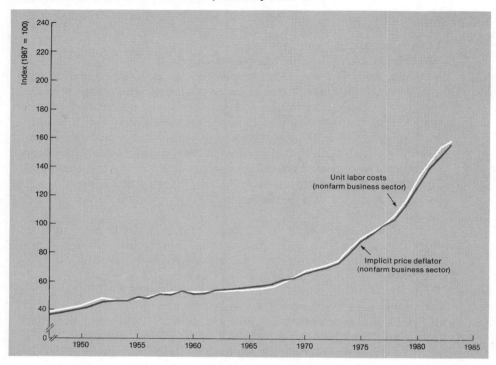

This shows the movement of unit labor costs and of the implicit price deflator for the private nonfarm economy. While there is some variation from year to year, the two indexes move closely together over the long run.

INFLATION AND AGGREGATE DEMAND

While any existing rate of inflation tends to perpetuate itself, the inflation rate does change from year to year. It may change because of an OPEC oil price increase or some other supply shock, which we'll examine in a later section. But it may change also because of fluctuations in aggregate demand over the course of the business cycle.

Starting from the bottom of a recession, with much idle labor and plant capacity, output can be expanded for some time without affecting the inflation rate. But when we pass a certain point, which we'll try to define, the inflation rate begins to accelerate, and this acceleration will continue as long as the upswing continues. When the upswing comes to an end (and the Fed can always bring it to an end) and aggregate demand begins to fall, the inflation rate will also begin to fall. But the deceleration is slow, and inflation normally continues at a lower rate right through the recession. Let's look at these two phases in more detail.

Acceleration on the upswing

The course of events on the upswing is illustrated in Figure 9–2. Note first that in this figure, the initial inflation rate is not zero. It is a positive rate, P, inherited from the past. It is, in fact, the underlying rate of inflation which is perpetuating itself as explained in the last section.

Point A, corresponding to an output of Y, we can interpret as the low point of a recession. Output is well below capacity. The economy now enters a cyclical upswing. As aggregate demand and output rise,

FIGURE 9–2
A model with unemployment *and* inflation

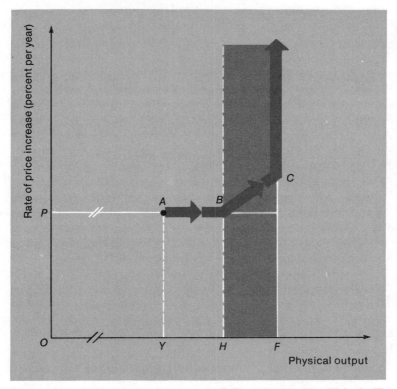

Current output is Y and capacity output is F. There is a positive ("inherited") inflation rate, P. Aggregate demand now begins to rise. When output reaches H, we enter a "high-employment zone," shown by the shaded area. The inflation rate begins to rise, and the closer output comes to F the faster it will rise. At outputs below F, there is some inflation *and* some unemployment.

this for a while will not affect the inflation rate. But beyond some point—shown here by B, corresponding to output H—as demand and output continue to rise, the rate of price increase accelerates. The closer we come to the maximum physical output F, the faster will be the rate of price increase.

The unemployment rate corresponding to point B and output H is usually called the *nonaccelerating inflation rate of unemployment* (NAIRU). Beyond this point, in the output range for H to F, we are in what may be called a *high-employment zone.* As we enter this zone, the inflation rate begins to rise, and the farther we penetrate into this zone, the faster it will rise.

The NAIRU is sometimes referred to as the "natural" rate of unemployment, but this label does not seem useful. It is no more natural than other rates, corresponding to other levels of aggregate demand. It may or may not be regarded as a desirable policy target. Moreover, as we will see in Chapter 13, the NAIRU can be shifted by measures designed to increase the employability of the labor force.

Why does inflation accelerate to the right of point B? We get a useful clue if we think carefully about the meaning of *capacity.* What do we mean by the capacity of a plant? This could mean the maximum it is capable of producing, often called *engineering capacity.* Pushing a plant to this point, however, would involve high production costs.

A more useful concept is the output rate which yields *lowest cost per unit of output.* This is called the *economic capacity* of the plant, and it is always below the physical maximum. Surveys of businesses suggest that economic capacity is typically in the neighborhood of 90 percent of engineering capacity. Output can be stepped up beyond this—to 92 percent, 94 percent, or whatever—but with the consequence of rising costs per unit of output; and producers will expect to be compensated for this by higher prices. This is one reason for increasing price pressure as aggregate demand rises.

A further reason is that the operating rates of different industries are never perfectly *synchronized.* During a recession, some may be operating at 70 percent of capacity, others at 75 percent, others at 80 percent. As aggregate demand rises, some have more production slack than others. Thus, while some industries are still underutilized, others will already have reached or passed the 90 percent point and will be coping with higher costs by raising their prices.[5] But some of the outputs of these industries are inputs for other industries, which will raise the latter's

---

[5] In March 1984, for example, the economy was in the midst of a cyclical upswing. The average rate of factory utilization, which had fallen as low as 69 percent during the 1981–82 recession, was back up to 81 percent. This *average* rate does not seem high enough to put upward pressure on costs and prices. In this same month, however, a number of individual industries reported markedly higher rates: motor vehicles 87.2 percent, textiles 88.2 percent, rubber and plastics 93.3 percent, electrical machinery 92.2 percent, paper and paper products 98.2 percent, basic aluminum 99.0 percent (*The Wall Street Journal,* April 17, 1984, p. 1).

production costs and eventually their prices. So on the upswing, price increases start off gradually, then accelerate as more and more industries reach economic capacity.

Since measuring the amount of unused plant capacity turns out to be complicated, perhaps we can do better by looking at the amount of unutilized labor. The published unemployment rate is often used as an indicator of labor force slack. But this measure has its own set of complications.

The unemployment rate, of course, can never be reduced to zero. There are seasonal fluctuations in agriculture, construction, and other industries which lead to some loss of labor time. In addition, there are always workers hunting new jobs—because they are entering or reentering the labor force, or have been laid off, or have quit an unsatisfactory job in the hope of bettering themselves. Finding new jobs takes time— time to inquire of friends and relatives, visit the state employment service, apply directly to companies, weed out acceptable from unacceptable jobs. Companies also need time to interview and test applicants and to select among them.

This unemployment in between jobs, resulting from normal turnover in the labor market, is called *frictional unemployment.* Suppose we estimate frictional (and seasonal) unemployment at 4 percent of the labor force. We observe that the actual unemployment rate is 7 percent. It would seem that the extra 3 percent constitutes "excess unemployment," resulting from a deficiency of aggregate demand.

Simple? Not so simple. First, the level of frictional unemployment itself depends partly on aggregate demand. New jobs will be found faster when vacancies are plentiful than when they are scarce. George Perry has estimated that at a national unemployment rate of 3 percent, a prime-age male worker would take an average of 4.3 weeks to find a new job.[6] At an unemployment rate of 6 percent, however, his average length of job search would be 6.6 weeks.

Next, the official unemployment rate is only one of several possible measures. It counts all those who have no job and are "actively seeking" work. But some of these may have been out of work a week and will shortly be reemployed, while others may have been out of work for a year. What about parttime workers who would like additional work? What about "discouraged workers" who have stopped seeking work because they are convinced that jobs are unavailable, and so are no longer counted as in the labor force?

Earlier, we defined the unemployment rate below which the inflation rate will begin to rise as the *nonaccelerating inflation rate of unemployment* (NAIRU). A good estimate of this rate is obviously important for policy purposes. Available estimates suggest that the NAIRU is considerably

---

[6] George L. Perry, "Unemployment Flows in the U.S. Labor Market," *Brookings Papers on Economic Activity,* no. 2 (1972), pp. 245–78.

higher today than it was a generation ago. One reason for this is a changed composition of the labor force. Because of the baby boom of 1945–60, plus the steady growth in the percentage of women choosing to work, the proportion of young people and women in the labor force is substantially higher today than it was in the 50s. In 1951, women formed 29.6 percent of the labor force, while by 1983 this had risen to 43.5 percent. The corresponding percentages for workers under 25 were 17.4 percent in 1951 and 21.7 percent in 1983.

These changes have tended to raise the unemployment rate existing at any level of aggregate demand. Women typically have higher unemployment rates than men, mainly because they leave and reenter the labor force more frequently, and new jobs are not found instantaneously. Teenagers have much higher unemployment rates than older workers, partly because of a good deal of job shopping and job changing is normal in the first few years of employment, partly because the minimum wage system and other legal requirements tilt the scales against inexperienced workers with relatively low productivity.

Another significant development is an improvement in the sources of support for unemployed workers. Unemployment compensation, welfare, food stamps, and other government transfer payments have increased in volume, and these payments are nontaxable. Thus there may be little difference between what a worker could earn, after taxes, in a low-wage job and the amount he or she can receive without working. Moreover, if husband and wife are working, which is increasingly the pattern, one person can keep the household going while the other is job hunting. The result is to make workers more choosy, more leisurely in searching the market, more willing to reject jobs which do not meet their wage and other requirements. From one point of view, it is desirable that the unemployed should not be pressured into accepting undesirable jobs. At the same time, this raises the amount of unemployment which can be regarded as normal.

These developments have substantially raised the NAIRU, that is, the rate below which the inflation rate will be not merely positive but *rising*. The tightness of the labor market is probably best judged by the unemployment rate for men aged 25–55. The noninflationary rate of unemployment for this group is estimated at about 3.0 percent. As of the 1950s, this would have corresponded to an overall unemployment rate of about 4.5 percent.

Because of the structural changes noted above, however, the gap between the two rates has widened. An unemployment rate of 3 percent for prime-age males now corresponds to about a 6 percent rate overall.[7]

---

[7] For estimates and supporting data, see Michael L. Wachter, "The Changing Cyclical Responsiveness to Wage Inflation," *Brookings Papers on Economic Activity,* no. 1 (1976), pp. 115–59; and Philip Cagan, "The Reduction of Inflation and the Magnitude of Unemployment," in *Contemporary Economic Problems,* ed. William Fellner (Washington, D.C.: American Enterprise Institute, 1977), pp. 15–22.

The alternatives facing policymakers today are thus more uncomfortable than they were a generation ago. It appears that we have to put up with unemployment considerably higher than what used to be considered normal, or with an inflation rate above the historical norm, or perhaps both together. At the same time, this line of reasoning provides some basis for optimism about future unemployment trends. Birthrates have fallen sharply since 1960, and from here on the proportion of young people in the labor force will be declining. This aging of the labor force should be accompanied by a downward drift of the NAIRU.

There have been efforts also to estimate the noninflationary (average) rate of utilization of plant capacity. This is currently estimated at about 86 percent, meaning that when the average rises above that level, enough plants will be operating in the 90+ range to produce a significant *increase* in the inflation rate.

Beyond the NAIRU point, we enter a *high-employment zone,* shown by the shaded area in Figure 9–2. The right-hand edge of the zone is maximum physical output, which is never approached in peacetime and so is a rather academic figure. The left-hand edge of the zone is the rate of output above which *the inflation rate begins to rise* because unemployment has fallen below and plant utilization has risen above the noninflationary level.

THINK ABOUT THIS

1. Suppose we had an accurate estimate of the NAIRU. Could we then say that government should not try to reduce unemployment beyond this rate? Why, or why not?
2. Find out what has been happening recently to the unemployment rate, the plant capacity utilization rate, and the inflation rate. Knowing these things, would you judge that government should be trying to raise aggregate demand, restrain aggregate demand, or neither?

Slow deceleration on the downswing

Output is not always growing. There is a business cycle. After several years of expansion, the upswing typically ceases and aggregate demand begins to fall. This will usually reduce the rate of price increase, but only gradually, and it will not necessarily bring it back to the level from which we started. *The path ABC is not reversible.*

To a limited extent, the wage-price-wage spiral goes into reverse during recession. As the labor market softens, the rate of wage increase slackens. Cost pressure on producers is further reduced by a drop in raw material prices. Some producers cut their markups a bit when demand is weak, either openly or through concealed price reductions. The rate of increase in the CPI declines somewhat, and this tends further to reduce the rate of wage increase.

This downward spiraling, however, is slow and sluggish. Statistical estimates suggest that it would take five years or more of high unemployment to cut the inflation rate from, say, 10 percent to 4 percent. In actuality, recessions typically last only for a year or so. Thus, before the inflation rate has had time to decelerate very much, the economy is off on the next upswing.

The behavior of the inflation rate and the unemployment rate during recent business cycles is shown in Figure 9–3. Several things stand out from this figure. First, recession does tend to reduce the inflation rate, though only moderately and with some lag. The recessions of 1953–54, 1957–58, 1969–70, 1973–75, and 1981–82, were each followed by a noticeable drop in the inflation rate. Second, the characteristic rate of inflation has drifted upward over the years—higher in the 60s then the 50s and still higher in the 70s. Third, the characteristic rate of unemployment has also drifted upward, from a range of 4–6 percent to one of 6–8 percent, partly for reasons already explained. The so-called discomfort index, obtained by *adding* the inflation rate and the unemployment rate, which before 1970 was typically below 10 percent, has recently been closer to 20 percent.

Inflation and market power

Are there any villains in the inflation picture? Business leaders and labor leaders tend to blame each other for keeping the process going. The public tends to blame both. Some economists argue that inflation arises from excessive demands by trade unions and business oligopolists, leading to a "cost push" on the price level. This has been termed *seller's inflation* and has been urged as an alternative to the demand explanation of inflation.

Two separate questions are involved: First, do unions and oligopolists accelerate the rate of wage and price increases on the upswing? Second, do unions and oligopolists prevent wage and price cuts on the downswing? The answers need not be the same.

On the upswing, unions might raise the rate of wage increase in two ways: (1) by demanding and winning larger increases for themselves and (2) by setting high wage targets which are then imitated by nonunion workers and employers—the so-called spillover effect. But neither of these things seems actually to happen. The evidence suggests that, on the upswing, wage increases in unionized establishments are somewhat *smaller* than in nonunion establishments. The reason is that union contracts normally run for three years, with annual wage increases scheduled in ad-

FIGURE 9–3
Clockwise circling at loftier levels

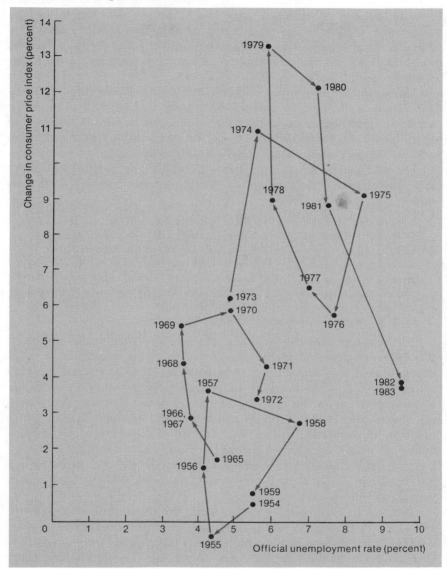

The recessions of 1957–58, 1969–70, 1973–75, and 1981–82 did bring a slowdown of the inflation rate but with considerable lag. Note also that each of these cycles is higher than the previous one—the "inherited" rate of inflation has been rising.

vance. So in a year of high employment, some of the wage increases in union plants were negotiated as long as two years ago when aggregate demand and the inflation rate were lower. Union wages lag on the upswing, and the advantage of union over nonunion workers decreases. There is no evidence either of a spillover effect from the union sector, which includes less than one quarter of American workers, to the larger nonunion sector.[8]

The sluggishness of union wages has an opposite effect during recession. Then, even though unemployment may be high and rising, large wage increases negotiated in previous prosperous years will still go into effect. Union wage increases tend to exceed nonunion increases, and union workers regain the advantage they lost on the upswing.

The evidence is similar as regards oligopoly price behavior. Scherer finds no evidence of a "profit push" in concentrated industries. He concludes:

> The weight of the statistical evidence suggests that concentrated industries do exhibit somewhat different pricing propensities over time than their more atomistic competitors. They reduce prices and (perhaps more importantly) price-cost margins by less in response to a demand slump and increase them by less in the boom phase. They may also pass on unit cost changes more slowly. . . . Statistical studies of price movements over the span of several business cycles confirm that concentrated industries have not increased their prices abnormally rapidly.[9]

To the extent that market power has an independent influence, then, this influence is felt on the downswing of the cycle rather than the upswing. Indeed, the main difference between pre-1945 and post-1945 price behavior involves the behavior of prices on the downswing. In earlier times prices rose on the upswing of the cycle, but they also fell during the downswing. In the 10 cycles which occurred between 1891 and 1929 (omitting the abnormal war period 1914–20), the average rate of increase in the wholesale price index during upswings was a bit under 4 percent per year. But prices fell in every downswing except one at an average rate of slightly over 4 percent per year, thus cancelling out the upside increases.

Today prices still rise on the upswing, but the decline on the downswing has vanished. What happens now is that prices move upward briskly during prosperity periods, rise a bit more slowly during recession, then accelerate again during the next expansion. This is often termed a *ratchet movement* of the price level, or *one-way flexibility* of prices.

It would be simplistic to attribute this changed behavior entirely to

---

[8] On this point, see Robert J. Flanagan, "Wage Interdependence in Unionized Labor Markets," *Brookings Papers on Economic Activity,* no. 3 (1976), pp. 635–82.

[9] F. M. Scherer, *Industrial Market Structure and Economic Performance,* 2d ed. (Chicago: Rand McNally, 1980), p. 357.

union and oligopoly power, but this must have contributed to it. Trade unions and oligopolies not only keep a firm floor under wages and prices but also keep them moving upward even during recession. They are encouraged in doing this by a belief that the recession will be short and that government will intervene promptly to "get this country moving again."

Inflation and money supply

Some monetary economists would say that this explanation of inflation is overelaborate and even wrong. Surely the basic source of inflation is much more simple: an unduly rapid increase in money supply. In Milton Friedman's classic phrase, "Inflation is always and everywhere a monetary phenomenon." We saw in Chapter 7 that the strong uptrend of prices since 1950 has been paralleled by a similar uptrend in money supply. What, if anything, can we conclude from this?

A statement that the price level could not have continued to rise without a parallel rise in money supply may be quite true, in an arithmetical sense, but may at the same time not be very useful. It doesn't really tell us how to get from an 8 percent inflation rate to a 4 percent or a zero rate. Nor does it demonstrate that the Fed should have acted differently than it actually did.

Consider the following situation, which is close to what the Fed actually faces. The underlying inflation rate is 6 percent. Real output is expected to grow in the year ahead by 3 percent. If Goldfeld's estimates are correct, the demand for money will rise by about 8 percent—6 percent to offset the price rise and an additional 2 percent because of the 3 percent increase in real income.

What is the Fed supposed to do in this situation? It could say that its main job is to maintain stable growth of output and employment. This can be interpreted as implying reasonable stability of interest rates. But interest rates will remain stable only if money supply expands at about the same rate as money demand. So the Fed might raise money supply by 8 percent and say that it is simply accommodating the demand for money built into the system. If it does this, it will probably be accused of aiding and abetting inflation.

Suppose, on the other hand, that the Fed says "our prime responsibility is to maintain a stable level of prices. An inflation rate of 6 percent is unacceptable, and we must try to bring it down." In pursuit of this policy, the Fed might try to hold the rate of money supply increase to 4 percent. With money demand growing at 8 percent, this will mean a rise in interest rates, which will have a braking effect on aggregate demand and perhaps bring on a recession. The slowing down of economic activity will tend to reduce the inflation rate, though only gradually. In this case, the Fed will doubtless be attacked for causing idle capacity and unemployment. James Tobin has underlined the dilemma:

> Clearly the rate of inflation would be much lower today if the path of *MV* ever since 1960 or even 1970 had been fairly steadily held to, say, 4 percent a year. . . . What is far from clear is that the paths of real variables—output, employment, investment—would have approached the paths actually realized. . . . The Federal Reserve would not have accommodated the fiscal stimuli of early 1960s, the fiscal excesses of the Vietnam War, the wage explosion of the early 1970s, the later shocks from increases in OPEC prices, and the inflationary pressures these events generated. Economists today differ, and economic historians doubtless will also, about the shape of such a counterfactual rerun of these two decades. I certainly cannot prove my suspicion that the path of real variables would have been disastrously worse. I do think that it is disingenuous to give the impression, so prevalent today, that the whole inflationary experience could have been costlessly avoided by conservative demand management.[10]

Those who adhere strongly to a monetary explanation of inflation are really saying that they prefer a policy of braking the money supply as hard and as long as necessary to bring the inflation rate down. This is a major policy issue, and we must leave further analysis of it to Chapters 12 and 13.

SUPPLY SHOCKS AND INFLATION

The traditional explanations of inflation—monetarist, neo-Keynesian, or whatever—emphasize the behavior of aggregate demand. During the 1970s, however, it became increasingly apparent that the price level can be jolted also by shocks from the supply side. Some of these came from the international economy, including jumps in crude oil prices and grain prices and a substantial decline in the value of the dollar relative to other currencies. On the domestic front, there was a marked slowdown in productivity growth, which is not directly under the control of government. But there were also government actions which added to business costs, and these were quickly translated into higher prices, notably a sharp increase in payroll taxes for social security and increases in the legal minimum wage. Such actions have been described as "self-inflicted wounds."

Recent studies by Jon Frye and Robert Gordon suggest that most of the acceleration of inflation during the 70s resulted from these supply side developments rather than from the behavior of aggregate demand:

---

[10] James Tobin, "Stabilization Policy Ten Years After," *Brookings Papers on Economic Activity,* no. 1 (1980), pp. 43–44.

Why was inflation so variable between 1971 and 1980? And why did inflation accelerate from 5 percent in early 1971 to 10 percent in early 1980? Our basic equation explains the high variance of inflation mainly as a result of swings in the effect of Nixon controls, the deviation of productivity from trend, the relative prices of food and energy, and the effective exchange rate, with an additional minor contribution made by the aggregate demand variables and by social security tax changes. The overall acceleration of inflation during the past decade is explained by the adverse contribution of most of the variables.[11]

The two oil price explosions

The oil story is well known. During the winter of 1973–74, a group of oil-exporting nations (the Organization of Petroleum Exporting Countries, or OPEC) raised the price of crude oil from $2 per barrel to around $10 per barrel. Since much of our crude oil consumption is imported, the price impact was substantial. In the northeastern states, the price of gasoline went up by about one third and the price of home heating oil doubled. Because of the widespread industrial use of oil as fuel and raw material, the indirect effects were also substantial. The costs of oil-fired power generating plants rose, so the price of electricity jumped sharply. Truckers' operating costs rose sharply, and so did their freight rates. Petroleum is the basis for a wide range of plastics and petrochemical products, the prices of which were also forced upward. All this added several percentage points to the CPI.

A second round of major price increases occurred in 1979–81, when oil supplies were disrupted by the Iranian revolution and the Iran–Iraq war. In 1979, prices doubled, from about $14 per barrel to $28 per barrel. They peaked at about $35 per barrel before declining moderately in 1982–83. Again, the price impact in the United States was substantial, contributing to double-digit inflation during these years.

Consider what happens when the United States is obliged to pay out many more billions of dollars to foreign oil producers. These dollars are available to be spent on American goods, and a large proportion of them are spent in this way. Our exports to the OPEC countries have risen somewhat in line with our oil imports. In large measure, we pay for goods with goods. But this means that a larger percentage of our national output is going abroad, and a smaller share remains for American consumers. The result is a decline in real income per capita and in American living standards.

---

[11] Jon Frye and Robert J. Gordon, "Government Intervention in the Inflation Process: The Econometrics of 'Self-Inflicted Wounds'," working paper no. 550 (Cambridge, Mass.: National Bureau of Economic Research, 1980), p. 17. See also, by the same authors, "The Variance and Acceleration of Inflation in the 1970s: Alternative Explanatory Models and Methods," working paper no. 551 (Cambridge, Mass.: National Bureau of Economic Research, 1980).

There is no way by which this cut in real income can be avoided. But will Americans understand this and be willing to accept it? Will they simply pay the higher prices for petroleum products without demanding offsetting wage and salary increases? If they do, the inflationary impact will be confined to petroleum products. But very likely they will not. The idea that any price increase can be and should be offset by at least an equivalent wage increase is deeply ingrained. It is built into many union contracts, into social security pensions, and into other forms of income. So the oil impact will probably spread to the general wage-price level and will raise the underlying rate of inflation. This happened in 1973–74 and again in 1979–81.

A further effect—or perhaps the same effect viewed from another angle—is that U.S. consumers who are forced to spend more of their income on gasoline, heating oil, electricity, and so on will have less to spend on other things. There is a negative effect on demand, output, and employment in nonoil industries. Thus it is quite possible to have an increase in the unemployment rate and the inflation rate at the same time. Such a situation of "stagflation" or "slumpflation" has caused a vast outpouring of words over the past decade. It is often said that the rules of the economic game have changed and that economists no longer know what they are doing. This is a misunderstanding. The pre-1973 rules are still in place, but something new has been added.

This kind of supply shock worsens the dilemma facing policymakers. How should the Fed respond to the jumps in petroleum product prices? It could adopt a permissive policy and simply increase money supply enough to accommodate the higher price level. But this will be criticized by many as an inflationary policy.

Suppose, on the other hand, that it is determined to enforce price stability. This would mean forcing *down* the price of nonoil products enough to offset the unavoidable increase in oil product prices. It would mean severe restraint on money supply and a marked rise in interest rates, which would intensify the slump side of the slumpflation problem. The Fed did lean in this direction in 1973–74, and again in 1981–82, which helped to make these two recessions the most severe of the postwar period.

Instability of grain prices

A second channel through which the international economy affects the U.S. inflation rate is the sharp fluctuations in prices of wheat, corn, and other food grains. The United States and Canada are now the only major grain exporters, and most other countries are importers. So a major crop failure anywhere in the world, or a poor crop year in North America, can drive up grain prices suddenly and sharply. Food products have a weight of about one quarter in the CPI. So if the price of foodstuffs jumps by 20 percent, this alone will raise the CPI by 5 percent. Such an increase tends to generate wage increases and to get built into the underlying rate of inflation in the same way as an oil price increase.

Between January 1973 and December 1974, retail food prices rose by about 36 percent, raising the CPI by about 8 points. Behind this were two years of poor crops (1972 and 1973) in many of the less-developed countries and also in the Soviet Union. This led to a large increase in foreign purchases of U.S. grain, which reduced our grain reserves to a very low level. The price of wheat shot up from $2 to $5 a bushel, while corn rose from $1.50 a bushel to $3.50. Since cattle and hogs are fed partly on grain, livestock producers' costs rose rapidly and so did meat prices.

A second spurt of about 50 percent in farm prices occurred in 1978–80. Grain crops in 1980 were below normal in the United States and much below normal for the largest importer, the Soviet Union, and world grain reserves were once more seriously depleted. Food price shocks, like oil price shocks, are independent of the level of aggregate demand in the United States and are not readily countered by the usual weapons of monetary policy.

The dollar exchange rate

Until 1971, the U.S. dollar had a fixed value in relation to foreign currencies. A dollar bought about 4 German marks, 5 French francs, 350 Japanese yen, and so on. In mid-1971, this system broke down, for reasons which will be discussed in Chapter 16. The world moved to a system of *flexible* or floating exchange rates, under which the value of a currency moves up or down in response to changes in supply and demand. Under this system the value of the dollar floated gradually downward during the 70s. By 1979, the dollar was down about 20 percent relative to a basket of major foreign currencies and down about 50 percent relative to such strong currencies as the German mark, the Swiss franc, and the Japanese yen.

This aggravated the inflation problem by raising the prices of goods which we import from other countries. Suppose that in 1970, a VW car was selling in Germany for 10,000 marks. With $1 = 4 marks, the import price in the United States was 10,000/4 = $2,500. Suppose that in 1980, the car was still selling for 10,000 marks (though actually, prices have been rising in Germany as everywhere else). But by 1980, a dollar would buy only about two marks. So the import price would be 10,000/2 = $5,000. Any car shopper knows that German and Japanese cars were much more expensive in 1980 than in 1970. The same was true of other imported goods, and all this went to boost the CPI.

Since 1980, on the other hand, the dollar has strengthened considerably. By the end of 1983, its value relative to a basket of foreign currencies was about 25 percent higher than in 1980. Reversing the arithmetic used above, you can see that imported goods would now be cheaper than before—or at least, in an inflationary world, their prices would be rising less rapidly. This was an important factor in the decline of the U.S. inflation rate between 1981 and 1983.

Slower productivity growth

Another supply-side development which has aggravated the inflation problem is a reduction in the rate of productivity growth. Since 1970, the rate of increase in output per worker-hour has been only half as high as it was from 1950–1970, and in some recent years, productivity has actually declined. The reasons for this slowdown have not yet been sorted out. Several things may have contributed: some decline in research and development activity as a percentage of business sales; some decline in the rate of increase in the nation's capital stock; a more rapid increase in the labor force, which further reduces the growth of *capital per worker* on which output per worker depends heavily; and a higher proportion of young and inexperienced workers in the labor force.

Whatever the reason, slower productivity growth contributes to inflationary pressure. If productivity is rising at 3 percent a year, then a 7 percent rate of wage increase will mean an increase of $7 - 3 = 4$ percent in unit labor costs and presumably in the price level. But if productivity is rising at only 1 percent a year, the same 7 percent rate of wage increase will raise unit labor costs and prices by 6 percent. So, either wage expectations have to be lowered, the inflation rate has to be higher, or some combination of the two will occur.

Improvement in real income per worker has to come mainly from increased output per worker. Because of slower productivity growth, living standards for the average American have recently been rising more slowly than we have been accustomed to in the past. This is naturally an unpleasant development, hard for most people to understand and accept. It may account for some of the restiveness over wages and incomes during the 70s. Many people may have responded to a slower growth of real income by demanding more money in the hope that this would somehow yield more goods.

THINK ABOUT THIS

Would you expect the inflation rate in the 80s to be about the same as in the 70s? Higher? Lower? Explain.

Does the inflation rate which you expect have any bearing on your own financial planning?

The 1981–83 disinflation: Good management or good luck?

The economy is full of surprises. The rate of increase in the GNP price index, after peaking at 9.8 percent in 1980, fell to 6.4 percent in 1982 and 4.3 percent in 1983. The Reagan administration naturally took credit for the drop in inflation, but much of the credit belongs elsewhere.

The Federal Reserve followed a generally restrictive policy from late 1979 through 1981, and the rate of increase in M1 fell from 8.3 percent in 1979 to less than 5 percent in mid-1982. This helped to bring on a six-month recession in 1980 and a larger recession from mid-1981 to the end of 1982. This by itself would have lowered the inflation rate somewhat. While the administration did not instigate this monetary restraint (which indeed had begun in the Carter presidency), it did not object to it either, and signified its general approval by reappointing Paul Volcker as Chairman of the Fed in 1983.

But there was good luck as well. Most of the adverse supply shocks which we noted as operating in the 70s turned into favorable supply shocks in the early 80s. As consumer nations moved to conserve oil by substituting other fuels, an oil glut developed and the price of crude oil dropped about 20 percent from 1981–83. Grain prices at the farm also fell about 10 percent in 1981 and 1982 because of bumper crops, which slowed the rise of food prices to consumers. The U.S. dollar rose substantially in value compared with foreign currencies, for reasons to be explained in a later chapter, which reduced the dollar cost of imported goods. Productivity growth remained low through 1982 but revived strongly in 1983.

These favorable supply developments—which unfortunately are reversible—may explain half or more of the recent inflation slowdown.

INFLATION AND ITS CONSEQUENCES: WHO GAINS AND WHO LOSES?

What are the consequences of inflation? Whom does it benefit and whom does it hurt?

We must distinguish at the outset between *anticipated* and *unanticipated* inflation. If inflation were perfectly anticipated, it need not hurt anyone because people could protect against it. If it were certain that the price level will be 5 percent higher a year from now, a union bargaining for a wage increase could simply add 5 percent to whatever *real* increase it is demanding. Similarly, a bank considering a loan, and wanting a *real* return of 5 percent on this loan, could simply set the *money* interest rate at 10 percent.

But in actuality, the inflation rate varies from year to year, and so inflation is never fully anticipated. To the extent that it is not, it brings about a redistribution of *real income* and *real wealth*. There is a redistribution of real income, because while most people's money incomes will be rising during an inflation, they will not rise at the same rate. Suppose that this year the CPI goes up 10 percent. Some people will have had an income increase of 15 percent: they are winners. But others will have had an increase of only 5 percent: they are losers. The principle is this: *Increases in the general price level bring about shifts in the distribution of real income from those whose dollar incomes are relatively inflexible to those whose dollar incomes are relatively flexible.*

While this principle has been known for a long time, it has proved difficult to sort out actual winners and losers. One earlier idea—that wages typically fail to keep up with prices, so that wage earners lose and profit recipients gain—has not stood up well against the evidence. In actuality, wage earners seem on the average to more than hold their own. A more recent surmise is that losers are found mainly among the very poor and the very rich. The rich depend heavily on fixed interest payments from bonds, whose real value shrinks with inflation. Many of the poor depend on government transfer payments, whose money value does not get adjusted upward as rapidly as prices rise.

How does inflation bring about a redistribution of *real wealth?* Consider a simple example, exaggerated to emphasize the point: Ms. A borrows $100 from Mr. B for one year at 6 percent interest. Suppose that during the year the price level doubles. Then when Ms. A pays Mr. B the $106 she owes him, she is paying with dollars which are worth only half as much in real purchasing power as the dollars which she borrowed. Ms. A is repaying with the equivalent of $53 at the old price level. Obviously, Ms. A will have gained real wealth and Mr. B will have lost. Here the principle is: *Inflation brings about a redistribution of real wealth in favor of debtors at the expense of creditors.*

A less obvious effect of inflation is that it redistributes income from the private sector to government. This is because taxes are based not on real income but on money income, and for the personal income tax, the rate rises as one moves up to higher brackets. Wage-price inflation moves people up into higher money income brackets, whether or not their real income has risen. The proportion of income paid in taxes rises, and government revenue increases faster than GNP. The fact that the Treasury benefits from inflation may be one reason why political leaders are not as hostile to it as they profess to be.

It has been suggested that this effect could be offset by "indexing" the brackets in the income tax schedule. If the CPI went up 10 percent, the minimum of each bracket would also go up 10 percent. Thus, people would not automatically be shifted into higher brackets, and the real burden of taxation would remain unchanged. Indexing of tax brackets was put into effect in Canada several years ago. A similar system for the United States was enacted by Congress in 1981 as part of the Reagan tax-reduction package. It is scheduled to become effective in 1985. But since it involves a loss of revenue, and since prospective federal budget deficits are very large, this action may possibly be reversed by some later Congress.

Inflation distorts business calculations of cost and profit. Profits are overstated in at least two ways. First, under some methods of inventory valuation, a rising price level raises the value of a company's holdings of raw materials and goods in process, even with no change in the physical quantities. This appears on the books as a profit, though it has nothing to do with production operations. A second problem involves depreciation allowances, a business cost intended to provide for replacement of plant and equipment. Say a company pays $1 million for a machine with a 10-year operating life. Each year the company dutifully sets aside $100,000 for depreciation, and at the end of 10 years it has $1 million available to buy a new machine. But surprise! The machine now costs $2 million, so the depreciation reserve is inadequate. The company has deducted too little from profits each year to replace its equipment. Its apparent profit has thus been overstated.

Why does this matter? Partly because the corporate income tax is based on reported money profit rather than adjusted or true profit. To the extent that profits are overstated, companies, like individuals, are being overtaxed.

Inflation, or more correctly *expected inflation,* raises the level of nominal interest rates. A lender is naturally interested in the *real* rate of return on the loan. If the inflation rate is 2 percent, then a nominal interest rate of 7 percent will yield a real return of $7 - 2 = 5$ percent. But if the inflation rate is 10 percent, it will take an interest rate of 15 percent to yield the same real return. So interest rates will be marked up to reflect lenders' expectation of inflation in the year ahead. Only on this basis can one understand the lending rates of 15 and even 20 percent which were common in the late 70s. People considering buying a house on mortgage or a car on time will look at, and possibly be deterred by, the high nominal rate they must pay; and it will not be much comfort to explain to them that the real rate is much lower.

There is a considerable cost from frequent price and wage adjustments. Most prices and wages are not simply determined by an impersonal market. They have to be made by deliberate decision. In an atmosphere of price stability, where one can rely on custom and precedent, this is fairly easy. There are customary differentials between wages for different kinds of labor, customary price-cost margins for businesses, and so on. But under inflation, decisions have to be made more frequently, with less clear precedent, and often generating greater antagonism among contending groups. Moreover, since decisions are made at different times, some prices and wages will always be out of balance at a particular time. The price signals which we count on for effective allocation of resources are distorted.

The popular perception that rapid inflation is an expensive nuisance thus has a solid foundation. The economy works better when everyone expects price stability and when this expectation turns out to be right. What can be done to control the price level will be discussed in Chapters 12–13.

THINK ABOUT THIS

1. How would you evaluate the economic costs of inflation as compared with the economic costs of unemployment? Which should government work harder to reduce? Does this depend on what the rates are at a particular time?
2. Can you think of any actions government could take which would reduce *both* the unemployment rate and the inflation rate? (More on this in Chapter 12, but it's a good idea to start thinking about it now.)

NEW CONCEPTS

inflation
inflation, demand
inflation, cost (or sellers')
inflationary bias
wage-price-wage spiral
underlying rate of inflation
unit labor cost
oligopoly
administered price
markup pricing
capacity, engineering
capacity, economic
capacity utilization
unemployment rate

unemployment, frictional
unemployment, demand
unemployment, nonaccelerating
    inflation rate of (NAIRU)
high employment
high-employment zone
supply shock
inflation, anticipated
inflation, unanticipated
income redistribution, through
    inflation
wealth redistribution, through
    inflation

SUMMARY

1. Inflation is a rise in the general price level or a decline in the real purchasing power of the dollar. It is measured by the price indexes discussed in Chapter 3.

2. The American economy now has a marked inflationary bias, in

the sense that the general price level continues to rise even during periods of slack demand.

3. Any existing rate of inflation tends to perpetuate itself through the wage-price-wage spiral. The rate of increase in unit labor costs, that is, the rate of wage increase minus the rate of productivity increase, is usually called *the underlying rate of inflation.*

4. As output rises during an economic upswing, the inflation rate will eventually begin to rise. The point at which this happens can be estimated either in terms of the average utilization rate of plant capacity or in terms of the nonaccelerating inflation rate of unemployment (NAIRU). The NAIRU is currently estimated at about 6 percent.

5. As output levels off or falls during an economic downswing, the inflation rate tends to fall, but only moderately and with some lag.

6. The influence of sellers with market power—trade unions and oligopolists—is felt mainly on the downswing rather than the upswing. By resisting wage or price reductions, and indeed continuing to make substantial increases, they help to maintain inflationary momentum even during a recession.

7. The price level and the money supply tend to move upward together. But this does not reveal the chain of causation, nor does it provide a clear guide to Federal Reserve policy.

8. The inflation rate may rise also because of supply shocks, such as OPEC oil price increases, increases in the world price of food grains, or increases in the dollar price of imported goods because of the declining value of the dollar. Such shocks are especially hard to counter by the usual monetary instruments.

9. Unanticipated inflation redistributes real income from those whose dollar incomes are relatively fixed, and it redistributes real wealth from creditors to debtors. It tends to redistribute resources from the private sector to government through a rise in tax collections as a percent of GNP. Inflation also distorts business calculations of cost and profit and has other harmful side effects.

TO LEARN MORE

The subject matter of this chapter is covered in the standard texts on macroeconomics listed in Chapter 4. For a perceptive discussion, see Robert M. Solow, "The Intelligent Citizen's Guide to Inflation," *The Public Interest,* Winter 1975, pp. 30–66.

■ 10 ■

Taxes, Public Spending, and Public Debt

Let us all be happy and live within our means, even if we have to borrow the money to do it with.

ARTEMUS WARD

INTRODUCTION

Government affects aggregate demand in three main ways:

1. It buys goods and hires labor to produce *public goods*. This is mainly an activity of state and local governments, which produce education, health services, police and fire protection, streets and roads, and a great variety of other goods. Federal production of public goods is dominated by the defense budget.

Total output by all levels of government is shown by the *G* schedule in the aggregate demand diagrams of Chapter 5. A rise in the *G* schedule raises aggregate demand, while a reduction lowers demand.

2. It makes *transfer payments* to individuals. This is mainly a function of the federal government. The largest items are pension payments under Social Security and medical cost payments under Medicare and Medicaid. Other important items are transfers to farmers under agricultural programs, unemployment compensation, aid to families with dependent children (AFDC or "welfare"), food stamps, and housing subsidies.

This has been much the fastest growing part of the federal budget. In 1958, transfer payments by the federal government were only $22 billion. In 1983, they amounted to some $450 billion.[1] This compares with federal purchases of goods and services of only $275 billion in 1983. The federal government is thus engaged mainly in redistributing income, and only secondarily in producing public goods.

In government budget accounting, transfers are classified as an expen-

---

[1] This includes interest payments on the federal debt of about $90 billion, which are classified in the national accounts as transfer payments. But it does not include some $85 billion in grants-in-aid to state and local governments, part of which goes into transfer payments at those levels of government.

diture, because government must find money to finance them. For economic analysis, however, we use a different classification:

Government expenditure means government purchases of goods and services, which equals output of public goods. Transfer payments are negative taxes, which reduce total tax payments.

Government expenditure determines the height of the G schedule. Transfer payments, on the other hand, go into consumers' disposable income and thus affect the C schedule. An increase in transfer payments, like a cut in tax rates, tends to *raise* the C schedule. A cut in transfer payments, or an increase in tax rates, tends to *lower* the C schedule.

Positive tax payments minus transfer payments we define as *net taxes*. This figure shows the net amount which government is taking out of consumers' pockets.

3. In order to finance government expenditure and transfer payments, government levies *taxes* on businesses and individuals. The federal government relies mainly on the payroll tax, the personal income tax, and the corporate profits tax. State governments rely mainly on sales and income taxes, while local governments get most of their income from personal property taxes.

All tax payments are borne eventually by individuals. Taxes which are paid by businesses in the first instance, such as payroll taxes and corporate profit taxes, are shifted mainly to consumers or employees. Anything which cannot be shifted to these groups is borne by the stockholders of the corporation. Different types of taxes, of course, fall on different groups of individuals, which is why there is always so much controversy over the tax system.

Because government is so prominent in the economy, its activities are studied in both microeconomics and macroeconomics, but the focus of attention is different. Microeconomics is concerned with the components of government expenditure and tax revenue. It asks questions such as: How can we judge whether we are producing too much or too little of a particular public good? How do transfer payments change the distribution of income among households? Is there any economic basis for judging the desirability of these changes? Who pays each kind of tax— for example, the payroll tax levied on businesses? How should the tax burden be distributed among different types of taxes and among households?

Macroeconomics, on the other hand, is concerned with the *aggregates*. How do changes in total expenditure and in tax rates affect the G and C schedules? To the extent that revenues and expenditures differ in a particular year, there is a budget *surplus or deficit*. How does the size of this surplus and deficit, and the methods used to finance it, affect aggregate demand?

The budget totals are best judged, not by the billions of dollars in-

TABLE 10-1

Social accounting measures of government activity (percentage of GNP, selected years)

	1953–56 Eisenhower	1961–64 Kennedy–Johnson	1968–72 Nixon	1977–80 Carter	1981–84 Reagan†
Government purchases					
Federal: Defense	10.8	8.5	7.0	4.8	6.1
Federal: Other	1.8	2.3	2.3	2.5	1.9
State and local	7.5	9.8	12.5	12.9	12.6
Total	20.1	20.6	21.8	20.2	20.6
Transfer payments*					
Federal	4.7	6.1	7.8	10.8	15.5
State and local	1.0	1.1	1.3	1.1	0.5
Total	5.7	7.2	9.1	11.9	16.0
Revenue					
Federal	17.1	16.4	16.1	16.4	19.6
State and local	8.3	11.0	14.3	15.2	14.4
Total	25.4	27.4	30.4	31.6	34.0
Budget surplus (+) or deficit (−)					
Federal	−0.2	−0.5	−1.0	−1.7	−4.2
State and local	−0.2	+0.1	+0.5	+1.2	+1.3
Total	−0.4	−0.4	−0.5	−0.5	−2.9

* Including interest on public debt.

† Federal 1984 receipts and expenditures and 1984 GNP are estimates. State data cover only 1981–83.

volved, but by these dollars as *percentages of GNP.* An increase in these percentages means that government is becoming relatively more important in the economy, while a decrease carries the opposite message. The actual totals for selected periods since 1950 are shown in Table 10–1.

The trends shown by Table 10–1 speak for themselves. Output of public goods as a percentage of GNP has been quite stable at around 20 percent, but the composition of the total has changed substantially. State and local output, which was well below federal output in 1953–56, was much above federal output in 1981–84. The long-run decline of the federal share is entirely a reduction in the relative importance of defense expenditure, whose percentage of GNP was cut more than half between the Eisenhower and Carter presidencies.

The upsurge in transfer payments also stands out in the table. These payments, largely at the federal level, more than doubled in relative importance, reaching almost one sixth of GNP by 1981–84.

The rise in total outlays was roughly matched by an increase in tax collections, but with a significant difference among levels of government. At the federal level, tax revenue fell increasingly behind outlays. The federal budget deficit, near zero in 1953–56, had risen to 1.7 percent of GNP by 1977–80, and then jumped to 4.2 percent of GNP in 1981–83.

The large tax reduction program initiated by the Reagan administration was not matched by an equivalent reduction in federal outlays, and by 1983 the deficit had risen to nearly $200 billion. State and local governments, on the other hand, showed a budget surplus, which was growing as a percentage of GNP up to 1980. This healthy fiscal situation, to be sure, partly reflects large grants-in-aid from the federal government.

The fact that tax payments now amount to almost one third of GNP, while it may have undesirable aspects, has one favorable effect which we noted in Chapter 5. It increases the *stability* of the economy. This arises from the fact that taxes constitute a leakage from the income stream—considerably larger, indeed, than the leakages into personal and business saving. Part of any increase in national income is drained off into tax payments, and part of any drop in national income is offset by a reduction in tax payments. The tax leakage *reduces the size of the multiplier,* so that any autonomous change in spending has a smaller effect on the equilibrium rate of GNP.

The tax structure thus has a stabilizing effect on the economy, tending to moderate both upswings and downswings of economic activity. Further, this effect occurs *automatically,* without requiring decisions by Congress or the administration. This effect of the tax system is usually called the *built-in stabilizer.*

In this chapter, we focus on the federal budget. The reason is that state and local revenues must usually cover expenditures. There is some state and local borrowing, but this is limited by state constitutions. The federal government is subject to no such limitations. Its ability to borrow is virtually unlimited, so it is freer to vary tax rates and expenditure levels. In practice, as we've seen, the federal budget is usually in deficit, and so we must examine how deficits are financed and how this affects the working of the economy.

We'll look at the following issues:

1. The budget deficit (or surplus) in a particular year depends partly on the *fiscal program* in effect, that is, the level of government output and the rates set for various taxes and transfer payments. But the deficit depends also on the rate of GNP during the year. The same tax rates will yield more revenue (and hence a lower deficit) at a high GNP than at a low one.

2. A federal deficit must be financed by selling federal securities. It is often argued that this will necessarily raise the rate of interest, which will have a negative effect on private investment. Thus a deficit, which on the surface appears as a stimulus to aggregate demand, may be less stimulating than it appears. What is the evidence on this point?

3. As deficits accumulate year after year, there is a steady rise in the total of the *federal debt.* Growth of the public debt tends to be regarded as unfavorable, as "a burden on future generations." How much is there to this line of reasoning?

THE MEANING OF A FISCAL PROGRAM

The public tends to judge government budget policy by the size of the surplus or deficit. But this can be quite misleading. The surplus or deficit is partly a result of policy—planned government expenditure and the level of tax rates and transfer payments. But it also depends on the rate of GNP during the year. This is an important point which requires full explanation.

A *fiscal program* consists of two parts: *(a) A planned rate of government expenditure* which, once decided, is taken as a constant. (Note that in each of the fiscal programs shown in Table 10–1, the expenditure level G is constant for all GNP rates.) *(b)* A set of *net tax rates*—personal income tax rates, corporate income tax rates, rates of social security pensions and other transfer payments. These tax *rates* are taken as constant, but the net tax *revenue* which they yield is not constant. Rather, it varies with the rate of GNP prevailing during the year. (Note that for each of the fiscal programs shown in Table 10–2, net tax revenues rise as the rate of GNP rises—more income, more tax payments.)

Let us now compare the impact of the three fiscal programs shown in the table. With Fiscal Program A, government purchases are $100 billion per year, and the next tax structure is such that the budget would be balanced only if the rate of GNP turns out to be $1,200 billion, and there will be a fiscal surplus if GNP is greater than $1,200 billion.

Fiscal Program B is clearly *more expansionary* than A, for while government purchases are the same, B's tax structure is such that it takes a $6 billion per year smaller bite out of GNP income at each rate of GNP. Program B involves a considerably larger fiscal deficit (or smaller surplus) *at each rate of GNP.*

Program B will bring about a higher rate of aggregate demand than will A. Thus, if inflation is the problem, A would be a more appropriate

TABLE 10–2
Alternative fiscal programs (billions of dollars per year)

	Fiscal Program A			Fiscal Program B			Fiscal Program C		
GNP	T_n	G	$(T_n - G)$	T_n	G	$(T_n - G)$	T_n	G	$(T_n - G)$
1,150	90	100	−10	84	100	−16	90	106	−16
1,160	92	100	−8	86	100	−14	92	106	−14
1,170	94	100	−6	88	100	−12	94	106	−12
1,180	96	100	−4	90	100	−10	96	106	−10
1,190	98	100	−2	92	100	−8	98	106	−8
1,200	100	100	0	94	100	−6	100	106	−6
1,210	102	100	2	96	100	−4	102	106	−4
1,220	104	100	4	98	100	−2	104	106	−2
1,230	106	100	6	100	100	0	106	106	0
1,240	108	100	8	102	100	2	108	106	2
1,250	110	100	10	104	100	4	110	106	4
1,260	112	100	12	106	100	6	112	106	6

fiscal program than B. On the other hand, if unemployment is the problem, B would be better than A.

One cannot judge how expansionary fiscal policy is merely by observing the surplus or deficit. One might think that an increase in the deficit means that policy has become more expansionary. But this is not necessarily true. Suppose, for example, that Program A is in effect, GNP is $1,200 billion, and the budget is balanced. Now investment demand falls, and through the operation of the autonomous spending multiplier, GNP falls to $1,160 billion. There is now a deficit of $8 billion. One might think that there had been a shift to a more expansionary program. But there has been no shift—Program A is still in effect.

Suppose, on the other hand, that with GNP at $1,200 billion the government shifts from Program A to Program B. There is now a deficit of $6 billion instead of a balanced budget. This *is* a change of policy, a move in an expansionary direction.

To compare the impact of two different fiscal programs, one must compare their relative deficits (or surpluses) *at the same rate of GNP.* Thus we have seen that Program B is more expansionary than A because it generates a larger deficit (or smaller surplus) at each rate of GNP. But even this is not a completely reliable test. Compare Programs B and C in Table 10–2. Note that at any rate of GNP, net tax collections are $6 billion higher under Program C than under Program B, and government expenditures are also $6 billion higher. The surplus or deficit, at any rate of GNP, is precisely the same, and so one might think that the impact of the two programs is identical.

Actually, however, a shift from Program B to Program C is expansionary. The explanation is that the extra $6 billion of expenditure under Program C raises aggregate demand by a full $6 billion. The fact that net taxes are $6 billion higher, on the other hand, reduces aggregate demand by *less than* $6 billion. The reason is that part of the increased tax payments come out of saving rather than consumption. The consumption schedule falls by only, say, $4 billion—the actual amount depending on the marginal propensity to consume disposable income. So, the positive effect of the G on aggregate demand outweighs the negative effect of the lower C, and the net effect is expansionary.

The high-employment fiscal surplus

A common yardstick for comparing fiscal programs is the surplus or deficit they would yield if the economy were operating at what is sometimes called "full employment." It is probably better to substitute the term *high employment.* The economy never operates at full employment in the sense of maximum physical output. We can take "high employment" as meaning operation at the NAIRU as defined in Chapter 9, say, at an unemployment rate of 6 percent.

Suppose that this year, operating at the NAIRU would mean a GNP rate of $3,000 billion, shown by the right-hand edge of Figure 10–1. Other lower rates of GNP are shown along the horizontal axis, while the vertical axis shows the size of the budget surplus or deficit. *A, B,* and *C* illustrate alternative fiscal programs. Note that for each program the deficit varies with the rate of GNP, for reasons already explained. We can compare the impact of these programs by observing the point at which they hit the high-employment line. Program C is most expansionist, since there would still be a budget deficit even at high employment. With Program B, the budget would be exactly balanced at high employment. Program A is least expansionist, since if the employment target were reached, there would be a sizable budget surplus.

The behavior of the high-employment fiscal surplus since 1950 is charted in Figure 10–2, which also shows the actual budget surplus each year. This figure reveals several things. First, there is usually a deficit in the actual budget, and since 1970, these deficits have been unusually large. Second, the actual deficit is usually larger than the high-employment deficit. This means that the economy is usually operating below the

FIGURE 10–1
The high-employment fiscal surplus

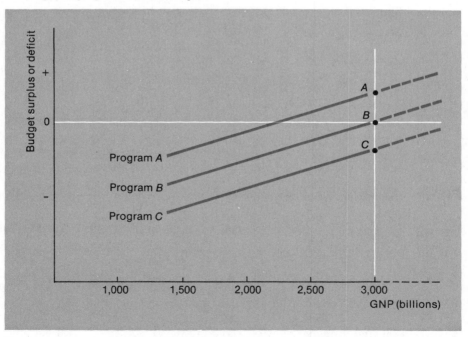

Fiscal programs can be compared in terms of the deficit or surplus each would yield if the economy attained a high-employment target, here taken as a GNP rate of $3,000 billion. The dotted lines show the effect of keeping the same fiscal program in effect when GNP is increasing.

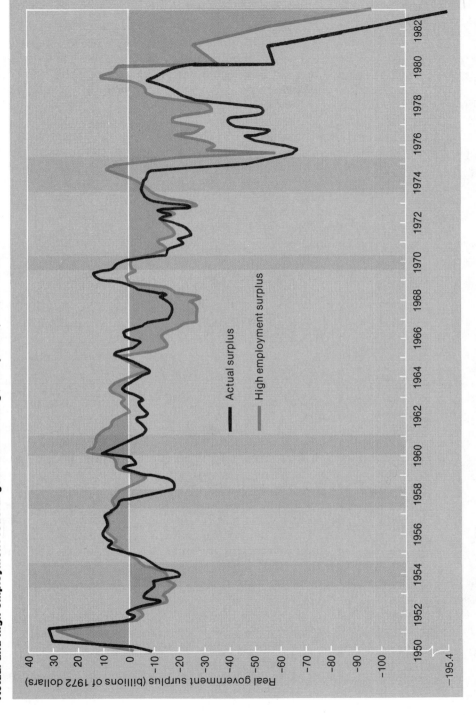

FIGURE 10-2

Actual and high-employment federal government budget surpluses, 1950–1983

Real government surplus (billions of 1972 dollars)

40
30
20
10
0
-10
-20
-30
-40
-50
-60
-70
-80
-90
-100
-195.4

1950 1952 1954 1956 1958 1960 1962 1964 1966 1968 1970 1972 1974 1976 1978 1980 1982

—— Actual surplus

—— High employment surplus

NAIRU rate. At the height of the Vietnam War, however, the economy operated for a while at "more-than-full employment," and the actual deficit was *less* than the high-employment deficit. Third, the actual deficit increases sharply during a recession because of the drop in tax collections. This happened in the recessions of 1957–58, 1968–70, 1974–75, and 1981–82.

In 1981, the Reagan administration proposed, and Congress approved, a reduction of 25 percent in personal income tax rates over a three-year period. This reduction, combined with the effect of the 1981–82 recession, meant that federal revenues in fiscal 1983 were no larger than in 1981. Meanwhile, budget outlays continued their inexorable upward course, rising by about $140 billion between these two years. Thus the deficit rose from $58 billion in 1981 to $195 billion in 1983.

The economic recovery which began in 1983 was expected to shrink the deficit somewhat. But it was estimated that a deficit of over $100 billion would remain even at high employment. It became fashionable to refer to this as a *structural deficit,* that is, a deficit which will not be removed by a return to high employment, but requires corrective action by Congress. In terms of Figure 10–1, the economy in 1983–84 was operating on something like Program *C.* The structural deficit is shown by the distance *BC.*

We can use Figure 10–1 also to make an interesting point about changes over the course of time. Suppose that the output capacity of the economy is growing at 3 percent a year. Then a high-employment output of $3,000 billion this year will grow to $3,090 billion next year, $3,183 billion the year after, and so on. The right-hand edge of Figure 10–1 keeps moving to the right, and as this happens, tax revenues continue to increase.

Thus, even if fiscal Program B is in effect, with the budget balanced at the old high-employment output, there will now be a fiscal surplus, and this will grow steadily larger as we move up to higher GNP rates. Note also that the same thing will happen even if real output is not rising but the money value of GNP is being pushed up by increases in the price level. This is one of the side effects of inflation noted in the last chapter. Since government revenues rise with money GNP, and in fact rise faster than GNP, inflation sweeps a larger percentage of money income into the federal treasury.

This tendency for the fiscal surplus to grow as GNP rises is called a *fiscal dividend.* What can or should be done with this dividend? One possibility is to do nothing. Keep the old tax rates and expenditure rates in effect, and let the fiscal surplus drift upward. But this means that in the private sector investment must exceed saving by larger and larger amounts if high-employment output is to be maintained. If private investment actually is this vigorous, fine. But if not, the rising tax drain will make it harder and harder to maintain high employment. This phenomenon is usually called *fiscal drag.*

Fiscal drag is not a serious problem in practice, because it is so easy (and popular!) to reduce the fiscal surplus by the alternatives of raising the government expenditure rate G or declaring a dividend to taxpayers in the form of lower tax rates or increased transfer payments. Choice among these alternative involves judgment about social priorities at a particular time.

A rule for budgetmaking?

Each year Congress and the administration must work out a federal budget for the coming fiscal year. They are urged by commentators to exercise fiscal responsibility. What does this mean? Are there any general principles on which policymakers can rely?

A traditional view in public finance is that the budget should be balanced in each fiscal year. This rule, generally observed at the state and local levels, has now been set aside at the federal level. But many people believe that the federal government, too, should observe it. Indeed, some 30 state legislatures have passed resolutions calling for a constitutional convention which would write into the constitution a requirement for annual budget balance.

The urge behind this proposal is to restrain federal spending by saying to Congress, "If you want to spend, you've got to tax." But even if one sympathizes with the objective, the proposal is impractical. A look at Figure 10–1 will show why. Suppose the economy is operating a high employment, Program B is in effect, and the budget is balanced. Now a recession sets in, output and tax revenues fall, and there is a budget deficit. If Congress were forced by law to get the budget back into balance, it would have to raise taxes or cut expenditures. Either action would reduce aggregate demand and intensify the recession. Output and tax revenues would fall more, and it might prove impossible to balance the budget no matter how hard one tried. President Hoover worked hard at balancing the budget during the Great Depression, but this worsened the depression and helped to guarantee the Roosevelt landslide of 1932.

Recognizing the difficulty, some people, including the Committee for Economic Development (a group of leading business executives), have espoused the principle of a *balanced budget at high employment.* Under this proposal, government purchases would first be determined on the basis of economic priorities. Next, one would estimate the high-employment level of output. Finally, one would set tax and transfer rates such that *if high-employment GNP were actually achieved,* tax receipts would just equal expenditures.[2] So long as the economy was below this level,

---

[2] The CED formulation is actually a bit more conservative than this. "It should be the policy of the government to set its expenditure programs and tax rates so that they would yield a constant, moderate surplus under conditions of high employment and price stability." Committee for Economic Development, *Fiscal and Monetary Policy for High Employment* (New York, 1962), p. 26.

there would be an automatic deficit, which would have an expansionist effect on aggregate demand. Program B in Figure 10–1 would be in accordance with this rule.

Under this rule, the budget surplus, $T_n - G$, would be zero at high employment. But for the economy to be in equilibrium, there must be enough investment demand to absorb the desired savings of businesses and individuals at a high-employment rate of output. Can we be sure that this requirement will always be met? Business investment is buoyant in some years, depressed in others. It seems likely that the condition for high-employment equilibrium would be met at some times but not at all times.

For this reason, many economists feel that government cannot safely tie itself to any fixed formula. We cannot prescribe a zero level, or any other level, of high-employment surplus as equally appropriate to all occasions. Rather, government must retain flexibility to adjust the surplus upward or downward to offset fluctuations in the private economy.

THINK ABOUT THIS

1. Because the federal budget is so large, a large share of any increase or decrease in GNP is reflected in change in net taxes. Early in the chapter we referred to this (approvingly) as constituting a built-in stabilizer. Later on we referred to it (disparagingly) as constituting fiscal drag in a growing economy. What is going on here? Can both views be correct?
2. For the last 20 years Japan's GNP has been growing rapidly, often at 10 percent per year. Almost every year the Japanese government cuts income tax rates. Are these two things connected?

FINANCING THE DEFICIT

Until about 1965, many economists wrote optimistically about using changes in the federal budget to steer the economy toward desirable targets for output and employment. The prescription seemed simple enough. If aggregate demand and output are too low, raise demand by some combination of higher public goods output, larger transfer payments, and lower tax rates. If aggregate demand is too high and inflation seems threatening, turn the prescription into reverse: reduce public goods output, cut transfer payments, or raise tax rates.

Today, most economists are less hopeful about the feasibility of using fiscal policy as a stabilizing device. This is partly for practical reasons to be examined more closely in Chapter 12. Budgetmaking, which touches the voters' money nerve, is bound to be political. When members of

Congress vote on tax or expenditure changes, economic stabilization is not uppermost in their minds. Partly because of the unavoidable political infighting, a final vote sometimes takes many months. Fiscal policy is not very nimble.

In addition, monetary policy, which Keynes and his early followers tended to play down, has reemerged as a major stabilization tool. Monetarists and also many nonmonetarist economists now regard it as the prime instrument for regulating aggregate demand. They question whether fiscal policy can do anything which monetary policy could not do as well or better.

Beyond these general considerations, the strength of fiscal policy has been questioned on two main grounds. First, the effect of a tax change on consumer spending seems to depend on how the change is made, and especially on whether consumers view it as temporary or permanent. There is considerable evidence that spending decisions are related to expected *permanent income*. If there is a structural change in the tax system, such as the permanent lowering of federal income tax rates which occurred in 1981–83, consumers will conclude that their permanent income has been increased and will raise their planned spending. But if the change is viewed as temporary, it may have little effect on spending plans. A temporary increase in taxes will mainly be taken out of saving, and a temporary tax cut or a cash bonus will flow mainly into saving.

An analysis by Alan Blinder concludes that

> the point estimate suggests that a temporary tax change is treated as a 50–50 blend of a normal tax change and a pure windfall. Over a one-year planning horizon, a temporary tax change is estimated to have only a little more than half the impact of a permanent tax change of equal magnitude, and a rebate is estimated to have only about 38 percent of the impact.[3]

There have even been episodes in which the effect was close to zero. An example is the temporary income tax surcharge imposed in mid-1968 to contain the inflation resulting from the Vietnam War, a surcharge which was scheduled to expire after 18 months. Between the first half of 1968 and the last half, tax payments as a percentage of GNP rose by 1.5 points. But saving as a percentage of GNP fell by 1.5 points. The surcharge was paid by reducing saving, and consumption was little affected.

Even a permanent tax change produces its effect only gradually because

---

[3] Alan S. Blinder, "Temporary Income Taxes and Consumer Spending," *Journal of Political Economy* 89 (February 1981), pp. 26–52. Another study by Hall and Mishkin estimated the marginal propensity to consume food out of temporary and permanent income changes. For temporary income, the MPC was found to be less than one third as large as for permanent income. Robert E. Hall and Frederic S. Mishkin, "The Sensitivity of Consumption to Transitory Income," *Econometrica* 50 (March 1982), pp. 461–81.

it takes time for consumers to readjust their spending plans. The Blinder study estimated that about one third of the effect is felt within three months and about two thirds within a year. At the end of a year, consumer spending will have risen by 56 percent of the amount of a permanent tax reduction.

A second consideration is that cutting taxes or increasing spending to stimulate the economy will usually create a budget deficit or increase the size of a preexisting deficit. The deficit must be financed, and this will have monetary consequences.

Suppose we are starting from a position of monetary balance in which people are holding just the amount of money they want to hold relative to their incomes. Now the federal government cuts taxes by $20 billion in order to stimulate the economy. Expenditures remain unchanged. The Treasury finances the increased deficit by selling $20 billion of government bonds to the public. The money supply is unchanged, because every dollar which the government raises through the bond sales is returned to the private economy as the government spends in excess of its tax receipts.

But why should people be willing to buy the additional bonds? They will do so only if they are compensated by a *higher rate of interest.* Or to look at it a bit differently, throwing a large block of federal securities on the market will drive down securities prices, which is the same thing as a rise in interest rates.

There is another reason why interest rates will rise. As the tax cut raises the consumption schedule, and as this raises total output and income, people will want to hold more money to keep the normal ratio of money to income. They will try to increase their money stocks by selling securities, and this will lower security prices and raise interest rates.

The rise in interest rates, in turn, will reduce investment in houses, commercial buildings, and industrial plant and equipment. If the *MEI* schedule is quite flat, the cut in investment will be large. This drop in investment will at least partially offset the stimulating effect of the tax cut. This is usually called the *crowding out effect*—private borrowing being crowded out of the market by government spending.

How important is the crowding out effect in practice? This depends partly on the strength of private investment and private borrowing. During recession, when private demand for loans is slack, government borrowing may not raise the interest rate very much. But when investment and aggregate demand are already high, the effect may be substantial. A case in point was the sharp increase in federal spending and the federal deficit as the Vietnam War deepened. During 1966, real government expenditure rose by $27 billion. The real money supply remained almost unchanged. The result was a marked rise in the interest rate and a drop in real investment (mainly housing investment) which offset about 76 percent of the increase in government expenditure.[4] Again in 1984, continuation of heavy federal borrowing, together with a strong economic upswing which raised private demand for credit, brought a rise in interest rates.

The crowding out effect may be mitigated in either or both of two ways. If interest rates in the United States rise appreciably above those in other countries, there will be an inflow of foreign funds, which will help to finance U.S. borrowing and to ease the upward pressure on interest rates. This was an important factor in the early 80s. Further, the direct effect of the deficit is to raise aggregate demand and GNP. This raises domestic saving, which helps to meet borrowing needs. As the economy approaches full employment, however, the possibility of any further rise in real saving decreases, and the crowding out effect may be close to 100 percent.

The upshot is that the multiplier effect of a tax cut or an expenditure increase may be considerably smaller than one would conclude from the simple multiplier analysis of Chapter 5. If the money supply is held constant, the interest rate will rise, and the stimulative effect of a larger deficit will be offset in greater or lesser degree by adverse effects on private investment.

But, you may say, this result can readily be avoided by increasing the supply of money. True. The Fed, by adding to the monetary base, can increase money supply sufficiently to prevent any rise in the rate of interest. The Fed could even buy the new government bonds itself. In this event, the government would receive deposits at the Fed equal to the value of the bonds, and, as these deposits were spent, they would be converted into commercial bank reserves. The monetary base would rise by the amount of the bond sale. This process is called *monetizing the debt.*

Actually, the Fed has shown no strong tendency to accommodate the Treasury in this way. A study by Alan Blinder[5] concludes that Fed behavior has come far closer to no monetization than to full monetization. Indeed, when inflation has been high, the Fed has typically reduced bank reserves in spite of government deficits (i.e., monetization has been *negative*).

THE QUESTION OF THE DEBT

A federal deficit must be financed by borrowing, and a continuing series of deficits means a rise in federal debt over the long run. What

---

[4] This episode is described in Robert J. Gordon, *Macroeconomics* (Boston: Little, Brown, 1978), pp. 127–29.

[5] Alan S. Blinder, "On the Monetization of Deficits," working paper no. 1052 (Cambridge, Mass.: National Bureau of Economic Research, December 1982).

are the economic consequences? Should growth of government debt be a matter of concern?

A word first on the size of federal debt. While it is very large, it is not as large as newspaper accounts may suggest. Confusion arises because part of the debt is held by the federal government itself in special trust funds, such as the social security fund and the highways trust fund. An additional amount is held by the Federal Reserve System.

The amounts involved are shown in Table 10–3, which presents data on the debt of the U.S. government at the end of selected calendar years up to 1970 and selected fiscal years since 1970. Column (2) shows what is called the "total debt." But the name is misapplied. It would be more accurate to label the column "the debt of the *general fund* of the U.S. Treasury," for that is exactly what it is. Column (2) does not provide information on the operations of the special trust funds.

These funds, particularly the social security fund, typically take in more in tax receipts than is paid out. What happens to this surplus or these excess tax receipts? They are used to buy government securities. Column (3) shows how much of the government debt was held by these trust funds or *by the U.S. government itself* at the end of each year. Note that by the end of 1983, the U.S. government owned more than $240 billion of *its own debt.*

Column (4) of the table shows the *net debt* of the federal government. It is the total debt less that portion which is held by the government in its special trust funds or special accounts. Thus, the *net debt is a measure of the debt of the entire federal government establishment,* not just the debt of the Treasury's general fund.

But there is something else. Column (5) shows how much of the federal debt was owned by the Federal Reserve banks. These banks are privately owned, but they are run almost as if they were part of the

TABLE 10–3
The debt of the federal government, 1940–1983 (billions of dollars)

(1)	(2)	(3)	(4) = (2) − (3)	(5)	(6)
Year	Total Debt	Held in Federal Government Accounts	Net Debt	Held by Federal Reserve Banks	Held by Private Investors
1940	45.0	6.7	38.3	2.2	36.2
1945	278.1	23.9	254.2	24.3	230.0
1950	256.7	36.0	220.7	20.8	199.9
1955	280.8	49.0	231.8	24.8	207.0
1960	290.2	52.8	237.4	27.4	210.0
1965	320.9	59.7	261.2	40.8	220.5
1970	370.1	95.2	274.9	57.7	217.2
1975	533.2	145.3	387.9	84.7	303.2
1980	908.2	193.4	714.8	121.5	593.3
1983	1,381.9	240.1	1,141.8	155.5	986.3

Source: *Economic Report of the President, 1984*, p. 305.

federal government. They own a large amount of federal securities. But of the interest they receive on these securities, almost all is paid right back to the Treasury.[6]

Finally, column (6) shows how much federal government debt was actually owned by private investors. A big increase occurred between 1940 and 1945. After that, it went down somewhat and then back up, so that by 1970 it was about the same as in 1945. Since 1970, however, private holdings of government debt have risen rapidly.

Another misconception about the debt is that at some point in the future it must be "paid off." I must eventually repay my house mortgage and other personal debts. Must not the U.S. government do the same? The answer is emphatically no. Personal debts have to be repaid because people are mortal. My creditors want to make sure that I pay off my debts before I die. But nations do not suffer from this human frailty. So there is no reason why national debt must be paid off, and in fact it rarely is. It may be reduced a bit in years of budget surplus. But for the most part, as old debts mature, the government simply "refunds" the debt by issuing new securities in place of the old. Recently, these refunding operations have been in excess of $100 billion a year. The art of doing this smoothly and successfully is called "debt management," and the operations are handled by a division of the Treasury Department.

All this is an accepted part of our financial system. Banks, insurance companies, colleges, and wealthy individuals hold large amounts of government securities. To them, these certificates of national debt appear as *assets*. And they are preferred assets because of the ease with which they can be converted into cash and the negligible risk of default. If the supply of such assets ever shrank materially through retirement of the national debt, large investors would be hard pressed to find substitutes for them which are as riskless.

As federal debt has grown, interest payments on the debt have also grown. The most significant figure here is perhaps the percentage of national income which must be raised in taxes to pay interest on the debt. The behavior of this figure since 1940 is shown in Table 10–4. It shot up during World War II, which involved large deficits and heavy federal borrowing. It then remained rather stable through 1970. Since then it has tended to rise because of large federal deficits and unusually high interest rates.

To what extent do these interest payments constitute a burden on the people of the United States? We must distinguish, first, between private and social points of view. From a private viewpoint, most of the federal debt is owned by individuals and businesses within the United States. So most of the taxes raised to pay interest on the debt come

---

[6] The Federal Reserve banks are not legally required to make these payments to the government. But they have been doing it for so long, it has become a de facto requirement. If they were to stop, the Congress would quickly make it a legal requirement.

TABLE 10–4
Net interest payments on the federal debt, 1940–83

(1)	(2)	(3)	(4)
		Net Interest*	Net Interest
	GNP	Payments	Payments as a
Year	($ billions)	($ billions)	Percent of GNP
1940	99.7	0.7	0.70
1945	211.9	3.3	1.56
1950	284.8	4.5	1.58
1955	398.0	4.9	1.23
1960	503.7	7.1	1.41
1965	684.9	8.7	1.27
1970	976.8	14.0	1.42
1975	1,528.8	23.3	1.52
1980	2,627.4	64.5	2.45
1983	3,309.5	89.8	2.72

* Does not include interest paid to the Federal Reserve banks and then returned to the government.
Source: *Survey of Current Business,* August 1965, pp. 36–37; *Economic Report of the President,* 1972, p. 273; and *Economic Report of the President,* 1984, p. 305.

back into the pockets of people in this country. At most, one can say that having to levy additional taxes always harms the private economy to some extent. "There are no good taxes." This inconvenience arising from additional taxation is often called *tax friction.* It is true also that a minor but growing proportion of federal debt is owned by residents of foreign countries. Interest payments to other countries must basically be met by export of goods, and these impose a burden on Americans similar to that imposed by payment for oil imports.

From a social viewpoint, whether a debt increase can be viewed as a burden depends partly on the purposes for which the money was used. There is a useful analogy here between private and public debt. Recently, IBM issued several billion dollars worth of bonds on which it will have to pay many millions in interest each year. We don't regard these interest payments as constituting an undue burden on IBM. Why is this? The reason is that the money was put into plant and equipment which will increase the company's net revenue in future years. IBM must have estimated that the increase in net revenue would at least equal the increase in interest payments. If it is right, it is as well off as before and possibly better off.

Similarly, money borrowed by government could be put into projects which yield a continuing flow of benefits to the citizens in future years. This typically is true of state and city borrowings, which go mainly to finance construction projects—schools and colleges, hospitals, sewage systems, highways, and so on. A good deal of federal money also goes into physical structures as well as research, education, and other forms of human investment. In this case, if the citizens value the future benefits at least as highly as the tax money they pay out for interest charges, no real burden is involved.

The case is different if borrowed money is used to pay for current expenditures which yield no future benefit. Here the citizens in future years are making tax payments for which they receive nothing in return, and this can reasonably be considered a burden.

We must bear in mind also the possibility that, at certain times, government borrowing may crowd out some private investment. The fact that business investment in a particular year was lower than it otherwise would have been means that the nation's capital stock in future years is also lower than it would have been. This reduction in capital stock, which must mean a lower GNP in future years, constitutes a real cost of the government borrowing. The most dramatic examples occur in wartime. From 1941–45, our resources were channeled mainly to war purposes. We wore out our previous stock of plants, machinery, buildings, houses, automobiles, and entered 1946 with a substantially smaller capital stock than we would have had with five years of normal growth. This was the main economic burden imposed by the war.

THINK ABOUT THIS

Find out the rate of federal expenditures and tax receipts for the fiscal year during which you are studying this chapter. In view of the current state of the economy, do you think that the federal fiscal program for the *next* fiscal year should be more expansionist or less expansionist than that for the current year? Why?

What specific tax and/or expenditure changes would you recommend to achieve the desired effects?

NEW CONCEPTS

built-in stabilizer	crowding out effect
fiscal policy	federal debt, total
fiscal program	federal debt, net
high-employment fiscal surplus	federal debt, privately held
fiscal dividend	tax friction
fiscal drag	tax payments, net
monetizing the debt	structural deficit
debt management	

SUMMARY

1. A change in government expenditure (G) raises or lowers aggregate demand by the full amount of the change. A change in net taxes (T_n) raises or lowers consumers' disposable income. If the change is viewed

as permanent, there will be a substantial impact on consumer spending and hence on aggregate demand; but if it is viewed as temporary, the effect may be small.

2. The existence of the tax leakage reduces the size of the multiplier and thus increases the stability of the economy. This effect of the fiscal system is called the *built-in-stabilizer*.

3. A *fiscal program* includes a rate of planned government expenditure and a set of tax rates. How much tax revenue these rates will yield in a particular year, and the consequent budget surplus or deficit, depends on the *rate of GNP* during the year.

4. One fiscal program is more expansionist than another if, *at the same rate of GNP,* it yields a larger deficit or a smaller surplus. A common standard of comparison is the high-employment fiscal surplus—that is, the surplus or deficit which a particular fiscal program would yield at a specified target rate of GNP.

5. It is not desirable to balance the federal budget in each year. That would require raising taxes during a recession, which would make the recession worse. A more reasonable rule is that the fiscal program should yield a balanced budget at *high employment*.

6. A tax cut or expenditure increase will increase the federal deficit, which must be financed by selling federal securities. If money supply remains unchanged, this will raise interest rates, which will reduce spending on investment and durable consumer goods such as automobiles. This *crowding out effect* will partly offset the initial stimulus to aggregate demand.

7. Government debt imposes a real burden on the economy only to the extent that past government borrowing has crowded out private investment, leading to a lower capital stock and a smaller GNP than could have been achieved otherwise. Beyond this, the need to raise more taxes to meet interest payments on the debt imposes an inconvenience usually called *tax friction*.

Part Two

Macroeconomic Policy

■ 11 ■

Fluctuations in National Income

All Mathematics would suggest
A steady straight line as the best,
But left and right alternately
Is consonant with History.

        —W. H. AUDEN

In later chapters we will be talking about what government can do to influence the rate of output and the level of prices. But it is important to realize that the economy has a rhythm of its own, independent of government action. Output and employment, instead of growing regularly year after year, follow an irregular pattern. Periods of rising output, averaging three or four years in length, are followed by a leveling off or decline of output for a year or so. These fluctuations are usually called *business cycles.*

The purpose of this chapter is to explain what goes on during the business cycle, with special attention to fluctuations in investment which are a prominent feature of the cycle. One of the more puzzling questions is why an upswing which has been going on for several years eventually comes to an end. We will also say something about efforts to forecast future changes in GNP. These efforts have not been very successful as yet, but there is always a possibility of improvement.

ECONOMIC FLUCTUATIONS: WHAT GOES ON

Some people don't like the term *business cycle* and prefer to speak simply of *economic fluctuations.* The reason is that "cycle" suggests greater regularity than actually exists. If expansions and contractions followed each other at regular intervals, there would be no forecasting problem.

241

The thing which keeps one sitting on the edge of one's chair is uncertainty about when the next turn will come. Some economic expansions (1942–46, 1927–29, 1958–60) peter out after a couple of years. But the 1938–45 expansion associated with World War II lasted almost seven years, and the strong upswing which began in 1961 lasted almost nine years. The average duration of an upswing is something like three years. But an average is not an insurance policy.

In popular usage, periods of economic expansion go by such varied names as "recovery," "prosperity," "boom." Periods of declining activity may be called "slumps," "recessions," "depressions." All this is rather confusing. Let us agree, therefore, to call a period of rising activity an *upswing* and a period of declining activity a *downswing*. The point at which an upswing ceases and reverses itself we shall call the *upper turning point*. The end of a downswing is the *lower turning point*. A complete fluctuation, then, consists of a lower turning point, an upswing, an upper turning point, and a downswing. If this sounds less exciting than boom and slump, it has the advantage of saying exactly what we mean.

What goes on during one of these fluctuations? The most striking thing about them is the divergent movement of different elements in the economy. During a downswing, some things fall a lot and others fall a little, while some go right on rising. In general, the things which fall most on the downswing also rise most on the upswing. It is necessary to say a bit about these differences in movement, since they provide some clues to why the fluctuations occur.

Some things fluctuate widely

Among the things which show sizable fluctuations are:

1. *Business inventories* of raw materials, goods in process, and finished products. Businesses typically add substantially to inventories on the upswing and try to reduce them on the downswing. The sharp changes in this item are clear from Figure 11–1. In this figure, *P* indicates a cycle peak or upper turning point, while *T* indicates a trough or lower turning point.

2. *Business plant and equipment* expenditures also normally rise on the upgrade and fall off during contraction, though the swings are not as wide as those in inventories.

3. *Housing construction* is heavily influenced by mortgage interest rates. As interest rates rise during an upswing, housing typically levels off and turns down *before* the downturn of business in general. Similarly, as interest rates fall during recession, housing usually turns up *before* the end of the recession. This pattern is evident from Figure 11–1.

4. *Consumer spending on durable goods,* such as automobiles, furniture, and household appliances, is postponable and financed partly by borrowing. During a period of economic uncertainty, some families are unable

FIGURE 11-1
Economic fluctuations are mainly investment fluctuations

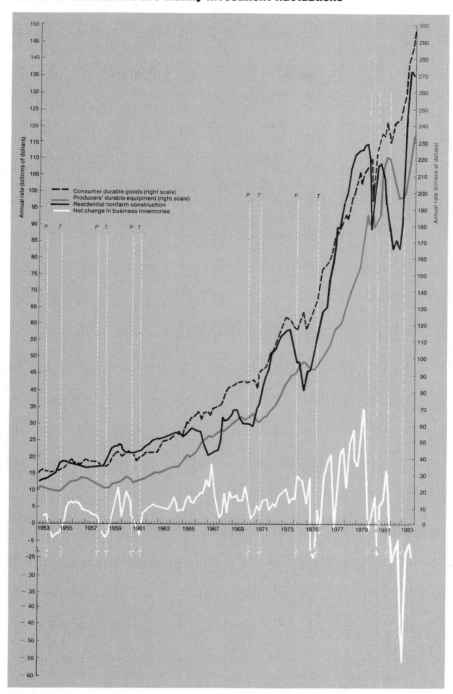

P indicates a cycle peak or upper turning point. T indicates a cycle trough or lower turning point. The dating is that used by the National Bureau of Economic Reserve.

Source: *Economic Report of the President, 1984.*

to borrow and postpone their purchases to a more favorable time. So durable goods purchases are bunched up on the upswing and contribute to the upswing.

5. *Federal military purchases* fluctuate considerably, contributing to the instability of the economy. These fluctuations, however, do not follow the general business cycle. Rather, they are associated with war periods, such as the Korean War and the Vietnam War, or with military buildups arising from a "Soviet scare."

6. *Production of durable goods* declines on the downswing. With business spending on plant and equipment, housing activity, and consumer spending on durable goods all falling, it stands to reason that output of durable goods must fall on the downswing. A downswing is mainly a decline in construction, steel, metals, machinery, automobiles, and other durable goods. Recession unemployment is concentrated in these industries, and other industries are little affected.

Some things always go up

The main things which do not fluctuate appreciably with general economic activity are:

1. *Government nonmilitary purchases.* State and local expenditures, which are twice as large as federal expenditures, have risen consistently since 1945, and the rise has continued right through the downswing periods. This is true also of federal purchases outside the defense area.

2. *Consumer spending on nondurable goods and services* also rises consistently, even during recession. This is a very large item, amounting to more than half of GNP. Its massive stability reflects the fact that recessions since 1945 have been brief and mild, slowing down the rise of consumer incomes but not stopping it.

EXPLANATION: THE ROLE OF INVESTMENT

There are two main things to be explained. First, after the economy has started moving up or down, why does it build up momentum and keep going in the same direction for a considerable time? Second and more difficult, why does the movement reverse itself after a while? After production has been rising for several years, the production index levels off and then starts to decline. Why doesn't expansion continue indefinitely?[1]

---

[1] The great center of research on this subject is the National Bureau of Economic Research. Anyone who wants to delve into detail will find a wealth of publications by Wesley C. Mitchell, Arthur F. Burns, Geoffrey H. Moore, Solomon Fabricant, and other past and present members of the bureau staff.

Autonomous investment: Reasons for irregularity

Since economic fluctuations are centered in the investment industries, we must look further into the short-run behavior of business investment. A basic distinction here is between *autonomous* and *induced* investment. The latter is capacity-oriented investment, occurring in response to changes in consumer demand. Demand for shoes rises 10 percent. If the shoe industry is presently operating at capacity, it will have to increase its capacity 10 percent to keep up with the expanding market.

Autonomous investment, on the other hand, is independent of current consumer demand. An example is investment in the early automobile factories. There was no prior demand for the product, since the product didn't exist. But some business executives believed that by starting to turn out this new product, they could tap a potential desire for it and develop an effective demand. New-product investment, then, is autonomous; and so is a good deal of the investment in cost-reducing improvements. Scientists and engineers are every day turning up improvements in production methods which are so profitable that they will be adopted even if consumer demand is not rising.

Autonomous investment could conceivably go on at a steady pace year after year, but this is unlikely to happen in practice. True, invention and innovation are going on all the time. But there are major and minor innovations. At one end of the scale is the small adjustment on a machine which increases its efficiency by 5 percent and which earns someone a $100 prize from the company suggestion system. At the other extreme are the inventions which led to the railroad, electric power production, telephone communication, and the automobile.

A major innovation gives rise to a wave of capital investment. First, a few pioneers demonstrate that the new technique is feasible and that the public will take the product at profitable prices. After this, imitators swarm into the new industry. Investment is heavy, plant capacity and output grow rapidly. But eventually the potentialities of the new industry are fully exploited, output tapers off to a plateau, and investment falls.

To sustain the upward momentum of the economy, one would need a series of major innovations, following each other at regular intervals, so that as the force of one new development tapers off, there is something else to take its place. But this cannot be counted on. No matter how many well-financed research laboratories there may be, one cannot be sure of producing the equivalent of a new automobile industry every decade. Putting more money into scientific training and research should raise the *average rate* of invention, but it cannot make it completely regular. Significant discoveries cannot be turned out on an assembly line.

The late Professor Joseph Schumpeter regarded the irregularity of autonomous investment as the main explanation of economic fluctuations. An upswing is a period during which business leaders are swarming into one or more new fields of activity. As capacity catches up with demand for these products, prices and profits fall, investment declines, and we enter the downswing.

Induced investment: The acceleration principle

If autonomous investment is likely to fluctuate, induced investment is certain to fluctuate. This can be explained by a simplified illustration. Table 11–1, which is charted in Figure 11–2, shows a company operating in an industry in which technology is such that it takes $2 of plant and equipment to produce $1 of product per year. When the scene opens in Year 1, the company is operating at capacity, producing $100 million of goods per year from a plant costing $200 million. We suppose that $10 million of the company's equipment wears out each year and has to be replaced just to keep capacity unchanged. This appears as *replacement investment* in column (4). To increase capacity requires additional *net investment,* shown in column (3). *Gross investment* is the sum of the two and appears in the final column.[2]

We do not try to explain the sales figures in column (1). We simply assume that sales behave irregularly, first rising for a while and then falling. What we intend to show is that because of the fluctuation in sales, there will be even larger fluctuations in investment. This is usually called *the accleration principle,* because sales variations are magnified or "accelerated" into wider swings of investment.

TABLE 11–1
The acceleration principle applied to a plant (millions of dollars)

Year	(1) Sales	(2) Desired Stock of Capital	(3) Net Investment (change in column 2)	(4) Replacement Investment	(5) Gross Investment (columns 3 + 4)
1	100	200	0	10	10
2	110	220	20	10	30
3	125	250	30	10	40
4	135	270	20	10	30
5	140	280	10	10	20
6	140	280	0	10	10
7	130	260	−20	10	−10
8	125	250	−10	10	0
9	125	250	0	10	10
10	135	270	20	10	30

---

[2] Strictly, it would be more correct to treat each year's depreciation as a fixed percentage, say, 5 percent of the capital stock at the beginning of the year. On this basis, replacement investment would by Year 11 have risen to $15 billion. This adjustment would not, however, change the conclusions to be drawn from the table.

FIGURE 11-2
The acceleration principle

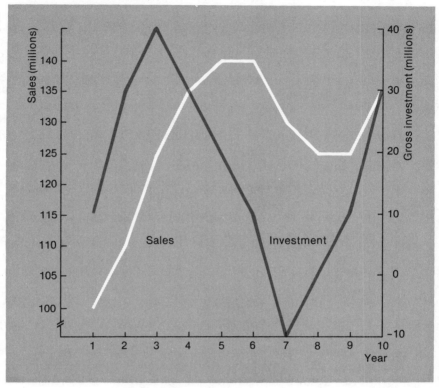

Note that investment turns down or up *before* sales and fluctuates more widely in percentage terms.

In Year 1, sales and capacity are in balance, so the company invests only the $10 million needed to replace worn-out equipment. In Year 2, however, sales rise by $10 million, requiring new plant capacity of $20 million. Adding this to the $10 million of replacement gives gross investment of $30 million for that year. The course of events in subsequent years can be traced by working down the table. Note that positive net investment occurs only in years when sales are rising. Note also that in some years net investment becomes negative. Why is this? Because in these years sales are falling. The company can afford to let its plant wear out and its capacity shrink, since it still has enough capacity to produce all it can sell.

Two points deserve special emphasis: First, the fluctuations in demand for the product produce magnified or accentuated fluctuations in gross investment. An increase of 25 percent in sales between Year 1 and Year 3 produces a *fourfold* rise in gross investment.

Second, the *level* of gross investment depends on the *rate of increase* in sales. In Year 4, a slowing down of the rate of increase of sales as compared with the previous year causes an actual *drop* in investment. So the downturn of investment in column (5) *precedes* the downturn of sales in column (1), even though sales are the causal factor. This is the most interesting feature of the accelerator, and it helps to explain why a business upswing may slow down and eventually topple over.

Note that this principle works on the downswing as well as the upswing. In Year 8, sales are still falling but falling *less rapidly* than in Year 7. So gross investment *increases* from −10 to 0, and in Year 9 even though sales are level, investment increases again to 10. The upturn in investment *precedes* the upturn in sales. This rise in investment, of course, has a multiplier effect on GNP. It helps to explain how a downswing comes to an end and turns into an upswing.

The acceleration principle applies also to other types of investment— for example, investment in business inventories. Since inventory fluctuations play an important role in business cycles, we give a simplified example in Table 11–2.

A common principle of inventory management is to keep inventories at a constant ratio to current sales. The department stores in Table 11–2 tries always to maintain a 2 to 1 ratio. As its sales fluctuate, and it has unintended additions to or withdrawals from inventory, it will try to bring inventories back to the desired level. In period 1, the store is running along smoothly, with sales at 100 and inventory at 200. It will order from manufacturers just enough to replace the goods it has sold (i.e., 100 units) as shown in the final column. In period 2, however,

TABLE 11–2
The acceleration principle applied to inventories

Period	Sales during Period	Desired Inventory at End of Period	Orders to Adjust Inventory	Orders to Replace Goods Sold	Total Orders
1	100	200	0	100	100
2	115	230	30	115	145
3	130	260	30	130	160
4	145	290	30	145	175
5	150	300	10	150	160
6	140	280	−20	140	120
7	130	260	−20	130	110
8	130	260	0	130	130
9	140	280	20	140	160
10	150	300	20	150	170

sales rise to 115 units, requiring an inventory of 230 units. To reach this level at the end of the period, it will have to order 115 units to replace the goods sold plus 30 units to build up inventory, or a total of 145 units. So an increase of 15 percent in the store's sales raises its orders to manufacturers by 45 percent—the accelerator once more.

The buildup of inventories continues through period 5. In period 6, however, sales drop, and the accelerator goes into reverse. The store now wants to reduce inventories, to engage in *inventory disinvestment.* How does it do this? Simply by ordering fewer goods than it is currently selling. In period 6, it sells 140 units but buys only 120, so inventories drop from 300 to 280. Investment drops again in period 7. Just as on the upswing, a small change in sales produces a large change in orders to manufacturers.

Note that the turning points in new orders *precede* the turning points in sales. In period 5, sales are still rising, but the *rate of increase* has diminished. This brings a decline in new orders because of the slackening of inventory investment. Again, in period 8, sales are at the same level as in the previous period. Orders begin to rise, however, because the store has stopped disinvesting in inventories.

By working the accelerator and the multiplier together, we can generate a "built-in" business cycle. True, there must be a push to set the machine going, an autonomous increase in spending from one source or another. Given this, the multiplier generates increased income and additional spending by consumers. As sales begin to increase, the inventory accelerator takes hold, and manufacturing activity rises even faster. This generates additional income, sales rise some more, and the rush to invest in inventories gains momentum. As manufacturing plants begin to near capacity, the plant and equipment accelerator takes hold, and investment rises some more. Through the multiplier, this generates still more income, sales rise again, and so on.

To keep the upswing going, sales of finished goods must continue to rise. Moreover—and this is what really matters—they must *rise at a constant or increasing rate.* Any slackening of the rate of increase in sales, as we have seen, is sufficient to cause a decline in both inventory investment and plant and equipment investment. If this happens, the multiplier goes into reverse and income begins to fall.[3] Maintaining an economic upswing is rather like racing a motorcycle up a steep slope. As soon as the machine loses momentum, it is in danger of toppling over.

---

[3] This impressionistic account can be made more precise by using some simple algebra. Well worth reading is the classic article on the subject by Paul A. Samuelson, "Interactions between the Multipler Analysis and the Acceleration Principle," *Review of Economics and Statistics,* 1939, pp. 78–88 [reprinted in the A.E.A. *Readings in Business Cycle Theory,* ed. Gottfried Haberler (Homewood, Ill.: Richard D. Irwin, 1944)]. By selecting different values for the multiplier and the accelerator, one can generate a violent cycle which becomes progressively wider, one which repeats itself indefinitely, or one which becomes progressively milder.

The mechanism of expansion

With these principles as background, let us look more concretely at what goes on during economic fluctuations. Let us ask first how an upswing feeds on itself and develops enough momentum to continue for several years at a time. We break into the cycle just after the lower tuning point, and ask what happens early in the upswing and what happens later.

At the very beginning, the upswing is centered in inventories and in consumer durable goods. Rapid increases in these sectors are readily explained on accelerator grounds. Inventories have been run down during the previous downswing. As soon as sales begin to rise, there will be an effort to rebuild inventories, so that new orders will rise even faster than sales. Similarly, consumers who have let their stock of automobiles and other durables goods wear out during the downswing now come back into the market. There is typically little change in the other sectors of aggregate demand. Fixed business investment lags behind the general cycle, and may still be declining in the early stages of the upswing. Government purchases maintain their customary uptrend, and consumer purchases of nondurables and services rise in proportion to the increase in consumer incomes.

The rise of real GNP is unusually rapid in the first year or so of the upswing. During the five upswings between 1949 and 1972, GNP rose in the first five quarters at an average rate of 7.5 percent—much above the long-term trend. Employment also rise, but less rapidly than output, as people who were kept on the payroll through the downswing now become more fully employed. Meanwhile, the labor force is increasing year by year. So unemployment may show little change during the first year or more of recovery. The ratio of profits to GNP rises rapidly and reaches a peak early in the upswing. Overhead costs per unit of output fall as output rises. Labor costs per unit of output may also fall, since productivity is rising rapidly as workers become more fully employed. Some product prices may be raised in response to rising demand. But even without this, the combination of more units sold and a wider price-cost margin per unit produces a sharp recovery of profits.

The first, very rapid, period of growth comes to an end after a year or so, mainly because of a decline in inventory investment. The inventory accelerator goes into reverse. This stands out clearly in Figure 11–1. The force which comes in now to keep the upswing going, though at a slower rate, is fixed business investment.

Fixed business investment depends heavily on financial factors: the size of the corporate cash flow, the level of interest rates, and the extent of monetary "tightness." But fixed investment also responds sluggishly to change, so that only after conditions have been favorable for several quarters will one see an actual upturn. After a year or so of upswing, the stage is set. The rise in profits has fattened the corporate cash flow. Interest rates have come down in the previous downswing. Bank reserves are ample and credit rationing slight. The recovery of output has raised the rate of capacity utilization, so that more and more companies begin to feel that capacity should be increased. The fixed investment accelerator takes holds and carries on from where the inventory accelerator left off.

The extent of the rise in fixed investment depends mainly on the rate of capacity utilization at the beginning of the second phase of expansion. The higher this rate, the sharper will be the rise in investment. But even if capacity utilization is rather low, there will be investment for plant modernization and also autonomous investment from new industries, which find this a favorable time to begin operations. The multiplier effect of this investment is sufficient to keep the economy moving forward for a year or two at about its long-term trend rate. In postway upswings, the rate of GNP increase in the *third* year of expansion was about 4.5 percent, compared with the 7.5 percent in the first year.

The upper turning point

Just when people have become confident about continued economic expansion, the rug is pulled from under them, and the economy heads downward into recession. Why is this? Must the upswing come to an end? Couldn't a downturn be prevented, if only we were sufficiently clever?

Even after the rise in investment has lost momentum, the economy may be given another upward boost by a cut in tax rates or a rise in government expenditure. An example is the substantial cut in personal income tax rates in 1964, which helped to sustain the upswing which had begun in 1961. Shortly thereafter, sharp increases in Vietnam War expenditures in 1965 and 1966 carried the expansion forward until 1969, though at the cost of accelerating inflation.

The public sector can obviously act as a depressant as well as a stimulant. The sharp drop in Korean War expenditures brought on the downswing of 1953–54, and the tapering off of Vietnam War expenditures was a factor in the downswing of 1969–70. This does not in itself prove that war is necessary to maintain prosperity. It does indicate that adjustment from wartime to peacetime conditions, which involves substantial changes in the composition of aggregate demand, is hard to manage without a temporary drop in output.

If we rule out such changes and look only at reactions within the private economy, we must conclude that a downturn after a few years is to be expected. It is quite unlikely that business fixed investment can go on rising at the same rate year after year. There is a bunching up of new investment projects early in the second phase of expansion. These usually take a year or two years to complete. As they are completed, and unless new projects come along at just the right rate, investment will taper off. Moreover, as more and more new plants come into operation, the rate of capacity utilization will level off or fall, and this discourages the construction of additional capacity.

Here is another thing to consider: The feasible rate of investment is limited in the short run by the capacity of the capital goods industries and by the supply of metals, machinery, building materials, skilled construction labor, and so on. These industries enter the upswing with much idle capacity, and so for a while their production can expand rapidly. If the upswing carries to the point at which the capital goods industries are working to capacity, however, investment must level off and then creep along the capacity ceiling.

Thus, investment *may* level off or decline even before the capital goods industries are working at capacity. If the upswing carries these industries to capacity, investment *must* taper off for physical reasons. And this implies that the increase in GNP will also taper off.

But what is wrong with this? Why can't the economy taper off at a high level and move along a gently rising full-employment plateau? Basically, because a reduced rate of increase in aggregate demand cuts induced investment via the accleration principle. A drop in investment then leads, via the multiplier, to a drop in national income.

The tendency for the fixed-investment accelerator to go into reverse after a while is reinforced by financial factors. There is usually a squeeze on corporate profits in the later stages of expansion. As the labor market tightens and the price level begins to move upward, wage increases become larger. But as the rate of increase of demand slows down, it becomes harder to pass this on to buyers in higher prices. So price-cost margins tend to shrink, and total profits stagnate or decline. This is typically not passed back to stockholders in lower dividends but is simply absorbed by corporations as a reduced cash flow.

In the latter stages of expansion, too, the Federal Reserve usually becomes concerned about the rate of inflation and puts on the monetary brakes. Interest rates rise rather sharply and credit rationing is intensified. This reinforces the squeeze on companies' cash position and reduces their ability to carry out investment programs.

Remember, too, that several other props for expansion have already been removed. Residential construction usually turns down midway through an upswing, due mainly to rising interest rates and reduced supply of investment funds. Inventory investment has been declining since the start of the second expansion phase, and purchases of consumer durables have usually also turned downward. So, when business fixed investment turns down, or even if it ceases to rise substantially, the balance of forces becomes negative and a downswing ensues.

The downswing

The most interesting feature of the downswing is its relative brevity. While upswings average about three years in length, cycle downswings since 1945 have averaged a bit under one year.

What breaks the force of the decline and brings about an upturn within a relatively short period? First, tight money changes very rapidly to loose money. As output falls, business demand for loans also falls, banks find themselves with ample lending capacity, and interest rates fall. This is helpful especially to residential construction. We noted earlier that residential construction typically begins to decline in the middle of the upswing, as mortgage money becomes scarcer and more expensive. But it begins to revive early in the downswing and is moving upward well before business in general.

A second favorable factor is the behavior of inventory investment. This has also been moving downward in the second phase of the upswing and is usually negative in the first few months of the downswing. But it then changes course. As inventory investment rises back toward zero and then becomes positive, new orders for goods increase, and this helps to end the downswing. Government expenditure also maintains an even course. In recessions since 1945, it has continued to rise right through the downswing.

In post-1945 downswings, unlike the "bad old days" before 1940, the drop in GNP has never exceeded a few percent. The decline is concentrated in consumer durable goods and plant and equipment investment, and in steel and other industries which provide materials for these sectors. Output of nondurable consumer goods and services as well as government output tend to go on rising right through the downswing.

So we are back where we started: at the beginning of the next upswing.

FORECASTING

What's going to happen next on the economic front? Everyone would like to know. Economic forecasting has become a favorite indoor sport of journalists, commentators, sales managers, and public officials. The quality of these forecasts varies greatly. Many are so vague or loaded with weasel words that the forecaster can hardly lose, but by the same token the user of the forecast can hardly benefit.

A good way to judge whether a forecast should be taken seriously is to see whether it uses numbers. Economics is a quantitative subject, and masses of current statistical information are now available. Unless an economic writer indicates a grasp of this material and is willing to spell out predictions in figures, the forecast cannot be taken seriously.

"And when this button lights up it's time to readjust for inflation."

From The Wall Street Journal, *with permission of Cartoon Features Syndicate.*

Barometric forecasting: Leading indicators

This method does not require any theorizing about the causes of economic fluctuations. It is purely inductive. It rests on the observation that things have happened in a certain way in the past and a surmise that they may happen similarly in the future.

The best known example is the work of the National Bureau of Economic Research. Research workers at the bureau have analyzed the movement of several hundred economic variables over a long period in the past, beginning in some cases as early as 1870. Particular attention has been paid to upper and lower turning points in each series, which presumably reflect the rhythm of overall economic fluctuations. From an examination of this material, the bureau has established a precise year and month for each upturn and downturn in general economic activity. By comparing the turning points of a particular series with that for business in general, one can discover whether the series typically reverses itself earlier than general business, at about the same time, or later.

On this basis, the series have been classified into three groups:

1. *Leading series,* which typically turn up and down in advance of general business. Included in this group are business failures, stock prices, new orders for durable goods, building contracts, average workweek in manufacturing, new incorporations, and sensitive wholesale prices.
2. *Roughly coincident series,* which turn at about the same time as general business. This group includes employment, unemployment, industrial production, GNP, freight carloadings, corporate profits, and wholesale prices (except farm and food products). This amounts to saying that these are the series to which the bureau attaches greatest weight in

defining the turning points in general business, and also that these major indicators move quite closely together.

3. *Lagging series,* which move somewhat behind the swing of general business. Among this group are personal income, retail sales, consumer installment debt, manufacturers' inventories, and bank rates on business loans.

How can this kind of information be used by the economic forecaster? It is no use to look at the lagging series, which are always behind the course of events. Even the coincident series do not help on prediction, though they can *confirm* a turning point two or three months after it has occurred. The only way to obtain an advance tip-off is to look at the leading series, which normally move ahead of general business. If five or six of these have already changed direction, one can reasonably conclude that a turning point in economic activity is near.

Since particular interest attaches to leading series, their past performance is shown in Table 11–3. The titles of the indicators are self-explanatory, with the possible exception of "accession rate," which simply means workers added to the payroll as a percentage of those already employed. Note that two of the series—the layoff rate and business failures—move in the *opposite* direction from national income. To use them as indicators, therefore, they must be "inverted," charted upside down.

TABLE 11–3
Behavior of 12 leading indicators at business cycle peaks and troughs

Indicator	Median Lead (−) or Lag (+) (months)	Longest Lead (months)	Lag
Sensitive employment and unemployment indicators			
Average hours worker per week, manufacturing	−6	−20	+5
Gross accession rate, manufacturing	−4	−35	0
Layoff rate, manufacturing, inverted	−6	−27	−1
New investment commitments			
New orders, durable good industries	−5	−35	0
Housing starts, number of new dwelling units	−6	−31	+8
Commercial and industrial building contracts, floor space	−2	−32	+3
Net change in number of operating businesses	−4	−33	+21
Profits, business failures, and stock prices			
Business failures, liabilities, inverted	−7	−28	+7
Corporate profits after taxes	−2	−20	+1
Common stock price index, industrials, rails and utilities	−4.5	−21	+9
Inventory investment and sensitive commodity prices			
Change in business inventories	−10	−26	+1
Industrial materials spot market price index	−2	−29	+9

Source: Geoffrey H. Moore, ed., *Business Cycle Indicators,* vol. 1 (Princeton, N.J.: Princeton University Press, 1961), p. 56.

The first column shows the average number of months by which each series has been ahead of general business at downturns and upturns. Thus, we see that new housing starts change direction, on the average, six months ahead of total output, while common stock prices are four to five months ahead. These averages, unfortunately, conceal a good deal of variation from one cycle to the next, as is evident from the last two columns. Thus, while common stock prices are usually a good indicator of a turning point in the near future, on one occasion they changed direction almost two years before general business, and on another occasion they moved nine months *later* than economic activity. Reliance on any one indicator, then, can be quite misleading.[4] A particular series will sometimes "flash the signal" a good deal too early, while in other cases there may be no signal at all until after the fact.

There are two main reasons why a series may be a leading series:

1. It may measure something which foreshadows a change in productive activity. An increase in building contracts normally means a rise in construction work a few months later. A rise in new orders for durable goods leads to increased activity in the metals and machinery industries. An increase in incorporations means that the new businesses will shortly be spending money on plant and office facilities.

2. A series may express the combined opinion of experienced observers about what lies immediately ahead. When large investors become convinced that a downswing is "bottoming out" and will soon end, they will buy securities immediately to get in at the bottom. Thus, the stock market will turn up before the upturn in physical production. The same is true of raw material prices and other items included in the "sensitive wholesale price" index.

The barometric approach rests on economic logic. There are good reasons why the leading series *are* leading series on the average. But the method also involves certain weaknesses:

a. The variability in the behavior of individual series has already been noted. A series which is "well behaved" most of the time may deceive you in a particular case by reversing itself too early or too late.

b. Most economic series show small, irregular fluctuations from month to month. If an index declines in a particular month, one cannot tell immediately whether this is a real turning point or a minor variation which will be reversed next month. It may take two or three months to be reasonably sure, and this cuts into the forecaster's precious margin of time.

The pioneering work of the National Bureau was taken over in 1961 by the U.S. Department of Commerce, which now collects the data and publishes them every month in the *Business Conditions Digest*. The move-

---

[4] The movement of a large number of economic indicators is published monthly by the U.S. Census Bureau in *Business Conditions Digest*.

ment of the individual series is averaged to provide a single "index of leading indicators," which you will see cited in the newspapers. An analysis[5] of the performance of this index over the years 1948–75 suggests that, while not fully reliable, it is distinctly better than nothing. At cycle peaks, it turned down on average five months before GNP turned down, and it failed to turn down in advance only once out of nine times. At cycle troughs, it turned up on average seven months before GNP began to rise, and again there was only one failure out of nine cases.

Econometric forecasting

Suppose that the economy has passed a lower turning point, and an upswing is underway. It is important for business and government planning to estimate what is likely to happen during the next year or so. Specifically, one needs estimates of (1) the growth rate of money GNP, or GNP in current dollars; (2) the inflation rate, that is, how much of the increase in money GNP will be due simply to rising prices; and (3) the increase in physical output or real GNP. The three figures must of course be consistent. If money GNP is estimated to rise by 10 percent and physical output by 3 percent, the remaining 7 percent must be the inflation rate.

Because of the demand for such estimates, economic forecasting has now become a large business. A half-dozen major concerns and a good many smaller ones prepare forecasts and sell them to customers. This kind of work involves:

1. Assumptions about fiscal and monetary policies over the year ahead: the government expenditure rate, tax levels, and rate of increase in money supply. Because these things are subject to change during the year, it may be necessary to prepare several alternative forecasts.

2. A guess about external shocks which may hit the economy during the year. Will foreign demand of U.S. goods rise or fall next year and by how much? How much will OPEC raise oil prices? And so on. The poor record of forecasters in 1974–75 was due partly to failure to foresee the size and effects of the first oil price crunch.

3. An *economic model,* which specifies the relations among major variables in the economy. While we cannot discuss such models in depth, their spirit can be conveyed by an example. Business investment in plant and equipment is an important component of GNP, so we want some way of predicting its value. We theorize that plant and equipment investment *(PE)* depends on the rate of interest *(R)*, the corporate cash flow *(L),* and the change in output between last year and this year *(Y −*

---

[5] Philip A. Klein and Geoffrey H. Moore, "The Leading Indicator Approach to Economic Forecasting—Retrospect and Prospect," working paper no. 941 (Cambridge, Mass.: National Bureau of Economic Research, July 1982).

Y_{-1}), which brings in the influence of the accelerator. This gives us an equation of the form

$$PE = f(R, L, Y - Y_{-1})$$

in which the dependent variable PE is related to three independent variables.

We next want to know *how much* a change in each of the independent variables will change PE. For example, how large a change in PE will result from a one point change in the rate of interest. To learn this, we resort to statistical estimation, which mean looking at figures over, say, the last 20 years to see what the average relation has been in the past. The equation is thus tested and reduced to quantitative form.

To get a forecast of PE for the coming year, we put into the equation specific values for R, L, and $Y - Y_{-1}$ (which are not pulled out of the air, but are themselves derived from other equations in the model). We then push the button, and the computer tells us the probable value of PE. The procedure assumes, of course, that the future will resemble the past, that relations derived from past experience will operate with the same strength in the future. To the extent that this is not strictly true, some forecasting error is inevitable.

The larger forecasting models include 300 to 400 equations—some aimed at predicting components of aggregate demand, some aimed at supplies, and others aimed at predicting wage and price movements. These are constantly being tested, revised, and brought up to date by dozens of economists and statisticians using elaborate computer equipment.

The forecasting record

Economic forecasting has not yet reached a high level of reliability. The fallibility of the procedure is suggested by the degree of variation among forecasts. Consider, for example, the following forecasts for 1981, all produced by large and reputable organizations:

TABLE 11–4

Organization	Money GNP (percent change from 1980)	Real GNP (percent change from 1980)	Inflation Rate (GNP deflator)	Unemployment Rate (percent)
Chase Econometrics	10.2	0.7	9.4	8.3
The Conference Board	9.6	−0.4	10.0	8.2
Data Resources	10.8	0.8	9.8	7.9
Evans Economics	11.5	1.9	9.4	7.6
Wharton Econometric Forecasting	11.2	1.9	9.2	7.6

Source: Reproduced from the *New York Times*, January 18, 1981.

These estimates are in the same ball park, but some are distinctly more optimistic than others as regards growth of real GNP. You can now, if you wish, look at the actual 1981 figures and judge which forecaster performed best.

Many researchers have played this game for past years, comparing forecasts made in advance of the year with actual results during the year. These studies suggest that forecasters tend to predict more stability than actually exists. They overpredict output on the downswing and underpredict it on the upswing, and similarly for price fluctuations. Still, the forecasts track events fairly closely except in years of severe external shocks, such as the oil price explosions of 1973–74 and 1979–80.

How far can forecasts be made more reliable in the future? The models themselves may be improved by further experience and testing. But the main sources of error arise at earlier steps of the procedure—assumptions about policy settings in government and guesses about external shocks. Unexpected changes in these areas will always confound the forecasters to some extent.

Still, forecasting services will continue to flourish and make money. Where there is so much demand, there is bound to be a supply.

THINK ABOUT THIS

1. Take the most recent turning point which has occurred in the economy at the time you read this chapter. Look up in *Business Conditions Digest* each of the leading indicators listed in Table 11–3 and determine *their* turning points. How well did they perform as predictors on this occasion?
2. Around the beginning of each calendar year there are numerous published forecasts for the year ahead—in the *Annual Economic Report of the President,* in the monthly economic newsletters of leading banks, in newspaper financial pages, and so on. Look at these carefully, and try to figure out how they were put together.

NEW CONCEPTS

business cycle
economic fluctuation
upswing
downswing
upper turning point
lower turning point
autonomous investment
induced investment

acceleration principle
lagging series
leading series
coincident series
barometric forecasting
econometric forecasting
recession
depression

SUMMARY

1. Fluctuations in national income are concentrated in the various components of business investment.

2. The *acceleration principle* is helpful in explaining these fluctuations. As applied to plant and equipment investment, the principle states, first, that fluctuations in product sales will be magnified into larger fluctuations in investment. Second, a *decline in the rate of increase* of sales can cause an absolute decline in investment. The acceleration principle is applicable also to investment in housing and in business inventories.

3. On this and other grounds, one can readily explain why, once an upswing is underway, it will build up momentum and continue for some time in the same direction. It is harder to explain the *turning points,* particularly the upper turning point. Review the section on the upper turning point for some clues on this matter.

4. A simple method of *barometric forecasting* involves the use of leading series which typically turn up or down in advance of general business. But this method is not entirely dependable, and at best it predicts only the *date* of turning points, not the *magnitude* of upward or downward movements.

5. *Econometric forecasting* involves developing statistically tested equations for relations among key variables in the economy. But it also involves assumptions about fiscal and monetary decisions by government and guesses about supply shocks and other external events. Because of surprises on these fronts, forecasts are bound to be somewhat in error.

TO LEARN MORE

You will find it educational to check the movement of key economic aggregates—GNP components, wages, prices, money supply, interest rates—over the past year or two, and see how their behavior compares with the "typical" behavior outlined in this chapter. The standard statistical sources mentioned in the "To Learn More" sections in previous chapters will be helpful. Another useful source is the *Brookings Papers on Economic Activity,* published three times a year by the Brookings Institution, Washington, D.C. The articles in this journal focus on analyzing recent macroeconomic behavior.

■ 12 ■

Macroeconomic Policy: Strategy and Tools

If to do were as easy as to know what to do, chapels had been churches, and poor men's cottages princes' palaces.

— WILLIAM SHAKESPEARE, THE MERCHANT OF VENICE

In earlier chapters, we were describing how the economy operates. Now we turn to what government can do to improve its operation.

There is a general principle that to achieve a given number of targets, one needs an equal number of instruments. This principle is not confined to economics. A car driver wants to arrive at a point on the map, located in two dimensions. The driver has two instruments, an engine and a steering wheel. But if he were flying an airplane, and operating in three dimensions, he would need a third instrument to control altitude.

The key objectives of macroeconomic policy are a high level of *output and employment* and a stable level of *prices*. The two tools available are money supply and the federal budget. If we add a third objective, equilibrium in our balance of payments with other countries, we need a third instrument, the exchange rate between the dollar and other currencies. Here we focus on the price and output objectives, leaving balance-of-payments problems to Chapter 15.

A desirable rate of *economic growth* is often listed among the objectives. Actually, economic growth is usually not a direct objective of policy. But anything the government does in pursuing price and output objectives is likely to have side effects on the growth rate. We will consider some of these side effects here and explore the growth problem more thoroughly in Chapter 14.

Since the Great Depression, economists generally have argued that government should adjust its monetary and fiscal policies to offset economic fluctuations. If output is undesirably low, stimulative policies are in order. If output is above the NAIRU point and the inflation rate is rising, restrictive policies are called for. This deliberate adjustment of policy to achieve desirable output and price level targets is usually called *fine tuning*.

We shall consider first the characteristics of a good policy tool, for fine-tuning purposes: speed of decision and application, strength and predictability of results, and so on. Next, how does monetary policy operate in practice? And how does fiscal policy operate? How far do these two tool sets meet the requirements for a "good" policy tool laid down at the outset?

In actuality, monetary and fiscal decisions are both being taken all the time. This poses a need for *coordination* of policy, so that the right hand at the Fed is not undoing what the left hand at the Treasury is trying to accomplish. We shall ask how far coordination exists at present and what might be done to increase it.

Finally, we shall consider a basic policy dispute between economists who favor fine tuning and those who prefer *fixed rules* for monetary and fiscal policy. We shall look at the factual issues involved in this dispute and the evidence available on them.

Characteristics of a good policy instrument

Suppose that you are a federal administrator and that you believe in fine tuning. What kind of policy tools would you like to have available, in an ideal world?

The following characteristics are usually considered desirable:

1. Speed of application.   Events move rapidly in the economy. A business cycle peaks out and turns into recession in a matter of weeks. The time from the peak of an upswing to the trough of a recession is typically less than a year. So how quickly a decision can be reached is quite important.

There is, first, an unavoidable *information lag*. It takes time for economic statistics to be collected and processed, so it is usually one to two months after an economic change has occurred before policymakers know that it has occurred. Then it takes additional time to determine whether last month's change was an erratic fluctuation or a continuing trend. A common rule of thumb is to require movement in the same direction for three months before accepting it as significant. Thus, the information lag, for both monetary and fiscal decisions, can scarcely be less than four months or so.

Even after the economic situation is known, it takes time to discuss and get agreement on what policy actions are appropriate. This is the *decision* lag. After a decision is reached, there may be a further *applica-*

tion lag, during which steps are taken to make the decision effective.

The sum of these three lags is usually called the *inside lag* of economic policy, because it occurs within the government machinery. Whether it is short or long can make the difference between a sharp instrument and a blunt one.

2. Speed of impact.   After a policy action is taken, it will take time for it to affect private decision makers and be reflected in output, employment, and prices. This lag between action and consequences is called the *outside lag* of economic policy. Typically, the impact is not felt at one point in time but is spread over a considerable period of time. There may be little effect for several months, then an increasing effect up to a year or so, then diminishing effects for a long time after that. This pattern is called a *distributed lag* in statistical analysis.

It is desirable that the outside lag be short, so that policy becomes effective rapidly. It is desirable also that the aftereffects not linger on into a phase of that cycle at which they are no longer appropriate.

3. Predictability of impact.   A policy instrument must "work" in the sense that there actually is an impact in the desired direction. In addition, one should be able to predict the size of the impact within reasonable margins of error. Unless we can do this, we are working in the dark.

4. Neutrality.   By this we mean neutrality among businesses, industries, and sectors in the private economy. The object is to ensure full use of resources, but without distorting the allocation of resources which reflects private preferences. This is doubtless a counsel of perfection. Probably no government action can be strictly neutral in this sense. But the side effect of an action on resource allocation and on income distribution should be analyzed and weighed before the action is taken.

MONETARY POLICY

How monetary policy operates

The structure and powers of the Federal Reserve System were discussed in Chapter 6. The Fed's day-to-day policy tool is *open market operations* (i.e., purchase or sale of federal securities with a view to raising or lowering bank reserves).

Monetary policy operates quite indirectly. The ultimate object is to affect the level of output and employment and, at times, the rate of inflation. But the Fed cannot get at these goals directly. It cannot even control the money supply with any precision. What it can (largely) control is bank reserves. The subsequent chain of events can be outlined as follows:

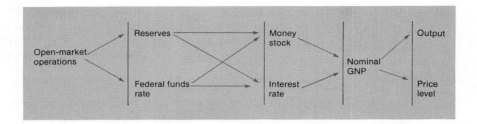

The direct effect of an open-market operation is to raise or lower the reserves of the banking system. We saw in Chapter 6 that a bank which is short of reserves can borrow from the Fed or, more commonly, from another bank which has excess reserves at the moment. The interest rate on these interbank loans, called the *federal funds rate,* is a sensitive indicator of money market conditions. If the Fed is draining reserves from the system, more banks will be forced to borrow, and the federal funds rate will rise. If, on the other hand, the Fed is supplying reserves faster than the banks need at the moment, the federal funds rate will fall. Since the Fed does not announce publicly what strategy it is following, and since stock market operators are very eager to figure out this strategy, they watch changes in the federal funds rate as a clue.

We saw in Chapter 6 that a change in bank reserves will lead, through the *money multiplier,* to a larger change in the money stock. Since the multiplier is somewhat changeable, the impact on money supply cannot be predicted precisely, but the direction of change is certain. Since the supply of money together with the demand for money determine the rate of interest, there will also be an effect on that rate. If demand remains unchanged, a rise in money supply means a fall in the interest rate, and conversely.

At the next stage, the money supply change affects the level of nominal GNP. Again, the size of the effect cannot be predicted exactly because of changes in the velocity of money, which usually rises sharply during economic upswings and falls on the downswing. Indeed, studies of cycles since 1945 show that changes in velocity are more important than changes in the growth rate of money supply in explaining the cyclical ups and downs of nominal GNP.

Finally, the change in nominal GNP is distributed between a change in output and a change in the price level. We saw in Chapter 9 that the main short-run effect is on output; but both effects are present, and the split depends somewhat on the level of output, with price effects increasing in importance as output approaches or passes the NAIRU point.

The moral is that there are many possible slips 'twixt cut and lip. A push or pull by the Fed on the open-market lever will ripple through the economy. But what will come out at the end of the chain, and how long it will take to come out, is only roughly predictable.

The choice of targets: Money supply versus interest rates

Policy makers at the Fed are, of course, concerned with the end of the chain, with the level of output and employment, and with the rate of inflation. But they cannot get at these things directly. So they must choose some *intermediate target* as a guide to day-to-day policy.

The two main candidates for this target role are the money stock and the rate of interest. The Fed can aim at a certain rate of increase in M1, M2, and so on; *or* it can aim at a certain level of interest rates. It cannot, as we explained in Chapter 8, do both things at the same time. If it aims to increase M1 at 6 percent per year or some other regular rate, then interest rates will fluctuate with changes in demand for money. If, on the other hand, it tries to hold interest rates steady, it loses control of the money supply. The interest rate will be stable only if money supply is increased to match any increase in money demand.

The relative merit of money stock targets and interest rate targets has been debated for a long time, with no end in sight. Most economists, and monetarists in particular, seem to prefer a monetary target on several grounds. Money supply is somewhat more measurable, partly because there are a great variety of interest rates and because it is not easy to get from nominal interest rates to the real (inflation-adjusted) interest rates which are more significant. Monetarists also believe that the money supply → nominal GNP linkage is more direct and predictable than the interest rate → nominal GNP linkage. In the background, too, is the fact that the interest rate is a politically sensitive price, with the political pressures usually favoring lower interest rates rather than higher. Thus, a policy of stabilizing interest rates can easily lead to excessive growth of money supply with inflationary consequences. So economists who are leery of inflation are apt to be equally leery of interest rate targets.

The man in the street, however, and especially the man in Wall Street, looks at things differently. The reason is the direct linkage between interest rates and securities prices. A fall in interest rates is equivalent to a rise in bond prices, and stock prices tend to move in sympathy. An interest rate drop is thus bullish for the market, while a rise in interest rates is bearish. So the favorite guessing game in Wall Street is: Which way will interest rates move next? And the Fed is under considerable pressure not to let interest rates change rapidly, especially in an upward direction, since that would tend to depress security prices.

Because of these practical consequences, the Fed has historically given considerable weight to interest rate stability as well as to money supply growth. In October 1979, however, there was a rather sharp shift of policy, brought about by unusually rapid money stock growth, double-digit inflation, and a drop in the value of the dollar on foreign exchanges. The Fed announced a strong anti-inflation program, part of which was a decision to emphasize monetary targets and to control money stock growth more firmly than before. A natural consequence was increased variability of interest rates, which at times in 1980 and 1981 reached unheard-of highs. Despite considerable complaint, the Fed in general held its ground, continuing to emphasize monetary targets and lowering the target growth rates gradually over the years.

Beginning in 1975, Congress also came into the picture. The Chairman of the Board of Governors is required to come before Congress four times a year to reveal the Fed's money growth targets and to answer questions both about these targets and about the past record of monetary growth. There have been occasional proposals that Congress should be empowered not only to listen but to prescribe what the growth rates should be. The Fed has naturally opposed such proposals, and they have never gotten off the ground.

Because of the unpredictabilities emphasized above, the money targets are always stated as a *range* rather than a single figure: say, an annual growth rate of 5 to 8 percent for M1, and 7 to 10 percent for M2. It is generally recognized, too, that the growth rate cannot be controlled closely from week to week or even from month to month. Quite often, the actual result for a calendar quarter falls outside the target range. When this happens, the Fed tries to lean in the opposite direction in the following quarter. The record of hitting the range is considerably better over year-long periods than over shorter periods.

While money supply is now in the center of the stage, the Fed still keeps a weather eye cocked at the movement of interest rates and particularly the federal funds rate. The practical reason for this is the effect of any sharp change in interest rates on stock and bond prices. So some critics maintain that the Fed is still secretly addicted to interest rate stability, and that it has not gone far enough in focusing on money supply as the prime target for policy.

What the Fed is actually trying to do, as is evident from the causal chain shown earlier, is to influence the growth rate of nominal GNP. So why not target nominal GNP directly? This has been suggested by some monetary scholars, but the Fed has shown no inclination to move in this direction. The technical problem is that to go from a money stock target to a nominal GNP target requires predicting changes in the velocity of money, which are sizable but uncertain. (The Fed obviously *cares* about nominal GNP, and so must have predictions of V in the back of its mind; but it prefers not to drag these out into the open.) The Fed can also say with some reason: "We are not in the business of controlling GNP. We are in the business of regulating money supply, which is something we know about and for which our tools are appropriate." To announce a target for nominal GNP would come close to announcing a target for employment and unemployment, which is politically sensitive and could easily land the Fed in hot water.

Evaluating monetary policy

How far does monetary policy meet the criteria for a good policy instrument set forth earlier? What is the evidence on length of the inside lag, length of the outside lag, predictability of impact, and neutrality among sectors of the economy?

The information lag cannot be avoided, but the decision lag is short. The Federal Open Market Committee meets every month and is in telephone communication during the month. The scale of open market operations can be adjusted from day to day by instructions to the trading desk at the Federal Reserve Bank of New York. This short inside lag is a decided advantage of monetary policy.

The outside lag, on the other hand, is quite long. The average lag, that is, the time from action to peak effect, has been estimated at eight to nine months, with effects lingering on for two years or so. One reason is that interest rate changes affect mainly construction activity—housing, factories, and commercial building—which takes considerable time to plan and complete.

Predictability of impact is not as high as may appear at first glance. What the Fed can control precisely is the size of bank reserves. But there is uncertainty at later links in the causal chain sketched above. Because of variability in the money multiplier, a given change in reserves may translate into a larger or smaller change in money stock. Because of variability of velocity, a given change in money stock may mean a larger or smaller change in spending, in nominal GNP. And how this change will be divided between output and prices is also somewhat uncertain. The Fed uses an econometric model of the economy, as well as informed hunches and intuition, in an effort to make the best possible forecast of results. But quite often it undershoots or overshoots and then has to correct by tacking in the opposite direction.

Experienced Fed watchers draw two conclusions about monetary policy in practice. First, it clearly is counter-cyclical. Expansionist action is taken soon after the beginning of a downswing, and restrictive action is often taken toward the top of an upswing. Second, up to the policy shift of 1979, policy was rather tolerant (the polite word is "accommodative") toward inflation. Monetary targets were set so as to take account of the built-in rate of inflation as well as expected growth of real GNP, so that there was little downward pressure on the inflation rate. Since 1979, the Fed has taken a tougher stance, and it deserves much of the credit for deceleration of inflation from more than 10 percent in 1980 to 4.3 percent in 1983.[1] The cost, of course, was a 6-month recession in 1980 and a 15-month recession in 1981–82, with substantial unemployment and loss of output.

What about the neutrality of monetary policy? A tightening of policy makes borrowing harder, partly by a rise in interest rates but also partly through *credit rationing* by the banks. When the Fed is reducing bank reserves, the banks respond both by raising interest rates and by rationing credit, that is, refusing to accommodate all of those who are willing to borrow at the going rate. Conversely, when the Fed raises reserves, the banks both lower interest rates and accept a higher percentage of loan applications. Both things help to increase borrowing and to raise aggregate demand.

This is often described as an impersonal, thermostatic device, which produces its effects through the market mechanism. If the Fed succeeds in raising interest rates and restricting credit, some would-be borrowers will be left unsatisfied. But the Fed does not say which borrowers or which projects will be dropped from the list. This is left to negotiations between private borrowers and lenders.

But the argument that monetary policy is neutral should not be pushed too far. True, the Fed does not set out deliberately to discriminate against certain businesses or groups. But is not a rise in interest rates and restriction of credit inherently discriminatory? It is argued that this may be true in at least two respects:

1. Some types of spending are inherently more interest-sensitive than others. This is true notably of house building, which is financed mainly through mortgages, with the level of mortgage rates having a large effect on housing demand. It is true of other large construction projects which are financed mainly on credit. And it is true of consumer purchases of durable goods, notably automobiles, where most of the purchase price is usually borrowed. It is no accident that the 1981–82 recession, during which interest rates were pushed unusually high, had a severe impact on the automobile and construction industries.

2. Some companies have larger internal resources than others and hence are less dependent on external credit. In addition, some businesses have a higher credit rating and better banking connections than others. When the banks are forced to restrict loans, they will still try to accommodate preferred borrowers with high credit ratings. Thus, the impact of restriction falls more heavily on smaller and newer businesses which are regarded as less creditworthy. Statistical studies suggest that small concerns do suffer somewhat more than big ones during periods of tight

---

[1] As noted earlier, there are several price indexes, which differ somewhat in movement. The rate of increase in the consumer price index fell from 12.4 percent in 1980 to 3.8 percent in 1983. The rise of the producer price index fell from 11.8 percent to 0.6 percent, and the GNP deflator covering all output fell from 10.2 percent to 4.3 percent.

money, both because of lower credit standing and smaller internal resources.

FISCAL POLICY

The meaning of fiscal policy

Fiscal policy means adjusting the federal budget year by year to steer
the economy toward a desirable level of output and employment. If aggregate demand is too low, it can be raised by either an increase in federal
purchases or a reduction in net taxes. If aggregate demand is too high,
which will usually mean too high a rate of inflation, the prescription
goes into reverse: cut federal purchases and/or raise net taxes.

While in principle fiscal policy can mean either varying expenditures
or net taxes, in practice it means mainly the latter. There is rather wide
agreement that government purchases *should not* be varied to offset short-
term fluctuations in national output. This is partly because it is difficult
to vary public construction programs quickly. But more basically, it is
because the proper level of government output depends on long-term
priorities. A new school or highway needed next year is needed just as
much whether the year happens to be a good one or a poor one. Leaving
potholes unfilled to provide jobs during the next recession would mean
a lot of broken springs in the meantime.

The main burden of fiscal policy, then, falls on net taxes. If aggregate
demand threatens to be too high, leading to undue inflation, tax rates
can be raised and transfer payments reduced. Conversely, if demand is
insufficient, tax rates can be cut and transfer payments increased. This
happens automatically to some extent, because a recession means larger
unemployment compensation payments as unemployment rises. But in
addition, a recession usually brings proposals in Congress for a personal
income tax cut, a cash bonus to taxpayers, extension of the normal 26-
week period for unemployment compensation to 39 or 52 weeks, hiring
workers for special public works programs, and other measures to aid
the unemployed and raise private spending.

Budget making in practice

The federal budget year runs from October 1 to October 1. Thus
October 1, 1985–October 1, 1986 is "fiscal 1986." Preparation of a proposed 1986 budget by the executive branch began about a year in advance.
In the fall of 1984, each department and agency submitted its request
for 1986 to the Office of Management and Budget, which operates directly
under the president. These requests are normally larger, often considerably

larger, than actual expenditures in the previous year. Each agency feels entitled to *at least* as much as it currently has and is prepared to bargain only over the size of next year's increase. President after president has told the agencies that they are not "entitled" to anything and must justify next year's budget from the ground up, a policy called "zero-base budgeting." But this has not yet had much impact on seasoned federal administrators.

The OMB bargains at length with each agency and eventually submits a draft budget to the president. The president, after deliberation and additional bargaining, sends his proposals to Congress in late January in the annual Budget Message. Congress, of course, has final authority on taxes and expenditures, subject to the rarely used presidential veto. Procedure in Congress is complex and at times bewildering. Tax legislation originates in the House Ways and Means Committee, but the Senate Finance Committee eventually becomes involved. Expenditure appropriations are reviewed by specialized committees and subcommittees in both the House and Senate. Until the 70s, strange as it may seem, neither house voted on the budget as a whole. This was changed in 1974 by creation of an overall Budget Committee, supported by a sizable economic staff. The committee recommends, and Congress is obliged to vote on, an overall expenditure ceiling for the coming fiscal year. The numerous appropriations committees are then pressured to tailor their spending recommendations so as to fit within the approval total.

"Always remember this, grandson: there's no such thing as a free lunch. But . . . properly handled, they can be tax deductible."

From The Wall Street Journal, *with permission of Cartoon Features Syndicate.*

Experience has revealed several facts of life about fiscal behavior, which should be considered in evaluating its usefulness as a stabilization tool. First, the pressures impinging on congressmen and congresswomen are mainly pressures to increase expenditures and transfer payments. Steps in these directions are always popular, while steps to raise taxes or reduce expenditures are unpopular. The system is thus biased in the direction of larger deficits than would be warranted on stabilization grounds alone. Since 1960, there has been only one year (1969) of budget surplus. In 1979, at the peak of a business cycle, the federal deficit was still close to $30 billion. Deficits approaching $200 billion are projected for 1984 and 1985, despite an expected high level of output. The lesson that deficits are unavoidable and even desirable on the downswing seems to have been learned more thoroughly than the message that restraint is desirable on the upswing. Our political institutions, as well as our economic institutions, have an inflationary bias.

Second, it has proven impossible in practice to separate decisions about tax *levels* from decisions about tax *structure.* On paper, it may seem simple to make a clean, quick, across-the-board reduction or increase in taxes as the state of the economy may require. But there are a lot of taxes, which impinge differently on people with different income sources and at different income levels. So a proposal for a tax cut immediately raises the question of *who* is to benefit and by how much. The issue of the equity of the existing tax structure arises inescapably.

Partly because of arguments over tax equity and tax reform, discussion of tax bills is complicated, politically charged, and usually lengthy. Tax reductions can easily take six months or more, and the less palatable tax increases can take even longer.

Evaluating fiscal policy

Just as in the case of monetary policy, we must ask how fiscal policy measures up to our criteria for a good policy instrument. The inside lag, as just suggested, is substantial—certainly longer than in the case of monetary policy. The outside lag is also substantial. A change in personal income or social security tax rates affects disposable income almost immediately through the payroll withholding system, but it then takes time for consumers to adjust their spending patterns. We cited earlier Blinder's finding that about two thirds of the effect is felt within the first year after a tax change.

What about the *predictability* of fiscal actions—say, a reduction in personal tax rates? Writing about this is more cautious today than it was 20 years ago. Whether a tax cut increases consumer spending, and by how much, depends on how the cut is interpreted by consumers and particularly on how far it is viewed as a *permanent* increase in incomes.

The evidence suggests that a temporary change, whether upward or downward, has a smaller effect on spending than a permanent change.

Further, if spending does increase, there will be a multiplier effect on GNP. This increase in income will raise the demand for money. But since we have assumed no accompanying monetary action, the money supply is unchanged. Thus, the interest rate must rise, which will tend to reduce business investment, houseing construction, and sale of consumer durables. This crowding-out effect will at least partly offset the stimulating effect of the tax reduction.

The size of the crowding-out effect depends on things discussed in earlier chapters—the slope of the money-demand schedule, the rate at which this schedule shifts with a change in income, and how sensitive investment is to the rate of interest (slope of the *MEI* schedule). Since the slopes of these schedules can't yet be estimated accurately, the extent of crowding out can't be predicted accurately either. But there is evidence that the effect is substantial, especially in periods of high employment.

What about *neutrality?* Fiscal actions seem certain to be nonneutral. The reason is that the tax structure is complex, and hardly anyone is fully satisfied with it. Each congressman and each lobbyist has different ideas about desirable reforms, and what comes out is always a mixture of changes in tax *structure* and tax *levels.* The structure changes are likely to be nonneutral, first, as between consumption and investment. A reduction in business taxes is investment oriented, while a reduction in personal taxes is consumption oriented. Second, changes are usually nonneutral as regards the distribution of income. There are many ways of allocating a tax cut among people in different income brackets, and right-wing Republicans are not going to agree with liberal Democrats about which should be chosen.

So we will probably never see a tax package designed *solely* to affect the level of aggregate demand. What we will see are packages aimed partly at this objective but which also include a variety of other objectives.

Up to this point, we have considered fiscal policy as affecting aggregate demand. Recently, however, there has been increasing attention to the effect of fiscal actions on supply and on business costs. Increases in business costs resulting from government action—such as higher social security taxes, higher minimum wage rates, higher prices for agricultural and other raw materials, and higher costs of meeting regulatory requirements—are likely to be passed through fully and rapidly to consumers, adding to the inflation rate. By the same token, contrary fiscal actions—say more use of income tax revenues and less use of payroll taxes to finance the social security system—could reduce business costs and thus reduce inflationary momentum.

In a longer time perspective, tax measures designed to stimulate business investment and research and development activity might make possible a faster growth of our output capacity over the years. This is the important element of truth in the not-so-new "supply-side economics."

THINK ABOUT THIS

1. The Reagan administration proposed, and Congress approved, a large tax-cut program in 1981. How far was this program nonneutral, and in what direction?
2. The size of the crowding-out effect depends on the shapes of the money demand and *MEI* schedules.
   a. Construct a set of assumptions which would lead to a *strong* crowding-out effect.
   b. Construct another set of assumptions which would lead to a *weak* crowding-out effect.

POLICY MIX AND POLICY COORDINATION

Fiscal and monetary actions are both being taken all the time. To some extent, they are substitutes for each other. For example, if one wants to raise aggregate demand by 10 percent, different combinations of monetary and fiscal stimulus might be capable of doing this. So, what combination should be chosen? This is a problem of the *policy mix.*

Next, whatever mix is chosen, it should be possible to carry it through. Monetary and fiscal actions should fit together into a coherent strategy. This is the problem of *policy coordination.*

Let's look briefly at several kinds of situations: (1) Monetary policy used in support of fiscal policy; (2) fiscal policy used in support of monetary policy; (3) fiscal and monetary policy used together to achieve two separate objectives; and (4) a policy conflict.

1. A case of the first sort has already been encountered in discussing the crowding-out effect. Suppose aggregate demand is judged to be too low. The government adopts a more expansionist fiscal program, involving a larger deficit. This will tend to raise nominal income. But with an unchanged stock of money, interest rates will rise, which in turn tends to reduce private investment. Since the purpose is to stimulate the economy, this adverse effect on investment is counterproductive. It can be avoided, provided the monetary authority follows an *accommodative policy.* If the Fed increases the money supply at a rate sufficient to keep interest rates from rising, the crowding-out effect need not occur.

2. The second type of situation may be illustrated by the problem of restraining an inflationary boom. This could be done by relying entirely on monetary policy. But to reduce aggregate demand sufficiently might

require pushing interest rates very high, with severe strain on financial markets and serious discomfort to some types of borrower. These strains can be reduced by shifting part of the burden to fiscal policy. Government can move to a more restrictive fiscal policy, involving a reduced deficit or a budget surplus. Thus, aggregate demand can be lowered to the desired level with a smaller rise in interest rates.

3. To illustrate situation (3), suppose that one wanted to raise the growth rate of the economy. A low-interest policy would stimulate investment and thus be helpful in achieving the growth objective. But this might also raise aggregate demand to an inflationary level. What to do? One might apply a more restrictive fiscal policy to curtail aggregate demand. This strategy amounts to using an expansionist monetary policy to stimulate growth, while relying on tight fiscal policy to avoid inflation.

Consider another situation of the same kind. Under the present system of flexible or "floating" exchange rates, the value of the dollar floats up or down relative to foreign currencies. Suppose that the dollar has been falling. The administration regards this as undesirable and wants to "defend the dollar." One way of doing this is to hold U.S. interest rates at a high level compared with interest rates in other countries. People and businesses will then shift money from other countries to the United States to earn higher interest. This creates a demand for dollars which, like any demand increase, tends to raise the price of the dollar.

The high interest policy, however, will have a depressing effect on aggregate demand and output in the United States. To offset this, it may be desirable to inject some fiscal stimulus through tax reductions.

4. Consider, finally, the possibility of a direct policy conflict. The White House and the Treasury are pulling in one direction, while the Fed is pulling in the other. Considering that the Fed is not subject to direct orders from either the president or Congress, this has to be admitted as a possibility, and there is evidence that at times it has become an actuality. A recent study of the period 1958–73 concluded that "the Fed and the administration acted much more in unison when a Republican was in the White House than when a Democrat was. Indeed, the correlation was consistently negative during the Kennedy-Johnson period, suggesting that the Fed tried to offset the impact of fiscal policy more often than it tried to accommodate it . . . the abstraction of a single authority conducting stabilization policy in the United States is just that—an abstraction with little or no empirical validity."[2]

The question of policy coordination is a thorny one. Within the executive branch, there is frequent consultation among key economic officials— the secretary of the Treasury, the director of the Office of Management and Budget, the chairman of the Council of Economic Advisers, and others.

---

[2] Allan S. Blinder and Stephen M. Goldfeld, "New Measures of Fiscal and Monetary Policy, 1958–73," *American Economic Review,* December 1976, pp. 780–96.

But Congress, jealous of its power over taxes and appropriations, does not necessarily go along with the administration. And then there is the Fed, not directly responsible to either the president or Congress.

The independence of the Fed, however, should not be exaggerated. In a sense, the Fed can preserve its independence only by not pushing it too far. Its actions have political consequences, and so it must walk a narrow chalk line. It has even been accused on occasion of tailoring its policies to an incumbent president's desire for reelection.

There is already a practice under which the chairman of the Board of Governors appears frequently before the Joint Economic Committee of Congress to explain and defind Federal Reserve policies. There have been proposals to go farther than this, by permitting Congress to specify monetary targets or by integrating the Fed into the executive branch. But the Fed, fearing that this would politicize its operations and reduce its ability to combat inflation, has so far successfully resisted such proposals.

THINK ABOUT THIS

Would it be a good idea *(a)* to make the chairman of the Board of Governors of the Federal Reserve System directly responsible to the president, or *(b)* to require the System to hold money supply growth rates and changes in interest rates within guidelines prescribed by Congress? Why, or why not?

FIXED RULES *VERSUS* FINE TUNING

All the discussion to this point has assumed the desirability of frequent monetary and fiscal changes aimed at "fine tuning" the economy. But this assumption is not universally accepted. An important body of thought holds that the economy would perform better if government followed *fixed rules* for monetary and fiscal policy and did not try to offset short-run fluctuations in the private economy. What are the issues in dispute, and what evidence do we have concerning them?

There are, in fact, three possible policy positions:

1. *Fixed rules* for money supply and the federal budget, which would remain unchanged for quite long periods of time. The favorite rule for money supply is that it should grow steadily at a rate equal to the long-term trend of real GNP, say, 4 percent a year. A commonly proposed fiscal rule is that the high-employment budget surplus should be zero.

Fixed-rule people tend also to be monetarists, though this connection is not logically necessary. They place main emphasis on steady growth of money supply and treat fiscal actions as secondary. So from here on we will refer to this school as *monetarists.*

2. *Fine tuning,* that is, frequent adjustment of monetary policy and the budget balance to offset instability in the private economy. A downswing in output and employment would be countered by lowering interest rates and tax rates, while the opposite actions would be taken to check undue inflation. The gas pedal and the brakes would be constantly in use, or at least constantly under consideration, rather than locked in fixed positions.

It is not quite accurate to label these people nonmonetarists, since almost everyone now regards money as a central force in the economy. Nor is it useful to call them post-Keynesians, which everyone now is. Let's instead call them *activists,* since they favor frequent active government intervention.

3. *Activist rules,* sometimes also called "formula flexibility." There would be a definite rule for monetary and fiscal policy at any moment, but the rule would be adjusted to changes in economic activity. For example, fiscal experts have often proposed an automatic variation of income tax rates within prescribed limits. A reduction of 1 percent in real GNP would trigger a reduction of 1 percent, or some other set figure, in the first-bracket tax rate. Tax rates would rise again on the next upswing.

A similar rule could be constructed for monetary policy. The operation of such a rule is illustrated in Figure 12–1. Suppose output capacity is growing at 4 percent a year and that we want money supply to grow on the average at this same rate. Suppose the nonaccelerating inflation rate of unemployment is judged to be 6 percent. Then the rule might provide that money supply growth will be adjusted upward if the unemployment rate rises above 6 percent and adjusted downward if unemployment falls below 6 percent. Under the formula illustrated in Figure 10–1, a 1 percent change in unemployment would trigger a 2 percent change in money supply growth. A different rule would change the *slope* of the M line, and a different decision about the NAIRU would shift it leftward or rightward.

This intermediate approach would allow economic policy to shift from time to time in the direction which activists regard as desirable. But the shifts would be predictable, which would be helpful to private decision makers. This approach removes the element of human discretion, which should reduce human error.

Whatever attractions the approach may hold on paper, however, it seems unlikely to be accepted by Congress or the Fed. So from here on we'll structure the discussion as a debate between positions 1 and 2. First, we'll review the main planks in the monetarist platform and the response which activists would make on each point. Then we'll review the available evidence.

FIGURE 12-1
An activist monetary rule

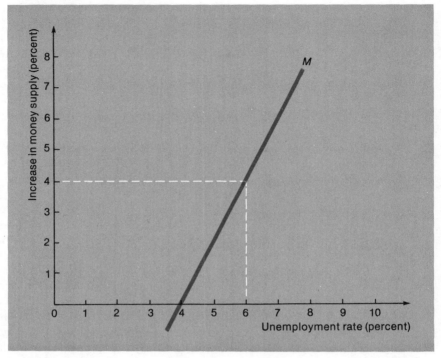

In this illustration, a 1 percent change in the unemployment rate, upward or downward, would trigger a 2 percent change in the growth rate of money supply in the same direction.

Monetarists and activists: The key issues

The policy differences among economists are not just whimsical or political. They rest on differing views of how the economy operates and on differing judgments of administrative feasibility. Here are the main issues:

1. Monetarists regard the private economy as basically rather stable. They think it would be even more stable if government bound itself to fixed rules which business executives and consumers could count on. Erratic government actions are at least as important a source of instability as variations in private spending.

Activists disagree. They point to instability in most components of investment—plant and equipment, business inventories, housing—and also in purchases of automobiles and other durable consumer goods. Fluctuations in spending on these items seem to set off a downswing every three or four years, which cannot be left to drift and possibly get out of hand. Instead, prompt action is needed to reverse the drop in output.

2. Even if the private economy is somewhat unstable, monetarists argue that it has built-in corrective mechanisms which will bring it back on course. A downswing tends to reduce money demand and interest rates, which brakes the decline in investment. A recession also produces downward pressure on wages and prices, which is helpful as regards both inflation and employment. (A drop in the price level means an increase in *real* money supply, which is expansionist.)

Activists retort that these corrective mechanisms are not very strong. In particular, downward flexibility of wages and prices has almost vanished from the economy. In addition, these correctives operate slowly and would take a long time to restore high employment. Why should we suffer underemployment year after year when employment can be raised quickly by activist measures?

3. Fine tuning, which involves actions aimed at the future, requires accurate estimates of the future. Monetarists believe that our forecasting ability is limited and point to a long record of forecasting errors. Activists argue that forecasting, even if imperfect at present, can be improved.

4. Monetarists emphasize also the *lags* and *uncertainties* involved in fine-tuning actions. The effects of a monetary or fiscal action are spread out over a long period in the future. An action taken to stimulate the economy at one point in time may still be stimulating it two years later, when restraint rather than stimulus is needed. Thus, at any moment, government is about as likely to be doing the wrong thing as the right thing.

The uncertainty about the effects of any action and uncertainty about what government may suddenly decide to do next month also create problems for private decision makers. Businesses would be able to plan more effectively and run their own operations more steadily if government followed consistent, credible policies on which everyone could rely.

Activists reply that these problems are overstated and that active intervention can on balance do more good than harm. So at any point in time, one will usually find activists saying "do something," while monetarists are apt to say "do nothing." (The exception is that one often finds monetarists saying "do something—to slow down the growth of money supply.")

5. This leads to a further point: a difference in the time horizon of the two groups. Activists tend to look at what can be done to improve the economy in the next 6 or 12 months. Monetarists think we should pay less attention to the short run and concentrate on policies which will pay off in the long run. They feel especially this way as regards inflation. They believe that over the long run, the growth rate of money supply is fully reflected in the price level. Thus, any serious anti-inflation

policy involves reducing this growth rate and holding it down for as long as necessary to produce the desired result.

6. A new line of argument which has come into play recently stresses the possible *ineffectiveness* of government action. It is associated with, though it is not the same thing as, the theory of *rational expectations*. Briefly, this theory holds that individual and business plans are based on expectations of the future. Further, these expectations are rational in the sense of taking into account all available information, *including information about expected government actions*. If government is following any predictable line of action, people will already have figured this out and adjusted their plans accordingly. So when government takes the expected action, *it will have no additional effect.*

Example. There is a drop in aggregate demand. By the usual supply-demand reasoning, one might expect this to lead to reductions in prices and wages. But people expect (correctly) that government will take prompt monetary action to restore aggregate demand to its previous level. So they will keep prices and wages unchanged or may even try to raise them.

So, people are smart—they will outguess the government. Thus, any consistent or predictable government actions will be ineffective. Government can have an effect only by surprising the public, by doing the unpredictable.

There have already been several efforts to test this hypothesis against available data.[3] The results are not very comforting to the theory. They suggest that even predictable government actions do have an effect—indeed, the effect seems to be about as strong as for unpredictable actions. Further, the models used by the rational expectations theorists are quite unrealistic, typically assuming complete flexibility of wages and prices. Thus, a 10 percent increase in aggregate demand would mean an *immediate* increase of 10 percent in the wage-price level, with no change in output, and conversely for a drop in demand. This is not the way the economy seems to operate. The main immediate effect of a change in aggregate demand is on output, as we explained in Chapter 9.

A review of evidence

In 1950, debate on these issues was largely in abstract terms. But we now have several decades of experience, mountains of statistics, and

---

[3] See in particular Robert J. Gordon, "Price Inertia and Policy Ineffectiveness in the United States," *Journal of Political Economy* 90 (December 1982), pp. 1087–1117; and Frederick Mishkin, "Does Anticipated Monetary Policy Matter? An Econometric Investigation," *Journal of Political Economy* 90 (February 1982), pp. 22–51.

a great deal of research. Some of the evidence has been reviewed in earlier chapters. Let's try to summarize what we've learned.

First, how unstable is the private economy? Early Keynesians worried mainly about a collapse of business confidence leading to a sharp drop in plant and equipment investment such as occurred in the Great Depression. This particular menace has not been important since 1945. Fixed investment has moved up rather steadily, falling a bit in recession years but soon reversing itself.

The main fluctuations in demand have been associated with:

1. Housing construction, which shows large cyclical swings. Note, however, that these are partly policy induced rather than "normal." During an upswing which reaches and passes the NAIRU, the Fed becomes concerned increasingly about inflation and raises interest rates to cool the economy. The cooling effect is particularly noticeable in housing, which is heavily dependent on borrowed (mortgage) money and so is very sensitive to mortgage rates.

2. Purchases of consumer durable goods, especially automobiles. These are financed heavily by borrowing and so are sensitive to interest rates. In addition, the automobile industry seems to have its own three- to four-year rhythm, arising partly from major model changes. Thus, sales of consumer durables fluctuate substantially, while sales of nondurables continue to rise right through a recession.

3. Business inventories fluctuate substantially, as will be remembered from Chapter 11. If businesses become nervous about future sales, they may conclude that they are overstocked and try to cut down inventories. Conversely, they usually rebuild inventories during early recovery. The short three- to four-year business cycles which have marked the economy since 1945 are in fact often referred to as "inventory cycles."

4. Federal expenditures, especially military expenditures, have sometimes had a destabilizing effect on the economy. During the mid-60s, Vietnam War expenditures rose substantially without any offsetting tax changes, helping to force the economy beyond full employment and to generate sustained inflation. During the early 70s, as the war wound down, military expenditures were allowed to dwindle without any offsetting adjustments. In 1981–84, military expenditures were once more raised sharply without corresponding tax increases—indeed, in the face of large tax reductions.

Despite these elements of instability, fluctuations in autonomous spending have been moderate. Equally important, as we noted in Chapter 5, the multiplier is smaller today than in earlier times, due mainly to the large income leakage into tax payments. So a change of $1 billion in autonomous spending now produces a smaller change in equilibrium GNP than was true before 1940.

Monetarist economists would not deny some degree of instability in private spending. But they argue that there are corrective mechanisms in the system which will bring it back on course without any need for fine tuning. What does experience tell us about this?

One such stabilizer operates through the monetary system. As the economy goes into recession and business demand for loans slackens, short-term interest rates begin to fall, followed in time by long-term rates. And economic activity does respond. Building construction, in particular, typically turns up midway through a recession and helps to bring the recession to an end. But it is an exaggeration to say that all this happens naturally. The Fed is in there nudging interest rates downward, trying to keep money supply growing. How the system would operate without any fine tuning by the Fed is an open question.

The other stabilizer on which neoclassical economists relied was wage-price flexibility. A recession would bring downward pressure on wages and prices, which would tend to brake the drop in employment and output. This has turned out to be a very weak reed. The postwar economy has shown strong resistance to any decline in wages and prices, or even any decline in the rate of inflation; and this downward inflexibility seems to have been increasing over the course of time. Here activists score a substantial point.

Another major area of dispute is how well fine tuning can work in practice as against how it might work ideally. The monetarist criticism of activism leans heavily on (1) the lack of accuracy in forecasting future movements of the economy and, hence, in judging what policies are appropriate; (2) the difficulty of judging the impact of any Federal Reserve action, because of variability of the money multiplier and the velocity of money; and (3) the fact that this impact is spread out over a considerable period of time.

There are problems here, but they do not seem to be as serious as some monetarists have suggested. Economic forecasting is imprecise, but not hopeless. Indeed, as Robert Gordon points out,[4] errors in forecasting nominal GNP for a year ahead have been relatively small, usually within 1 to 2 percentage points of the actual figure. The main errors have been in predicting the inflation rate. If inflation is underpredicted, then the increase in real output will be overpredicted, and vice versa.

Turning to uncertainties along the monetary base $\rightarrow$ money supply $\rightarrow$ nominal GNP chain, the most important fact of life is variations in the velocity of money. In a study of business cycles from 1945–82, Gordon found that changes in the growth rate of V as between upswings and downswings were much larger than changes in the growth rate of M and were thus mainly responsible for fluctuations in total spending (nominal GNP).[5] But the variations in V are systematic, hence somewhat pre-

---

[4] "Using Monetary Control to Dampen the Business Cycle: A New Set of First Principles," working paper no. 1210 (Cambridge, Mass.: National Bureau of Economic Research, October 1983).

[5] Ibid.

dictable. Because of the variability of V, Gordon argues that it makes more sense to use MV (nominal GNP) as a policy target than to use M by itself.

As regards the length of time needed for monetary policy to become effective, we noted earlier that much of the impact is felt within two quarters and most of it within a year. The lag is short enough to allow the Fed to take corrective action if the economy seems to be overshooting the original target.

The postwar policy record

There has been much research on the actual record of monetary and fiscal action since 1945.[6] Were the effects typically in the right direction, as activists would hope? Or were they frequently perverse, which would strengthen the monetarist case?

The record of fiscal policy is mixed. One can find several occasions, mostly before 1965, on which fiscal policy was applied intelligently in the right direction. Immediately on the outbreak of the Korean War, President Truman raised taxes to offset increased military expenditure. Government expenditures were increased appropriately at the outset of the 1958 recession. The 1964 tax cut program, applied at a time of substantial excess capacity, is generally credited with a classic multiplier effect on GNP. More recently, the 1975 tax reduction package seems to have been helpful in pulling the economy out of recession.

But one can cite other situations in which fiscal policy was not used effectively or not used at all. Most notable was the failure to raise taxes in 1965–66 to finance increased Vietnam War expenditures. The belated tax surcharge of 1968 appears to have had little effect in reducing consumer spending and restraining inflation. From 1968 to 1973, real federal expenditure was allowed to decline continuously, with no attempt at countercyclical timing. In the middle and late 70s, there were numerous government actions which accelerated the inflation rate: increases in farm price supports, sharp increases in payroll taxes for social security, indexing of social security benefits to the CPI, and increases in the minimum wage. Such actions have been called self-inflicted wounds. The Reagan taxcut program of 1981–83 was clearly too large. It generated a large high-employment deficit, now often called a "structural deficit," which forced the Fed to be more restrictive than it might have been otherwise and kept interest rates high.

The record of monetary action is, if anything, even more spotty. In 1959–60, when the Eisenhower administration was tightening fiscal policy, the Fed was also reducing money supply, and continued to do this even

---

[6] See in particular the summary by Robert J. Gordon, "Postwar Macroeconomics: The Evolution of Events and Ideas," in *The American Economy in Transition*, ed. Martin Feldstein (Chicago: University of Chicago Press, 1980).

after the economy went into recession. There was an irresponsibly rapid expansion of money supply from 1965–68, even when the economy was beyond full employment and inflation was accelerating. Partly because of this rapid earlier expansion, there was a sharp cutback in 1969, which contributed to the 1969–70 recession. During 1972–73, money supply was once more allowed to grow too rapidly, which some believe was not unconnected with the Nixon reelection campaign of 1972. The Fed reacted to the oil price shock of 1973–74 by braking money supply, which may not have been a correct response to supply-side inflation, and in any case intensified the 1973–75 recession. From 1974–79, the velocity of money was rising, so even though money supply grew at a rather stable rate, MV shot up faster than was desirable.

Monetary policy has certainly has an impact. Accelerations and decelerations in monetary growth have regularly preceded movements in nominal GNP of roughly the same size. But as Gordon concludes, "Monetary policy has not only been potent but also inept, bearing responsibility for the unnecessary recession of 1960, the excessive expansion of nominal GNP growth of 1967–68, the recession of 1969–70, and the second episode of excessive growth in 1972–73."[7]

Monetarists can take comfort from this spotty record. On the other hand, activists are entitled to turn the tables and ask: "Suppose the fixed rules which *you* favor had been in effect. Would the economy have performed better or worse than it actually did?"

It is hard to research what might have been. But not impossible. Set up a computer model of the economy, with equations specifying the relations among money supply, interest rates, investment, consumption, the price level, and so on. Then, instead of the actual rate of increase in money supply, feed into the system a steady percentage rate of increase—4 percent a year, or whatever. Activate the computer and see what will happen. Do you come out with smaller fluctuations in real GNP, or larger ones?[8] Thus far, such experiments suggest that a fixed monetary rule would lead to wider fluctuations of output and employment than we have actually experienced. So it is still possible to argue that, however imperfect fine tuning may have been up to now, the fixed-rule alternative is still more imperfect.

It is useful also to distinguish two quite different policy problems. Suppose the economy is operating at the NAIRU rate, and that the inherited or underlying rate of inflation is 3 percent. Suppose also that the output capacity of the economy is growing at 3 percent a year because of growth in labor and capital supplies plus productivity growth. Then there would seem to be a simple policy rule: raise nominal GNP at 3 + 3 = 6 percent a year. Real output can then rise at 3 percent a year,

---

[7] Ibid., p. 72.

[8] For an account of one such experiment, see James Tobin, "Stabilization Policy 10 Years After," *Brookings Papers on Economic Activity,* no. 1 (1980), p. 43. See also Franco Modigliani, "The Monetarist Controversy, or Should We Forsake Stabilization Policies?" *American Economic Review,* March 1977.

"Mitchell! I've found two economists that agree!"

From The Wall Street Journal, *with permission of Cartoon Features Syndicate.*

keeping the economy at the NAIRU point, and (if there are no supply shocks) there will be no tendency for the inflation rate to rise. This is the kind of situation which "fixed rule" advocates seem to have in mind.

But this is not the situation which policy makers usually face. They are riding the swings of the business cycle. Unemployment is usually above the NAIRU rate or, more rarely, below that rate. Suppose the NAIRU rate is 6 percent and the actual umemployment rate is 9 percent. The problem of moving from 9 to 6 percent resembles that of an airplane pilot coming down to a runway. A fixed rule—always come down 300 feet per minute—will lead to crashing into the runway. Frequent adjustment is needed to achieve the proper glide path. This is where activist policy changes come in.

A practical footnote: Whatever the intellectual merit of the two positions, it seems likely that federal policymakers will continue to make fine-tuning adjustments rather than adopting fixed rules which would put them out of business. Even if some rule, such as the often-proposed constitutional amendment requiring a balanced budget, were placed on the statute books, it would almost certainly be twisted to permit flexibility in practice. Neither Congress nor the Fed would actually remain locked in by formula, but would find ways of getting around any rule in response to changing economic circumstances and political pressures.

NEW CONCEPTS

fine tuning   activist rule
activist   fixed rule

information lag   policy mix
decision lag   policy coordination
application lag   intermediate target
inside lag   rational expectations
outside lag   policy ineffectiveness
neutrality

SUMMARY

1. The desirable characteristics of a policy instrument include speed of decision and application (short "inside lag"), speed of impact (short "outside lag"), predictability of impact, and neutrality between individuals and businesses.

2. Tax changes have a sizable inside lag, but a short outside lag. The effect is not highly predictable and is always nonneutral.

3. Monetary actions have a short inside lag but a sizable outside lag. The effect is reasonably predictable. While neutral on the surface, monetary policy is actually not as neutral as it appears.

4. Monetary and fiscal actions can support each other, or they can conflict. Different monetary-fiscal combinations may have about the same effect on aggregate demand, but one may be preferable to another in terms of some other objective, such as a high rate of investment or maintenance of the value of the dollar.

5. There are frequent proposals to coordinate Federal Reserve policy more closely with that of other branches of government. But the Fed, fearing that this would distort its policies toward political objectives, has resisted such proposals.

6. Some economists favor *fixed policy rules,* such as a constant growth rate for money supply (CMGR) and a zero fiscal surplus at high employment. Other economists, whom we've called *activists,* favor *fine tuning,* that is, frequent policy adjustments to raise or lower aggregate demand.

7. There is also a difference between those who regard money supply as the main or even the only policy tool, who are called *monetarists,* and nonmonetarists who think that fiscal policy is also quite important. Monetarists tend also to favor fixed rules, though this association is not logically necessary.

8. Fixed-rule advocates argue that private spending is reasonably stable, that the economy has built-in corrective devices, and that because of lags and uncertainties, efforts at fine tuning are likely to be counterproductive. Activists are skeptical about the inherent stability of the economy and argue that even though fine tuning is imperfect at present, it is capable of improvement. The evidence does not warrant a clear verdict for either group.

13

Coping with Underemployment and Inflation

Twenty years ago, macroeconomic policy was said to involve a choice of evils. If you want a low level of unemployment, you must pay for it by accepting a high rate of inflation. On the other hand, if you want a low inflation rate, you must pay for it by accepting higher unemployment and less output. There is a simple trade-off and a single choice.

Today it seems better to view inflation and unemployment as related but separable problems. There are ways of reducing the unemployment rate with little or no effect on inflation. Similarly, curbing aggregate demand and creating unemployment is one way of reducing the inflation rate, but it is not the only way. A 6 percent unemployment rate is compatible with 10 percent inflation, but it could also be compatible with 2 percent inflation. It is this more complex world which we have to explore.

Another way of putting the matter is to say that the monetary and fiscal instruments discussed in Chapter 12, while certainly the major policy tools, are not the only policy tools. There are several auxiliary tools which can play a useful role. The NAIRU can be reduced, and the feasible level of employment raised, by a variety of *labor market policies*. The inflation rate can be reduced by steps to reduce production costs and raise productivity. Some economists also believe that inflation can be reduced by direct controls or pressure on wages and prices, usually called *incomes policy*. There have been several experiments in this direction since 1940, and the effects need to be examined.

COPING WITH UNDEREMPLOYMENT

The problem: Output loss

We should be clear first that the problem is not unemployment per se. There is always a certain amount of unemployment, usually called "frictional" unemployment, arising from normal turnover in the labor market. Many millions of people are in the market each year because they want a better job, have lost their old job, are entering the labor force for the first time, or are reentering after a period out of the labor force. Even in good years, it typically takes a month or so to find a new job. So the proportion of people seeking jobs times the amount of time needed to find jobs defines a minimum unemployment rate.

A good deal of the time, unemployment is above this minimum level. There is *excess unemployment*. This can involve hardship for the unemployed, though it need not do so. Most workers now have sufficient resources from family or government sources to tide them over during short spells of unemployment. The main problem is that the labor force is being underutilized. This is accompanied by underutilization of plant capacity, and the result is a substantial loss of output. There are fewer goods available for investment, personal consumption, and public services.

The size of this "output gap" can be roughly estimated (see Figure 13–1, which is the same as Figure 3–1). On the basis of long-run trends in hours of labor available and output per hour, we estimate that the potential output of the economy is growing at, say, 3.5 percent per year. This is shown by the straight white line in the upper part of Figure 13–1. Against this we chart the growth of actual output, shown by the blue line. Except for a few years during the Korean and Vietnam wars, actual output has run below capacity output. The gap widens during recession—as in 1957–58, 1969–70, 1974–1975, and 1981–82—then narrows again during the subsequent upswing. Economic downswings involve a large loss in national output which could have been produced had the economy remained on a steady growth path. At present GNP rates, an output gap of 5 percent means a loss of more than $150 billion of output per year. This is a lot of output—goods which might have been used for investment, for private consumption, or for expansion of public services.

The NAIRU as an employment target

What do we mean by excess unemployment? Some benchmark is needed. In fact, a benchmark was needed to draw the output capacity line in Figure 13–1. Defining capacity requires a figure for labor supply,

FIGURE 13-1
Actual and potential GNP, 1950–1983 (billions of 1972 dollars)

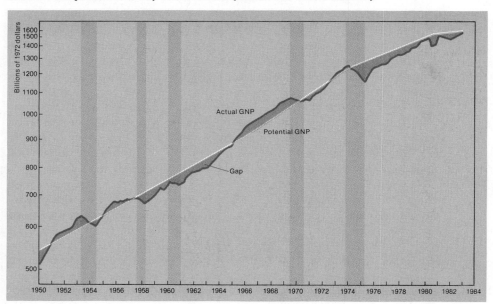

Source: *Economic Report of the President* and *Survey of Current Business*, November.1980, p. 17.

and this requires an assumption about the percentage of the labor force which is normally employed.

We saw in Chapter 9 that as demand and output rise during a business cycle upswing, the underlying rate of inflation will eventually begin to accelerate. The point at which this happens can be estimated either in terms of plant capacity utilization or labor force utilization. In labor terms, we define the NAIRU as the unemployment rate below which the inflation rate will accelerate.

Many economists now regard the NAIRU as a reasonable target for demand management. If the unemployment rate is higher than this, there is excess unemployment, and aggregate demand should be raised by monetary-fiscal measures. But as unemployment drops toward the NAIRU, the expansion should be tapered off, with the object of hitting the target without overshooting.

This is a policy judgment, of course, not a fact of nature, but it can be defended in at least two ways. Suppose the NAIRU at present is 6 percent, and suppose someone argues that the unemployment rate should be pushed down to 5 percent to secure additional output. Suppose further that this would raise the underlying inflation rate by 2 percentage points.

A defender of the NAIRU target might say that the gain in output is more than offset by the losses from a higher rate of inflation. This is a policy judgment, but not one which is clearly foolish.

A more basic argument, and the one on which NAIRU exponents mainly rely, is that the gain in output from a lower unemployment rate is only temporary. While the immediate effect may be to raise inflation by only 2 percent, the longer run effect will be to raise it by more than that as the wage-price-wage spiral takes hold. Accelerated inflation will reduce real income and real demand for goods, which will tend to reduce output and raise unemployment back toward the NAIRU rate. A related argument, political rather than economic, is that as inflation accelerates, the Fed will take alarm and apply the monetary brakes, again leading to lower output and higher unemployment.

How convincing these arguments are the reader must judge. Let's be clear also that to say that the NAIRU is a reasonable employment target and that the NAIRU is presently 6 percent does not mean that we must live with 6 percent unemployment for all time to come. The NAIRU itself is changeable, as we'll explain in a moment. But to reduce the NAIRU to 5 percent by labor market policies and then reduce actual unemployment to that level is one thing. To force unemployment down to 5 percent *without* altering the NAIRU is quite another.

Employment targets and output targets

There is a further problem, less obvious, but quite important in practice. Suppose, after weighing the considerations outlined above, government chooses 6 percent unemployment as a desirable goal. The current rate of unemployment is 8 percent. How large an increase in aggregate demand is needed to achieve the 6 percent goal?

This question is trickier than it appears. One might think that only a 2 percent increase in demand is needed. But this is wrong and would set the output target a good deal too low. Arthur Okun has estimated that "in the postwar period, on the average, each extra percentage point in the unemployment rate above 4 percent has been associated with about a 3 percent decrement in real GNP."[1] Thus to cut unemployment by 2 points, one must raise real GNP by about 6 percent. The capacity gap is substantially larger than the visible employment gap. This principle has been called Okun's law.

There are several reasons for this. First, there is considerable evidence that the labor force fluctuates in response to the level of aggregate demand.

---

[1] Arthur M. Okun, "Potential GNP: Its Measurement and Significance," *1962 Proceedings, Business and Economic Statistics Section, American Statistical Association* (reprinted as Cowles Foundation Paper 190, Yale University, 1963).

"Rose colored glasses in place?"

From The Wall Street Journal, *with permission of Cartoon Features Syndicate.*

As the economy goes into recession and jobs become harder to find, many people who are near the margin of decision as to whether to hunt jobs or not decide against doing so. Since they are no longer looking for work, they are not counted in the labor force and so cannot be considered unemployed.[2] True, during a recession, unemployment of the household head may force some other family member to go to work and thus add to the labor force. But the number of such "additional workers" seems to be swamped by the number of "discouraged workers." Dernburg and Strand found that "over the period of 1947–62, a fall in employment of 100 is, on balance, associated with withdrawal from the labor force of 38 workers. The recorded increase in unemployment of 62 therefore understates the increase in unemployed manpower by 38."[3]

We even know a good deal about *whose* participation in the labor force fluctuates with employment opportunities. There is little variation among men in the prime working years, almost all of whom are in the labor force continuously. But a rise in the unemployment rate has a marked discouraging effect on women workers and an even stronger effect on boys 14 to 19 and men 65 and over.[4] These last two groups pop into

---

[2] Our estimates of unemployment come from a sample survery conducted monthly by the Bureau of the Census. A person is counted as in the labor force is he or she either has a job or is "actively seeking work." For each person in the labor force, the survey then determines whether he or she was working full time, working part time for one reason or another, or had no job at all. Since the actively seeking work criterion is a bit vague, the count of the labor force is not completely accurate and so neither is the unemployment figure.

[3] Kenneth Strand and Thomas Dernburg, "Cyclical Variation in Civilian Labor Force Participation," *Review of Economics and Statistics,* November 1964, pp. 378–91.

[4] See, on this point, William G. Bowen and T. A. Finegan, "Labor Force Participation and Unemployment," in *Employment Policy and the Labor Market,* ed. Arthur M. Ross (Berkeley: University of California Press, 1965).

and out of the labor force in large numbers as employment opportunities vary.

When the economy is operating below capacity, then, there are many people not currently in the labor force who would be available for work if the demand for labor were higher. The reservoir of available labor is larger than the rate of visible unemployment suggests.

In addition to this flexibility in numbers, the labor force is flexible in terms of hours worked. During years of low employment, many people are forced to work shorter hours than they would prefer. In 1982, for example, in addition to an average of 10.7 million wholly unemployed, there were 5.9 million reported as "working part time for economic reasons," that is, not out of personal preference but because that was all they could find. The working hours of fully employed workers are also somewhat adjustable to the level of demand. Periods of peak output are met partly by additional overtime work, and hours are reduced again as demand falls.

Finally, there is evidence that a rise in aggregate demand brings a sharp increase in output per hour. "The record clearly shows that hourly productivity is depressed by low levels of utilization, and that periods of movement toward full employment yield considerably above average productivity gains."[5] Thus, a 1 percent increase in employment during an upswing produces considerably more than a 1 percent increase in output. Or, to put the point in reverse, a 1 percent rise in output can be obtained with considerably less than a 1 percent increase in labor. Eckstein and Wilson estimate that as of 1960 a rise of 1 percent in output called for only 0.52 percent more hours of labor.[6] This is partly because managerial, clerical, and other nonproduction workers are typically not laid off when business slackens. For this group, a 1 percent rise in output requires only 0.28 percent more hours. The interesting thing is that even for production workers the rise in labor requirements is only 0.6 percent.

These results help to explain events which might otherwise seem puzzling. Between the first quarter of 1975, the low point of the 1974–75 recession, and the last quarter of 1979, near a cycle peak, real GNP rose by 29 percent. Yet over this same period the rate of full-time unemployment fell from only 8.9 percent to 5.9 percent. How could output rise by 29 points while unemployment fell by only 3 points? The answer is partly that the labor force is growing each year through population increase (and was growing unusually fast in the 70s because of high birthrates 20 years earlier), partly that labor supply rises unusually fast during an upswing for the reasons already noted, and partly that labor requirements per unit of output are falling because of productivity increases.

---

[5] Okun, "Potential GNP."

[6] Thomas A. Wilson and Otto Eckstein, "Short-Run Productivity Behavior in U.S. Manufacturing," *Review of Economics and Statistics*, February 1964, pp. 41–54.

> **THINK ABOUT THIS**
>
> Check the behavior of the unemployment rate and the inflation rate over the past year. Considering what you find, should government be trying to stimulate aggregate demand at this point or trying to restrain it?

Reducing the NAIRU

To understand what determines the NAIRU and how it might be changed by labor market policies, we should recall two facts of life about unemployment. First, it is not spread evenly over the labor force. Some groups have much higher unemployment rates than others. The situation at the end of 1983, when the overall unemployment rate was 8.1 percent, is shown in Table 13–1. Black workers typically have higher rates than white workers, partly because they are more heavily concentrated in blue-collar occupations that are more subject to unemployment. Young people, especially black young people, have much higher rates than older workers.

The higher rates for young people do not seem to arise from longer periods of job search. They find jobs about as fast as adult males, the average period being four to five weeks. The difference is that they are in the market more frequently. Young workers change jobs more frequently than older workers in the process of shopping around and trying to locate the best job possibilities. Whenever this happens, it takes time to locate a new job. It is more spells of unemployment, rather than more time lost per spell, that accounts for the greater unemployment of youths.

As we noted in Chapter 9, the NAIRU rose between 1960 and 1980

TABLE 13–1
Selected unemployment rates, December 1983 (percent)

Age	Male	Female
White:		
16–19	20.2	18.3
20–24	13.8	10.3
25 and over	6.5	5.6
Black:		
16–19	48.8	48.2
20–24	31.4	31.8
25 and over	13.4	10.9

Source: U.S. Department of Labor, Bureau of Labor Statistics, *Employment and Earnings*, January 1984.

by something like 1.5 percentage points. The largest reason was the growing proportion of women and young people in the labor force. Other factors which may have contributed include larger unemployment compensation benefits and other sources of support for unemployed workers, which encourage more leisurely job search and a higher asking wage; the fact that the unemployment compensation system makes it cheaper for employers to lay off workers than to reduce hours in periods of slack demand; and increases in the minimum wage, which may have reduced employment opportunities, especially for young workers.

The first of these factors, of course, has now gone into reverse. Because of falling birthrates since 1960, the inflow of young people into the labor force will be much smaller in the 80s than in the 70s. So the NAIRU, which was drifting upward before 1980, should now drift downward again, perhaps by half a percent or more.

The second fact of life is that even while there are large numbers of unemployed people, there are also large numbers of vacant jobs. Even in periods of slack demand such as 1974–75 or 1980–81, there were plenty of job openings for secretaries, draftsmen, machinists, computer programmers, television repairmen, electronics engineers, oil well drillers, industrial hygienists, and lab technicians. How can vacant jobs and unemployed workers continue to coexist month after month? The answer must be that many of the unemployed do not have the skills and abilities which would qualify them for the vacant jobs. This kind of unemployment is often called *structural*. It has also been termed *mismatch* unemployment— a failure of workers' qualifications to match job requirements.

The nature of the problem can be illustrated by a simple diagram (Figure 13–2). The vertical axis shows the number of job vacancies in the economy, while the horizontal axis shows the number of unemployed workers. Along the 45-degree line *OF*, the number of vacancies equals the number of unemployed, which has sometimes been suggested as a working definition of full employment.

The *location* of curves such as E_1 or E_2 indicates the degree of mismatch in the labor market. E_1 indicates more serious structural maladjustment than E_2, because for any level of vacancies we choose, there will be more unemployment with E_1 than with E_2. Given the location of the curve, where the economy will operate on it depends on aggregate demand. During an upswing, vacancies are increasing and unemployment is falling, so we travel up the curve to the left. On the downswing, we move back down to the right.

Thus, there are two different ways of reducing unemployment, which can be regarded as complementary. Suppose the economy is operating on E_1, representing a particular degree of structural maladjustment. Demand management can move the economy up this curve, say from A to B. This would reduce the unemployment rate from U_1 to U_2.

If we could reduce the structural mismatch by labor market policies, it might be possible to shift the whole curve downward, say to E_2. It

FIGURE 13–2
Two kinds of employment strategy

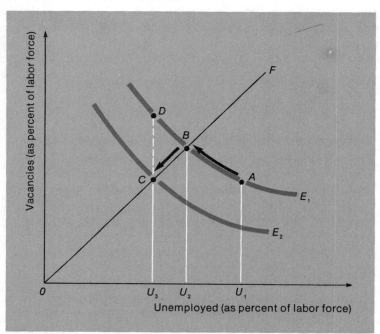

The location of a curve such as E_1 or E_2 indicates the degree of structural maladjustment in the labor market. Where the economy will operate on the curve depends on the level of aggregate demand. If the economy is operating on E_1, demand management can shift it from A or B, reducing unemployment from U_1 to U_2. But labor market policies may be able to shift the curve from E_1 to E_2, reducing unemployment further to U_3.

reduction of unemployment from U_2 to U_3. But if one tried to achieve unemployment as low as U_3 *without* any labor market changes, that is, while still operating on the old curve E_1, the economy would have to be pushed up to D, with an excess of vacancies over unemployed which would be highly inflationary.

Whether a point such as C actually is a NAIRU point is of course something one would have to investigate. Because of the marked inflationary bias of the economy, it might be necessary to offset this by maintaining a moderate excess of unemployed over vacancies, that is, aiming at a point somewhat to the right of C.

When we speak of "labor market policies," what do we mean concretely? What might be done to shift the E curve downward to the left? The possibilities, in rough priority order, include:

1. Better schooling.   The core of the problem is that part of the labor force is undereducated and underqualified for the jobs that are appearing in an increasingly complex, technical, white-collar economy. Many teenagers drop out of school, or even get a high school diploma while unable to spell, write a sentence, or make simple calculations. They can qualify only for low-paid, unattractive, dead-end jobs. Faced with such jobs, it is not surprising that some choose idleness, street crime, or other underground activities.

2. More in-plant training.   Young people who leave school with no skills have to acquire skills somewhere. A good way to do this is through working. On-the-job training has the advantage that a trainee who completes the program successfully can usually go on working for the same employer. Some government money is now available to pay part or all of trainees' wages, but more money for training subsidies would be useful.

3. Vocational education and apprenticeship.   Many high school students now go through academic programs but do not actually go on to college, and many others follow a general program which is neither academic nor vocational. Such students might be better served by entering a vocational track. Even those who go through supposedly vocational programs are often learning obsolete skills or using antiquated equipment. Vocational programs need to be geared to the labor market and to emphasize expanding rather than declining occupations. For the skilled trades, there are post-high-school apprenticeship programs operated cooperatively by technical colleges, trade unions, and employers; but the number going through such programs could usefully be doubled.

4. Educational loans.   In the past, it has been much easier to borrow to buy physical capital than to acquire human capital. This is unnecessary and undesirable. Any student who, because of lack of family support or because he or she must contribute to family support, cannot afford an extended period of training at low or zero wages should be able to borrow for this purpose. This is increasingly possible at the college level, but it should be possible at lower levels as well.

5. Reduction of employment discrimination.   It is now illegal to discriminate in recruitment, hiring, training, or promotion on grounds of race or sex, and government agencies have been set up to enforce this policy. But discrimination has by no means disappeared. Continued reduction of discrimination would improve the employment situation by diverting some of the demand pressure from (presently) more preferred to less preferred groups in the labor force.

6. The teenage minimum wage.   There is evidence that the cost of employing a teenager, which includes not only the minimum wage but social security and other contributions, is a substantial barrier to teenage employment. Many jobs which they might fill are simply not created because the employer regards the hourly cost as greater than the hourly productivity. There is merit in proposals for a lower teenage minimum, a practice which is common in other countries.

7. Aids to geographic mobility.   Jobs have a way of vanishing in some parts of the country and reappearing in others, and workers have to get from here to there. Millions of them do this now under their own power, but the flow could be expedited. The state public employment services already have a system for interstate clearance of vacancies, especially for technical and professional jobs, and this could be further computerized and improved. People should also be eligible for government grants or loans to cover costs of seeking work in other areas and of moving their families when a job has been found.

COPING WITH INFLATION

The inflation problem today is different from the problem as it appeared 20 years ago. Then the inflation rate was low, and one had only to discuss the steps needed to keep it low. Today, high inflation has been with us for more than a decade. Double-digit inflation occurred in 1974 and again in 1979–80.

Today's problem, then, is to reduce the inflation rate substantially. This is a tougher problem than simply maintaining a low rate once that has been achieved.

Another new development since 1970 is the appearance of supply shocks, which can occur independently of events in the American economy. We suggested in Chapter 9 that it may not be sensible to try to offset these price increases completely, which would mean forcing actual reductions in prices other than food and oil products. If this view is accepted, then we can no longer aim at zero inflation as a policy goal but must be more modest in our expectations.

Three approaches are available for reducing the inflation rate: (1) Restricting aggregate demand by monetary and fiscal policies so as to create slack in the economy and raise unemployment above the NAIRU rate. This does reduce inflation, though only slowly and with a high cost in lost output. (2) Trying to reduce production costs, or at least to reduce the rate of increase in production costs. Measures of this sort focus on supply rather than demand. (3) Direct pressure on wages and prices, usually called incomes policy. A difficulty in discussing incomes policy is that it can take different forms, ranging from a purely voluntary program to mandatory wage and price controls. These different possibilities must be examined.

Another possible response to inflation is indexing of incomes so that they rise automatically with increases in the consumer price index. Social security pensions are now indexed in this way, rising each July by the percentage increase in the CPI during the previous year. Many union contracts contain cost-of-living adjustment (COLA) clauses, under which hourly wages rise so many cents for each point increase in the CPI. Farm price supports are related to an index of the prices farmers pay, under the so-called parity price system.

Indexing is not a remedy for inflation. It is a way of living with inflation, widely used in countries such as Brazil where high inflation has been a way of life for a century. If American policymakers eventually give up on inflation and decide to accept it as a permanent feature of the economy, then wider extension of indexing should be considered. At present, only selected groups in the population have such protection, a situation which seems unfair to the majority who are not covered.

Creating economic slack

This is the traditional remedy, applied mainly by the Federal Reserve system. To a considerable extent, recessions are now deliberate, policy-induced recessions aimed at reducing the inflation rate.[7] We have seen earlier that a recession does reduce inflation, though only modestly and with some lag. This remedy is unpopular, however, and when recession sets in there is strong pressure to shift to an expansionist course—lower interest rates, tax cuts, and so on.

But suppose the brakes were kept on. Could the inflation rate be reduced by as much as we wish? The answer (ignoring external supply shocks) appears to be yes—at a price. The price would be excess unemployment and substantial loss of output for a period of several years. Economists who have analyzed the problem distinguish two possible policies, sometimes called "cold turkey" and "gradualist." The cold turkey policy calls for cutting the growth rate of aggregate demand sharply, at one step, to a much lower rate compatible with the new inflation target. (For example, a zero inflation target would mean reducing the growth of demand to the same rate as the growth of output capacity.) The gradualist policy would involve a more moderate restriction of demand, aimed at working down inflationary expectations gradually over a period of years. Unemployment would not rise as high as under cold turkey, and the path of movement toward the new equilibrium would be smoother, but the adjustment might take longer to complete.

Under either strategy, the time required to reach the new target infla-

---

[7] An interesting concept which has surfaced in this connection is that of the *political business cycle.* The idea is that a newly elected president (or prime minister), if he wants to attack inflation, should bring on a recession early in his administration. Then, after applying this medicine for a year or so, he can begin to raise aggregate demand so that employment and output are moving briskly upward by the time of the next presidential election. Models of voting behavior suggest that the vote for an incumbent president is strongly influenced by the rate of change in output and employment during the year before the vote. President Carter mistimed his recession by letting it occur in election year.

tion rate depends heavily on the behavior of *expectations*. We saw in Chapter 9 that the inflation rate depends partly on what people expect it to be. If everyone behaves as though prices next year will rise 10 percent, then prices probably will rise by about that amount. The object of restraining demand through a tight monetary-fiscal policy would be to get people's expectations down this year from 10 percent to 8 percent, then next year from 8 percent to 6 percent, and so on. Inflationary expectations are stubborn, and reducing them is bound to take time.

How long it takes may depend partly on whether government policy is *credible* to the public. Suppose government announces that it will use monetary restraint to whatever extent needed to reduce inflation to, say, 2 percent per year. *If people really believed this,* their inflationary expectations, and the actual rate of inflation, might drop quite rapidly. This would reduce the cost of the adjustment in terms of lost output and employment. But given the past variability of policy, people are likely not to believe what the government says. They know, or think they know, that excess unemployment for any extended period will lead the Fed to loosen the reins.

The recipe of containing inflation through monetary restraint arouses varying responses among economists. Monetarist economists like it, and many would prefer the cold turkey version. Cut the growth rate of MV sharply and hold it thereafter at a rate geared to the growth of output capacity. This would be painful in the short run, but eventually it would be compatible with stable prices and a return to high employment. They believe that the Fed has been consistently soft on inflation and has simply accommodated to a rising price level rather than tried to curb it. The Fed's fine-tuning efforts, in addition to being mistimed and often counterproductive, have shown a strong inflationary bias.

A leading activist, James Tobin, argues that the Fed has been adjusting to genuine pressures and that the alternative policy of following a constant growth rate rule for money supply might have had disastrous effects on output and employment:

> Throughout the 1970s accommodation has been the agonizing issue repeatedly facing the monetary authorities. The practice of describing monetary policy in terms of observed growth rates of M_1 is misleading. It does not make sense to say that the policy was or is x percent money stock growth as if that number was something the central bank chooses arbitrarily and gratuitously. . . . when the authorities have chosen policies supportive of continued inflationary growth of MV, they have not done so from ignorance of arithmetic, indifference to inflation, or in my opinion political pressure. They have done so, rightly or wrongly, mainly because of the perceived consequences of nonaccommodation on the real performance of the economy. The inertia of inflation in the face of nonaccommodative policies is the big issue. To discuss the roots of that inertia and the sources of nonmonetary pressures for accommodation—administered

prices, contracts, collective bargaining, distributive conflict, supply shocks, OPEC—is not to commit any vulgar errors.[8]

As a practical matter, it is doubtful whether any administration, let alone Congress, would accept high unemployment for four or five years. The loss of output would run to many hundreds of billions, and the impact would be unevenly distributed over industries and members of the labor force. This is why most economists would prefer not to rely only on demand restriction but to bring in the auxiliary devices discussed below.

The Fed might straddle the credibility issue by announcing what amounts to an activist monetary rule: We will, on average over the years, hold monetary growth to a rate compatible with price stability, *but* we will also, on occasion, deviate from this rule to counter swings in the business cycle. (This may not be too far from what the post-1979 Fed has been trying to do.) Economists could certainly understand, and most might approve, such a mixed rule. But whether the public would understand and believe it, whether it meets the credibility test, is less certain.

At best, containing inflation by *demand management alone* seems likely to involve a substantial output cost. This has led economists to look around for auxiliary devices which, if used in conjunction with demand management, might reduce the cost. The leading candidates here are: greater attention to supply and costs of production, and direct intervention in wage and price setting, usually termed *incomes policy*.

Supply and costs

While emphasis in the past has been on mangement of aggregate demand, supply should not be neglected. If aggregate demand is rising 5 percent a year, the inflation rate will be lower if aggregate supply is rising at 4 percent than if it is rising at 2 percent.

Government can do a variety of things to encourage research and development, stimulate business investment, raise productivity, increase the human capital stock, and otherwise raise the growth rate of output capacity. Such proposals, much publicized in the media as supply-side economics, are not at all new and will be discussed more fully in Chapter 14. We should realize that these measures are slow moving. Over 10 or 20 years, they might raise output capacity considerably. They will not do much to lower the inflation rate this year or next year.

Measures with greater short-run impact are to be found partly in the fiscal system. For example, the payroll tax on employers for social

---

[8] James Tobin, "Stabilization Policy Ten Years After," *Brookings Papers on Economic Activity,* no. 1 (1980), pp. 19–72.

security is treated as a business cost and passed on in prices to consumers. Large increases in this tax in 1980 and 1981 contributed to rising costs and prices. Freezing or lowering this tax, while making up any deficit in the social security fund from income tax revenues, would have an anti-inflationary effect. Federal and state excise taxes on gasoline, cigarettes, alcohol, telephone service, airline travel, and so on raise the prices of these goods, and tax reductions would lower prices. At the state level, sales taxes raise the cost of almost everything consumers buy.

Earlier in this chapter, we argued that well-designed labor market policies could increase the effective labor supply and reduct the NAIRU. The same line of reasoning can be applied to product markets. During an economic upswing, some industries hit capacity earlier than others. Price increases in these bottleneck industries—which are often industries producing raw materials, machine tools, or other producers' goods—then become cost increases for other industries, intensifying upward pressure on the price level. To foresee such capacity bottlenecks and to avert them by building new capacity in advance of demand is mainly the responsibility of the companies involved. But government can play a useful monitoring and advisory role and can sometimes provide incentives for capacity increases which would not otherwise be undertaken. (French experience with "indicative planning" since the 1950s suggests the usefulness of systematic consultation between government and industry experts to compare demand and supply estimates for some years ahead and to consider the amount of investment needed to avert supply bottlenecks.)

Government itself is the most important price fixer in the economy. It sets minimum wages, whose impact ramifies up through the lower levels of the wage structure. It sets minimum prices for many farm products through the price support system; tariff rates and import quotas which raise the price of many manufactured goods; minimum rates for rail, air, and truck transportation; maximum prices for electric power and telephone service.

Pressure on government to adjust these prices comes mainly from producer groups and is consistently in one direction—upward. Thus on the one hand, political leaders denounce inflation as a national evil, while at the same time their microeconomic actions contribute to inflation. This paradox cannot be removed entirely. But it could be ameliorated by anything which would reduce the political influence of producers, would build up counterpressure from consumers, or would permit systematic intervention by agencies concerned with macroeconomic objectives in making micro decisions. The recent progress of deregulation is encouraging and has already lowered prices in such areas as air transportation.

The logic of the approach suggested in this section has been well summarized by Lindbeck:[9]

---

[9] Assar Lindbeck, "Stabilization Policy in Open Economies with Endogenous Politicians," *American Economic Review,* May 1976, pp. 1–19.

it is important to stress that there are at least two different kinds of "fine tuning." *One* type is that the government tries continuously to keep aggregate demand very close to the capacity ceiling of the economy, which tends to create a situation with excess demand ["bottlenecks"] in many sectors simultaneously with excess supply ["slack"] in others. It was this type of fine tuning which ran into severe difficulties in the late 1960s and early 1970s.

A *different* type of fine tuning . . . is to be very "modest" with expansions of aggregate demand after a rather high, but not quite "full," level of capacity utilization has already been reached, and instead try to achieve full employment by way of factor mobility policies and selective demand and supply management.

Incomes policy

But isn't there another way out? Why can't we, like King Canute, wave our arms at the incoming tide of wage and price increases and say "Stop." Efforts to impose direct restraint on wage and price increases, by various combinations of persuasion and coercion, are usually called *incomes policy.*

The central idea is to convince the different groups in the economy who are contending for larger incomes that there is only so much to go around. People's *real* incomes can increase year by year only by as much as the *real* output of the economy rises. Efforts to get more than this by raising *money* incomes are bound, for society as a whole, to be self-defeating. Inflation can be regarded, indeed, as a process of adjustment of the economy to a set of inconsistent claims, with some groups being disappointed at each point in time. Somebody *has* to be disappointed if money claims add up to more than the economy can produce.

European countries have experimented extensively, though not very successfully, with incomes policy since World War II. In the United States, there have been two main periods of experimentation. In 1962, President Kennedy's Council of Economic Advisers advanced the concept of "guidelines" for wage and price behavior. The central idea was that hourly compensation of employees should rise no faster than average output per worker hour in the economy, in which case unit labor costs and the average level of prices could remain constant.

The guidelines, of course, had no legal force, and the Kennedy and Johnson administrations never attempted to apply the concept throughout the economy. Instead, they chose to intervene in selected situations, usually involving large unions and large, concentrated industries, whose wage-price decisions receive wide publicity and may be expected to have substantial economic influence. The tactics of persuasion and publicity used in these cases came to be known as "jawboning." Statistical studies suggest that the policy did have a mild downward effect on the rate of wage and price increase over the period 1961–65.[10] But after 1965, the rising Vietnam War expenditures, combined with President Johnson's reluctance to admit the cost of the war and to levy taxes to cover it, produced irresistible inflationary pressure and the guideline experiment broke down.

The second experiment was initiated by the international monetary crisis of August 1971, when the United States abandoned convertibility of the dollar into gold, ushering in a period of fluctuating exchange rates instead of the fixed-rate system which had prevailed earlier. President Nixon imposed a three-month freeze on wage and price increases, followed by a comprehensive control system from November onward. Wages were placed under the jurisdiction of a tripartite Pay Board including industry, labor, and public representatives, while prices were monitored by a Price Commission including only public members. Companies in the largest size category were required to ask *advance permission* for wage and price increases, medium-sized companies were required to *report* wage and price changes after the fact, and the smallest companies (with less than 1,000 employees) were simply expected to observe prescribed wage and price guidelines and were subject to spot checks for compliance. The program continued, with changes in detail, through 1973. Postaudits of the program suggest that it did hold down the price level moderately during 1971–73, but that this effect was fully reversed in 1974–75 after controls were abandoned, leaving the price level about where one would expect on economic grounds.[11]

Another brief episode of voluntary restraint was initiated by the Carter administration in late 1978. Wage increases during 1979 were to be held to 7 percent, and price increases by sellers were to be smaller in 1979 than in 1978. This program was blown apart by the oil price explosion of 1979. As inflation soared to double-digit levels, the 7 percent wage target became less and less plausible, and the control effort crumbled.

The policy dilemma is this: At one extreme, mere coaxing of companies and unions to "be reasonable" cannot have much effect. Everyone will pay lip service to the desirability of avoiding inflation, but then they will go ahead and do whatever self-interest dictates in the circumstances. At the other extreme, a comprehensive system of legal controls over wages and prices, such as was used during World War II and again during the Korean War, is unfeasible under peacetime conditions.

The obvious political objection to comprehensive wage and price control is that business and labor leaders are resolutely opposed to it, and

---

[10] An effect of the order was 1 percent per year in the case of wages and 0.6–0.7 percent per year in the case of prices. See George L. Perry, "Wages and the Guideposts," *American Economic Review,* September 1967, pp. 897–904; and Robert M. Solow, "The Wage-Price Issue and the Guideposts," in *Critical Issues in Employment Policy,* ed. F. H. Harbison and J. D. Mooney (Princeton, N.J.: Industrial Relations Section, 1966).

[11] See Robert J. Gordon, "The Effect of Aggregate Demand on Prices," *Brookings Papers on Economic Activity,* no. 3 (1975), pp. 613–62.

so it cannot win either congressional approval or the degree of voluntary compliance needed to supplement legal procedures. But equally serious, from an economic standpoint alone such a system would have undesirable side effects. The reason is that, in a market economy, *specific* wages and prices typically change at different rates, depending on supply and demand shifts in particular markets. These diverse movements serve the function of balancing the quantities supplied and demanded in each market in the short run and of reallocating productive resources in the long run. A control system, which tends to impose uniform rules based on "fairness," retards these desirable adjustments and may even prevent them.

There are many reasons why wages for a particular kind of labor may rise more (or less) rapidly than wages in general. For example, it is natural and desirable for wages in a particular occupation to rise faster than other wages if: (1) demand for this kind of labor is rising rapidly, so that higher wages are needed to recruit additional workers; (2) there has been a change in the nature of the job—it has become harder or more unpleasant, or it has become more skilled, requiring a longer period of training; (3) there has been a shift in workers' tastes away from the kind of work in question—fewer people want to be coal miners or domestic servants. One would expect wages for these jobs to rise faster than wages in general because of the shrinkage of supply.

Now suppose a control board lays down the principle that no wage shall rise by more than 4 percent a year, and suppose that market conditions for a particular job call for a 6 percent increase. Then, as we saw in Chapter 3, the fact that the wage rate is pegged *below* the market level will lead to a shortage of labor for that job. The free flow of labor in response to market conditions has been blocked.

The same reasoning applies to product prices, which are typically changing at quite different rates. If the CPI is rising at 4 percent per year, some prices will be falling, others rising at 2 percent, others at 6 or 8 percent. The basic reason, over the long run, is differing behavior of production costs. Some industries are more successful than others in raising productivity and reducing cost through technological progress.

These differential price movements serve a valuable economic function. Industries which manage to reduce their selling prices relative to other industries can increase their sales to consumers, expand their production facilities, and make still further gains in productivity in a continuing "virtuous circle." Conversely, products whose costs and prices remain relatively high will find their market shrinking. Thus, productive resources flow toward those sectors of the economy in which technical progress is most rapid. A price control system need not permanently block such adjustments, but it does tend to retard them.

There is the further difficulty, noted in Chapter 2, that a price fixed below the equilibrium level creates a shortage of the good in question. The quantity demanded exceeds the quantity supplied. So, whose demands will be satisfied and whose will not? Unless a rationing system is introduced, this will be decided by informal, haphazard methods— for example, by motorists lining up at the gas pumps. There will also be a strong incentive for sellers to charge black market prices above the legal maximum, and to prevent this will require a substantial enforcement staff. War conditions apart, it seems doubtful that the benefits are worth the administrative costs plus the disruption of the market mechanism.

If we reject coaxing as ineffective and wage-price controls as undesirable, are there any intermediate approaches which might be useful? It is interesting to think about possible ways of getting a handle on the rate of increase in money incomes. It is income increases, after all, which on the supply side push up business costs and prices and on the demand side provide the money with which to pay these higher prices. A lower rate of income increase should lead to a lower rate of price increase, though with some lag (and again overlooking the possibility of external supply shocks). Getting at prices indirectly through income restraint seems to be the commonest meaning of the term *incomes policy.*

It would be inappropriate to outline a specific program here. But in thinking about program possibilities, several points should be borne in mind.

1. Incomes policy is not a continuing program. It is typically used as part of a temporary crash program designed to achieve a sharp reduction in inflationary expectations. It cannot be maintained, and indeed may not be needed, for more than two or three years.

2. Incomes policy is not a separate program but rather part of a policy package. The centerpiece of any inflation-control program must be monetary and fiscal restraint. Without this, any effort to restrain the growth of incomes will quickly be blown apart. But given monetary-fiscal restraint, incomes policy can be a useful auxiliary tool, speeding the transition to a lower inflation rate and reducing the cost in lost output.

3. To be fair, the program should include every form of money income—wages, salaries, professional fees, self-employment income, dividend and interest payments, and other income from property. Some types of income, notably farm income, would no doubt be hard to control, but an effort could be made.

4. Incomes policy could be made more effective by judicious use of the fiscal system, possibly including a *real income guarantee.* Suppose everyone agrees to an incomes policy under which income increases are held to 5 percent per year. But then the CPI rises by 7 percent, so that everyone suffers a 2 percent loss in real income. Fear of such losses is one reason why many people oppose an incomes policy.

Knowing that a tax rebate would replace any loss of real income could remove this fear. In the example above, personal income tax rates could be reduced by 2 percent, or there could be a 2 percent reduction in the employee payroll tax for those covered by the social security system.

This sort of proposal is usually called a *tax-based incomes policy* (TIP). Such a program was actually recommended to Congress by President Carter in late 1978 as part of his voluntary control effort. Congress did not approve it, but the idea remains alive partly because of the lack of any attractive alternative.

A somewhat different TIP program, proposed by Henry Wallich and others, would use the corporate tax system to restrain wage increases. Suppose the wage target for a particular year were set at 5 percent. Then a company which gave a wage increase of, say, 7 percent would not be able to deduct the extra 2 percent as a cost of production in calculating its profit tax liability. This would make wage increases above the target roughly twice as expensive to the company and would reduce employers' willingness to give them.

Incomes policy is highly controversial. Business and labor leaders generally oppose it as an infringement on private economic decisions. Many economists, perhaps most economists, also oppose it on the ground that the inflation-reducing effect is only temporary, since the long-run trend of prices is dominated by money supply, while the side effects on resource allocation are harmful.

The idea remains alive, however, because the inflation problem will not go away and because containing inflation by monetary-fiscal restraint alone involves a substantial cost.

THINK ABOUT THIS

After considering the arguments for and against some sort of incomes policy, what is your position? If on balance you favor such a policy, how would you set it up?

NEW CONCEPTS

output, potential	labor market policy
output gap	indexing
Okun's law	incomes policy
unemployment, structural	tax-based incomes policy

SUMMARY

1. Unemployment and inflation are related but separable problems.
2. The loss from underemployment is essentially an output loss, measured by the gap between actual and potential output.

3. The unemployment rate gives a misleading impression of the output gap. It takes an increase of about 3 percent in GNP to reduce the unemployment rate by 1 percent. The reason is that labor force participation, average hours of work, and productivity per hour all fall during a downswing and rise during an upswing.

4. Structural unemployment arises from a mismatch between unemployed workers and available vacancies. Labor market policies designed to reduce this mismatch can increase the effective labor supply and lower the NAIRU.

5. Creating economic slack through a tight monetary and fiscal policies can gradually lower the inflation rate. But to get the rate down close to zero by this method alone would take a number of years and a large output loss.

6. Fiscal and other measures to reduce business costs and increase supply can have a useful anti-inflationary effect.

7. Efforts at direct wage-price restraint have not achieved much thus far, but experiments in this direction are likely to continue. The most interesting recent proposal is for a tax-based incomes policy (TIP), which would use the fiscal system to reward noninflationary behavior.

TO LEARN MORE

Clip your daily newspaper and also the *New York Times* and *The Wall Street Journal* if available. You will find plenty of complaints about what Washington is or is not doing and proposals for what ought to be done. It will be educational to form your own judgment on such proposals. The macroeconomics texts listed in earlier chapters also contain extensive discussions of stabilization policy.

14

Long-Term Growth: The Past and The Future

The rule is, jam tomorrow and jam yesterday—but never jam today.

—Lewis Carroll, Through the Looking Glass

One of the great themes of economics concerns the long-run growth of national output. This has been called "the nature and causes of the wealth of nations" (Adam Smith), "the theory of economic development" (Joseph Schumpeter), and "modern economic growth" (Simon Kuznets).

We will point out first that growth of GNP does not mean an equal growth in consumers' welfare. The two are related, but they are not the same thing.

Next, we'll look at the growth record over the past century or so. We'll see that growth in the Western industrial economies was abnormally high from 1945–73 but has now fallen to about the long-run average. It's interesting also that socialist and capitalist economies have grown at about the same rate.

The sources of economic growth can be divided into (1) growth of *factor supplies*—amounts of labor and capital in use—and (2) growth of *factor productivity*, often called *technical progress*. In the United States, the growth of productivity has slowed down considerably since the late 60s, and we'll look at possible explanations of this fact.

Finally, we'll speculate about growth prospects for the future. We'll find reasons to expect that growth from 1980–2000 will be slower than from 1945–73. But predictions that growth must cease entirely because of natural resource scarcities or environmental problems have been exaggerated.

GNP DOES NOT MEASURE WELFARE

It's a truism that consuming more does not necessarily make people happier. But having said this, there's not much more we can say. Since we can't measure happiness directly, we fall back on measures of production and consumption as providing clues if not definite answers.

What do we mean by economic growth? Suppose that a country's population is increasing at 3 percent per year while GNP is also increasing at 3 percent per year. This is growth in a sense. The economy is getting larger. This kind of development, often termed *extensive growth,* is a common pattern in today's less developed countries. Many of these countries are just managing to raise national output at about the same rate as population.

We can speak of growth in a more significant sense, however, when we find GNP rising *faster* than population. Suppose GNP is rising 5 percent a year and population only 2 percent. Then output per capita is rising 3 percent per year.

The growth rate of an economy is defined as its rate of increase in output per capita.

When we use the term *growth* without qualification, this is what it means.

If GNP per capita is rising at, say, 3 percent a year, it is natural to suppose that people are getting "better off" at this same rate. We pointed out in Chapter 3 that this is not necessarily so, but we must explain this point more fully.

GNP is a measure of production, not consumption. Economists, preoccupied with the determinants of productive capacity, have been slow to develop measures oriented toward consumer welfare. Recently, there have been efforts to adjust the conventional GNP figures to come closer to what Jan Tinbergen has termed a measure of "gross national happiness."

Three main adjustments are required:

1. Reclassification of final output. Many items conventionally classified as "consumption" should really be regarded as investment. This includes much of health and education expenditure, which contributes to "human capital formation," and also automobiles and other durable consumer goods. (The *services* yielded by these goods during a certain time period constitute consumption, but purchase of the goods does not.) There are also important types of government output which, while usually counted as "public consumption," really come under Kuznets's heading of "regrettable necessities." The leading example is defense expenditure. No one really "demands" or "buys" national defense, and there is no indication that additional defense expenditure adds anything to citizens' satisfaction. If anything, this is an overhead cost of living in a world of complicated weaponry and virulent nationalism.

When one reclassifies output in this way, the true consumption share of GNP is a good deal smaller than usually thought, and it does not necessarily rise as fast as GNP rises.

2. Correction for the services yielded by durable consumer goods, for the value of leisure time and for home-produced output.   While the corrections under heading (1) reduce the consumption total, these corrections increase it substantially. Leisure time certainly has value, though estimates of this value are necessarily rough; and the amount of leisure is rising over time as hours of work decline. The amount of home output is also large and may even be increasing with the spread of do-it-yourself activities.

3. Economic growth produces an increased output of "bads" as well as "goods."   There is growing damage to the environment—air and water pollution, devastation of large areas through strip mining, laying waste of forests by clean cutting—for which the producers in question are not charged. The damage done to consumers should be deducted from GNP as an uncounted cost of production.

Life in large cities rather than rural areas or small towns also involved disamenities—noise, dirt, lack of privacy, increased risk of crime and violence. As a large percentage of the population becomes concentrated in urban complexes, the importance of these negative factors is rising, and some correction should be made for them. The gap in real wages between small towns and metropolitan areas could be regarded as a necessary offset to the disamenities of urban life and, hence, as a crude measure of them.

William Nordhaus and James Tobin have tried to estimate these corrections and to arrive at a more accurate measure of economic welfare (MEW).[1] Their figures, while preliminary and subject to revision, indicate that MEW is quite different from conventional measures of national output or personal consumption. Further, while MEW has been growing, it has been growing less rapidly than NNP. The authors estimate that over the period 1929–65, NNP rose at 1.7 percent per year while MEW rose at 1.1 percent. Thus, the progress indicated by the conventional national income accounts is partly mythical but not entirely so. MEW and GNP tend to move *in the same direction*, though not necessarily *at the same rate*.

We are now ready for the substance of the chapter, which consists of three parts: (1) We shall look briefly at the historical record of economic growth in the United States and other major industrial countries. This tells us something about how fast national economies tend to grow over the long run. (2) We shall examine the main forces responsible for this growth. How much of it has been due to a more skilled and educated

---

[1] William Nordhaus and James Tobin, "Is Growth Obsolete?" in *Economic Research: Retrospect and Prospect, Fiftieth Anniversary Colloquium, V, Economic Growth* (New York: National Bureau of Economic Research, 1972).

labor force, how much to a growing stock of physical capital, and how much to progress in science and technology? (3) We shall look at a variety of antigrowth arguments which have appeared in recent years. Is the growth rate bound to slow down in the future because of environmental problems, exhaustion of natural resource supplies, or other reasons? If the growth rate does not decline of its own accord, should government try to force it down as a matter of deliberate policy?

THE RECORD OF ECONOMIC GROWTH

The leading student of long-term growth is Simon Kuznets, who has made estimates for 14 of the Western industrial countries, covering roughly the century 1860–1960.[2] The average growth rate of output per capita in these countries has been quite moderate. It ranges from a bit above 1 percent per year in the slowest growing countries (United Kingdom, Netherlands, Australia) to a bit under 3 percent per year in the fastest growing countries (Sweden and Japan). The industrial countries are relatively rich today, not because they have grown very fast but because they have been growing for a long time.

The long-term average for the United States is a bit under 2 percent a year. Thus, we have not been the fastest growing economy, as we sometimes tend to think. Several other countries, notably Sweden and Japan, have outdone us in this respect. The U.S. growth rate has also fluctuated a good deal from decade to decade, being as high as 4 percent in some decades, as low as 1 percent in others, and slightly negative during the Great Depression of the 1930s.

Most countries grew considerably faster after 1945 than they had before (Table 14–1). During the 50s, the average growth rate of per capita output in the Western industrial countries was close to 3 percent. During the 60s, it was even higher, at about 4 percent. As usual, there was considerable variation among countries, with Japan at the top of the league and Britain and the United States toward the bottom.

High growth rates continued in most countries through 1973. In 1974, partly because of the oil price explosion, most of the Western countries went into recession at about the same time. Recovery was sluggish, and a new recession developed in 1980–81. In addition, the oil-importing countries were obliged to turn over a larger share of their national output in payment for oil. Thus, the growth rate of goods available for domestic use was even lower than the growth rate of output.

It seems likely that 1974 marked a real turning point and that the unusually high growth rates of 1945–73 will not return. But we'll go into future prospects in a later section.

---

[2] See Simon Kuznets, *Modern Economic Growth: Rate, Structure, and Spread* (New Haven, Conn.: Yale University Press, 1966), especially Chap. 2.

TABLE 14-1

Annual percentage increase in total and per capita output, selected countries, 1950–60, 1960–73, and 1973–80

	1950–60		1960–73		1973–80	
Country	Output	Output per Capita	Output	Output per Capita	Output	Output per Capita
Japan*	8.0	6.8	9.9	8.7	4.2	3.1
Italy†	5.5	4.9	5.8	5.1	2.7	2.1
France	4.4	3.5	5.5	4.5	3.0	2.6
Norway	3.6	2.7	4.8	4.0	4.8	4.3
Sweden	3.6	2.9	4.0	3.3	1.5	1.2
Denmark	3.2	2.5	4.5	3.8	2.0	1.7
Canada	4.0	1.2	5.5	3.8	3.1	1.9
West Germany	7.7	6.6	4.5	3.6	2.6	2.8
United States	2.9	1.2	4.1	2.9	2.8	1.8
Australia‡	4.3	2.0	5.6	3.4	2.5	1.2
South Africa	4.4	1.9	5.5	2.7	3.0	0.3
Switzerland	4.2	2.9	4.2	2.8	0.0	0.2
United Kingdom	2.7	2.3	2.9	2.4	1.4	1.4

 * 1952–60.
 † 1951–60.
 ‡ 1953–60.
 Source: *U.N. Yearbook of National Account Statistics 1981.*

To add some global perspective, we may note that post-1950 growth rates in the Soviet Union and the East European socialist countries average out to about the same as the average for the Western industrial countries.[3] Total output in the socialist group has grown at about 5 percent per year, per capita output at between 3 and 4 percent per year.

These results are rather surprising. In the socialist countries, rapid growth is a central objective of economic policy. Labor resources are fully mobilized to this end. The percentage of GNP devoted to capital formation is higher than in the capitalist countries. One might expect, therefore, that the rate of increase in GNP would also be higher. Yet it is not. Many economists infer from these facts that the higher growth rate of factor inputs is offset by deficiencies in economic planning and administration, and perhaps also by a lower rate of technical progress. Overstraining of the economy by excessively high output targets, the cumbersomeness of centralized production planning and materials allocation, and the efforts of plant managers to protect themselves by hoarding labor and materials all produce frequent slowdowns and interruptions of production. Growth rates are respectable, but they are not consistently above capitalist levels.

The less developed countries (LDCs), on the other hand, have grown

[3] Maurice Ernst, "Postwar Economic Growth in Eastern Europe," in *New Currents in Soviet-Type Economies,* ed. George R. Feivel (Scranton, Pa.: International Textbook, 1968); and Bela Balassa, "Growth Performance of East European Economies and Comparable West European Countries," *American Economic Review Proceedings,* May 1970, pp. 314–20.

more slowly than the other two groups in total output, and much more slowly in output per capita. Their population growth rates are much higher than in the more developed countries, typically in the range of 2.5–3.5 percent per year. Kuznets concludes that between 1954–58 and 1964–68, GNP per capita rose in the LDCs by only 1.4 percent year.[4] Thus, the income gap between the richer and poorer nations has been widening over the course of time.

There has also been great diversity of experience within the less developed world. National growth rates differ more widely than within either the capitalist or socialist groups. There are a dozen or more successful LDCs which had 1960–80 growth rates in the range of 3 to 5 percent per year and thus fully kept pace with the developed world. But there are many countries in which output growth has done little more than keep up with population growth, and some in which output per capita has actually declined.

THINK ABOUT THIS

1. The United States has the highest per capita income in the world (except for a few oil-producing countries and, possibly, Sweden). Yet several other countries have had a higher growth rate over the past century. Can you explain why?
2. It is often argued that steps should be taken to close the growing income gap between the richer industrialized countries and the less developed countries. Is this desirable? Feasible?

THE SOURCES OF ECONOMIC GROWTH

Economic growth is a very old problem in economics, associated with such names as Adam Smith, David Ricardo, Karl Marx, and Joseph Schumpeter. But space limits compel us to leave their ideas to the historian of economic thought. We pick up the story with the strong revival of interest in growth theory around 1950.

Modern growth theory sorts the sources of economic growth into two boxes: (1) increase in *factor supplies,* that is, worker-hours of labor used in production and the size of the capital stock and (2) increase in *factor productivity,* that is, the amount of output per unit of factor inputs. Suppose that labor and capital inputs are growing at 1 percent a year, but output is growing at 2.5 percent. The difference, 1.5 percent a year,

---

[4] "Problems in Comparing Recent Growth Rates for Developed and Less Developed Countries," *Economic Development and Cultural Change,* January 1972, pp. 185–209.

is the growth rate of factor productivity. We will see later that this mechanical separation of growth into two components oversimplifies a complex process. But it is a starting point.

What this approach tries to explain is the growth of an economy's *output capacity,* the "output ceiling" line which we drew in Chapter 13. Actual output will normally be below the ceiling. But experience justifies us in assuming that actual output, while fluctuating from year to year, will rise at about the same average rate as output capacity.

Growth and factor supplies

In most economies, the supply of the factors of production is increasing. The labor force is growing, mainly because of population increase. The capital stock is also rising, since construction of new capital goods exceeds the wearing out of old ones. The rate of net capital formation varies widely among countries, but rarely does it fall to zero. It would be surprising, then, if total output were *not* growing. How much of the observed increase in output can be explained simply by the increase in factor supplies?

Let us give a rough, commonsense answer. Suppose supplies of the basic productive resources, labor and capital, are increasing at the same rate—say, 1 percent per year. If nothing else is happening—no change in products, no improvement in methods of production—one would expect output to rise at about the same percent per year. Note that this would be merely *extensive* growth as defined earlier. It would not involve any increase in output per worker and, hence, no improvement in living standards.

Suppose on the other hand that capital is increasing faster than labor, as is typically the case in advanced industrial economies. Labor supply is increasing at, say, 1 percent per year and capital supply at 3 percent. This means that each worker has more machinery and other capital goods to work with, year after year. Capital per worker is rising. Thus, one would expect output per worker, or *labor productivity,* to also be rising. Here we do have a source of economic growth and of improvement in living standards.

Measures of labor productivity are obtained by dividing physical output in a year or a calendar quarter by the number of worker-hours used in production during that period. These figures, reported frequently in the newspapers, are interesting, but they are also likely to be misunderstood. In the short run, they are much affected by cyclical upswings and downswings. We noted in Chapter 13 that when output drops during a recession, employment does not drop as fast. People are kept on the payroll in expectation of an early recovery. The result is that output per worker-hour typically falls during a recession.

In the early stages of an upswing, on the other hand, output rises faster than employment. Remember Okun's law. So output per worker-hour is likely to rise unusually fast at such times.

When we average out these swings, output per worker-hour normally rises over the long run. But the phrase productivity of *labor* is a bit misleading. The increase does not necessarily mean that workers are getting more skillful or are working harder. In large measure, it means that each worker has more and better capital goods to work with. A better productivity measure, then, is output per unit of labor and capital combined. This measure is usually called *total factor productivity.*

To get this figure, we must first measure the growth rate of *labor and capital combined,* or *total factor inputs.* But how can we add labor and capital? Labor is usually measured in hours, and we figure out that available hours increased last year by, say, 1 percent. Similarly, we can estimate that the total amount of capital equipment increased by 3 percent. But how fast did the supply of *labor plus capital increase?* To answer this, we must decide how important labor is in production relative to capital.

The accepted rule is that each factor's contribution to output is measured by the share of national income it receives. So if labor receives three quarters of national income and capital one quarter, we say that labor is three times as important. Hence the growth rate of labor is given a weight of three quarters and the growth rate of capital a weight of one quarter in calculating the combined growth rate.

Example. Suppose labor receives three quarters of national output and capital one quarter, and suppose labor supply is growing 1 percent a year and capital supply 3 percent. Then the growth rate of *labor plus capital* was

$$\frac{(3 \times 1) + (1 \times 3)}{4} = 1.5 \text{ percent per year.}$$

Suppose that over whatever period we are studying, GNP grew at 3.5 percent per year. Then the growth rate of *total factor productivity* was $3.5 - 1.5 = 2.0$ percent.

Improvement of factor productivity: The residual

What we have called total factor productivity has also been called *the residual*—the difference between the measured growth rate of inputs and outputs. Professor Moses Abramovitz has called it "a measure of our ignorance."

The leading student of long-term changes in productivity is John W. Kendrick, whose results are summarized in Table 14–2. Several things

TABLE 14–2
Growth of U.S. output and inputs, 1929–78

		Annual Percentage Increase in	
Period	GNP	Total Factor Inputs	Total Factor Productivity
1929–48	2.6	0.3	2.3
1948–66	3.9	1.1	2.8
1966–73	3.5	1.9	1.6
1973–78	2.4	1.6	0.8

Source: John W. Kendrick, "Productivity Trends and the Recent Slowdown," in *Contemporary Economic Problems,* ed. William J. Fellner (Washington, D.C.: American Enterprise Institute, 1970), pp. 17–70.

stand out from this table: the unusually rapid growth of GNP from 1948–73 and the markedly lower growth rate since 1973; the increase in growth of factor inputs after 1966, due mainly to a sharp increase in labor inputs as young people born during the baby boom of 1946–60 began to enter the labor force; and the sharp drop in total factor productivity after 1966, whose causes we examine in the next section.

EXPLAINING THE RESIDUAL

Recognition that increases in total factor productivity account for a large share of output growth has stimulated study of the source of these increases. Part of the answer must lie in the fact that the American economy shows a high rate of technical progress. So at this point we look briefly into the economics of technical change.

The economics of technical change

What is technical change? It is the discovery and application of techniques which produce either a new product, an improved product, or the same product at lower cost. It involved the introduction of new production functions.

Technical change comes from several sources: (1) *Basic scientific research,* which lays the foundation for new products and techniques, is done mainly in universities. In agriculture, medicine, and atomic energy, however, government laboratories are important; and some large companies also do basic research. (2) *Applied research,* aimed at converting general knowledge to specific uses, and (3) the design of products and pilot production units which is termed *development.* The two latter activities are carried on mainly by business concerns. The lone-wolf inventor is still important but relatively less important than some generations ago.

TABLE 14–3
R & D expenditure, selected industries

	R&D Expenditure as Percent of Sales
Aircraft and missiles	24.2
Electrical equipment	10.4
Instruments	7.3
Chemicals	4.6
Machinery	4.4
Primary metals	0.8
Paper	0.7
Textiles and clothing	0.6
Forest products	0.5
Food	0.3

Research and development, usually shortened to R&D, is one of the fastest growing activities in the economy. Expenditures on R&D have risen more than 20-fold since 1940. Most R&D activity goes on in industrial laboratories, though universities and government installations also participate. Of the amount spent in industry, however, more than half comes from the federal government, mainly in industries producing military supplies.

Some industries spend more on research and development than others. R&D expenditures as a percentage of industry sales is a good indicator. Table 14–3 lists a few of the highest and lowest industries.[5]

About 90 percent of the research on aircraft and missiles and 60 percent of that on electrical equipment are paid for by the federal government and devoted mainly to military products. The research done by instrument, machinery, and chemical producers (along with most other industries) is financed mainly from company funds.

Only about 4 percent of industrial R&D expenditure goes for basic research, while 20 percent is spent on applied research and 76 percent on development. Most of the effort goes into development of *products* rather than production *processes*. In a survey of large manufacturing companies on this point, 47 percent said their main purpose was to develop new products, 40 percent said that it was to improve existing products, and only 13 percent reported a major interest in processes. But one industry's product often affects another industry's production methods. If a

---

[5] Edwin Mansfield, *The Economics of Technological Change* (New York: W. W. Norton, 1968), p. 56. Much of the information for this section is derived from Mansfield. Another good general source is Richard R. Nelson, Merton J. Peck, and Edward D. Kolachek, *Technology, Economic Growth, and Public Policy* (Washington, D.C.: Brookings Institution, 1967).

manufacturer of textile machinery develops an improved loom, this leads to higher productivity in the textile industry. Thus, the consumer goods industries, which do little research of their own, do not show an abnormally low rate of productivity increase. They benefit from the research of companies which supply them with machinery and materials.

Inventions do not just come out of the blue, falling unpredictably on all sectors of the economy. Applied research is largely an organized activity conducted for profit. Economic factors are important. Technical change seems to be most rapid in areas where it will be most profitable.

Where demand is rising rapidly, for example, a cost reduction will yield greater profit than where demand is stagnant. Studies of several industries over a long period show a marked relation between the number of patents issued in an industry and the rate of increase in its sales.[6] Again, if one input is becoming more expensive relative to other inputs, one would expect special effort toward reducing the use of this input. Labor has been this kind of input in the United States, and there is considerable evidence that technical change has been oriented in a labor-saving direction.

Company scientists and engineers usually suggest far more research projects than can be undertaken with the resources available. In deciding which items shall be included in the annual R&D budget, company officials estimate the cost of each project and the total profit it might yield if successful. A project will usually not be undertaken unless it is expected to pay for itself within three or four years. By the nature of inventive activity, the results of any one project are highly uncertain. Only a small percentage of the ideas on which preliminary research is undertaken ever reach the stage of being tried out in production. But the profits from one major discovery, such as nylon, can pay for a company's research department for many years.

Technical change, then, need not be interpreted as something coming from outside the economy at a rate which we cannot explain. To some extent, additional technical change can be produced by additional research effort. One of Mansfield's studies finds that "holding size of firm constant, the number of significant inventions carried out by a firm seems to be highly correlated with the size of its R&D expenditures. Thus, although the output from an individual R&D project is obviously very uncertain, it seems that there is a close relationship over the long run between the amount a firm spends on R&D and the total number of important inventions it produces."[7] If this is true for individual firms, it is probably true also for *total* R&D expenditure in the economy.

---

[6] Professor Jacob Schmookler, of the University of Minnesota, has been a pioneer in the analysis of patent data as an indicator of inventive activity. See his study, *Invention and Economic Growth* (Cambridge, Mass.: Harvard University Press, 1966), and numerous shorter papers.

[7] Edwin Mansfield, *The Economics of Technological Change* (New York: W. W. Norton, 1968), p. 67.

Disembodied technical progress

How does technical change contribute to the growth of output? It has sometimes been viewed as falling like manna from heaven, mysteriously raising the productivity of the factors without changing their form. This possibility, no doubt of some importance, is usually called *disembodied technical progress.*

What would disembodied technical progress look like, concretely? The most plausible illustration would be improvements in management, which do not change the characteristics of labor or capital, but simply enable these factors to be used more effectively. Management methods in 1890 were still casual and traditional. The scientific management movement after 1890 brought major advances in production and personnel management, and the movement later spread to marketing, finance, and other areas. Developments in organization theory have improved the overall coordination of large enterprises. Most recently, mathematical methods (operations research, econometrics, linear programming) have been used with increasing success in management decision making.

Organizational improvements need not be confined to the enterprise. Improvement of economic information and markets may lead to better overall coordination of the economy, with a consequent rise in factor productivity.

Embodied progress and factor quality

While disembodied technical change can be defined, it is not easy to think of concrete examples. This suggests that technical change usually is embodied in physical form. It is not something to be added on *after* the growth of labor and capital supplies. Rather, it is *incorporated* in the growth of labor and capital inputs. Where technical change is occurring, capital and labor will increase in quality as well as in quantity.

This is perhaps most obvious in the case of capital. Invention leads not just to more machines but to different and better machines. As old equipment wears out, it is replaced by equipment with greater productive capacity per dollar of cost.

The effort to take account of this in growth theory has led to the concept of *vintage capital.* Each part of the nation's capital stock is dated by its year of origin, and it is assumed that each year's capital is x percent more productive than that of the year before. (Note that this is the reverse of vintage wines, where the newest is least good!) For example, if capital is improving at 3 percent per year, then capital of 1980 vintage would be more than twice as productive as capital of 1950 vintage and would get more than twice as much weight in the total capital stock. When you sum up the nation's capital stock year by year on this basis, you get a faster rate of increase than you would get otherwise.

Labor as well as capital has improved over time in the American econ-omy. Indeed, this can be viewed as a different kind of capital formation, an increase in the nation's stock of *human capital,* resulting from a combi-nation of formal education, on-the-job training, and work experience. Americans today have, on the average, more than twice as many years of education as their grandparents. Their level of skill and experience has risen. A much larger proportion of the labor force today consists of skilled craftsmen, white-collar workers, executives, and professional peo-ple.

One way to adjust for this improvement in the quality of the labor force is to use earnings level as an indicator. If supervisors earn twice as much as laborers, their hours can be diven double weight in the national total, and professional people might receive a weight of four or five. If the makeup of the labor force is shifting toward the higher occupations, such an adjusted index of total hours will rise faster than a crude index in which everyone's labor is taken as equal. Another possibility is to use years of education as an indicator of labor force quality and to give greater weight to hours worked by more highly educated people.

Thus, one can develop vintage measures of labor supply similar to the vintage capital measures. Total labor supply, adjusted for quality in this way, rises a good deal faster than the crude total of hours worked.

Statistical work by Griliches, Denison, and others has shown that improvement in factor quality is sufficient to explain most of the increase in national output, reducing the "residual" to minor proportions.[8]

Learning and technical progress

A somewhat different approach, developed particularly by Kenneth Arrow and Nicholas Kaldor, views progress as a process of learning through experience in production:

> The hypothesis is that improvements in technique do not become available from the passage of time as such, but by familiarity with the problems involved. Learning is the product of experience. If experience in this con-text can be measured by the amount of a commodity produced, then the higher is production, the greater will be the opportunities for learning and the faster the rate of technical progress.[9]

---

[8] Edward F. Denison, *The Sources of Economic Growth in the United States and the Alternatives before Us* (Washington, D.C.: Committee for Economic Development, 1962); Edward F. Denison, *Why Growth Rates Differ* (Washington, D.C.: Brookings Institution, 1967); Zvi Griliches, "The Sources of Measured Productivity Growth: U.S. Agriculture, 1940–60," *Journal of Political Economy,* August 1963, pp. 331–46; and "Research Expenditures, Education, and the Agricultural Production Function," *American Economic Review,* December 1964, pp. 961–74.

[9] F. H. Hahn and R. C. O. Matthews, "The Theory of Economic Growth: A Survey," *Economic Journal,* 1964; reprinted in *Surveys of Economic Theory,* vol. 2 (New York: St. Martin's Press, 1965), pp. 1–124.

It is well known that this happens for particular products. The case of air-frame production has been especially well investigated. The first few units of a new aircraft type are very expensive. Design problems have to be worked out, defects corrected, workers trained, and production method developed. As more and more units are produced, however, costs fall substantially, and they continue to fall, though more slowly, throughout the lifetime of the model. There is a predictable "learning curve."

If the economy produced only one product, all possibilities of learning might eventually become exhausted. But with new products being introduced continually, each subject to its own learning curve, the possibilities of progress through learning are continually renewed, and this must contribute importantly to the sustained rise of output in a progressive economy.

The idea that productivity improvement is related to experience in production can perhaps be extended from particular products to *output in general*. It may be that a high growth rate of GNP opens up more possibilities for technical improvement, so that rapid growth of output and rapid growth of factor productivity tend to go together. (Which is cause and which is effect, however, may be difficult to untangle.) It is significant that Japan and West Germany, which have had unusually high rates of GNP growth since 1950, have also had high rates of productivity increase—well above that in the United States. It may be significant also that the sharp drop in the growth rate of U.S. GNP after 1973 was paralleled by a sharp reduction in productivity growth.

The recent productivity slowdown: A passing phase?

We noted earlier the slowdown in the growth of both output and productivity which set in around 1973. This was not confined to the United States. It occurred in all the advanced industrial economies and, in fact, was sharpest in Japan. The experience of several key countries is shown in Table 14–4.[10] Output per worker, which is not as good a measure as total factor productivity but is more readily available, fell by more than half in most countries and by almost two thirds in Japan.

The reasons for the slowdown are still being studied and debated. Several factors were probably important:

1. Some features of the 1945–73 period, particularly favorable to productivity growth, could not be repeated on the same scale in later years. In the 50s and 60s, labor was still being reallocated on a large scale from lower-productivity jobs in agriculture to higher-productivity jobs in other sectors. By the 70s, this reservoir was running dry. World trade grew

---

[10] Adapted from R. C. O. Matthews, ed., *Slower Growth in the Western World* (London: Heineman, 1982), p. 21. See also Assar Lindbeck, "The Recent Slowdown of Productivity Growth," *Economic Journal* 93 (March 1983), pp. 13–34.

TABLE 14–4
Growth rate of output and output per worker for selected countries (percent per year)

Country	Output		Output per Worker	
	1960–73	1973–81	1960–73	1973–81
France	5.6	2.5	4.7	2.2
Germany	4.5	2.0	4.4	2.6
Japan	9.9	3.7	8.5	3.0
United Kingdom	3.1	−0.8	2.8	1.4
United States	4.1	2.3	2.2	0.4

at an unprecedented rate because of reduction of tariff barriers, rapid reduction of transport and communications costs, creation of the European common market, and other factors which could not continue at the same pace. The large technological lead of the United States as of 1950 left wide room for catching-up by other countries, a process which by the 70s had been largely completed. As these uniquely favorable circumstances faded away, some slowdown of productivity growth was to be expected.

2. The slowing down of output growth after 1973, combined with high rates of inflation, tended to erode business profits in the way described in Chapter 9. The fall in profit rates reduced both the funds available for investment and the inducement to invest. The food and oil price shocks, and the uncertainty associated with inflation, were also discouraging to investment. Thus, the growth rate of the capital stock and of capital per employed worker slowed down considerably. In the United States, for example, capital per worker rose at about 3 percent per year in the 50s and 60s. In the years 1973–80, this fell to less than 1 percent. Since productivity depends partly on how much capital labor has to work with, one would expect this to result in a deceleration of productivity growth.

In addition, the oil price revolution and the shift toward production methods using less energy made a certain amount of capital obsolete before its time. The amount of *effective* capital thus rose even less rapidly than the amount of capital on the books. Moreover, an increasing amount of capital during the 70s was directed toward pollution control, which no doubt added to welfare but did not raise measured GNP.

3. Depressed demand and underutilization of plant capacity were also important. The recessions of 1973–75 and 1981–82 were the most severe of the postwar period. We saw in Chapter 13 that in periods of slack demand, workers are not laid off as rapidly as output falls, so that productivity growth is often negative. Thus, the fact that Table 14–1 shows a sharp reduction after 1973 in both output and output per worker is no accident.

What can we expect in the decade ahead? Much clearly depends on the course of demand, on whether the vigorous growth of output in 1983–84 is sustained in later years. Something depends also on government policy—a possible reduction in the antisaving bias of the tax system, continuation of a moderate rate of inflation, adequate funding of scientific education and research. A reasonable guess is that GNP growth and productivity growth may return to something intermediate between the unusually strong performance of 1950–73 and the weak performance of 1973–82.

THE FUTURE OF ECONOMIC GROWTH

How rapidly will U.S. GNP per capita rise over the next 50 years? Will growth come grinding to a halt because of food shortages or exhaustion of mineral resources? Should government be trying to do anything about the growth rate? Can government, indeed, do anything about it? We are bound to speculate about such questions even if we can't get precise answers.

To simplify our task, we'll talk mainly about the outlook for the United States. If we were considering Brazil or Kenya or Bangladesh, the growth problem would appear different, and we would come to different conclusions.

Population and food supply

The determinants of population growth are still not very clear, and the track record of population forecasters is not good. As birthrates fell in the 20s and 30s, there were predictions that the U.S. population would soon level off and then decline. The upsurge of the birthrate after 1945 led to projections of a much higher population. Now birthrates are down again, and there are predictions that we will achieve zero population growth by 2020 A.D.

A precise prediction of U.S. population growth, however, is not very important. Because of our large land supplies and productive agricultural technology, we can easily feed any population we are likely to have in the foreseeable future. This does not quite end the discussion, because many other countries are in a less fortunate position. In many of the developing countries, population is outgrowing local food supplies and leading to rising demand for food imports. This is true also in China and the USSR, which have become large food importers because of lagging agricultural productivity.

The United States and Canada are now the only major grain exporters. As growing world demand converges on our limited supplies, it seems likely that prices of farm products in the United States will be bid up faster than prices in general. This is in fact already foreshadowed by the farm price spurts of 1973–74 and 1979–80. American farmers, of course, will welcome this development, but consumers will not. There will probably be political pressure to restrict our food exports to other countries. But this will strike some as a hard-hearted policy, and farmers will oppose it for obvious reasons. There may be major controversies over this issue in the years ahead.

Natural resource supplies

The idea that economic growth must encounter a barrier set by limited natural resources is not new. It was prominent in the writings of Ricardo, Malthus, Mill, and other classical economists. But recently, it has experienced a strong revival in popular economic writing.[11] It is easy enough to show that if world consumption continues to grow at recent rates, the known supplies of copper or oil or aluminum will be exhausted after 30 years, 50 years, or whatever. The question is what one can conclude from such projections.

Quite apart from the possibility of future resource discoveries—which are uncertain and in any case would only postpone the day of reckoning—this approach ignores two familiar facts of economic life. The first is technical change and substitution. Technical change may shift demand away from an item long before the supply has been exhausted. This seems likely to be the case with coal. With the present rapid pace of technical change, it is not of much use to predict resource shortages 40 or 50 years ahead, since no one can really say what will be a resource at that time.

Not only is one natural resource substitutable for another, but there is evidence that labor and capital are substitutable for resources in general. This is obviously true of land, where yields per acre in the developed countries (and even in some LDCs) have risen dramatically through application of modern technology. It is true also in industry, where amounts of fuel and raw materials used per unit of output have fallen substantially over the last several decades. Ironically, the complaint from the countries producing raw materials is not that we are putting too much pressure on their resource supplies but rather that our demand is rising too slowly because of substitution of synthetic products and other results of technical change.

The second fact of life is the role of prices in guiding resource use.

---

[11] See, for example, Donella H. Meadows, Dennis L. Meadows, Jorgen Randers, and William W. Behrens, III, *The Limits to Growth* (New York: Universe Books, 1972). For a critique of this and similar models, see Peter Passell and Leonard Ross, *The Retreat from Rides: Affluence and its Enemies* (New York: Viking Press, 1974).

If the supply of a particular resource rises less rapidly than demand, its price will rise. This, on the one hand, stimulates exploration for a new supplies and, on the other, encourages researchers to discover ways of using less of the material or of substituting other materials for it. All else failing, the price of products embodying the scarce resource will rise relative to prices in general, and this will reduce the quantity demanded and produced. The economy does not go charging blindly forward, determined always to produce the same outputs by the same methods. Both outputs and methods are responsive to price changes which signal resource scarcities.

As we should have learned from Chapter 2, to speak of a shortage of something independently of its price makes no sense. Supply and demand must be regarded not as *amounts* but as *schedules*. Over short periods, the supply schedule of a natural resource product can be taken as vertical, and the (downward sloping) demand schedule tends to shift to the right as growing industrial output demands more raw materials. But over a period of decades, the supply schedule also keeps shifting to the right through resource discoveries, while the demand schedule keeps getting batted back down through material-saving innovations and possibilities of substitution. Whether supply is losing out in the race can be judged only by looking at the behavior of *price.*

Prices of minerals and other natural resource products fluctuate widely over the business cycle. But over a long period, say 1900–80, there has been no tendency for these prices to rise relative to prices of manufactured goods. So apparently the scarcity point is not yet in sight—at least in the minds of the business leaders and government officials who must be assumed to look at least some distance into the future.[12] The recent spectacular increase in the price of crude oil resulted not from any shortage of supplies but from a discovery by the producing nations that they could exercise monopoly power. The United States has a problem of paying for imported oil. But for the world as a whole, *there is no oil scarcity.* On the contrary, there is a surplus of production capacity over quantity demanded, and oil storage tanks around the world are overflowing.

If and when prices of some materials do experience a sustained uptrend, this will raise production costs and prices of finished goods in which they are an important ingredient. It is quite possible, for example, that metal-using products will become gradually more expensive relative to

---

[12] Strictly speaking, for present estimates of future scarcity to be reflected accurately in prices requires the existence of *futures markets,* on which oil, copper, rubber, and so on could be traded for delivery at various future dates. Such markets exist for some commodities, but the delivery dates do not run very far into the future. The possibility that these markets could be further developed and the time horizon extended has been debated a good deal. See, for example, William D. Nordhaus, "The Allocation of Energy Resources," *Brookings Paper on Economic Activity,* no. 3 (1973), pp. 529–70; and Robert M. Solow, "The Economics of Resources or the Resources of Economics," *American Economic Review,* May 1974, pp. 1–14.

other goods. This will induce consumers to use less of those products, which will also restrain demand for the metals on which they are based. But one should not confuse reduced output of *some things* with a reduction of output *in general*. Consumers will simply allocate their spending power in other directions.

Our economy is quite capable of making such shifts, and in fact is making them all the time. Kuznets and others have shown that as a country's output per capita rises, the proportion of *goods* in this output decreases steadily, while the proportion of *services* increases. The real growth industries in the United States today are things like health care, travel, and entertainment. Production of services, which involves mainly the use of skilled labor, is neither very resource-consuming nor very environment-polluting.

The natural resources argument perhaps comes down to this: It is quite possible, perhaps even probable, that demand pressure will in time produce a *relative* increase in the prices of minerals and other raw materials. Since we import large quantities of these materials, we will face a problem of paying more for them to other countries, similar to the problem we already face of paying OPEC. This will mean larger transfers of U.S.-produced goods to those countries, which will slow down the growth of U.S. consumption.

Can the growth rate be manipulated?

Turning to growth policy, there are two main issues: (1) Can the growth rate be altered by government action and, if so, by what means? (2) To the extent that the growth rate can be manipulated, what are the considerations favoring a higher or lower rate of growth?

The answer to the first question seems to be yes, but not very much. The reason is the highly decentralized structure of the American economy. The growth of factor supplies, the rate of technical progress, and the pattern of outputs depend on millions of separate decisions which can be influenced only indirectly by government. During the heyday of "growthmanship" in the 60s, paper programs were developed to show how the GNP growth rate might be raised by 1 percent a year, and one could doubtless construct counterprograms which might lower it by 1 percent. But this is probably an outside estimate of government's potential impact, and it would require concerted effort over a period of years.

One possible lever is expenditure on industrial research and development. There is much evidence that research does accelerate the rate of productivity growth, and a large share of financial support for research comes from the federal government. So government could step up (or reduce) its support for research in an effort to attain a higher (or lower) growth target. Stepping up support for research, of course, would require a parallel increase of support for educational institutions training scientists and engineers, since the amount of research that can be done is limited by the number of people available to do it.

The other obvious lever is the rate of business investment. We pointed out in Chapter 12 how investment could be stimulated by combining an easy monetary policy, involving low interest rates, with a tight fiscal policy to restrain inflation. The opposite policy mix—a loose fiscal policy accompanied by tight monetary policy and high interest rates—would tend to reduce investment. The structure of corporate taxation is another important instrument. The tax treatment of depreciation allowances, corporate profits, and dividend payments must affect investment, though the size of the effect is hard to estimate.

The second question of what government *should* do is more difficult. What constitutes a desirable growth rate for the economy? If one could put this question to the public in a referendum, one would not get meaningful results. To most people, the question would seem academic, remote from their daily lives, and they would not have either the interest or the information to address themselves to it effectively.

The traditional attitude has doubtless been that growth is good, and the more of it, the better. Most people hope to be better off tomorrow than they are today, and this is easier to achieve if national output is rising. The expectation of continued growth contributes to business optimism and investment. Patriotic and military considerations—keeping up with the Russians or whoever—also enter in.

More recently, there have been doubts about whether growth at past rates is desirable or even feasible because of the natural resource and environmental constraints discussed above. We have suggested that such fears are exaggerated, but it would be irresponsible to write them off as groundless.

So, what constitutes a desirable growth rate is a fine subject for class discussion and college debate, but given the unsettled state of information and opinion, it is not something on which a text writer should lay down the law. Having said this, let me add two mildly progrowth comments.

First, we should be clear that growth in a country's productive capacity does *not* imply a corresponding increase in material consumption. What it does is to enlarge the options open to individuals in the economy. One such option is leisure. Another is increased consumption of education, recreation, and cultural activities. How these options are exercised is, in our society, a matter for individual choice. It is perfectly open to anyone to work as little, spend as little, and live as ascetically as he or she prefers. But it is illegitimate to take the further step of saying "others should do as I do." It is a reasonable guess that the large majority of Americans who still live below the upper middle-class level would not agree that they have nothing to gain from increased consumption.

This leads to a further consideration in thinking about economic growth. Personal income in the United States is still very unequally distributed. There is considerable consensus that extreme poverty should be eliminated and that all families should be brought up to some minimum income. Many would argue that we should try also to reduce income disparities above the poverty level.

How to do this? So long as total income is growing, a feasible strategy is to divert a large part of this growth to the lower income groups. Redistribution can be (and in fact is being) achieved by low incomes rising faster than high incomes but without anyone actually losing what they now have. But if the income pie were to become fixed in size, higher incomes for the poor could be achieved only by an absolute reduction in other incomes. This kind of redistribution would be difficult and divisive. The fact that economic growth permits income redistribution without generating excessive social tensions is a substantial advantage.

The future of the growth rate

Regardless of how one might like the growth rate to behave, it is interesting to ask what is most likely to happen over the years ahead. The future is somewhat speculative, but not entirely so.

We start from the basic determinants examined earlier in the chapter: the growth of labor inputs, the growth of the capital stock, and the rate of technical progress. As regards labor supply, what is likely to happen to labor inputs *per head of population?* Overall, will the population be putting in more work or less?

Here there are conflicting forces at work. The percentage of women who are in the labor force has been rising for several decades and will continue to rise. This *increases* labor inputs per head of population. On the other hand, people are tending to stay longer in school and college and to retire earlier (and even the 1978 law prohibiting compulsory retirement before age 70 may not change this very much). These trends *reduce* labor input per head. In addition, the workweek and work year have been falling steadily over the long run. Weekly hours have fallen from 60 to 50 to 40, and the 30-hour week is now in sight. Vacation periods have grown longer, paid holidays are on the increase, and some industrial workers now get "sabbatical leaves" of several months' duration. All this makes economic sense. As wage levels rise, most people prefer to receive part of the benefit in the form of greater leisure rather than increased income. Because of this tendency, we should expect labor input per capita to continue falling in the future.

There is no reason to expect any marked change in the growth rate of the capital stock. Gross capital formation as a proportion of GNP has held close to 20 percent for more than a century. There is a marked cyclical fluctuation, however, with the capital formation rate falling on the downswing and rising on the upswing. So the future course of events depends somewhat on how effectively we are able to check downswings and keep the company operating close to capacity. Assuming reasonable success on this front, we may expect the total capital stock to rise as rapidly as in the past. This would mean that capital stock *per hour worked* would rise somewhat faster because of the slowdown of labor inputs.

Technical change is by nature unpredictable. It has been more rapid in recent decades than in the early 20th century. There seems no reason why it should not continue at recent rates or even accelerate further. But it seems unlikely that it will accelerate enough to offset the long-run decline in labor inputs per capita. Thus, the most likely prognosis is for a modest decline in the growth rate of output per capita in the next several decades.

This also seems to be the opinion of Simon Kuznets, the leading student of long-term growth in the Western industrial countries. He concludes that these countries have tended to pass through three phases: an early phase in which the growth rate rises markedly, a long period of more or less constant growth, and finally a phase of slower growth. He finds the reason for eventual decline of the growth rate on the side of demand rather than supply:

> there are no inherently *compelling* reasons for the rate of growth of per capita product to decline . . . technological and other limitations on the *supply* side can hardly be viewed as an important factor. The major reason would therefore lie on the demand side. A long-term rise in real income per capita would make leisure an increasingly preferred good, as is clearly evidenced by the marked reduction in the working week in freely organized, nonauthoritarian advanced countries. One could argue that after a high level of per capita income is attained, the pressure on the demand side for further increases is likely to slacken.[13]

It should be reemphasized that this does not mean a slower rate of increase in economic welfare, of which leisure is an important component. The fact that workers choose a reduction in hours means that they value the increase in leisure more highly than the additional income they could have obtained by working the old hours.

THINK ABOUT THIS

1. The last section views a continued rise of per capita output in the United States as feasible and, on the whole, desirable. Is this too optimistic? Are there reasons for being apprehensive about continuation of economic growth at past rates? You should worry about this. The author may be wrong!
2. Should government try to raise (or lower) the growth rate? Explain why, or why not.

---

[13] Simon Kuznets, *Six Lectures on Economic Growth* (Glencoe, Ill.: Free Press, 1959), p. 38.

NEW CONCEPTS

output growth, total

output growth, per capita

economic growth

total factor input

total factor productivity

technical progress, disembodied

technical progress, embodied

human capital

vintage capital

vintage labor

learning curve

economic welfare, measure of

SUMMARY

1. The growth rate of an economy is defined as its rate of increase in output per capita.

2. GNP per capita is not an accurate measure of consumer welfare. Efforts to estimate a measure of economic welfare (MEW) suggest that welfare has been rising over the long run but more slowly than GNP per capita.

3. Over the past century, output per capita in the developed industrial countries has risen on the average at about 2 percent per year, but 1950–70 growth rates were above this long-term average.

4. Natural output rises partly because labor and capital inputs are increasing. We can estimate the growth of *total factor inputs* by determining the growth rates of labor supply and capital stock and then weighting each by the proportion of national income going to that factor.

5. National output usually rises considerably faster than total factor inputs. The gap between the two rates is a measure of the increase in *total factor productivity,* also called "technical progress" or simply "the residual."

6. Technical progress comes increasingly from organized research laboratories, mainly operated by industry but financed partly by the federal government. There is evidence that increased expenditure on research and development increases the flow of useful inventions.

7. Technical progress can be regarded as *disembodied* or as *embodied* in one or both of the factors. Improvement in the quality of capital over time has been recognized in the concept of *vintage capital.* There have also been efforts to measure the rate of increase in *labor force quality* resulting from education, job training, and work experience.

8. Growing scarcity of some raw materials, leading to an increase in the relative price of goods based on these materials, would result in changes in the *composition* of national output but need not reduce the *growth rate* of output.

9. While a decline in the growth rate is not inevitable for this reason, it probably will occur for other reasons, notably a continued decline of labor inputs per capita.

10. Government probably *could* raise (or lower) the growth rate moderately by increasing (or reducing) federal expenditure on industrial research and development and by monetary and tax policies to raise (or lower) the rate of business investment. Whether government *should* try to raise or lower the growth rate is a controversial issue on which there is no consensus at present.

TO LEARN MORE

The record of long-term growth in the industrialized countries is analyzed in Simon Kuznets, *Modern Economic Growth* (New Haven, Conn.: Yale University Press, 1966). Growth in the poorer third-world countries since 1945 is analyzed in Part Two of Lloyd Reynolds, *Image and Reality in Economic Development* (New Haven, Conn.: Yale University Press, 1977). The recent "limits of growth" controversy was set off by Donella H. Meadows and others, *The Limits to Growth* (New York: Universe Books, 1974). Other lively contributions to this debate are Peter Passell and Leonard Ross, *Retreat from Riches: Affluence and Its Enemies* (New York: Viking Press, 1973); and William Nordhaus and James Tobin, "Is Growth Obsolete?" in *Economic Research: Retrospect and Prospect, 50th Anniversary Colloquium, V, Economic Growth* (New York: National Bureau of Economic Research, 1972).

Part Three

The International Economy

■ 15 ■

The Basis of International Trade

*Our interest will be to throw open the doors of commerce,
and to knock off its shackles, giving perfect freedom to
all persons for the vent of whatever they may choose to
bring into our ports, and asking the same in theirs.*

— THOMAS JEFFERSON

The purpose of this chapter is to explain why countries trade with each other and how a country can gain from trade. We will make several main points:

A country normally exports goods which it can produce most efficiently, that is, at lowest cost relative to other countries; and it imports goods in which other countries are relatively more efficient. This is called the *principle of comparative advantage.*

When countries exchange goods on the basis of comparative advantage, they all gain. The source of the gain is that world output is larger when each country specializes in the goods it can produce most efficiently.

The goods in which a country will have comparative advantage depends partly on supplies of the factors of production. A country with much rich agricultural land will tend to export agricultural products. A country with abundant and cheap labor may have comparative advantage in labor-intensive manufactures.

Comparative advantage is influenced also by research and invention. The United States, because of its relatively heavy expenditure on research and development, tends to have comparative advantage in new goods embodying advanced technology.

Comparative advantage changes over the course of time, and a country should expect the makeup of its exports and imports to change accordingly.

Introduction

Even those who believe in free competition within a country often question the extension of this principle to international trade. Competition among American business concerns may be all right, but let's not admit foreign nationals to the game. Let's "buy American" and "keep American dollars at home." There is something about foreign trade which seems mysterious and different.

One obvious difference is that factors of production move more freely within countries than between countries. If the productivity of labor is higher in California than in Oklahoma, and if California workers consequently ean more, labor will flow from Oklahoma to California. If capital yields more in southern textiles than in northern textiles, investment will grow in the South and shrink in the North. Factor mobility can be expected to reduce differences in rates of return within a country. But movement of labor from country to country is severely restricted by immigration laws, and capital movements are also restricted in various ways. As a consequence, there is no reason to expect equalization of wage levels and interest rates among different countries.

How freely commodities move among countries depends partly on transportation costs and partly on national policies. The great reduction of transportation costs over the past century and a half has been a powerful force swelling the volume of world trade. National policies have varied, tending at times in the direction of free trade and at other times placing severe restrictions on trade.

A country's participation in world trade is influenced by the size of its economy. A country with a limited resource base and a small internal market cannot possibly produce all the goods it may wish to consume. It usually exports a few products for which it has natural advantages and imports a wide array of other goods from the rest of the world. Countries which normally export 30 percent to 50 percent of their GNP include Belgium, the Netherlands, Eire, Iceland, Cuba, Panama, Jamaica, British Guiana, Peru, Venezuela, Ceylon, and Ghana. At the other pole are very large countries with diversified resources and a vast trading area within their own borders. These countries can be largely self-sufficient. The list of countries whose exports are normally less than 10 percent of GNP includes the United States, the USSR, China, India, Pakistan, and Brazil. International trade is important even to these countries. For the smaller countries, it is vital.

In this chapter, we ask *why* countries trade with one another and what determines *which* goods a country will export and import. Can we show that there is normally a gain from trade and explain how this gain is divided among the participants?

THE BASIS OF TRADE: COMPARATIVE CHEAPNESS

Why do nations export certain goods and import others? In some cases the reason is clear. It would not be sensible to try to grow enough bananas and coffee in the United States to meet our needs, so we buy them abroad. In other cases, our raw material supplies are insufficient for our needs, so we buy copper from Chile, iron ore from Canada and Venezuela, and oil from the Middle East. But why do we buy large amounts of manufactured goods from Britain, Western Europe, and Japan? We are ourselves a great manufacturing nation. In fact, we export large amounts of manufactures *to* these same countries. What are the reasons for this kind of trade?

One's first thought might be that a country will export goods which it can produce cheaply, and since wages are a large part of production costs, a country with a low wage level will have an advantage. Imagine, for example, that trade is opened up for the first time between the United States and Japan. Will Japan, with its lower wage level, be able to undersell us in everything? Suppose for a moment that this were to happen. Japan is exporting large amounts of merchandise and importing nothing. What would be the consequences?

Japan might be willing for a time to ship us goods on credit, but this could not continue forever. Eventually Japan would begin to want payment. To pay for our imports, we will have to buy Japanese yen. The demand for yen will rise, and if exchange rates are responsive to supply and demand, the price for yen in terms of dollars will rise. Thus, Japanese goods will become more expensive in the United States, while at the same time American goods will become cheaper in Japan.

Suppose that at the beginning the exchange rate is $1 = 100 yen. Now because of the great demand for yen the rate changes to $1 = 50 yen. (This is an *increase* in the value of the yen, which is now worth 2 cents instead of 1 cent, and it is a *decrease* in the value of the dollar.) So a product selling for $100 in the United States, which originally cost 10,000 yen in Japan, will now cost only 5,000. American goods are becoming cheaper and hence more attractive to the Japanese. On the other hand, a Japanese product selling at 1,000 yen, which used to cost Americans $10, will now cost $20 at the new exchange rate.

As the value of the yen continues to rise, more and more Japanese goods will be priced out of the American market. Conversely, more and more American goods will move into the Japanese market as their price (in yen) declines. So Japan's exports will shrink and its imports will rise until the flow of trade is balanced. At this point, the exchange rate will become stabilized.

What goods will Japan still be exporting to us when equilibrium has been reached? Isn't it clear that these will be the goods which it can produce most cheaply *relative to other Japanese goods?* Similarly, we will ship to Japan goods in the production of which we are unusually efficient. The basis for trade is that a country's labor, capital, and other resources are not equally effective in every line of endeavor. The goods for which a country's production resources are especially effective, and which consequently have relatively low unit cost and price, are the ones which will be exported, while goods which are relatively expensive to produce at home will be imported.

AN ILLUSTRATION OF COMPARATIVE CHEAPNESS

The principle of comparative cheapness can be illustrated by the hypothetical figures in Table 15–1. The table shows for each product the U.S. price in dollars, the British price in pounds, and the ratio of the dollar price to the pound price. Note that we cannot say whether any product is actually cheaper in the United States or in Britain. This depends on the rate of exchange, which we do not yet know. But even without this we can say something about *comparative* cheapness. Looking at the right-hand column, we see that the ratio of the dollar price to the pound price varies greatly. Items toward the top of the table are comparatively cheap in the United States. Items toward the bottom are comparatively expensive in the United States and comparatively cheap in Britain. We get the same result by looking down each of the first two columns. In the United States, a bicycle is worth 90 times as much as a dozen radio tubes, while in Britain it is worth only 10 times as much. Again, we reach the conclusion that bicycles must be comparatively cheaper in Britain.

Given these relative prices, the movement of trade depends on the rate of exhange. Suppose the rate were £1 = $10. Then everything would be absolutely cheaper in the United States. Radio tubes would be worth $1 a dozen in the United States, but $10 a dozen in Britain. Wheat would be worth $2 a bushel here, $10 a bushel there; and so on. All six items

TABLE 15–1

Comparative prices, United States and United Kingdom

Commodity	U.S. Price (dollars)	U.K. Price (pounds)	Price Ratio (dollars/ pounds)
Radio tubes (dozen)	1	1	1
Wheat (bushel)	2	1	2
Coal (ton)	30	10	3
Wool cloth (100 yards)	150	30	5
Shoes (dozen pairs)	280	40	7
Bicycles (each)	90	10	9

would be exported from the United States to Britain. This situation clearly could not continue. There would be a great supply of pounds and no demand, and the price of pounds would fall.

Conversely, suppose the exchange rate were £1 = $0.50. This would make everything cheaper in Britain. Radio tubes would be worth $1 a dozen in the United States, $0.50 a dozen in Britain. Wheat would be worth $2 a bushel here, $0.50 a bushel there; and so on. Trade would move solely from Britain to the United States, and so this also turns out to be an unfeasible exchange rate.

There must be some intermediate exchange rate, however, which will permit two-way trade. Suppose the rate were £1 = $4. Now radio tubes are $1 a dozen in the United States, $4 a dozen in Britain. Wheat is also cheaper in the United States, and so is coal. When we come to wool cloth, we find that it costs only $120 per 100 yards in Britain, but $150 in the United States. Shoes and bicycles are also cheaper in Britain. So the United States will *export* the first three items which are cheaper here and will *import* the last three items, which can be obtained more cheaply from Britain.

Prices reflect costs of production. If a good is relatively cheap in the United States, this must be because we are relatively efficient producers of that good, and if we can buy something more cheaply from another country, this must be because that country is a relatively efficient producer. Both countries gain by producing and exchanging the products in which each is relatively more efficient. *This is the main point of this chapter.* It will take a few pages to explain and illustrate it, but if you become lost at any point, it may help to recall what the story is all about.

THE PRINCIPLE OF COMPARATIVE ADVANTAGE

We have argued that trade depends on the comparative cheapness of products in different countries. But on what does cheapness depend? If goods are produced under competitive conditions in each country, prices will reflect money costs; and these costs reflect quantities of land, labor, capital, and other resources used in production. If radio tubes are relatively cheap in the United States, this means basically that they are cheap *in terms of the physical resources required to product them.* To put the matter in reverse, American productive resources are particularly well adapted to production of radio tubes, more so (still following Table 15–1) than they are to production of bicycles. The United States has a *comparative advantage* in radio tube production, while Britain has a *comparative advantage* in bicycle production.

This does not tell us, and we need to know, anything about *absolute* levels of productive efficiency in the two countries. U.S. productive resources may have higher productivity in each and every line of production.

Now if the United States were exactly twice as productive as Britain in every line of activity, there would be no basis for trade and no trade would occur. (The ratios in the right-hand column of Table 15–1 would all be the same.) But in actuality our productivity advantage is *uneven*— much greater in some lines than in others. So it pays us to concentrate on products in which our productivity advantage is greatest, in which we have a *comparative advantage,* and to import those in which our advantage is least.

The idea of comparative advantage is so important that we shall illustrate it from several points of view. The principle applies to production and exchange within countries as well as between countries. We shall look at three examples: (1) farms with different production possibilities; (2) two regions of the United States with different production possibilities; and (3) two countries, the United States and Switzerland, with different production possibilities. These cases look different on the surface. But we come out in each case with the same conclusion: the farm, region, or country gains by devoting its resources to products in which it has comparative advantage.

Case 1. There are five farms, each of which has the option of feeding beef cattle for market or of growing corn and fattening hogs. The amount of beef each farm could produce if it concentrated entirely on beef is shown in the first column of Table 15–2, the amount of pork which could be produced by concentrating on pork production appears in the second column, and the ratio of potential beef output to pork output appears in the right-hand column.

What will each farm produce? We cannot tell without knowing the prices of beef and pork? A farm will specialize in beef if its prospective receipts are greater in that line, that is, if potential beef production $\times$ price of beef $>$ potential pork production $\times$ price of pork. This is the same as saying:

$$\frac{\text{Potential beef production}}{\text{Potential pork production}} > \frac{\text{Price of pork}}{\text{Price of beef}}$$

TABLE 15–2
Comparative advantage in farming

Farm	Potential Beef Production (tons per acre)	Potential Pork Production (tons per acre)	Beef/Pork Ratio
A	5	50	0.1
B	40	200	0.2
C	50	150	0.33
D	30	75	0.4
E	30	60	0.5

Suppose beef is selling at $1 a pound and pork at $0.30 so that the second ratio is 0.3. Then farms C, D, and E, whose beef/pork production ratio is greater than this, will produce beef. Farms A and B will find themselves better off producing pork. The price ratio slices through the middle of the table, just as the exchange rate did in our earlier case, and determines the most profitable line of production for each farm.

Note that the farms specializing in each product need not be those which are *absolutely* best in that line. Farm A is the poorest pork producer in the group. Yet it will cling to pork production longer than anyone else, even if pork prices are only a little more than one tenth of beef prices. The reason is that while farm A is a poor pork producer, it is an even worse beef producer. Comparative advantage can mean *either* that one is particularly good at the product in question or particularly bad in other things. The fact that certain mountain areas in Nevada concentrate on sheep grazing does not mean that these areas are absolutely best for this purpose, but since their productivity in other lines would be close to zero, they have a *comparative advantage* in sheep production.

Case 2.   This involves trade between regions of the United States. Why doesn't each region produce everything it needs? Why not keep New England money at home? Why are some kinds of production located mainly in one region, others mainly in another?

Regional specialization arises because a product can usually be produced more efficiently in some parts of the country than in others. For primary products, this may be due to climate, soil fertility, or natural resources. In manufacturing, it may be due to a highly skilled labor force, development of subsidiary industries supporting the main industry, long managerial experience, closeness to materials, or closeness to markets.

Suppose Texas and New England were separate countries, with no trade between them, and suppose that the productivity situation was as shown in Table 15–3. We use labor input to represent input of resources in general, and suppose that within each region products will exchange according to the ratio of labor input. Then, in New England, a pair of shoes will exchange for two pounds of beef. In Texas, however, the "beef price" of a pair of shoes will be much higher—five pounds of beef instead of two.

TABLE 15–3
A case of interregional trade

	Beef Production (pounds per day of labor)	Shoe Production (pairs per day of labor)	Price Ratio Beef/Shoes
Texas	200	40	5
New England	40	20	2

Suppose now that trade is opened up between these "countries." Surely it will occur to some New Englander to ship shoes to Texas, where their beef price is higher than at home, and to ship beef in the opposite direction. Ship 200 pairs of shoes to Texas, where they can be exchanged for 1,000 pounds of beef, bring this back to New England and trade it for 500 pairs of shoes, export these to Texas and get 2,500 pounds of beef, and so onward to riches. But as our trader gets to work, the price of shoes will begin to rise in New England and fall in Texas. Overlooking transportation costs, the price ratio will eventually become the same in both regions.

Table 15-3 does not tell us where the price ratio will settle down. To discover this, we would have to know the demand and supply curves for each product in each region. Suppose the price settles at 4:1, four pounds of beef exchanging for a pair of shoes. Then each region has gained from the opening up of trade. By concentrating on shoe production and importing beef, the New Englanders now get for a day's labor 80 pounds of beef (=20 pairs of shoes). Without trade, they could have gotten only 40 pounds. The Texans also gain by concentrating on beef production and importing shoes. For a day's labor they can now obtain 50 pairs of shoes (=200 pounds of beef), whereas formerly they could have gotten only 40 pairs. It appears that Texas has gained less than New England, but this is because we chose 4:1 as the new price ratio. If the ratio settled at a level more favorable to Texas, say 3:1, the Texans would gain more and the New Englanders less. But at anything between the original price ratios of 2:1 and 5:1, each region will gain something.

Note one curious thing about this case. Texas has higher productivity than New England in both products. One's first thought, then, might be that Texas will do best by producing everything for itself. Yet Texas actually gains by importing shoes and shipping beef in return. Texas has an *absolute* advantage in everything, but it has a *comparative* advantage in beef, where its absolute advantage is greatest. New England has a *comparative* advantage in shoes, where its absolute disadvantage is least.

This is not quite the end of the story. If economic resources are more productive in Texas in every line of endeavor, people in Texas will enjoy a higher standard of living. *Real* wage rates, which are based on absolute productivity, will be higher in Texas than in New England. If people respond to economic advantage, and if movement between the two regions is easy, one should see a migration of New Englanders to Texas to take advantage of the higher wage levels there; and there should also be an outward movement of capital from New England to take advantage of higher profit rates. The movement of labor and capital should continue until productivity levels and income levels have been brought close to equality in the two regions.

The results of this case may be summarized as follows:

1. Where two regions are linked by trade, each will export the products in which it has *comparative* advantage. This is true regardless of absolute productivity levels in the two regions.
2. The gain from trade is the increase in total output which results from each region specializing in the products in which it has comparative advantage.
3 The division of this gain between the regions depends on the price ratio which is established for the products exchanged. (In international dealings, this is called *the terms of trade,* defined most simply as the ratio of the prices a country receives for its exports to the prices it must pay for its imports. If a country's export prices rise relative to import prices, we say that its terms of trade have improved, and conversely.)
4. Over long periods, differences in *absolute* productivity levels among regions tend to be eliminated by movement of labor and other resources toward the high-productivity regions.

Comparative advantage: The international case

Case 3. If comparative advantage works for domestic trade, why not for foreign trade as well? Take two countries, each producing the same goods. (The classical writers usually chose England and Portugal, with cotton cloth and port wine as the products. But let us take the United States and Switzerland, with wheat and watches as the products.) The cost of producing each good in each country can be reduced to labor units, and within each country, the relative price of the products will equal their relative labor costs. Suppose also that each good is produced under constant cost conditions,[1] so that relative costs and prices are independent of how the country's resources are divided between its two outputs.

The United States has 200 labor-days available. It takes one labor-day to produce a bushel of wheat but four labor-days to produce a watch. So on the labor cost principle, one watch will be worth four bushels of wheat.

The U.S. production possibilities curve is shown in Figure 15–1. By putting all our labor into wheat production, we could grow $OA = 200$ bushels of wheat. If we produced nothing but watches, we could produce $OB = 50$ watches. Or we can produce various combinations of the two, shown by different points on AB. The steepness of AB indicates the relative price (= the relative labor cost) of the two products, which is 4:1. The fact that this ratio is constant (i.e., the AB is a straight line)

---

[1] This means that the total quantity produced has no effect on cost per unit of output.

FIGURE 15–1
Production possibilities in the United States

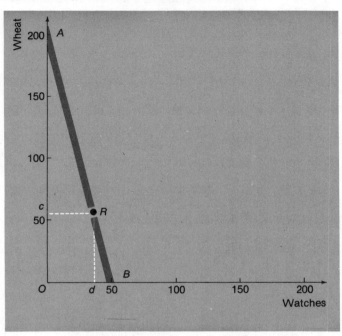

The line *AB* shows all combinations of wheat and watches which the United States can produce with the 200 labor-days available. For example, if it grows *Oc* bushels of wheat, it can also produce *Od* watches. The *slope* of the line *AB* measures the price of watches in terms of wheat, which is 1:4.

depends on our assumption that each good is produced under constant costs.

How much of each good will actually be produced cannot be determined from the cost ratios. We would also have to know the demand curve for each product. But we would undoubtedly produce and consume some combination, such as *Oc* + *Od*.

Now look at Switzerland, which also has 200 labor-days available. In Switzerland, as in the United States, one labor-day will produce a bushel of wheat. But Switzerland also has an unusually productive watch industry, in which one labor-day is enough to produce a watch. So in Switzerland the price ratio is 1 bushel = 1 watch.

The production possibilities curve for Switzerland is A_1B_1 in Figure 15–2. It is a straight line because of the constant cost condition, and its slope, which is 1:1, measures the price ratio of the two products. Once more, we cannot say where production will actually settle without having

FIGURE 15-2
Production possibilities in Switzerland

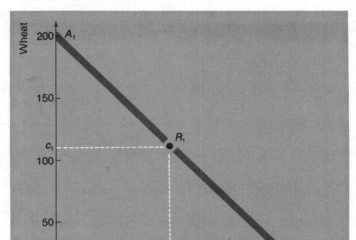

Here A_1B_1 shows all combinations of wheat and watches which Switzerland can produce—for example, Oc_1 of wheat plus Od_1 of watches.
As before, the slope of A_1B_1 measures the price of watches in terms
of wheat, which is 1 : 1.

demand information, but it might be at R_1, with Oc_1 of wheat and Od_1
of watches.

Now these two economies, which have previously been operating independently, are allowed to trade with each other, and it is clear that trade
will be profitable. The Swiss watch producers, who can get only one
bushel per watch at home, will see that they can get four bushels per
watch in America and will start exporting. The American wheat producers,
who can get a higher (watch) price in Switzerland than at home, will
also start exporting.

As trade continues, the price ratios will begin to shift. The relative
price of watches will fall in the United States as Swiss watches come
flooding in, while the relative price of wheat will fall in Switzerland. If
we overlook transportation costs, and if there are no tariffs, the price
ratio must eventually be *identical* in both countries. Why? Because they
have become in effect a single market, and under competition there cannot
be different prices in the same market.

The new price ratio will depend on the demand for each product in each country. But it will probably be at some point between the two previous ratios.

What will happen to production and consumption in each country? Look at Figure 15–3, which combines the information in Figures 15–1 and 15–2. There is a little trick about the construction of Figure 15–3: to get both countries on the same diagram, we locate their origins at opposite corners of the chart. The origin for the United States is at O, and its production possibilities curve looks just as before. But the origin for Switzerland is now located in the upper right-hand corner at O_1. (Study this a bit to make sure that you understand how it works.)

The new price ratio is shown by the line AS. Note that its slope is intermediate between that of the two old price lines, AB and A_1B_1. At this price ratio, it will pay the United States to produce only wheat and import all its watches. Out of a wheat production of OA we can consume, say, Of bushels. By trading the remainder, fA, at the new price ratio we can buy $Oe = fP$ watches. By comparing points P and R, one can

FIGURE 15–3
The gain from trade

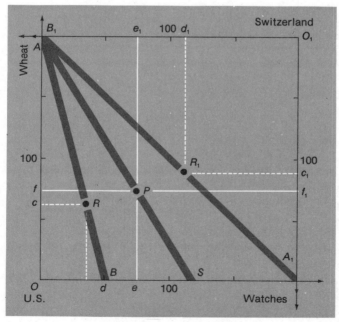

AB and A_1B_1 are the production possibilities curves shown in Figures 15–1 and 15–2, but the origin of the Swiss diagram is now located in the upper right-hand corner at O_1. Before trade begins, the United States is producing at point R and Switzerland R_1. With trade, it is possible to move to a point such as P, where each country has more of both products than before.

see that we now have *more of both wheat and watches than before.* We are now operating outside out old production frontier.

The Swiss on their side will specialize completely in watches. By selling us B_1e_1 (= *oe*) of watches, they can buy O_1f_1 (= *fA*) of wheat. So they also end up at *P,* above their old production frontier and with more of both products than before.

Each country has gained by concentrating on the product in which it has comparative advantage. The division of the gain between them depends on the new price ratio, that is, on the *terms of trade.* The further *AS* swings down toward *AB* (i.e., the higher the relative price of watches), the more of the gain will go to Switzerland. In the unlikely event that *AS* coincides with *AB,* all the gain would go to Switzerland and none to the United States. (The price of watches cannot go *higher* than the old U.S. price ratio. Why? Because then the United States would produce watches at home instead of importing, and trade would cease. Neither side can *lose* by trade, since it always has the option of not trading.)

From the fact that both countries are now able to consume more than before, it follows that total production must have increased. You can verify this from Figure 15–3 by adding up wheat and watch production before trade began and comparing it with the new levels after trade. Free international trade, by permitting each country to specialize according to its comparative advantage, tends to *maximize world production.*

In this simple example, we treated labor as the only factor of production, and we assumed by implication that a day's labor in one country was equivalent to a day's labor in another. This is obviously not true in actuality. But the assumption of equal labor quality is not essential to the argument. We can adjust for international differences in labor productivity in reasoning about international trade.

Suppose that over the economy as a whole, a labor-hour in the United States produces twice as much as in Britain. Since real wages depend on productivity, the general wage level in Britain will be about half that in the United States. Since the lower wage level is just offset by lower productivity, this does not per se give Britain a competitive advantage in world trade. So what will happen to trade? We come back to the principle that trade depends not on differences in productivity levels between countries but on productivity differences among different industries in the same country, that is, on *comparative advantage.*

U.S. workers are paid twice as much as British workers because *on the average* they are that much more productive. Relative American and British productivity, however, will differ a good deal from one industry to another. In producing electric light bulbs, say, American productivity may be four times as high as in Britain; so with American wages only twice as high, the unit cost and price of light bulbs will be lower in this country. We can successfully export light bulbs to Britain and undersell Britain in the markets of third countries. But suppose that in shoe production, our output per worker is just the same as in Britain. With British wages only half as high, they can undersell us and have a flourishing export trade.

This reasoning stands up well to statistical tests. Sir Donald McDougall of Oxford made a classic analysis of British and American productivity and exports as of the late 1930s. More recently, Professor Stern of Michigan has analyzed American and British exports of manufactured goods in 1950, at which time American wages were about three times the British level. His results are shown in Table 15–4. In most of the 15 industries where American output per worker was more than three times that in Britain, our exports were also larger than British exports. But in the 24 industries where our output per worker was less than three times the British level, they typically had an export advantage.

What determines the products in which a country will have comparative advantage? This is an old problem in international economics, and several hypotheses have been developed about it. Comparative advantage has been thought to depend on:

1. *Supplies of the factors of production.* A country will tend to export products which use factors which are relatively abundant, and therefore relatively cheap, in that country.
2. *Research and invention.* A country will tend to export products which have been developed there and in which the country can for a time maintain technological leadership.

THINK ABOUT THIS

1. Almost every country in the world has lower wage rates than the United States. It is often argued that a lower wage country poses a competitive threat to American industries, because it will be able to undersell us in our own market. We must restrict imports, therefore, in order to "protect the living standards of American workers." From what you have learned so far, can you see any defects in this argument?
2. "In popular discussions of international trade, exports are usually considered beneficial to the American economy while imports are regarded as a menace. Yet the truth is almost the reverse. Imports provide a *benefit*, because thereby we obtain goods more cheaply than we could produce them. Exports constitute a *cost* of obtaining imports and, like any cost, should be held to a minimum." Who is right?

---

3. *Domestic demand.* A country develops production in the first instance for the home market, and exports follow as an overspill from successful domestic performance.

These explanations are not mutually exclusive, and each may contain some measure of truth. Let us examine them in turn.

TABLE 15–4

	Total Number of Industries	U.S. Exports Larger than British	U.S. Exports Smaller than British
U.S. output per worker more than three times British	15	11	4
U.S. output per worker less than three times British	24	3	21

Source: Robert M. Stern, "British and American Productivity and Comparative Costs in International Trade," *Oxford Economic Papers*, October 1962, p. 288. The earlier MacDougall results appeared in the *Economic Journal*, 1951, pp. 697–724, and 1952, pp. 487–521.

Comparative advantage: Factor supplies

Natural resources sometimes provide an explanation of comparative advantage. A country with rich oil or mineral deposits will tend to export those products. The comparative advantage of Canada and the United States in grain production rests partly on fertile soil, adequate rainfall, and temperate climate. Some of the less developed countries (such as Thailand, Ivory Coast, and Mexico) also have large agricultural exports based on soil and climate.

Most discussion of factor supplies, however, focuses on capital and labor. Different countries have differing endowments of capital relative to labor, and the price ratio between capital services and labor services will differ accordingly. Perhaps this may help to explain the pattern of international trade. This line of reasoning was developed initially by two Swedish economists, Eli Heckscher and Bertil Ohlin, and has since been pushed further by Stolper, Samuelson, and others.

Consider a very simple two-country case. Each country is characterized by pure competition, full employment, and constant costs in all industries. Each factor is of the same quality in both countries. The same production techniques are known and available to both. There are no transportation costs and no barriers to trade.

The countries differ, however, in their endowment of the factors of production. Suppose one country has a large stock of capital relative to its labor force. Let us call this Industria. The other country is densely populated but has little capital. Call this Agraria. These differing factor proportions will be reflected in factor prices. In Industria, the wage level will be relatively high and the interest rate relatively low, whole Agraria will have high interest and low wages.

How will this affect the structure of production in each country? A basic consideration is that production of different goods requires different factor proportions. Suppose for each industry we calculate the amount of capital equipment used per labor-hour. We shall find some industries

"What do you think? If we buy a new American car, they'll throw in a new Japanese TV."

From The Wall Street Journal, *with permission of Cartoon Features Syndicate.*

in which this ratio approaches zero: custom tailoring, fine jewelry and gold-working, and other handmade quality products. These industries are very *labor-intensive.* At the other pole are industries, such as oil refining, in which the use of labor approaches zero, and so the capital-labor ratio approaches infinity. This is the *capital-intensive* pole. Every industry in the economy can be ranked along a scale running from one pole to the other.

In Agraria, labor costs little and capital costs much; so products lying toward the labor-intensive pole will be *relatively cheap.* (Any tourist can verify this observation. In the Orient, one gets low prices for haircuts, rickshaw rides, or hand-tailored suits, but durable consumer goods requiring much capital may be more expensive than in the United States.) In Industria, on the other hand, capital-intensive goods are *relatively cheap* and labor-intensive goods are expensive.

Agraria and Industria now discover each other, and trade develops between them. It is clear where comparative advantage will lie. Agraria has an advantage in labor-intensive products. These products will be exported to Industria, and their production within Agraria will expand. Agraria's production of capital-intensive goods will diminish, since it will import more of these from Industria where they are relatively cheap.

These changes in production in Agraria will react on factor prices. The capital-intensive industries, which are contracting in Agraria, will

release a good deal of capital but little labor. The expanding export industries, on the other hand, will demand much labor and only a little capital.
So total demand for labor will rise, and the wage level will move upward.
Capital, however, is now less scarce than before, so interest rates will
fall.

In a similar way, we can work out the sequence of events in Industria.
Because of import and export trends in Industria, and the consequent
changes in its structure of production, wage rates will fall and interest
rates rise. Industria's ability to import labor-intensive goods from Agraria
compensates for the scarcity of labor at home, reducing the essentiality
of labor and depressing its rate of return.

This means that, for each factor, the rates of return in the two countries
move toward each other. Wage levels in the two countries become more
nearly equal than they were before trade began, and so do interest rates.
If this went on long enough, the price of each factor could conceivably
become equal in the two countries. This is the result which would be
attained by free international movement of the factors themselves. Since
factor movements are restricted, *free movement of commodities serves as a
substitute for movement of factors* and affects factor prices in the same
direction.

This result has usually been called *the factor-price equalization theorem.*
But remember the thin ice of assumptions on which it rests. In this imperfect world, "It ain't necessarily so."

One major effort to test this reasoning has produced apparently para-
doxical results. Professor Leontief calculated the machinery-labor ratio
in American export industries and in import-competing industries, that
is, industries where we have some home production but also import from
abroad. In the first group of industries we presumably have a comparative
advantage and in the second group, a comparative disadvantage. One
would think that capital is the abundant factor in the United States,
while labor is scarce and expensive. So on Heckscher-Ohlin grounds,
we should have a comparative advantage in the more capital-intensive
industries. One would expect a *higher* machine-labor ratio in our export
industries than in import-competing lines.

Much to everyone's surprise, the results came out wrong. Leontief
found that the machine-labor ratio in the export group was slightly lower
than in the other group.[2] This has come to be known as "the Leontief
paradox."

Why the paradox? The answer may be that a two-way classification

---

[2] The results, in dollars of capital equipment per labor-year, were $11,622 for the export industries
and $13,658 for the import-competing industries as of 1947. For 1951, the results were $12,977 for the
first group, $13,726 for the second. See W. W. Leontief, "Domestic Production and Foreign Trade:
The American Capital Position Re-examined," *Proceedings of the American Philosoophical Society, 1953,*
pp. 332–49 (reprinted in *Economia Internazionale,* 1954, pp. 9–38); and W. W. Leontief, "Factor Proportions
and the Structure of Foreign Trade: Further Theoretical and Empirical Results," *Review of Economics
and Statistics,* November 1956, pp. 386–407.

of factors is too simple. Perhaps we need a three-way classification: physical capital, human capital, and raw (or uneducated) labor. The United States, with its high levels of education and technical training, may be relatively better endowed with human capital than with physical capital. If so, one might expect the United States to export goods which are human capital-intensive.

Research results seem to support this idea. As William Branson summarizes the research findings:[3]

> The United States exports chemicals and capital goods and imports consumer goods. . . . In this exchange the United States exports the services of human capital—i.e., skilled or educated labor—and perhaps physical capital and imports the services of unskilled labor. . . .
>
> Thus human capital and unskilled labor play a clear role in the formation of U.S. comparative advantage. Good examples are aircraft on the export side, which are extremely human capital intensive but not very intensive in physical capital, and consumer textiles on the import side. Physical capital plays a more neutral role, combining relatively more with human capital in exports and unskilled labor in imports. Good examples may be chemicals on the export side and consumer electronics on the import side.

Comparative advantage: Technology

The importance of technology derives from the rapid rate of change in products and production methods. In a static world, it would be plausible to assume that the methods used in one country would long since have been learned by others. But this is not the world in which we live. At any moment, there are recently developed industries whose technology is still evolving rapidly. The country which pioneered in developing a new industry will have comparative advantage in that field for some time. But not indefinitely. Technical ideas spread, and what one country has done, others can learn to do. So the original leader must be prepared to bow out eventually and move on to newer fields.

The classic case is the British textile industry, whose dominance in the world market originally earned Britain the title of "workshop of the world." But during the 19th century, factory production of textiles spread to the United States, Western Europe, and Japan. Britain is now almost out of the textile business. Japan will be displaced in its turn by other countries of Asia and Africa, where labor is even cheaper and more abundant, but Japan is shifting to electronics, machinery, and shipbuilding.

The United States has initially gained, and eventually lost, world pre-

---

[3] William H. Branson, "Trends in United States International Trade and Investment since World War II," in *The American Economy in Transition,* ed. Martin Feldstein (Chicago: University of Chicago Press, 1980), pp. 235–36.

dominance in one area of technology after another. But there has always been something new, and our total exports have kept on growing. For several decades we had almost a monopoly of automobile exports, but not any longer. We used to ship large amounts of heavy electrical generating equipment to Europe, based on the technical leadership of the American companies. After a time, innovation in the United States slowed down, competitors abroad caught up, and European companies can now compete effectively in the American market. We pioneered the development of the radio industry and built up a substantial export volume. But this is a light, labor-intensive industry, in which low-skilled assemblers are particularly effective. Now that the technology has spread throughout the world, good transistor sets are flowing back into the United States in large volume from Japan.

Kindleberger relates the story of

> a General Electric salesman who visited Japan on two occasions 10 years apart. On the second he sold no item which had been included in the first order, and many of these—light bulbs, household switches, etc.— were being made in Japan and exported to the United States. But since technology had not stood still in the United States, and since trade is based on differences in technology and new goods, his order the second time was larger than the first.[4]

Today, jet aircraft, computers, and other recently developed products continue to keep us in the forefront of world trade. Several studies have demonstrated that industries in which the United States has a comparative advantage are also industries in which scientific research and development are important. The results of one such study are shown in Table 15–5. Our competitive trade position in each industry is measured by our exports as a percentage of total exports by the Group of 10 countries.[5] Note that where our export percentage is high, employment of scientists and engineers and R&D expenditure as a percentage of sales, is also high. This suggests that the relatively large supply of scientists and engineers in the United States gives us an advantage in industries which are strongly science oriented.[6] Several industries in which our export position is less strong, and in which research activity is lower, are listed at the bottom of the table for comparison.

These strong export industries have other interesting characteristics. The skill composition of their labor force is unusually high. They employ

[4] Charles P. Kindleberger, *International Economics,* 3d ed. (Homewood, Ill.: Richard D. Irwin, 1963), p. 127.

[5] France, West Germany, Italy, Belgium, Holland, Sweden, United Kingdom, United States, Canada, and Japan.

[6] Data for Table 15–5 are drawn from Donald B. Keesing, "The Impact of Research and Development on United States Trade," *Journal of Political Economy,* February 1967, pp. 38–48. See also in the same issue, William Gruber, Dilect Melita, and Raymond Vernon, "The R and D Factor in International Trade and International Investment of United States Industries." pp. 20–37.

TABLE 15-5
U.S. trade performance related to selected industry characteristics

Industry	U.S. Exports as Percentage of Group of 10 Exports, 1962	R&D as Percentage of Sales, 1960	Selected Skill Categories as Percentage of Employment, 1960		
			Scientists and Engineers	Other Professional	Skilled Manual
Aircraft	59.5	22.5	13.0	9.4	25.6
Office machinery	35.0	n.a.	7.2	10.1	18.2
Drugs	33.0	4.8	6.6	12.7	10.0
Other machinery	32.3	4.3	4.0	4.5	29.4
Instruments	28.0	11.8	8.2	8.9	19.5
Chemicals, except drugs	27.3	4.1	7.4	7.7	17.6
Electrical equipment	26.7	10.9	7.2	8.0	16.7
Motor vehicles	22.6	3.1	2.6	4.2	23.2
Petroleum refining	20.6	1.1	6.1	9.9	23.3
Paper and allied products	15.8	0.7	1.5	3.6	17.2
Stone, clay, and glass products	15.2	n.a.	1.9	3.0	15.6
Lumber and wood products	11.7	0.6	0.2	1.1	12.6
Textile mill products	10.9	0.6	0.5	1.4	12.0
Primary ferrous metals	9.1	0.6	2.3	2.7	31.6

not only a high proportion of professional people but also a high proportion of skilled manual workers. They also have relatively large average size of plant, which suggests that economies of scale may be important in lowering production costs. They are not, however, unusually capital intensive. On the contrary, there is a clear inverse relation between R&D activity and capital-intensity, as measured by the capital-output ratio. This supports Leontief's finding that our export industries are (skilled) labor-intensive rather than capital-intensive.

Comparative advantage: The domestic market

National markets differ greatly in size. The United States has a very much larger domestic market than Denmark or New Zealand. Size matters because in many industries, a plant has to be large to achieve maximum efficiency, that is, lowest cost per unit of output. The most efficient size of plant also tends to increase over time with the progress of mechanization. Setup costs are often quite important. A plant which can spread these costs through long production runs on the same item will have lower unit costs than one which must shift frequently from one product to another.

A large economy, then, will tend to have comparative advantage in products requiring large plant size and long production runs. The traditional American advantage in automobiles and trucks, airplanes and airplane engines, heavy electric-generating equipment, and large computers is partly explainable on this ground. A further consideration is whether the product is standardized or differentiated. Even a small economy, such as Belgium or Sweden, may be able to achieve long production runs on highly standardized products with a world market. But differentiated products are more suitable to an economy so big that it can produce large quantities of each of a dozen varieties. Until recently, Britain produced more varieties of automobile than the United States. But since their market is much smaller, production runs were necessarily shorter and output per worker was only about 40 percent of the U.S. level.

Staffan Burenstam Linder, a Swedish trade theorist, argues that in order to export successfully, one must first attain a large enough output to reduce unit production costs. One must also master problems of quality control, test buyers' preferences, and gain experience in salesmanship and distribution. This experimentation is most easily carried out in the home market. Exports then follow as a normal spillover from successful domestic performance. Linder thinks that this argument is not only logically correct but is supported by historical experience (i.e., it is hard to find cases in which a country has built up large exports of a manufactured good for which there was no domestic demand).[7]

Rather similar is the theory of the "product cycle," which has been developed by Raymond Vernon and others.[8] American manufacturers begin to produce, say, refrigerators or home freezers for the relatively high-income American market. At the outset, they have a monopoly—high-income consumers in foreign countries will buy U.S. exports. But as incomes rise abroad, demand in some foreign countries will reach the minimum scale of an efficient plant. Domestic production will then begin, either by local producers or U.S. subsidiaries. As market size and production efficiency grows, these countries will reach the stage of competing with U.S. producers in third markets. Finally, they may be able to invade the U.S. market itself.

Most explanations of international trade stress *differences* among countries. This line of reasoning emphasizes *similarities,* in particular the importance of similar demand patterns at home and abroad. We shall see in the next chapter that the largest trade flow at present consists of an interchange of manufactured goods among the high-income Western economies. Similarity of income levels and consumer preferences may help to explain this interchange.

Interestingly, when these three apparently conflicting trade theories

---

[7] Staffan Burenstam Linder, *An Essay on Trade and Transformation* (Uppsala, Sweden: Almquist & Wiksells, 1961).

[8] For example, Louis T. Wells, Jr., "Test of a Product Cycle Model of International Trade: U.S. Exports of Consumer Durables," *Quarterly Journal of Economics,* February 1969, pp. 152–62.

are subjected to statistical tests, *each* of them yields quite a high correlation with actual trade flows.[9] This may be partly because the three sets of causal variables are not entirely independent but rather overlap to a significant extent.

Comparative advantage in practice

We can learn more about comparative advantage by examining what countries actually export and import. Professor Bela Balassa has made such an analysis for the major industrial countries. He calculates an "index of export performance" for each industry in each country. The index is defined as:

$$\frac{\text{Country A exports of product A}}{\text{World exports of product A}} \bigg/ \frac{\text{Country A exports of all manufactures}}{\text{World exports of all manufactures}}$$

For example, suppose countryA's share of world exports of manufactures is 10 percent. Its exports of product A, however, are 20 percent of the world total. Product A would then have an index of 20/10 = 2. When this has been done for all country A's exports, they can be ranked from those with the highest indexes to those with the lowest. Those at the top of the list are those in which country A has "revealed comparative advantage."

The top-ranking industries of the United States, the United Kingdom, and Japan are shown in Table 15–6.[10] Note on the U.S. list the prominence of machinery and heavy equipment, requiring large scale of plant, whose development has been facilitated by the large domestic market. Note also that most of the U.S. items embody advanced technology, confirming what was said earlier about the importance of U.S. technological leadership as a basis for comparative advantage.

Britain, like the United States, is now basically an exporter of machinery, vehicles, and other products of heavy industry, though woolen textiles continue as a carryover from earlier times. The Japanese list, on the other hand, still consists largely of textiles and other light consumer goods. Note that ships, trucks, and buses also appear on the Japanese list, and if we had fully up-to-date data, we would probably find that automobiles and steel products have now made the top 10. It is plausible to predict

---

[9] See for example, G. C. Hufbauer, "The Impact of National Characteristics and Technology on the Commodity Composition of Trade in Manufactured Goods," in *The Technology Factor in International Trade*, ed. Raymond Vernon (New York: National Bureau of Economic Research, 1970).

[10] Bela Balassa and Associates, *Studies in Trade Liberalization* (Baltimore: Johns Hopkins Press, 1967), Chap. 1; and Bela Balassa, "Revealed Comparative Advantage," March 1977 (mimeograph).

TABLE 15–6

Industries ranked by index of export performance, United States, United Kingdom, Japan

Rank	United States	United Kingdom	Japan
1	Aircraft	Tractors	Footwear
2	Agricultural machinery	Power-generating machinery	Cotton yarn, unbleached
3	Office machinery	Paints, varnishes	Synthetic fabrics
4	Power generating machinery	Explosives	Pottery
5	Photographic and cinematographic	Buses, trucks	Cotton fabrics
6	Inorganic chemicals	Woolen fabrics	Buses, trucks
7	Railway vehicles	Bicycles	Other woolen textile fabrics
8	Electrical power equipment	Nickel, wrought	Ships, boats
9	Bodies, chassis, and frames	Copper, wrought	Musical instruments
10	Scientific, medical, and optical	Fur clothing	Travel goods, handbags

that Japan's list in 20 or 30 years' time will look more like the British, German, or American list today.

More recent information on U.S. comparative advantage comes from the Branson study cited earlier. Judging by export performance during the 70s, our comparative advantage now lies mainly in three areas: agricultural products, chemicals, and capital goods. This last category includes a wide aray of products: electrical machinery, construction machinery, machine tools and other industrial machinery, tractors and agricultural implements, computers and other business machines, scientific and medical instruments, complete airplanes, and engines and parts.

In most consumer goods, we do not have comparative advantage and are net importers. This has long been true for soft goods—clothing, textiles, shoes, and so on. In other areas in which we pioneered—radio and television sets, electronic devices, household appliances—the product cycle has run its course, and other countries can now deliver high-quality goods at competitive prices. Even in automobile production, where we were a net exporter until the late 60s, we have now shifted to an import position.

There is little indication that our competitive position has weakened overall. Our share of world manufacturing production and world exports of manufacturers remained almost constant during the 70s. The rapid increase in our imports, due partly to the oil price explosion, was about matched by a rapid rise in exports of capital goods, chemicals, and farm products, keeping imports and exports roughly in balance.

THINK ABOUT THIS

1. Even without looking at statistics, could you list some products in which the United States is *(a)* likely to have comparative advantage and *(b)* likely *not* to have comparative advantage? What is the reasoning behind your lists?

2. In recent years, manufactured goods have constituted about two thirds of U.S. *exports.* But half our *imports* also consist of manufactured goods. Can you explain this apparent paradox?

NEW CONCEPTS

comparative advantage
terms of trade
comparative advantage, as related
    to factor endowment
comparative advantage, as related
    to scale economies
comparative advantage, as related
    to technological leadership

comparative advantage, as related
    to domestic demand
factor price equalization theorem
Leontief paradox
comparative advantage, revealed

SUMMARY

1. A country normally exports products which are comparatively cheap at home compared with prices abroad, and imports goods which are comparatively cheap in other countries. Underlying comparative cheapness of a good *in terms of money* is comparative cheapness *in terms of the physical resources required to produce it.* This is usually termed *comparative advantage.*

2. Trade that is based on comparative advantage leads to larger total output than if each country (or region) produced all its own requirements. This economic gain is usually divided between the trading partners, the exact division depending on the price ratio or terms of trade between their products.

3. When we take account of differing factor endowments, a country will tend to specialize in products requiring much of the factor which is relatively abundant (and hence cheap) in that country. For example, a country with abundant labor will specialize in labor-intensive products.

4. Because this specialization raises the demand for (and hence the price of) the abundant factor, the price of the same factor in different countries will be more nearly equal with trade than without trade. This is usually called the *factor price equalization theorem.*

5. In apparent contradiction to this prediction, U.S. exports of manufactured goods are somewhat more labor-intensive than U.S. imports. This may be due partly to the large amount of human capital embodied in the U.S. labor force.

6. Other considerations which may have an important influence on trade flows include: economies of scale, innovation and technological leadership, and patterns of demand in the home market.

TO LEARN MORE

Comparative advantage and its determinants are analyzed at a more advanced level in the references listed under "To Learn More" in Chapter 16.

16

External Balance and the World Monetary System

In Chapter 15, we talked about exchange rates between the dollar and the pound or the dollar and the yen. Where do these exchange rates come from? What determines them?

An exchange rate is the price of one currency in terms of another. Like any price, it is influenced by the pressures of supply and demand. Any transaction which obligates a foreign national to make payment to an American creates a *demand for dollars.* Any transaction which obligates an American to make payment to a foreign national creates a *supply of dollars.*

So we can construct supply and demand curves for dollars in terms of, say, German marks, and these curves determine an *equilibrium rate of exchange* between the two currencies. This equilibrium rate is constantly changing because of shifts in demand and supply. What happens next depends on whether countries are operating under a system of *fixed* exchange rates or a system of *flexible* ("floating") exchange rates.

To keep an exchange rate fixed when the equilibrium rate is changing, central banks must intervene in the market, buying a currency which is sinking or selling one which is rising. To do this, a central bank needs *international reserves* acceptable to other central banks. The traditional reserve was gold. Today however, reserves consist mainly of national currencies, chiefly U.S. dollars.

The system of fixed exchange rates established at the end of World War II (the "Bretton Woods system," administered by the International Monetary Fund) broke down in 1973. Since then, we have been on a system of floating rates, under which the market exchange rate is free to follow the equilibrium rate upward or downward. We will see, however, that central banks still intervene to restrain these fluctuations. This system of limited intervention is usually called a "dirty float."

That's the general message of this chapter. Now for the details.

THE MECHANISM OF INTERNATIONAL PAYMENTS

How do buyers of goods in one country manage to pay the sellers of goods in other countries? How do dollars get converted into pounds, lira, francs, and other currencies?

Consider an American importer who buys bicycles from a British exporter. The importer sells these to customers in the United States and receives dollars in return. But the British exporter, who bought the bicycles from a British manufacturer, has to pay for them in pounds. How is the importer, who has dollars, going to pay the exporter, who needs pounds?

The answer is that there are other people in these countries who are in the opposite situation. There are importers in Britain who have pounds, which they need to change into dollars to pay exporters in the United States. Suppose a British importer has bought raw cotton from an American exporter, and suppose that the value of the cotton happens to equal that of the bicycles. Then the four parties could get together and work out the clearing arrangement shown in Figure 16–1. The American exporter can receive pounds from the British customer and trade these for dollars to the American importer, who then uses them to pay off the British exporter. (Or the clearing could be done in Britain with dollars crossing the ocean instead of pounds.) Now everyone has been paid. American exports have paid for American imports, almost as though the cotton had been traded off against the bicycles in a single deal.

It would be awkward if each time an American importer needed 1,000 pounds, he or she had to hunt up an exporter who had exactly 1,000 pounds. Foreign transactions occur at different times and in varying amounts. The logical solution is to set up a clearinghouse which will undertake to buy or sell dollars or pounds in any amount to all comers.

FIGURE 16–1
Direct clearing of international payments

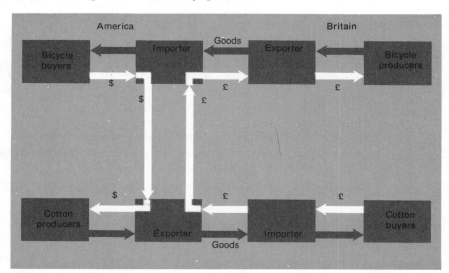

The nature of such a clearinghouse is shown in Figure 16–2. As in the previous diagram, colored lines indicate movements of goods, white lines show movements of money. The clearinghouse trades pounds for dollars at the top of the diagram and dollars for pounds at the bottom. As long as the two flows remain in balance, they cancel out and the system works smoothly. Actually, there will be a difference in the flows from day to day, and the clearinghouse needs some pounds and dollars of its own to tide over short periods of imbalance.

Note that it does not matter whether it is the American importer or the British exporter who buys pounds in exchange for dollars. They share a common interest. They are on the *same side* of the foreign exchange market. The American importer and the American exporter, on the other hand, are on *opposite* sides of the market, one selling dollars and the other buying them. The requirement for balance in the market is that American exports and imports should be equal in value, in which case they cancel out or "pay for each other."

In practice, there is no single clearinghouse for foreign exchange. The main dealers in foreign exchange are banks, chiefly banks in leading financial centers such as New York and London. The large New York banks keep checking accounts (in pounds) at the principal London banks. (The London banks have similar dollar accounts in New York, but it will be clearest to look at the process from the American end.) When a New York bank "sells pounds," it gives the customer a claim of so many

FIGURE 16-2
A clearinghouse for international payments

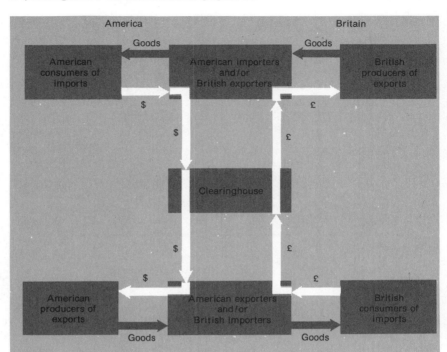

pounds on its London checking account, taking the dollars in return.
When it "buys pounds," these are added to its balance in London, and
it pays off by increasing the seller's dollar checking account in New York.
Checks rather than actual currency shuttle back and forth across the
Atlantic.

How does this work out? Suppose a New York bank finds that it
has more customers wanting to buy pounds than to sell them. As a result,
the bank's checking account in London will decline. Up to a point, the
bank may simply let this happen. But if the account becomes dangerously
low, the bank will have to replenish it by buying pounds somewhere.
It may buy from another American or British bank. Or it may go to
the Federal Reserve Bank of New York, where it has a checking account.
The Federal Reserve has an account at the British central bank, the Bank
of England. It can sell the New York bank pounds from this account,
deducting the dollar cost from the bank's account with it.

The foreign exchange market, in short, is an interconnected network
of private and central banks, which have checking accounts with each
other and can shift funds back and forth as needed. The mechanism is

TABLE 16-1
A simple export-import system

	Imports			
	A	B	C	Total exports
A		100		100
B			100	100
C	100			100
Total imports	100˙	100	100	300

(Left axis label: Exports)

basically the same as that through which checks are cleared between different regions of the United States.

Thus far we have considered only exchange dealings between Britain and the United States. But the clearinghouse principle which works for two countries can be extended to cover a larger group of trading nations. In this case, it is no longer necessary for U.S. imports from a particular country to be balanced by exports *to the same country.* It is sufficient if U.S. exports to *all countries* equal imports from all countries. If this is true for each country in the group, the system is in balance, and the clearinghouse mechanism will work. An extreme case is shown in Table 16–1. Country A exports only to B, B only to C, and C only to A. No country is in balance with any other single country, but each is in overall balance, with its exports equal to its imports. This recalls the famous "triangular trade" of the 18th century, in which the British West Indies shipped sugar to New England, which shipped rum to Britain, which shipped cloth to the West Indies.

THE BALANCE OF PAYMENTS

Now what determines how many pounds I can get for an American dollar? The price of one currency in terms of another is called *an exchange rate.* Like any price, it is influenced by supply and demand. An import of goods to the United States, for which we must make payment in dollars, creates a *supply* of dollars available for conversion into foreign currency. Conversely, an export from the United States creates a *demand* for dollars, since the foreign buyer must get dollars to pay for the goods. Thus, an increase in U.S. exports raises the demand for dollars, while an increase in U.S. imports raises the supply. In a free exchange market, the first development would raise the price of dollars in terms of other currencies, while the second would lower it.

Exports and imports are only one type of international dealing. Other transactions also affect the demand for and supply of dollars. Any transaction which obligates someone in the United States (an individual, business, or government agency) to make payment to someone abroad creates a *supply* of dollars. Conversely, anything which obligates someone abroad to make payment to Americans creates a *demand* for dollars.

The main kinds of transactions which create a *supply* of dollars are:

1. *U.S. imports of merchandise.*

2. *U.S. imports of services.* The main items under this heading are U.S. tourist expenditures abroad and payments to foreign ship lines for shipping services.

3. *U.S. military expenditures abroad.* These include expenditures by U.S. military personnel stationed abroad, purchases by our armed forces for their own use, and "offshore procurement" (purchase of equipment abroad for delivery to other countries under military assistance programs).

4. *Interest and dividend payments* to foreign owners of U.S. securities.

5. *Unilateral transfers and gifts* by Americans to other countries. It has long been customary for immigrants to the United States to send money to relatives and others in their home countries. But today the largest item under this heading is U.S. government grants to other countries under our international aid programs.

6. *Long-term loans and investments* by Americans to other countries. This includes U.S. government loans to other countries. On the private side, it includes purchase of plants and facilities abroad by U.S. businesses and purchase of foreign securities by Americans. These transactions are sometimes summed up as *capital exports*. (It seems odd at first that a capital export has the same effect on the foreign exchange market as a merchandise import. One way to remember this is to realize that an *export* of capital funds is an *import* of securities or titles of ownership, for which we are obliged to pay in dollars.)

7. *Net short-term investment or lending* abroad by Americans. If a U.S. bank makes a loan to a foreign company, or for that matter to a foreign subsidiary of a U.S. company, this increases the supply of dollars. So does a decision by a company or individual to shift part of the bank balance from New York to London or Paris.

If any of these transactions seems mysterious or difficult, look at it carefully. You will find that it meets th original test of obligating someone in the United States to pay dollars to someone abroad.

Each of these items has its counterpart on the other side of the balance sheet. The *demand* for dollars is increased by U.S. exports of goods or

TABLE 16–2
Balance of payments of the United States, 1982 (millions of dollars)

Item	U.S. Receipts	U.S. Payments	Net Balance
Current account	348,324	359,536	−11,212
Merchandise (excluding military)	211,217	247,606	−36,389
Travel	14,272	17,166	− 2,894
Transportation	12,437	11,638	799
Military expenditure	12,097	11,918	179
Unilateral transfers	—	8,034	
Interest and dividends	84,146	56,842	27,304
Other current items	14,155	6,333	7,822
Capital account	87,866	118,045	−30,179
Statistical discrepancy			41,390

Source: U.S. Department of Commerce, *Survey of Current Business*, December 1983, p. 52.

services, by foreign long-term investment in the United States, and by any other transactions which obligate foreign nationals to make payment to us.

Putting the two sides of the picture together, we get a statement known as the *balance of payments*. The U.S. balance of payments for 1982 is summarized in Table 16–2. Look first at item 1, the balance on current account. We normally import more goods than we export, and this was true in 1982. Our trade deficit was about $36 billion. But there are plus items as well, of which the largest is interest and dividends from overseas subsidiaries of U.S. corporations. Overall, then, the current account deficit was only 11 billion.

The deficit on capital account was considerably larger, more than $30 billion. The largest item here is short-term loans by U.S. banks to foreign governments and businesses. Short-term capital flows now dwarf the flow of long-term investment, though this is substantial and increasingly two-directional, foreign businesses investing in the United States while U.S. corporations invest abroad.

The lack of precision in these estimates is indicated by the large "statistical discrepancy" at the bottom of the table. As the world financial network has grown larger and more interconnected, flows of funds have become harder to trace, and many billions each year escape statistical measurement.

THINK ABOUT THIS

Like any accounting statement, the balance-of-payments table must always balance. So how can there ever be a "balance-of-payments problem"? What *is* the problem?

THE RATE OF EXCHANGE

Having seen what determines supply and demand for foreign exchange, we now ask how these forces influence the price of one currency in terms of another. This kind of price is called an *exchange rate*. It can be quoted in either of two ways. Suppose we are talking about the dollar and the West German mark, and that at a particular time $1 = 2 marks. We can equally say that 1 mark = $0.50. The two quotations are simple reciprocals of each other.

This can easily become confusing. Suppose the situation changes so that $1 = 1 mark. At first glance, it might seem that the value of the mark has fallen. But of course it is the value of the dollar which has fallen. The price of the mark has *risen* from $0.50 to $1.00. You will have to stop and think each time about which quotation is being used to be sure of what is going on. This is not because you are slow-witted. Exchange rates are just inherently tricky.

To reduce the confusion a little, we will henceforth talk only about the *price of the dollar in terms of foreign currency,* that is, we shall use quotations in the form of $1 = 2 marks (or 4 French francs, 200 Japanese yen, or whatever). Like any other price, this can be analyzed in demand-supply terms, in this case, demand curves and supply curves for dollars.

DEMAND AND SUPPLY OF IMPORTS AND EXPORTS

To do this, we must start with supply and demand for goods. Let's simplify the world by supposing that international transactions consist solely of exchanging goods and services, and we focus for the moment on trade between West Germany and the United States. Germans demand dollars solely to pay for imports from the United States. We supply dollars solely by importing goods and services from West Germany.

We start, then, from demand and supply curves for U.S. imports and U.S. exports. In the real world, of course, there are many individual products, each with its own demand and supply curves. But for illustrative purposes we reduce these to curves for a "representative bundle" of goods and services. At the beginning of our story, the exchange rate is $1 = 4 marks. At this rate, the demand and supply curves are shown by the thick lines in Figure 16–3.

Now suppose that the price of the dollar falls. The exchange rate changes to $1 = 3 marks. What will happen? Look first at U.S. imports. Our demand for, say, German automobiles does not change. But the supply curve shifts upward because *the price of German goods in dollars has risen* by one third. At the old exchange rate, a Volkswagen worth 12,000 marks in Germany would cost about $3,000 in the United States. But at the new exchange rate, it costs $4,000. The new supply curve,

FIGURE 16-3
A change in currency values changes quantities of imports and exports

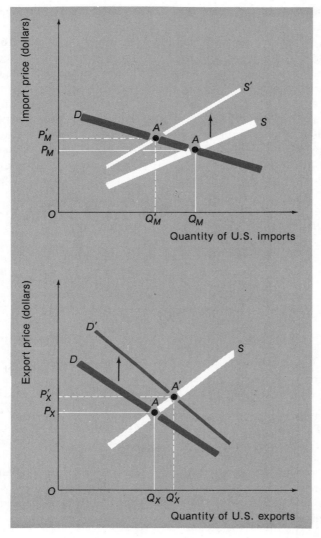

The thick lines correspond to an exchange rate of $1 = 4 marks. When the exchange rate changes to $1 = 3 marks (thin lines), this *raises* the dollar price of German goods in the United States and *reduces* the quantity imported. Total dollars spent on German goods will usually (though not necessarily) fall. The change *raises* the dollar price received by U.S. exporters for goods shipped to Germany and *raises* the quantity exported. Total dollars received by U.S. exporters will increase.

S^1, is higher than S by one third at any quantity level. The intersection of S^1 with D tells us that fewer German goods will be imported.

What will happen to the *supply of dollars,* that is, the total amount of money spent on imports from Germany? The total spent at the old exchange rate is shown by the solid rectangle $OP_M A Q_M$, and the total at the new rate by the dotted rectangle $OP^1_M A^1 O^1_M$. In Figure 16–3, the quantity spent is smaller than before. This is because we drew D as elastic[1] over the range $A^1 A$. If D were inelastic over this range, then the higher price of German goods would *increase* the amount spent on them.

There is good reason to think that the demand for imports typically is elastic. A major reason is that imported goods usually are in competition with similar goods produced at home. Thus, our demand for Volkswagens is much more elastic than our demand for automobiles in general. While the statistical evidence is still being debated, most studies show the demand for imports to be quite elastic. So we are on reasonably safe ground in concluding that:

> **A fall in the price of the dollar in terms of foreign currencies will normally reduce the quantity of dollars supplied, and conversely.**

The situation for exports is shown in the lower section of Figure 16–3. The supply curve of exports, S, will not be altered by the exchange rate shift. (Why, incidentally, does the supply curve slope upward? Partly because most export products can be sold either at home or abroad. As the price which exporters can get in foreign markets rises, the domestic price remaining unchanged, the incentive to export becomes greater.) But the demand curve for our exports shifts upward. Why is this? We have been exporting, say, large computer units for which we could get a price in Germany of 4 million marks. At the old exchange rate, this yielded our exported $1 million. But now the mark is worth more. At the new rate, the American exporter gets $1,333,333 for the computer. The new demand curve *in terms of dollars,* D^1, is above the old demand curve D by one third at each quantity level.

The number of dollars which Germand needed to pay U.S. exports at the old exchange rate is shown by $OP_X A Q_X$. At the new exchange rate, the total is $OP^1_X A^1 Q^1_X$. This must be larger than before, since both the quantity and the dollar price of U.S. exports has risen. We conclude that:

> **A fall in the price of the dollar in terms of foreign currency will increase the quantity of dollars demanded, and conversely.**

---

[1] Recall from Chapter 2 that a demand schedule is *elastic* if a small price increase, say of 5 percent, will reduce the quantity demanded by *more than* 5 percent. If, on the other hand, a 5 percent price increase reduces the quantity demanded by *less than* 5 percent, the demand schedule is *inelastic* over that range.

DEMAND AND SUPPLY OF DOLLARS

We are now ready to take the next step and examine the demand and supply for *currency* rather than for goods. Figure 16–4 shows supply and demand for dollars in Germany. The vertical axis shows the number of marks required to buy $1. The horizontal axis shows the number of dollars exchanged per year.

As we go down the vertical axis, the price of the dollar is falling. The quantity of dollars demanded will increase, and the quantity of dollars supplied will decrease, as explained in the previous section.

If D and S represent the market situation at a particular time, the equilibrium exchange rate will be R. At this rate, the number of dollars supplied just equals the number demanded. The foreign exchange market is in equilibrium.

Adjustment to change

But suppose now that there is a change in demand or supply conditions. For example, suppose the Germans decide that they don't like our products as much as they used to, or perhaps they decide that they can get some items cheaper from Japan. Their demand for U.S. exports falls, and so the demand for dollars shifts from D to D_1. At the exchange rate R, only RP dollars will be demanded while RT will be supplied. The market is in disequilibrium.

What will happen next? This depends on the rules of the game governing exchange rates. Governments might permit currency values to fluctuate from day to day in response to supply and demand changes. This would be a system of *flexible* or *floating* exchange rates. Under this system, the price of the dollar would fall to the new equilibrium rate R_1. At this rate, the market is once more in balance. This would be a *depreciation* of the dollar in terms of marks. Conversely, a rise in demand leading to a higher price for dollars would produce an *appreciation* of the dollar.

If national currencies are freely interchangeable, a depreciation of the dollar in terms of marks, with no other change, must mean a corresponding depreciation in terms of British pounds, French francs, and other currencies. Start from a situation in which $1 = 5 marks and $1 = 5 francs. Then, since things equal to the same thing are equal to one another, 1 mark = 1 franc. Now, suppose the dollar depreciates to $1 = 3 marks. Can the franc price of the dollar remain unchanged? If it did, foreign exchange dealers could make large profits by the following route: change $1 into 5 francs, then change the 5 francs into 5 marks, then change the 5 marks back into $1\frac{2}{3}$ dollars.

This kind of operation is termed *arbitrage*. Because of the possibility of arbitrage, a currency which is appreciating or depreciation must do

FIGURE 16–4
Demand and supply for dollars in Germany

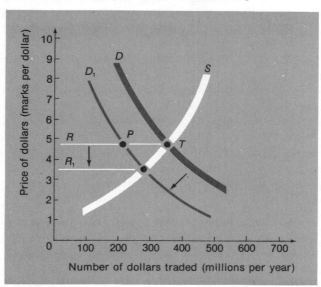

As dollars become more expensive in terms of marks, Germans
will demand fewer dollars to pay for imports from the United States,
while Americans will supply more dollars by importing more goods
from Germany. So D and S have the usual shapes and determine
an equilibrium exchange rate R. If demand for dollars falls, say
to D_1, the equilibrium value of the dollar will fall to R_1.

so equally in terms of all other currencies. In this case, the franc exchange
rate would quickly adjust to $1 = 3 francs; and similarly for the pound,
lira, yen, and so on.

But suppose that a country prefers not to have the value of its currency
fluctuating from day to day. So government, through the central bank,
intervenes in the foreign exchange market to maintain currency values
at some specified level regardless of short-term shifts in supply and demand. This is a regime of *fixed exchange rates*. Under it, a change in the
value of the country's currency relative to others requires a policy decision.
A downward change, for example, such as the British decision in 1967
to reduce the value of the pound from $2.80 to $2.40, is called a *devaluation*.
It is a sudden, one-time shift, as against the gradual depreciation which
might occur under a flexible rate system. The less common case of a
currency being increased in value is called an *upward revaluation*.

How does a govenment hold currency values stable when demand
and supply are fluctuating? Consider the case sketched in Figure 16–4.
Despite the downward shift of demand, it is desired to keep the mark
price of the dollar unchanged at R. At this price, there is an *excess supply*

of dollars equal to *PT*. The rate can be stabilized by the German central bank (the Deutsche Bundesbank) entering the market and buying these excess dollars, providing marks in exchange. The same effect could be achieved by the Federal Reserve coming in to the market to sell marks.

To intervene in the market in this way, a central bank must have something to trade with, and something which is generally acceptable to other countries throughout the world. It must have a supply of *international reserves*. Gold has traditionally been the main kind of international reserve. But in recent decades gold has been supplemented increasingly by holdings of national currencies which are widely used in international dealings. Before 1930, when London was the hub of the world money market, the pound was the main reserve currency. Since 1945, the U.S. dollar has played this role. But central banks also maintain holdings of other strong currencies such as the German deutsche mark, the Swiss franc, and the Japanese yen.

FIXED RATES: THE BRETTON WOODS SYSTEM

Before 1914, the major trading countries maintained fixed exchange rates with each other. Gold was the main form of international reserve and also circulated internally as currency in most countries. The world was on a full-fledged gold *standard*.

The interwar period 1919–39, which included the Great Depression, was one of considerable monetary confusion. Some currencies were floating for much of the period, revaluation of currencies was frequent, and many countries imposed restrictions on international capital movements.

The end of World War II ushered in a period of greater stability, which lasted until 1971. This was signaled by creation of the International Monetary Fund in 1944. The conference which drafted a charter for the IMF was held at Bretton Woods in New Hampshire, and the system which resulted is often called the "Bretton Woods system." Under this system, each Fund member pledged itself to maintain a fixed exchange rate for its currency in terms of gold, which meant also a fixed rate in terms of each other currency in the system. The rules permitted any fund member, however, to change the value of its currency by as much as 10 percent in order to correct a "fundamental disequilibrium" in the country's balance of payments, and changes of more than 10 percent could be made with the approval of the fund. This was called "the adjustable peg"—rates were pegged at any moment, but the peg could be changed occasionally for good cause. Changes in currency values were in fact infrequent up to 1971.

This system is usually called the *gold exchange standard*. It resembled the old gold standard in that each currency was defined as a certain weight of gold. Gold also continued to be an important component of central bank reserves and could be transferred among central banks in settlement of balance-of-payments deficits and surpluses. In practice, this meant mainly an outflow of gold from the United States to other countries. At the end of World War II, the great bulk of the world's monetary gold, about $26 billion, was concentrated in the United States. After 1950, however, we consistently ran balance-of-payments deficits, which required payments to other central banks. In large measure, other countries were content simply to increase their holdings of dollars. But occasionally they called for payment in gold, and so U.S. gold reserves fell gradually from the $26 billion of 1945 to about $11 billion.

But while gold continued important, it had been dethroned in two important ways. It no longer circulated internally as currency but led a shadowy existence only in the vaults of central banks, and even there, it formed a shrinking percentage of these banks' international reserves. This was partly because the need for international reserves, which is related to the volume of international trade and payments, has risen much faster since 1945 than the supply of monetary gold. The supply of newly mined gold depends mainly on production in South Africa and on how much the USSR finds it expedient to sell on Western markets, and from this, one must subtract the amounts drained off into industrial uses and speculative holdings.

The other side of the story is that central banks gradually discovered that they don't *have* to have gold. The currency of a major trading and banking nation can be used as a reserve asset, provided it continues to be generally acceptable throughout the world. During the 1920s, when London was still the world's leading financial center, many central banks began to use British pounds as a reserve asset. During the 1950s and 1960s, holdings of U.S. dollars assumed a predominant role.

The shift toward a "key currency" standard was in fact quite dramatic. In 1949, gold still constituted $33.5 billion of total world reserves of $45.5 billion, or about three quarters. By mid-1971, total reserves had risen to $104.8 billion. But more than half of this total, $55.5 billion, consisted of dollar holdings,[2] while gold holdings of $36.5 formed only one third.

This shift from gold to paper is comparable, on an international scale, to the earlier shift from metallic to paper currencies within individual countries.

While the gold exchange standard worked reasonably well in 1945–71, it presented several difficulties and could even be regarded as unstable over the long run. First, the supply of international reserves must keep pace with the growing volume of international trade and payments. With the supply of monetary gold rising only slowly, the task of providing

---

[2] This total concludes so-called Eurodollars, that is, dollar deposits in foreign branches of U.S. banks.

adequate reserves fell increasingly on national currencies and particularly on the dollar. American dollars provided about three quarters of the increase in world reserves between 1949 and 1970.

This meant that the United States was in a sense *obliged to run a balance-of-payments deficit*. Without this, foreign holdings of dollars could not increase at an adequate rate. It must be said that we more than did our duty on this score. During the 1950s, our annual deficits averaged $1.4 billion. This rose to $2.8 billion from 1960 to 1964 and to $3.5 billion from 1965 to 1970.

This could, of course, be considered a happy situation from our standpoint. It meant that other countries were accepting our IOUs, to the tune of almost $50 billion over this 20-year period, in return for their goods, services, and property. With the funds thus acquired, we financed large military expenditures abroad; bought up businesses and established new businesses on a large scale in Canada, Britain, and Western Europe; ran a large foreign aid program; and sent millions of tourists to all corners of the earth. But it is not surprising that some of our Western neighbors wondered at times *why* they were financing us to buy up their industries and to engage in military activities of which they didn't approve.

Further, while we were enabled and in a sense encouraged to run a deficit, it was essential that *this deficit not become too large*. For we remained legally obligated to redeem foreign dollar holdings in gold. The whole system rested on a belief that dollars were "as good as gold" and that gold would actually be provided on demand. This meant that, like any banker, we had to keep our reserves in some reasonable relation to our liabilities, and this we were unable to do. By mid-1971, our gold reserves were down to $11 billion. This compared with foreign dollar holdings of some $50 billion. Any large demand for conversion of dollars into gold would clearly cause a breakdown of the system.

The first tremors of change were felt as early as 1968. Until that time, the central banks stood ready to supply gold not only to each other but to the private market, at the official price of $35 an ounce. To many gold speculators, convinced that the price must eventually rise, this seemed a remarkably good deal. In early 1968, the outflow of gold from the banks rose to an alarming level. So the governors of the major central banks, meeting over the weekend in Washington, decided to stop furnishing gold to the private market at a fixed price.

This decision established a two-price (and two-market) system for gold. Central banks continued to exchange gold with each other at the official price, but they ceased to supply gold to the private market. The price in the private market gradually rose farther and farther above the official price. So all newly mined gold went into the private market, and the total gold holdings of the central banks remained frozen.

What finally brought down the system, however, was the growing size of U.S. balance-of-payments deficits, with no end in sight. Our traditional surplus of exports over imports shrank gradually to the point where in mid-1971 we experienced an import surplus for the first time in this century. Meanwhile, we continued to spend many billions each year on foreign investment by multinational corporations, large military expenditures, and steadily rising tourist expenditures. These unfavorable long-term trends were accentuated by the U.S. recession of 1969–70. This reduced U.S. interest rates well below European levels, causing short-term funds to flow abroad in search of higher earnings.

When it became clear in the spring of 1971 that the dollar was in serious trouble, there was heavy speculative selling of dollars in exchange for marks, yen, and other currencies. The world was deluged with dollars, and foreign willingness to accept dollars without question finally came to an end. There was a classic "run on the bank." Rumors circulated in August 1971 that some foreign central banks had asked for gold payments totaling several billion dollars. Faced with this situation, the U.S. government took the only feasible action, by "closing the gold window" to other central banks as well as to private buyers. The dollar, no longer convertible into gold, was left to find its own value in a fluctuating world market.

There was a short-lived attempt (the "Smithsonian Agreement" of December 1971) to return to a system of fixed exchange rates, with the dollar marked down to a lower value, but this broke down in early 1973 because of continued weakness of the dollar. Since that time, the major industrial countries have been on a system of floating exchange rates.

FLOATING RATES AND THE FUTURE OUTLOOK

Pros and cons of floating rates

Even in the days of Bretton Woods, many economists preferred floating rates to fixed rates, and the issue was debated at an abstract level. It may be useful to review these arguments before examining how the system has actually worked since 1973.

Those who prefer floating rates point out that trying to maintain a fixed rate when the equilibrium rate has changed can have awkward consequences. Look again at the imbalance in Figure 16–4, arising from a drop in demand for dollars. At the old exchange rate, there is an excess supply of dollars shown by the distance PT. The Fed can correct this for the time being by going into the market and buying up the excess dollars. But this cannot continue forever. Eventually the Fed would run out of reserves. So the monetary authorities cannot follow a purely passive policy of adjusting to the balance-of-payments situation. They must take active steps to alter the situation. In the present case, they must try to shift D_1 to the right and S to the left so that they will once more intersect at the exchange rate R.

The orthodox prescription for doing this is to restrict aggregate demand in the domestic economy through a tight monetary-fiscal policy—raise interest rates, restrict credit, raise taxes, or reduce government expenditures. Such measures will reduct demand for imports along with other things and will make for price stability, which will help to keep our exports competitive in foreign markets. Moveover, our exporters, finding demand reduced at home, may cultivate foreign markets more intensively. The rise in interest rates will also attract short-term funds from other financial centers. All these developments will help to close the balance-of-payments gap.

This is not a very palatable course of action, since it may mean holding aggregate demand below the high-employment level. There may be a direct conflict between internal and external considerations. A recession at home may call for expansionist monetary-fiscal policies, but these policies may worsen the balance-of-payments position.

Those who prefer flexible rates argue that a country brings this problem on itself by a misguided effort to maintain fixed exchange rates in the midst of a fluctuating world. Why not simply allow currency values to float in response to changing supply and demand? In this case, if the United States continued to run balance-of-payments deficits year after year, the value of the dollar would fall; and this, for reasons already explained, would tend to close the deficit. We would have an automatic, self-adjusting mechanism instead of a government-managed mechanism with its attendant possibilities of mismanagement.

A flexible exchange system would remove the balance-of-payments constraint on domestic economic decisions. No longer would we have to clamp down periodically on domestic expansion because of the danger or actuality of reserve losses. We could simply go ahead and promote full employment, leaving currency value to find their own level in the market.

This line of argument can also cut in the opposite direction. Those who are wary of a floating rate system argue that it would intensify the worldwide tendency toward inflation. Within each country, the central bank is usually the principal defender of price stability. Under fixed exchange rates, they have a powerful argument: "If we allow our price level to rise too fast, we will lose competitiveness in export markets. Our balance of payments will become unfavorable, and eventually we will have to devalue our currency. The only way to avoid this is to hold prices in check by monetary restraint." But if there is no fixed exchange rate to defend, this argument vanishes, and it becomes more likely that the proinflation forces will prevail.

Several other arguments are commonly brought against a flexible rate system. First, it is argued that the D and S curves will not always have the shapes shown in Figure 16–4. Suppose our demand for imports from Germany is inelastic. Then, as the mark price of the dollar falls, which means that the dollar price of German goods is rising, we shall spend *more* dollars on them rather than less. The balance-of-payments problem will get worse rather than better.[3] In answer to this, one can say only that while such a situation is conceivable, it is very unlikely to occur in practice.

A second objection is that fluctuating exchange rates involve increased uncertainty for producers and traders in exported and imported goods. The U.S. company which starts building a computer for export today cannot tell how many dollars it will receive when the computer is finished and delivered a year from now. But this difficulty is not as serious as it appears, because the company can protect itself by dealing in the *futures market* for foreign exchange. On this market, one can buy or sell any currency for delivery at a future date.

Example. The U.S. computer manufacturer negotiates a sales contract with a German buyer, who promises to pay 2 million marks when the computer is delivered 12 months hence. At today's exchange rate, this would yield the manufacturer $1 million, which is a satisfactory price. But the company is worried that the exchange rate may be different a year from now and that it may get fewer dollars than it expects. What to do? Simple enough. It can *sell* 2 million marks to a foreign exchange dealer in the futures market for 12-month delivery and get the $1 million at once. A year later, when the computer is finished and delivered, the German buyer pays the company 2 million marks, which it then turns over to the dealer with whom it made the futures transaction.

A third argument is that a regime of fluctuating exchange rates will attract speculators, whose operations will have a destabilizing effect on the market. If speculators see that the value of, say, the British pound is falling, they will say "Aha! It's going to fall farther—let's help it along and meanwhile make some money." So they will sell pounds in the futures market, and this increased supply will indeed cause the pound to drop some more. Of course, they may turn out to be wrong, and if the pound begins to move upward, they stand to lose heavily. There will then be a rush to buy pounds, and the price will shoot up. Thus, the normal price fluctuations in a free market may be exaggerated by speculative activity, and this is unsettling to exporters, importers, and investors.

What this argument overlooks is that the professional speculator is not an emotional plunger in the market. He is a cold-blooded expert. In order to survive over the years he has to be right more often than wrong. Further, since the future course of prices is uncertain, there will

---

[3] In this case, the foreign exchange market is said to be *unstable.* Technically, the market will be unstable if the sum of the U.S. elasticity of demand for imports from Germany and the German elasticity of demand for U.S. exports is less than one. This is usually regarded as a possible but very unlikely case.

be speculators operating on both sides of the market. As the price of a currency falls, more and more speculators will conclude that it is now too low and likely to rise, and so they will shift over to the buying side, which will tend to check the decline. Thus, contrary to popular opinion, informed speculation tends to *reduce* price fluctuations, in foreign exchange markets as well as securities and commodity markets.

THINK ABOUT THIS

1. What are the main differences between a fixed exchange rate and a flexible exchange rate system? Which system strikes you as preferable, and why?
2. Before 1971, under fixed exchange rates, Britain frequently had to check internal economic expansion in order to reduce its balance-of-payments deficits. Can you explain the nature of this dilemma? Can you explain also why the United States did not face the same problem, even though we consistently ran deficits?

Experience with floating rates

In the first few years after 1973, it was taken for granted that the floating rate system was temporary. Numerous international conferences were held to work out a new system with fixed exchange rates. These negotiations came to nothing. One reason was differences of national interest, particularly between countries with persistent balance-of-payments deficits (mainly the United States) and those with persistent surpluses, such as West Germany and Japan. But a more important reason for lack of movement toward fixed rates is that the floating rate system has worked better than many people predicted at the outset. As this has become apparent, fears about the system and pressure to change it have gradually subsided. There have been no general negotiations on the issue since 1976.

One reason why the system has worked acceptably is that it has turned out to be not a "clean float" with no central bank intervention but a managed or "dirty float" with a good deal of intervention. How does this work? Suppose that in a particular year the U.S. balance-of-payments deficit widens sharply. The supply of dollars increases. The equilibrium exchange rate for the dollar relative to other currencies falls, say, by an average of 10 percent. But the Fed and perhaps foreign central banks as well do not want the actual market rate to fall this much. So they come into the market to buy up dollars in exchange for marks, yen, and so on. By doing this on a sufficient scale, they hold the actual decline in the value of the dollar to 5 percent. Exchange rates move in the direction of the new equilibrium, but not all the way.

Under the new system exchange rates have fluctuated, as one would expect. There is considerable variation from day to day and month to month.[4] There have also been large swings over the years, notably in the value of the dollar relative to other major currencies. During the 70s, the United States continued to run large trade deficits. The value of the dollar floated gradually downward. By the fall of 1979, the dollar had fallen by about one third relative to a basket of other major currencies and by more than half relative to the strongest currencies, the Swiss franc and the German mark.

This was worrisome for several reasons. It raised the dollar cost of imported goods and contributed to U.S. inflation. It alarmed the OPEC countries, whose oil exports are priced in dollars and who saw their sales receipts falling in terms of other currencies. There was serious discussion of shifting away from dollar pricing to some more reliable currency. In an effort to check and perhaps reverse the decline, the Fed in October 1979 announced a shift in monetary policy. Money supply would now be regarded as the main policy target, and interest rates would be allowed to fluctuate more widely than before.

Under the new policy, U.S. interest rates rose sharply. Between 1979 and 1981, interest rates on long-term bonds rose between four and five points, while the banks' prime loan rate rose about six points. The 1982 recession brought reductions, but the level of interest rates in the United States has continued well above that in Western Europe and Japan. One result has been a large flow of funds from other countries to the United States to take advantage of these higher rates; and this increased demand for dollars has tended to raise the value of the dollar. By the end of 1983, the dollar had risen by some 30 percent on average, and was back close to the 1973 level.

The sharp increase in the value of the dollar, of course, has retarded U.S. exports by making them more expensive in other currencies, and it has stimulated imports to the United States by making them cheaper in dollars. We'll say something in Chapter 17 about the complaint that foreign trade is "deindustrializing America," and that many of our basic industries can no longer compete in the world market. But we should note here that much of the outcry arises not from any long-term loss of comparative advantage but from the movement of the exchange rate in recent years. There has also been complaint from other countries that high interest rates in the United States are forcing up interest rates in their countries and thus interfering with recovery from the 1981–82 recession.

We saw earlier that one of the arguments for floating rates was that

---

[4] Whether exchange rates have been "too volatile," and whether this has had harmful effects, is not easy to determine. On this point, see Jeffrey R. Schafer and Bonnie E. Lupesko, "Floating Exchange Rates After Ten Years," *Brookings Papers on Economic Activity* no. 1 (1983), pp. 1–70.

they would insulate policymakers in each country against events in other countries. One need no longer worry about international flows of trade and finance, since balance-of-payments deficits would be taken care of automatically by exchange rate movements. This has turned out not to be entirely true. What happens in other countries does matter. There is frequent consultation, and considerable arm-twisting, over macroeconomic policy among leaders of the leading industrial countries, though one cannot expect to see anything like full coordination of national policies.

While the floating rate system does not perform ideally, there does not seem at present to be strong sentiment for a return to fixed rates. This issue, quite prominent in the 70s, has now become rather a nonissue. The main problem of international finance is now the heavy indebtedness of some of the developing countries.

NEW CONCEPTS

balance of payments	currency appreciation
demand schedule, for a currency	currency depreciation
supply schedule, of a currency	arbitrage
exchange rate	international reserves
exchange rates, flexible	gold standard
exchange rates, fixed	gold exchange standard
devaluation	adjustable peg
revaluation	managed float

SUMMARY

1. International trading and financial relations require a *foreign exchange market,* in which the currency of one country can be converted into that of another. The chief operators in this market are large private banks and central banks. The price of one currency in terms of another is called an *exchange rate.*

2. A country's foreign transactions are summarized in its *balance of payments.* If the country's receipts from other countries exceed its payment obligation, it is said to have a *favorable* balance of payments. In the opposite situation, the balance of payments is *unfavorable.*

3. Deficits in a country's balance of payments are met by transfers of *international reserves.* When these balancing items are included, receipts and payments must always be equal.

4. The demand curve for a currency (say, the dollar) normally slopes downward to the right. The supply curve of a currency slopes upward

to the right. Review carefully what these statements mean and why they are normally true.

5. Under flexible exchange rates, the price of a currency in terms of others varies from day to day in response to supply and demand changes.

6. Under a system of fixed exchange rates, the fixed rate is maintained by central banks intervening in the market to buy or sell currencies as required. This means *(a)* that central banks must carry larger international reserves than would be necessary under flexible rates and *(b)* that they must take steps to correct an unfavorable payments balance in order to avoid being drained of reserves.

7. Under the *gold standard,* gold was the sole form of international reserves, and it also circulated internally as currency in most countries.

8. Under the *gold exchange standard,* gold was supplemented by holdings of *key currencies* (mainly British pounds in the 1920s and 1930s and U.S. dollars since 1945). This system is unstable in the sense that growth of reserves depends on balance-of-payments deficits in the key currency country, which eventually undermines confidence in the currency. This led to the "pound crisis" of 1931 and the "dollar crisis" of 1971.

9. Since 1973, the major industrial countries have been on a system of (managed) floating exchange rates. While this system also has some difficulties, it seems likely to continue for the foreseeable future.

TO LEARN MORE

International economics is a large enough subject so that entire courses and texts are devoted to it. If you want to pursue the issues raised in this chapter, you might look at the monetary chapters in such standard texts as Charles P. Kindleberger and Peter H. Lindert, *International Economics,* 6th ed. (Homewood, Ill.: Richard D. Irwin, 1978); or Herbert G. Grubel, *International Economics* (Homewood, Ill.: Richard D. Irwin, 1981).

A good data source is *International Financial Statistics,* published by the International Monetary Fund. U.S. balance-of-payments data are published by the U.S. Department of Commerce in *Survey of Current Business,* and summary data are reprinted in the *Economic Report of the President.* Current exchange rates are published daily in newspapers' financial pages.

■ 17 ■

Trade Flows and Trade Policy

*Free trade, one of the greatest blessings which a
government can confer on a people, is in almost every
country unpopular.*

—Thomas Babington Macaulay

This chapter deals with American trade policy and, particularly, with
proposals to restrict imports of goods which compete with American products. We will see that a tariff on imports or a quota restriction on imports
benefits companies and workers in the industry in question but hurts
the general public, who must pay higher prices. Restricting imports also
reduces our ability to export. It freezes resources in industries where
we do not have comparative advantage and prevents their transfer to
other industries in which we do have comparative advantage.

U.S. tariff rates have been reduced greatly over the past 50 years by
successive rounds of trade negotiations. But we have imposed import
quotas in a number of industries which are suffering from foreign competition, and there is continuing pressure to extend quotas to other industries.

At the end of the chapter, we'll discuss U.S. economic relations with
the less-developed countries (LDCs). Important issues here include: (1)
whether we should grant preferential treatment to exports of manufactured goods from the LDCs; (2) how much U.S. government money should
go for loans or grants to the LDCs; and (3) what can be done about
the LDC debt problem.

THE PATTERN OF WORLD TRADE

Europe has long been the hub of world trade, and this continues to
be true today (Table 17–1). About 40 percent of the world's exports origi-

TABLE 17-1
A world trade matrix, 1982 (millions of U.S. dollars, f.o.b.)

Origin \ Destination	North America	Europe	Japan	Other Developed Countries	Oil-Exporting Developing Countries	Other Developing Countries	Eastern Trading Area	Unspecified	World Total
North America	77,305	65,420	24,360	8,875	24,135	63,075	9,640	200	273,020
Western Europe	54,525	469,235	7,935	13,635	67,190	71,800	33,370	6,150	723,840
Japan	39,480	21,670	—	7,170	21,820	36,580	8,400	3,470	138,580
Other developed countries*	5,230	8,695	8,035	2,105	2,075	7,960	2,100	1,100	37,300
Oil-exporting developing countries	31,825	80,295	47,265	2,740	2,985	51,855	4,555	180	221,700
Other developing countries	71,560	60,005	24,445	4,550	19,070	57,700	15,105	3,065	255,500
Eastern trading area	3,245	48,360	6,255	400	11,000	21,320	94,440	7,980	193,000
Unspecified	—	—	—	—	—	—	—	—	—
World total	283,170	753,680	118,300	39,480	148,280	310,290	167,610	22,150	1,843,000

* Australia, New Zealand, and South Africa.
Source: GATT, *International Trade*, 1982–83, Table A23.

nate in Western Europe alone. Moreover, the bulk of European trade is with other European countries. This tendency has been accentuated by the development of the European Economic Community or "Common Market." This consisted initially of Belgium, Netherlands, Luxembourg, West Germany, France, and Italy but has since been enlarged to include Britain, Denmark, Ireland, and Greece. Reduction of tariff barriers within the group has stimulated the intercountry flow of trade.

Although U.S. trade is small relative to our own GNP, it forms about one sixth of total world trade. Our exports are double those of our nearest competitors, West Germany and the United Kingdom.

The communist countries as a group have about 10 percent of world exports. The USSR and the East European countries have tried to plan a systematic exchange of products through the Committee on Economic Cooperation (COMECON), intended as a rival to the Common Market organization. Nationalist sentiment has hampered this effort however, and each country still maintains a rather high degree of self-sufficiency. About two thirds of the trade by communist countries is with other communist countries, but trade with noncommunist countries has been increasing rapidly in recent years. The East European countries have long-standing trade ties with Western Europe.

The less developed countries furnish about 25 percent of world exports, but more than half of this is petroleum exports. If we exclude petroleum, only one eighth of world exports comes from the less developed countries. Considering that this group includes the bulk of the world's population, one might wonder why the ratio is not higher. The obvious answer lies in low productivity and low purchasing power. The trade of the less developed countries still consists largely of shipping primary products to the industrial countries and buying manufactures in return. There is still relatively little trade of the underdeveloped countries *with each other.* It may be true that there is a large potential in this direction, but it has scarcely begun to be tapped.

In terms of *types of commodity,* world trade is about evenly divided between manufactures and primary products. Manufactured exports come about 95 percent from the industrial countries. Even as regards primary products, the industrial countries' exports exceed those of the less developed countries. The reason is that the great agricultural exporters of the temperate zone—Canada, United States, Australia, New Zealand, Denmark—are all in the industrial group.

The trade of the industrial countries with each other forms about half of total world trade. Moreover, because of rapid output growth in the industrial countries since 1945, this proportion has been tending to rise, and the less developed countries' *share* of world trade (though not the absolute volume) has tended to decline. This has caused great concern in the less developed countries over how they can boost their exports or, alternatively, reduce their dependence on the advanced countries by developing their own manufacturing industries.

The United States, as a key member of the Western trading group, does most of its business with other members of that group. About three quarters of our exports go to Britain, Western Europe, Canada, Australia, and Japan. In terms of type of commodity, about two thirds of our exports are manufactured goods, though we are still an important exporter of food and raw materials. Interestingly enough, more than half of our *imports* are also manufactured goods. Remember the explanation in the preceding chapter of why one might expect to find a substantial interchange of manufactures among the richer industrial countries.

BARRIERS TO TRADE: THE TARIFF CONTROVERSY

We argued in Chapter 15 that trade between two regions or countries is mutually beneficial. It follows that barriers to trade will be harmful. Building a tariff wall between Texas and New England would hurt consumers on both sides of the wall.

Why, then, do most countries have tariff systems and other restrictions on free movement of trade? Are political leaders simply irrational? Did they not study elementary economics? The broad answer is that restriction of imports, while rarely in the interest of the population as a whole, is often in the interest of specific industries which are subject to import competition. These industries work hard to restrict imports, while the general public is apt to remain apathetic. Moreover, the arguments for trade restriction are easily intermingled with patriotic sentiment. It is easier to get the public aroused about protecting American labor and capital against foreign competiton than it would be to whip up sentiment for "protecting Illinois labor and capital" against "Alabamian competition," though the logic of the two cases is similar.

There are numerous types of trade restriction,[1] but the import tariff is historically the most important, and we shall concentrate on it here. Further, we shall concentrate on the protective aspects of the tariff rather than on the revenue which it yields. During the 1850s, about 90 percent of federal revenue came from customs duties. During the 1970s, however, less than 1 percent of federal revenue came from this source. Arguments

---

[1] A type which has been particularly important since the 1930s is the *import quota.* Here a country specifies how much of a particular commodity may be imported from abroad, and perhaps even how much may be imported from particular countries. This goes naturally with a system of exchange control, which requires importers to come to the government for their foreign exchange requirements. Exchange controls and import quotas are found particularly in the less developed countries of Asia and Latin America. But the United States also uses quota restrictions on oil, copper, lead, zinc, and certain agricultural products.

over the tariff today thus turn mainly on its price and production effects rather than on its revenue effect.

A tariff is a tax on imports. The importer is required to pay either a certain percentage of the value of the imported article (an *ad valorem* duty), or so many dollars and cents per physical unit imported (a *specific* duty). The effect of imposing a tariff on a product which is produced both in the United States and abroad may be illustrated by Figure 17–1. D and S are the demand and supply curves for the product in the United States. P is the "world price," the price at which the article can be imported from other countries. Under free trade, this will be the prevailing price in the United States. By seeing where the price line intersects the U.S. supply curve, we discover that Q of the product will be produced in the United States, American consumption will be Q_3, and $Q_3 - Q$ will be imported.

Now suppose the United States imposes a specific duty of PP_1 per unit. Importers must now pay the world price plus the tariff and will have to sell the product in the United States for P_1. Going across to D, we see that U.S. consumption of the product will decline from Q_3 to Q_2. U.S. production, however, will increase from Q to Q_1, which was

FIGURE 17–1
Effect of a tariff on imports

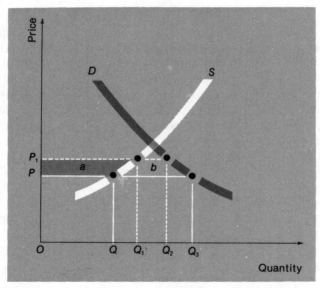

With free trade (solid lines) the product sells in the United States at the world price P. U.S. production is Q, consumption is Q_3, and imports are $Q_3 - Q$. A tariff of PP_1, per unit (dotted lines) raises the price of P_1. Consumption falls to Q_2, home production increases to Q_1, and imports fall to $Q_2 - Q1$.

presumably the point of putting on the tariff. With U.S. production up but consumption down, imports will fall to $Q_2 - Q_1$.

Tariffs: The gainers and losers

Who gains and who loses from the tariff? The direct effects are:

1. There is a *revenue* effect, an increase in the customs receipts of the government. This is equal to the rectangle b (Q_1Q_2 units of imports $\times PP_1$ tax per unit). This is of course not a gain from a national standpoint, since the customs revenues are paid by buyers of the product.

2. There is a *protective* effect, shown by the increase in domestic production from Q to Q_1. Some American producers who would not have been able to cover costs and survive at a price of P are able to keep going at P_1.

3. There is a *consumption* effect, shown by the reduction in sales of the product from Q_3 to Q_2.

4. There is a *redistribution* effect, a transfer of income from consumers to companies in the industry. The marginal producer, located right at Q_1, has production costs of P_1 and is just able to survive with the tariff protection. But everyone else in the industry is receiving more than he needs. The increased profit to the industry is shown by the shaded area a.

5. There is likely also to be an *export* effect. Putting a U.S. tariff on some item coming from abroad will probably lead other countries to retaliate by higher duties against U.S. exports. Even if there is no direct retaliation, a drop in U.S. payments for imports means that other countries have fewer dollars with which to buy goods from us. Unless we are willing to lend or give away more abroad, our exports will have to fall. Thus, against the increase in employment and profits in the protected industry one must set a drop in employment and profits in other U.S. industries which send part of their product abroad. Nor is this an even exchange from a national point of view. The export industries which are hurt are presumably those in which we have comparative advantage, while the protected industry presumably does not have comparative advantage in the world market. If it did, it would need no protection.

The effects may be summarized as follows: The industry which receives the tariff protection is benefited, other American industries engaged in export trade are hurt; total national output is reduced by a diversion of resources from products in which the United States has comparative advantages to products in which it does not; and consumers of the protected product get less of it at higher prices.

These effects are unfavorable on balance. Why, then, is tariff protection so widely practiced? Surely there must be some arguments in its favor. In reasoning about this, one must distinguish carefully between the interests of a particular industry and the interests of the national economy. A tariff is normally beneficial to producers of the protected product, and the higher the tariff, the better, up to the point at which imports are excluded entirely. Tariff increases enable the domestic industry to produce more, charge higher prices, earn more money, and employ more people. So it is not surprising that industries subject to import competition should lobby energetically for tariff protection.

Specious reasoning begins when an industry sets out to prove that "what's good for us is good for the country." This is typically done by focusing solely on benefits to the industry while ignoring or denying the injury to consumers and exporters. The argument is often supported by pseudoscientific reasoning. It is argued, for example, that it is fair to impose a tariff sufficient to equalize costs of production at home and abroad. If an item costs 40 cents to produce in the United States and can be bought abroad for 20 cents, then there should be a 20-cent tariff to "maintain fair competition between American and foreign producers."

This so-called scientific tariff principle has actually been written into law in some cases. Consider its implications. What is the standard for determining cost of production in the United States? Should one take the costs of the most efficient existing producer or of the least efficient producer? Should one consider the potential costs of new producers who might be able to survive at a higher price? A glance at Figure 17–1 shows that by going up the supply curve far enough one can justify any tariff one wants to, including a tariff high enough to exclude imports completely. In effect, the scientific tariff advocates are saying that whenever foreign producers can undersell *any* American company in *any* product, their advantage should immediately be canceled out by tariff duties. Whatever else this may be, it certainly is not scientific. It denies the principle of comparative advantage and in fact denies the possibility of any profitable trade among nations.

Tariffs: The national interest

If self-interested arguments are to be discounted, what about the national interest? Are there circumstances in which tariff protection can be justified on national grounds? There are several:

1. National defense.   Adam Smith, pioneer advocate of freer trade, nevertheless asserted that "defense is of more importance than opulence." The United States would be ill-advised to import long-range missiles or missile components. It can be argued that we need to preserve some watch production because watchmakers' skills are readily transferable to fuses and other military items. But one must not stretch the national defense argument too far. Everything which we might want to use in wartime need not be made within the United States in peacetime. Some stockpiling is feasible, and some foreign sources are reasonably secure. Maintaining an adequate number of watchmakers does not necessarily involve maintaining a large watch industry. We have many millions of trained military reservists, although only a fraction of this number are under arms at any one time. It shouldn't be any harder to organize a "watchmakers' reserve" than a naval air reserve.

2. Infant industries. This famous argument for protection, expounded in Alexander Hamilton's *Report on Manufactures,* has always been popular in countries in the early stages of industrialization. The argument is that a new industry may be relatively inefficient in its early years, while plants are being expanded to optimum size, labor and management skills developed, and market connections established. During this period it is vulnerable to low-cost competition from more experienced foreign producers. If it can be sheltered for a time by tariff barriers, however, efficiency can be raised to the point where it can compete with foreign producers on a free basis. The "infant" will have grown up, and the protective walls can be dismantled. This argument was used to justify protecting American manufactures against foreign (primarily British) competition during the early 19th century. It is widely used today by the countries of Asia, Africa, and Latin America which are trying to push industrialization in the face of competition from more advanced industrial countries.

This is an argument for *temporary* or transitional protection for industries which, when fully developed, will turn out to have comparative advantage in the countries concerned. It is not an argument for *permanent* protection. It is not applicable to industries which will never be able to attain a competitive position in world markets. Its application in a particular case, therefore, requires careful investigation of prospective costs and benefits.

Even in valid cases, there is the practical difficulty that the infants often refuse stubbornly to grow up. They get used to the high prices and profits guaranteed by the tariff wall and fight against its removal, even when fully capable of standing on their own feet. Protection which was supposed to be temporary thus often turns out to be permanent. Tariffs with a terminal date, or tariffs shrinking at a specified rate, might provide an answer to this problem.

Where temporary support to an industry seems desirable, a tariff is not the most efficient method of support.[2] A tariff raises prices, distorts consumer choice, and reduces consumption of the product. A direct subsidy to domestic producers would not have these undesirable effects. Look back at Figure 17–1. In the absence of a tariff (which we have

---

[2] For a demonstation of this point, see Harry G. Johnson, "Optimal Trade Intervention in the Presence of Domestic Distortions," in *Trade, Growth, and the Balance of Payments,* eds. R. Caves, H. G. Johnson, and P. Kenen (Skokie, Ill.: Rand McNally, 1965).

now decided *not* to impose), price will be *P,* consumption Q_3, and domestic production *Q.* Now domestic producers are given a subsidy of so many dollars per unit of output. This shifts *S* to the right, because producers can afford to supply any given quantity at a lower price than before. So *S* will intersect the price line farther to the right. The quantity supplied by domestic producers will rise and imports will fall, with consumption remaining unchanged. If the subsidy is large enough to shift *S* so that it intersects *D* at price *P,* domestic producers will be able to supply all of domestic demand.

Despite their disadvantages, tariffs continue to be the most common protective device. The argument for a tariff can be made to sound plausible, and the subsidy which it grants is indirect and concealed. A direct subsidy is more vulnerable to political attack.

3. Terms of trade. A country which is a large buyer of a certain product can sometimes alter the price to its advantage by imposing an import duty. Suppose the United States is the sole importer of coffee and Brazil the sole exporter. Suppose, further, that coffee supply in Brazil is completely inelastic. Coffee growers bring the same amount to market regardless of price. If the United States now imposes an import tax of 10 cents a pound, this will leave the price to U.S. consumers unchanged, but it will lower the price received by Brazilian producers by 10 cents. The Brazilians bear the full brunt of the duty while the U.S. Treasury gets the revenue. (Verify this if you wish by sketching a supply-demand diagram.)

Even if conditions were not this extreme—the United States simply the major importer, Brazil the major supplier, supply highly inelastic rather than completely inelastic—the United States could gain something from this sort of maneuver. This would not be regarded as a gentlemanly act by the Brazilians, however, and might lead to economic retaliation. It can scarcely be advocated as good national policy, particularly for an economically powerful nation such as the United States.

4. Antidepression measures. It was shown in Part One that if the United States were suffering from depression and if it could cut its imports without anyting happening to its exports, the result would be a rise in U.S. production and employment. On a commensense basis, "money which was being spent abroad will now be spent at home." Demand for domestic products will rise, and employment will rise with them. This works hardship on other countries, of course, since the reduction of imports by the United States will throw people out of work abroad. For this reason it is often termed a "beggar-my-neighbor" policy. It is doubtful also whether the policy is feasible for any length of time. Other countries would certainly retaliate to cut their imports from the United States, so that any advantage we might gain would be of short duration.

5. Making haste slowly. On a different plane stands arguments which relate not to imposing a tariff in the first instance but to removing it where it has been long established. Lowering a tariff amounts to forcing down product prices and may have a disruptive effect on the industry concerned. Plants may be closed down and workers faced with the necessity of moving to other jobs. These resource transfers are painful, and the economists' argument that it is all for the general good is likely to be received with ill grace. This is simply an argument for gradualism. Tariffs should be lowered gradually and judiciously—preferably during prosperity rather than depression, with due notice to all concerned and with advance planning to help plants and labor to convert to new uses.

THINK ABOUT THIS

1. Producers of goods for which the United States is a large exporter (farm products, jet aircraft, computers, machinery) typically favor reducing tariff rates throughout the world by negotiation with other countries. Producers of goods for which the United States is a large importer (textiles, clothing, shoes, steel) typically argue for higher tariffs or quota restrictions on imports. Do these opposing views cancel out? Or is one position stronger than the other?
2. Suppose tariffs and other import restrictions were completely eliminated, here and in other countries. What economic consequences would you predict?

ISSUES IN AMERICAN TRADE POLICY

Tariffs and quotas

Throughout the 19th and early 20th century, the United States was a strongly protectionist country. The peak of this era was reached with the Smoot-Hawley Act of 1930, which raised tariffs to an all-time high and led to retaliation by many other countries.

The Roosevelt victory of 1932 brought a sharp shift toward freer trade accompanied by a transfer of tariff-making authority from Congress to the executive branch. The Trade Agreements Act of 1934 authorized the president to negotiate with other countries for mutual lowering of tariff barriers, reductions by the United States to be matched by concessions of equal value by the other party. This act has been renewed and amended several times, most recently in 1974. Under it there have been a half-dozen rounds of negotiations with our major trading partners, which have gradually reduced tariffs to a low level.

These negotiations are carried on within the framework of the General Agreement on Tariffs and Trade (GATT). This is a multilateral agreement dating from 1948, which has been subscribed to by about 70 countries.

These include all the Western industrial nations, plus some of the larger less-developed countries, plus Poland, Czechoslovakia, and Yugoslavia from eastern Europe.

The main feature of GATT is the most-favored-nation principle: If a country makes a tariff reduction to any member of GATT, this is extended automatically to all other members. There is also an agreed-upon code of rules governing trade, designed to discourage quantitative import restrictions and export subsidies. GATT headquarters in Geneva, and the conferences held under its auspices, provide a forum for international discussion of trade matters.

Every few years, when the time seems propitious, there is a general conference or round of trade negotiations. Delegates come from each member country with lists of the tariff concessions they are prepared to make and with ideas of what concessions they would like to get in return. They then settle down for prolonged negotiation between pairs of countries over particular commodities. How much a country will concede to another country in these discussions is influenced by the fact that what it does for one it must do for all. Finally, at the end of the round, GATT compiles and publishes the new tariff schedules.

The United States is represented in these negotiations by the U.S. trade representative, an important official with a sizable staff, who is responsible to the president. The representative's actions are discussed with officials of the State Department and the Commerce Department, but this individual is not subordinate to them.

U.S. trade policy is defined in the Trade Reform Act of 1974. This is a complicated blend of trade-promoting and protectionist features, with the latter more prominent than in earlier legislation.

Following international negotiations, the president can abolish any tariff that is now 5 percent or less and can reduce any tariff now above 5 percent by three fifths. Thus, a 20 percent tariff could be reduced to 8 percent. He can also negotiate to alter or repeal nontariff barriers to trade, such as import quotas, in return for comparable concessions by foreign countries. Any agreements on nontariff barriers, however, must be submitted to Congress for approval.

The act authorizes the United States to join with other industrial countries in reducing duties to zero for many products from the less developed countries, but it also contains certain restrictions. A long list of items, such as shoes and textiles, cannot be granted zero duties if they are found to be "import sensitive." Countries joining cartels which restrict supplies to the United States are also barred from the new concessions. This provision was aimed at members of OPEC and at similar groups which may be formed in the future.

The act makes it easier for groups of workers to make a case that they have lost their jobs because of import competition. Claims for assistance, which previously went to the Tariff Commission, will now go to the presumably more sympathetic secretary of labor. If the scretary approves, the workers will be eligible for cash payments, retaining, and other benefits larger than those provided under previous law. Adjustment assistance is also made available to individual companies and, for the first time, to entire communities which can show that they have been damaged by import competition.

Two important protectionist features of the Trade Reform Act should be noted. It is substantially easier than before for domestic industries to make a case before the Tariff Commission (now renamed the United States International Trade Commission) that they have been injured by imports. If there is a finding of injury, the president is allowed some discretion in granting relief, including import restrictions. A further provision gives the president new powers to retaliate, by import restrictions, against countries that discriminate against U.S. trade. He is authorized, in a sense, to bargain upward as well as downward.

Some industries in which we no longer have comparative advantage— textiles, clothing, boots and shoes, radio and television sets, and other electronic products—have long suffered from import competition and have lobbied for increased protection. This can't take the form of raising tariff rates, since these are set by international agreement. Nor is it supposed to involve compulsory quotas on imports, which are forbidden by GATT rules. So what we have done is to negotiate "voluntary" quotas on imports of textiles, garments, TV sets, and some other products from Japan. Taiwan, Hong Kong, South Korea, and other Asian sources. These are voluntary in name only, because in the background is the threat that if other countries will not agree to limit their exports to us, legal import quotas will be imposed from our side, with or without GATT approval.

In addition to these long-standing pressures for protection, there have been pressures recently from the powerful steel and automobile industries. American automobile producers were slow in responding to the shift of demand toward smaller, more fuel-efficient cars, and this opened the door to large-scale imports of small cars from Japan and Europe. Imports have now carved out about 25 percent of the market, and this percentage seems unlikely to drop despite the belated move toward small cars by American companies. So the companies, supported by the United Automobile Workers, have urged that the United States negotiate voluntary quotas on imports, especially from Japan. In the spring of 1981, the Japanese government agreed to restrict auto exports to the United States, and this quota system was still in effect in 1984.

Basic steel imports, mainly from Europe and Japan, have been running at 15 to 20 percent of U.S. consumption, leading to layoffs and plant closings in U.S. steel mills. So the steel producers have also pressed strongly for protection. The Carter administration devised an ingenious system of minimum prices, called trigger prices, for specified steel products. Any foreign producer offering steel below these prices can be held guilty of "dumping" on the American market and subjected to a special import tax. This price floor enables U.S. companies to set their own prices at a profitable level.

The recent trend, then, has been toward creeping protectionism, taking the form mainly of import quotas rather than increases in tariff rates. But it is easy to show that the two are equivalent in economic effect. Both mean higher prices to consumers and higher profits for U.S. producers. Our earlier argument that tariff protection involves net economic loss to the nation applies equally to import quotas. They sacrifice national economic interest for the benefit of particular interests.

The effect of import quotas can be illustrated from recent experience in the automobile industry. In 1981, the Japanese government, under pressure from the U.S. government, agreed to limit the number of cars exported to the United States each year. Since the demand curve for Japanese cars was unchanged, the smaller number of cars commanded a higher price. Many buyers were willing to offer dealers a premium of $1,000 to $2,000 above the "sticker price." In addition, the Japanese auto companies, since they could export only so many cars, naturally slanted their exports toward the larger, more heavily equipped, more expensive, and more profitable cars. The substantial increase in the cost of Japanese cars enabled the U.S. companies to mark up their prices, which they did quite energetically. As a result of higher prices, plus rising volume during the 1983–84 recovery, profits of U.S. auto companies were higher than ever before. It seems likely that the United Automobile Workers will demand and obtain a share of these profits through wage increases. Thus, the industry's problems, which have been due partly to wage rates far out of line with manufacturing generally, will not have been solved, and the industry will continue to argue that import protection is essential. Meanwhile, the cost of import quotas to the U.S. consumer is estimated at about $5 billion per year.

THINK ABOUT THIS

U.S. companies frequently complain of unfair price competition from other countries. This was a key issue in the determination of "trigger prices" for imported steel products. So let us ask:

a. Is it unfair for a foreign company to offer goods in the American market at a price below that charged by U.S. producers?

b. Is it unfair for a foreign company to offer goods in the American market at a price below its own cost of production? below cost plus a reasonable profit markup?

c. Is it unfair for a U.S. company to sell goods in the United States below its cost of production? If this is not unfair for a U.S. producer, why should it be unfair for a foreign producer?

Is the United States de-industrializing?

Since the slowdown of economic growth after 1973, and especially during the depressed years 1980–82, there have been complaints that our basic manufacturing industries are withering under the impact of foreign competition and that steps should be taken to reverse this tendency by new types of government assistance. Proposals on this front are often called *industrial policy.*

It is necessary first to get the facts straight. It is quite normal for the composition of GNP to change as per capita income rises. The shift of productive capacity toward service production and away from goods production has been going on for a long time. Thus we should expect industry's contribution to GNP to fall gradually in *percentage* terms. But this is not inconsistent with large increases in *absolute* terms. Between 1950 and 1980, the manufacturing share of GNP did fall slightly, from 24.5 percent in 1950 to 23.8 percent in 1980. In absolute terms, however, manufacturing output rose by 170 percent. Manufacturing employment rises a good deal less rapidly than manufacturing output because of continuing technical progress. Employment rose by about one third, from 15.2 million workers in 1950 to 20.3 million in 1980.

Between 1980 and 1982, both manufacturing output and employment dropped substantially. This was due partly to worldwide recession, which reduced demand for manufactures both at home and abroad. In addition, a sharp rise in the value of the dollar penalized U.S. exports by making them more expensive in other currencies and stimulated imports by making them cheaper in the United States. These factors, however, are reversible rather than built in for all time to come.

What has mainly been happening in U.S. manufacturing is not a general decline but rather a shift in the relative importance of different branches of manufacturing. It is useful to classify manufacturing industries into (1) high-technology industries, which are characterized by relatively high employment of scientists and engineers and large R&D expenditures; (2) labor-intensive industries, such as clothing, footwear, and furniture; (3) capital-intensive industries, which produce standardized products and use a mature technology, such as steel and automobiles; and (4) resource-intensive industries, such as food products, lumber, paper, and petroleum.

While output in all these categories has been growing, it has grown most rapidly in category (1). Between 1960 and 1980, the high-technology share of manufacturing output rose from 27 to 38 percent. Further, this was due mainly to shifts in domestic demand rather than in foreign trade.[3] Between 1970 and 1980, domestic demand for high-technology products rose by 55 percent, while demand growth for the other three categories

---

[3] For a detailed analysis, see Robert Z. Lawrence, "Is Trade De-Industrializing America?" *Brookings Papers on Economic Activity* No. 1 (1983), pp. 129–61.

was in the range of 21–23 percent. Even the much-publicized difficulties of steel and automobiles are due mainly to a drop in U.S. demand rather than to import competition. The sharp rise in fuel cost brought a demand for fewer and lighter cars, using more aluminum and less steel. The shift to lighter metals for automobiles, household appliances, beverage containers, and other uses has brought a large and permanent reduction in demand for steel.

To a large extent, the foreign trade performance of different industries parallels this differential growth of domestic demand. There is little indication of an across-the-board decline of our comparative advantage in manufacturing. Rather, there is a continuing shift of comparative advantage. We long ago lost comparative advantage in textiles, clothing, shoes, and many other labor-intensive industries. More recently, we have been losing comparative advantage in some capital-intensive or "smokestack" industries, notably steel and automobiles. But in high-technology industries, U.S. comparative advantage is strong and even increasing. In addition to such obvious examples as aircraft, aircraft engines, computers, and heavy industrial machinery, our export performance has been strong in medical and pharmaceutical products, artificial resins and plastics, and professional, scientific, and control instruments.

Rather than a problem of general industrial decay, we face the usual problem of speeding the transfer of resources from declining to expanding sectors of the economy. The necessary shifts have perhaps been somewhat larger since 1973 than before that time, but they are not unusual, and the need for novel "remedies" is not clear.

A further question about "industrial policy" is: What does it mean? In particular, does it mean helping winners or bailing out losers?

On the first front, there is a question whether industries in a strong competitive position need special encouragement or support. Nor is it clear that government can select promising industries better than the market is able to do. The oft-cited Japanese Ministry of Trade and Industry (MITI) does gather information about potential growth industries and consults with industry leaders, labor leaders, banks, and outside experts about the best way of developing them. But government's financial contribution through research grants, tax concessions, low-interest loans, and so on is typically small compared with private investment and research expenditures. The record of picking winners and losers is also quite mixed. MITI has picked some industries that turned out to be winners but picked others (aluminum smelting, petrochemicals) that ended up as losers. It missed some big winners and it also picked industries which would have become winners without any help. In particular, the automobile, motorcycle, and consumer electronics industries became successes with little government aid. What the Japanese government mainly does is to maintain a generally favorable climate for private investment, through low profits taxation and other probusiness measures.

As regards losers such as steel, government might help to systematize the scaling-down of capacity which is occurring in any case. Antitrust restrictions on mergers might be relaxed, recognizing the fact that competitive pressure now comes mainly from abroad. In Japan, MITI has been successful in reducing excess capacity in a number of declining industries. The objective, however, should be to restructure and shrink the industry, rather than simply to keep it afloat through public subsidies; and restructuring should mean that capital owners and workers bear part of the cost.

THINK ABOUT THIS

1. What can government legitimately do to ease the competitive problems of industries such as steel and automobiles? What should workers, owners, and managers in these industries be asked to do in return?
2. What things should government *not* do in such cases? For example, should present automobile import quotas be continued?

East-West trade

Trade between the communist and noncommunist countries fell to a low ebb during the tensions aroused by the Korean War, but since that time it has increased rapidly. Exports to the communist countries from other countries rose from $1.4 billion in 1953 to about $70 billion in 1979.

The United States participated only slightly in this expansion. Our exports to the communist countries are far less than those of Germany, France, Britain, Canada, and Japan. One reason is that many American congressmen and congresswomen have been cool or hostile to commercial contacts with the communist countries. Their view has been that to sell to these countries or buy from them will strengthen their economies and that this is harmful to the United States. For products of direct military usefulness this view is doubtless valid, and there is a tacit agreement among the Western countries not to supply these products. But for consumer goods and capital goods in general, there seems no obvious reason why exchange of goods with a communist country should benefit their economy more than it benefits ours. In any event, these goods are normally available from other Western countries, which do not share our view of the harmful effects of trade. So we do not succeed in denying these goods to the communist world but simply penalize our own exporters and importers.

U.S. trade with the communist countries increased somewhat during the 70s, under the influence of détente with the USSR and the opening up of relations with China, but it is still subject to the ups and downs of political relations. Trade with the USSR is hampered by the fact that its exports to the United States have not been granted most-favored-nation status, which makes them subject to higher tariffs than imports from other countries. Congress has refused to grant equality of treatment to imports from the USSR unless that country will modify its policies concerning Jewish emigration, and the USSR has resisted this demand as an infringement on national sovereignty. More recently, the cooling of relations with the USSR following its invasion of Afghanistan has led to some discouragement of trade.

Trade with China has expanded rapidly in percentage terms but is small in absolute amount. China has a high demand for imports of machinery and other requirements for industrialization, as well as grain to supplement its own agricultural production. But its capacity to supply acceptable export products is still limited, and it is reluctant to go heavily into debt. Unlike the USSR, however, China has become a member of the World Bank and the International Monetary Fund and has begun to accept loans from those organizations.

THE UNITED STATES AND THE THIRD WORLD: SOME KEY ISSUES

Most of the world's population lives in the hundred or so countries which are variously described as "less developed countries" (LDCs), "third-world countries," or "countries of the South." These countries are extremely varied. They vary in size from Caribbean islands with 20,000 people to India with 600 million. Some of the small countries export half or more of their national output, while the largest LDCs may export only 5 to 10 percent. In terms of GNP per capita, some countries, such as those in tropical Africa, are very poor and almost entirely agricultural. But others, such as Mexico, Brazil, Argentina, and Chile, are medium-income, medium-industrialized countries. Some LDCs, mainly in Latin America and Southeast Asia, have experienced rapid economic growth since 1950. Others have stood still, raising output at roughly the same rate as population growth, and a few have been shipping backward.

Since 1973, there has been a further distinction between the OPEC countries and nonoil-producing LDCs. The OPEC countries have large revenues from oil exports. The nonoil LDCs, on the other hand, have been made even worse off by OPEC's success, since they have to import oil at greatly increased prices. This section deals only with the nonoil countries.

A key fact of life for the LDCs is the necessity to import. Since they are at an early stage of industrial development, they import many consumer goods, including even food in some countries. In addition, the effort to modernize and industrialize the economy requires imports of machinery, transport equipment, construction materials, chemicals and fertilizers, fuels, industrial raw materials, and intermediate products. In the more successful LDCs, imports are rising at 5 to 10 percent per year.

The money to pay for these imports has to come either from exports or from capital transfers from the richer countries—loans from the World Bank and other international agencies, loans and grants from national aid agencies such as the Agency for International Development (AID), short-term export credits and bank loans, and long-term investment by multinational corporations. Exports are much the most important source of funds. In 1982, total exports of the nonoil LDCs amounted to $255.5 billion. Net capital transfer—that is, the difference between total new loans and grants on the one hand, and LDC obligations for interest and repayment on old loans—amounted to $93.2 billion. More than half of this, some $56.6 billion, came from private sources. The remaining $34.3 billion was "official" transfers from governments and international agencies.[4]

In dollar terms, then, trade is three times as important as aid. So we begin with trade issues. What would the LDCs like the United States and other industrial countries to do in the trade area? Mainly two things: (1) cooperate in schemes to ensure stable and fair prices for LDC exports of primary products and (2) give preferential treatment in our market to the growing LDC exports of manufactured goods. A word on each of these points.

Pricing of primary products

The importance of exports has already been stressed. The next step is to recognize that exports, for the time being, means mainly exports of primary products. A few countries, mainly small countries in Southeast Asia and a few of the Latin American countries, are beginning to have sizable exports of manufactures. Most LDCs, however, still derive 80 percent or more of their foreign exchange from primary products.

The main problem is that revenue from primary exports fluctuates a great deal from year to year. Prices fluctuate widely, as we know from recent experience with coffee, cocoa, and sugar; there are also quantity fluctuations because of crop failure in some years and bumper crops in others. These variations in revenue, which can be sudden and unexpected, are obviously awkward. A country that was counting this year on $100 million of imports, much of this earmarked for ongoing development projects, and then finds its foreign exchange earnings cut suddenly to $50 million, is clearly in trouble.

---

[4] *Development Cooperation: 1977 Review* (Paris: Organisation for Economic Cooperation and Development, 1978), p. 172, Table A–9.

A skeptical observer might point out that revenues fluctuate upward as well as downward. There are years when export earnings are abnormally high, and when a prudent government might squirrel away part of the excess in increased foreign exchange reserves, to be drawn on later to cover a downswing of revenues. LDC governments do this to some extent, but there is a natural temptation to let imports rise when extra money is available, so that not enough reserves are available to cushion major downswings in earnings.

There are two lines of approach to cushioning such downswings. The first is to set up a credit facility from which a country can borrow at least part of the difference between its normal level of foreign exchange earnings and the actual reduced earnings in a particular year. The money is then repaid in some subsequent year when earnings rise above the normal level. The general effect is the same as if the LDC had itself set side reserves in a boom year and then drawn on these in a poor year. But governments being as they are, this type of plan is more realistic: A government is first allowed to get into debt, and is then put under pressure to repay the debt. The viability of the scheme depends, of course, on "normal earnings" being estimated at a realistic rather than an inflated level, and on the country being able to borrow only part of the foreign exchange gap rather than the whole amount.

The International Monetary Fund presently operates this kind of loan program but on a limited scale which falls well short of stabilizing foreign exchange earnings. There is agreement that the program could be expanded with benefit to all concerned, though there is disagreement on who should put up the money and take the risk of losses and on what constitutes reasonable loan terms. One advantage of an expanded loan program is that it might reduce pressure for stabilization of *individual commodity prices,* which is a trickier and more dubious proposal.

The traditional way of stabilizing the price of a particular primary product is through a *commodity agreement,* sometimes called a *cartel agreement,* among producer countries, binding them not to sell below the agreed price. The OPEC agreement is the most spectacular recent example. But there is a long history of commodity agreements involving tin, rubber, wheat, and coffee. Recently, there have been attempts to form such agreements for copper. bauxite, iron ore, sugar, and a variety of other goods. Some agreements, such as the tin agreement, provide for a price *range* rather than a single price and for a *buffer stock* of the commodity to meet fluctuations in world demand. If demand for tin is falling and the price is threatening to go through the agreed floor, the producing countries divert enough of their output into the stockpile to sustain price at the floor level. Later on, when rising demand has pushed prices up to the agreed ceiling, supplies are taken out of the stockpile to whatever extent is needed to keep prices from going through the ceiling.

The announced objective of such agreements is to prevent burdensome price fluctuations, to *stabilize* the price of the commodity. But stabilize it *at what level?* Lurking in the background is the objective of *raising* the average price of the commodity over the years, as the OPEC case amply demonstrates. The LDCs argue that in the past, prices of primary products have been "too low" relative to the prices they pay for manufacturers from the richer countries, and also that because of continuing inflation in the industrial countries, manufactured goods prices are rising so fast that the primary producers must make an organized effort to keep up. The debate is not unlike the traditional argument between farming and manufacturing interests in the United States or Canada, with the farmers maintaining that they are consistently exploited by the industrial monopolists. The primary producers can never be proven right (or wrong) in any objective sense. Once one departs from the test of the market, what constitutes a fair price becomes a matter of judgments about distributive justice. Still, feelings about fairness are strong; and this has accordingly emerged as a major issue in the "North-South" dialogue.

There are difficulties in maintaining a commodity agreement year after year, and many such agreements have broken down after a time. The main difficulty is that control of price implies control of production. At the price fixed for, say, rubber, only a certain amount of rubber can be sold. This amount is typically less than the participating countries can produce. So the question arises of which countries shall cut back production, and by how much. Even if the countries can agree on this touchy subject, application of production controls within each country may be difficult, particularly where there are many small peasant producers. Moreover, additional countries may begin to produce the product, attracted by the high cartel price. Unless these countries can be persuaded to join the cartel (which may be hard, since they can get the benefit of the high price without joining), they will take over more and more of the market, while members of the cartel will have to cut their production increasingly. At some point, the pressure of excess supply and excess production capacity may force abandonment of the fixed price.

The growth of commodity agreements confronts consumer nations such as the United States with a choice of strategies. We can discourage them, refuse to participate in any way, and hope that the evil creature will go away. This has tended to be the U.S. position in the past, though most of the other industrial nations have taken a more tolerant view. Alternatively, we may participate along with other consumer nations and use the opportunity to bargain over the level of the fixed price. In the past, most agreements have consisted of producer nations only. But some, including the former wheat agreement and the present coffee agreement, have included both consuming and producing countries. Whatever we do, it seems likely that commodity agreements will grow unless the other option of lending facilities to offset export fluctuations can be expanded.

Manufactured exports from LDCs

Many LDCs, with abundant and cheap supplies of labor, have a potential comparative advantage in labor-intensive manufacturing. We say "potential" because low wage rates do not by themselves mean lower costs of production. Capital costs are often high, management is often inadequate, and labor productivity may be low in the first instance. There is a problem of bringing nascent manufacturing industries up to an efficiency level at which they can compete effectively in world markets. So far only a limited number of countries—Mexico, Brazil, Colombia, South Korea, Taiwan—have made substantial progress in this direction. But there is a large potential in some other Latin American countries and in such Asian countries as Pakistan, India, Malaysia, and Thailand.

As wage rates continue to rise in the richer countries, one should expect that labor-intensive industries will migrate increasingly to labor-surplus countries with lower wage levels. This is in their interest, and also in ours, following the principle of comparative advantage. The United States and other leading industrial countries should be moving gradually out of light manufacturing and concentrating on high-technology products and products requiring large optimum scale. This has in fact been going on for a long time, but one can scarcely expect our textile, clothing, and similar industries to relish the prospect of eventual extinction.

The LDCs would like us to facilitate this transition by allowing their manufactured goods to enter our markets at lower tariff rates than those imposed on similar imports from developed countries, and preferably at zero rates. For better or worse, this idea of preferential tariffs has been largely accepted in the industrialized countries. We noted earlier that the most recent trade agreements act permits the United States to reduce tariffs on LDC products to zero, in concert with other industrial countries. Our nervousness about this, and the strength of the resistance of domestic industries, is indicated by the loophole provision for "import senstive" industries. Only time will tell which is more important in practice—the doughnut or the hole.

"Official" capital transfers

Ever since World War II, the developed industrial countries have been in the "aid business." They lend money directly to LDC governments, channel additional loan money through the World Bank group and other international institutions, and make outright grants on a limited scale. Part of this capital flow is properly regarded as aid, where it consists of grants or "soft loans" with generous interest and repayment terms. Most of it, however, is ordinary commercial lending at close to prevailing rates of interest.

The total flow of "official" capital from the developed capitalist countries has recently been in the range of $30 billion per year. The Soviet Union is in the aid business on a modest scale, and China on a much smaller scale. The Arab oil countries have recently become substantial aid contributors, at a rate of some $6 billion a year, which goes mainly to other Muslim countries.

U.S. activity in this area raises at least two policy issues. First, should this activity be regarded as investment or as charity? Should capital be allocated on the basis of productivity or on the basis of poverty and human need? Should a country which "cannot afford to borrow," that is, which has no reasonable prospect of repayment, receive any funds at all?

A strong argument can be made for productivity as the main criterion. This means allocating capital to countries which have demonstrated the ability to use it effectively. LDCs differ greatly in this respect, depending partly on the quality of political leadership and public administration. One advantage of the productivity approach is that it helps to answer the question: *How much* capital, on a world scale, should be transferred per year via official channels? Answer: As much as can be invested in projects yielding a reasonable rate of return. The charity approach, on the other hand, opens up a bottomless pit for income transfers from richer to poorer countries, with no assurance that this can bring more than a temporary alleviation of poverty in countries which lack internal growth capacity. A country which is really too poor to borrow and which shows no capacity for sustained development should perhaps be allowed to stagnate, as most countries have done through most of history.

A second policy issue is how much of whatever we decide to devote to official lending should be channeled through the World Bank group and other multilateral agencies, and how much should be allocated directly through AID and other U.S. government agencies. The argument for "do it yourself" is, first, that it's our money and should be used in our unfettered discretion. It enables us to decide what kinds of projects, in what countries, shall or shall not be financed. It enables us to tie U.S. aid allocations so that they can be used only for purchase of American goods (a practice used also by most other aid-givers), and this benefits our export trade. Finally, it is often thought that the power to give or withhold funds gives us greater leverage in international politics and enables us to win friends where we need friends. This hypothesis would be hard to test, and it s doubtful that there is much evidence to support it. Gratitude for favors received is not a notable feature of international relations, and the power of the purse has probably earned us as much ill will as goodwill abroad.

Most of what we put into LDC lending, therefore, should probably be channeled through the International Bank for Reconstruction and Development (popularly, the World Bank). This is now the largest single source of development finance, with annual lending of more than $5 billion. It is supported mainly by capital contributions from the Western industrial nations, though it is also authorized to sell its own bonds in the capital market and has done this on a considerable scale. It is a well-managed and businesslike institution, engaged mainly in long-term lending at commercial rates of interest. It has, in fact, accumulated substantial profits up to this point. There is also a soft-loan window for some of the neediest borrowers and a relatively small fund used to finance national development banks which make loans for *private* investment in developing countries.

While we have suggested that aid money should be devoted mainly to interest-bearing loans for productive investment and that outright grants of funds are not constructive, one would not want to rule them out entirely. There are types of assistance, involving mainly transfer of knowledge rather than a physical capital, which are useful and not very expensive. These might well be extended free to countries which are very poor and not creditworthy, in the hope of nudging them gradually toward sustained growth. One example is so-called technical assistance, which involves sending out teams of agricultural scientists, industrial engineers, medical scientists, or whatever to advise LDC governments in their respective fields. This is a constructive activity, which is carried on by developed country aid agencies and also by specialized agencies of the United Nations. Most LDCs are also poorly supplied with high-level technical and professional personnel, and they need to send students abroad on a substantial scale while developing their own university systems. Since we now have considerable slack in our higher educational system, it costs us little in real resource terms to provide scholarships for foreign students and to finance U.S. teachers to spend time teaching overseas.

Another legitimate use of grant money is to finance food transfers to meet famine emergencies. Eventually, of course, there should be a sizable world grain reserve, internationally financed and managed, which could be drawn on in poor crop years. This would not only be in the interest of food-needy nations but also in our interest, since it would smooth out foreign demands on our own grain supply and the sharp price fluctuations which these have caused in the past. There seems general agreement on the need for such a reserve, but steps to put it into operation have been slow.

Private lending and the debt problem

Private capital flows to the LDCs through a variety of channels. There is a certain amount of long-term investment by multinational corporations headquartered in North America, Europe, and Japan. This has aroused political arguments quite out of proportion to its quantitative importance. American multinational corporations invest mainly in other developed capitalist countries. There is limited investment in Latin America, very little in Africa or Asia. Most LDCs offer only a small market, often accompanied by management difficulties and serious political risks.

Most of the private capital flow consists of relatively short-term loans from commercial banks in Europe and the United States. The borrowing needs of the oil-importing LDCs increased rapidly after 1973, as the oil price explosion raised their import bills faster than their export receipts. The commercial banks, their coffers swollen with OPEC deposits, competed to find outlets for this money in the developing world. By the early 80s, the debts of some countries, including Argentina, Mexico, and Brazil, had reached a level which clearly could not be repaid at the rate originally planned. Even interest payments on the debt were consuming an unmanageable percentage of foreign exchange receipts.

What to do? To insist on repayment on schedule would have led to open default, which would have wiped out the capital of some of the lending banks and caused widespread bank failures. One is reminded of the old British saying: "If I lend a man 10 pounds, I own him. If I lend him a million pounds, he owns me."

To avoid outright default, the banks involved in loans to a particular country have typically gotten together and agreed with the borrowing country to "reschedule" the debt, a polite term for saying, "OK, you can pay us later." They have even agreed in some cases to lend new money to cover interest payments on the old debts. The International Monetary Fund has also usually come into the picture with emergency loans to help tide a country over for two or three years. In return, the Fund usually requires that the country improve its economic management—reduce budget deficits, lower the inflation rate, restrain wage increases, control imports, revalue its currency if necessary—to increase its self-sufficiency and reduce future borrowing needs. These austerity measures are naturally unpopular within the country and often lead to serious political turmoil.

To a considerable extent, the debt problem has been postponed rather than solved. The outlook is for continued haggling over repayment terms, a lower rate of new borrowings than has prevailed in the past, and (probably) a lower rate of economic growth in many LDCs than was achieved during the great boom of 1945–73.

THINK ABOUT THIS

1. Should the United States cooperate in price stabilization programs for primary products?
2. Is investment in the LDCs by multinational corporations on balance bene-

ficial or harmful to those countries? Should the U.S. government try to encourage or to restrict such investment?

3. Should U.S. government money be made available for loans to the LDCs? If so, should this be done:

   a. Directly, or through the World Bank group?

   b. At market rates of interest, or at lower rates?

   Assuming that demand for loans will exceed the funds available, how would you allocate funds among countries?

NEW CONCEPTS

tariff, specific
tariff, ad valorem
tariff, "scientific"
tariffs, infant industry argument for
import quota
less developed countries (LDCs)
multinational corporation
lending to LDCs, bilateral

lending to LDCs, multilateral
buffer stocks
commodity agreement
lending to LDCs, "hard" loans
lending to LDCs, "soft" loans
technical assistance
tariff preferences to LDCs

SUMMARY

1. The volume of international trade, after languishing from 1914 to 1945, has experienced a remarkable recovery since 1945. It is still only about 10 percent of world production, but many countries export 20 percent to 30 percent of their output.

2. The United States has shifted over the past century from being a food and raw materials exporter to being mainly an exporter of manufactured goods. Changes in factor supplies and technical progress have altered our comparative advantage.

3. A tariff is a tax on imports. It raises the price of the product, reduces consumption, and increases the proportion of consumption supplied by domestic producers. By reducing imports, a tariff system also reduces a country's export possibilities. It lowers economic efficiency by diverting resources from products in which the country has comparative advantage to products in which it does not.

4. One can justify temporary support for promising *infant industries* and continuing support for industries which are essential to national defense. In these cases, however, a direct subsidy is economically preferrable to tariff protection.

5. Since 1930, the United States has changed from being a high-tariff

country to being a rather low-tariff country. Average effective tariffs in the United States and other Western countries are now around 10 percent.

6. Important issues in our trade relations with the less developed countries include whether to participate in commodity control agreements and whether to grant tariff preference to LDC exports of manufacturers.

7. In the area of capital transfers, policy issues include: how much to allocate for loans and grants to the LDCs, how much of this should be channeled through the World Bank and other international organizations, and what criteria should be used by AID and other U.S. agencies in allocating the amounts under their control.

TO LEARN MORE

Issues of U.S. trade policy are discussed in the references listed under "To Learn More" in Chapter 16. For good discussions of economic relations between the more developed and less developed countries, see Harry G. Johnson, *Economic Policy toward Less Developed Countries* (Washington, D.C.: Brookings Institution, 1967); and Gerald Helleiner, ed., *A World Divided* (New York: Cambridge University Press, 1976).

Glossary of Concepts

Built-in stabilizer the U.S. tax structure reduces the slope of the consumption schedule, hence reduces the multiplier effect of any autonomous change in demand, 121, 223

Business a privately owned producer of goods, 4

Business cycle a term now out of fashion, suggesting periodicity or regularity in business upswings and downswings, 241–44

Business saving, gross retained earnings plus depreciation allowances, 66, 114

C

Capacity, economic rate of output which yields lowest unit cost of production, 202

Capacity, engineering maximum possible rate of output, 202

Capacity utilization actual output rate as a percentage of engineering capacity, 205

Capital machinery, buildings, and other produced means of production, 4

Capital consumption estimated depreciation of the nation's stock of capital goods in a given time period, 54, 72

Capital formation, gross total of new capital goods constructed during a specified period; also termed gross investment, 54

Capital formation, net gross capital formation minus capital consumption; also termed net investment, 54

Capital good a good which yields satisfaction indirectly, through production of other goods, 12

Capitalization procedure for deriving the value of an asset; consists in discounting the expected future income stream yielded by the asset, 175

Change in demand shift of the entire demand schedule to a new position, 35

Change in supply shift of the entire supply schedule to a new position, 42–44

Circular flow flow of income from business to households and back to business for purchase of goods, 4–6

Coincident series an economic magnitude which typically turns up or down at about the same time as total output and employment, 254

Commodity a material good, 3

Commodity agreement agreement among producer nations to control price and/or output of a primary product, 398–99

Comparative advantage expresses the fact that the efficiency of country A, relative to country B, varies from product to product. A country has comparative advantage in products for which its *relative* efficiency is highest, 333

Comparative advantage, as related to domestic demand the argument that manufactured exports tend to be a spillover from successful performance in the domestic market, 346–47

Comparative advantage, as related to factor endowment a country tends to have comparative advantage in products using factors which are relatively abundant and cheap in that country, 347–50

Comparative advantage, as related to scale economies an economically large country tends to have comparative advantage in products for which economies of large-scale production are important, 352

Comparative advantage, as related to technological leadership a country in which a new product is first developed will retain comparative advantage in that product for some time, 346, 350–52

Comparative advantage, revealed use of actual exports as an indicator of comparative advantage, 354–56

Constant money growth rule principle that supply of money should be increased at a constant percentage rate, 173

Consumer price index based on prices of goods bought at retail by urban consumers, 56

Consumption schedule, household amount which would be spent by a household at alternative rates of disposable income, 88–91

Consumption schedule, long-run observed statistical relations between annual data on disposable income and consumption expenditure, 94–95

Consumption schedule, national amount which would be spent by all households at alternative rates of disposable income, 91–92

Crowding out effect possibility that increased government borrowing might, by raising interest rates, reduce private borrowing, 232–33

Currency appreciation increase in the relative value of a national currency, under a flexible exchange rate system, 368

Currency depreciation decline in the relative value of a national currency, under a flexible exchange rate system, 368

Discount rate rate charged by a Federal Reserve bank for loans to member banks, 144–48

Double-counting a problem that arises because the value of inputs to production is included in the value of output; can be avoided by totaling only the value of final output, 54–55, 73

Downswing a pervasive downward movement in output and employment, 242

D

Debt management managing the sale of new federal securities to repay owners of maturing securities and to cover budget deficits, 127, 129, 134, 235

Decision lag time required to reach a policy decision after relevant information is available, 262

Deflation decline in the average price level; also refers to the technique of adjusting for price changes by use of a price index, 76

Demand a schedule of quantities which would be purchased at alternative prices, at a moment of time, 30–33

Demand deposit checking account; funds withdrawable on demand, 127, 129, 134

Demand schedule, for a currency relates the price of a foreign currency in terms of domestic currency to the quantity of that currency which will be demanded, 363

Dependent variable an economic quantity whose behavior is to be explained or predicted, 21

Deposit contraction results from an excess of loan repayments to commercial banks over new loans, 141

Deposit expansion results from an excess of new commercial bank loans over loan repayments, 137

Depreciation allowance for the wearing out, over a specified period, of capital goods existing at the beginning of the period; also termed capital consumption, 54, 72

Depression a severe decline in output and employment, not observed since 1940, 242

Devaluation reduction in the relative value of a national currency under a fixed exchange rate system, 369

E

Econometric forecasting employs behavioral relations (equations) linking many variables in the economy to obtain short-term projections of the future, 257–58

Economic fluctuation a broad upward or downward movement in output and employment, pervading most sectors of the economy, 241–44

Economic growth rate of increase in GNP per capita, 308–9

Economic model a simplified representation of an economy, or some part of an economy, 3, 16, 21–22

Economic prediction derived from an economic model and conditional on the features of the model, 21–22

Economic welfare, measure of the effort to adjust GNP data to arrive at a more meaningful indicator of changes in welfare per capita, 309

Equilibrium a state of balance which will continue until disturbed by some outside event, 43, 47

Equilibrium analysis, general mutual determination of price-output equilibria in a number of interrelated markets, 49

Equilibrium analysis, partial determination of price-quantity equilibrium in one market, assuming unchanged conditions in all other markets, 49

Equilibrium, full requires equilibrium in both the goods and the money market, 185

Equilibrium, goods market see *aggregate equilibrium,* 185

Equilibrium, money market exists when desired money holdings equals the amount of money in existence, 185

Equilibrium output that rate at which total expenditure on output equals total value of output, 95–96

Equilibrium price price at which quantity demanded and quantity supplied are equal, 40–41

Equilibrium quantity quantity demanded and supplied in a market at the equilibrium price, 40–41

Ex ante quantities planned or intended consumption, investment, etc., at the *beginning* of a time period, 107

Exchange rate the price of one currency in terms of another, 365

Exchange rates, fixed a system under which central banks intervene in the foreign exchange market to maintain fixed exchange rates, 359, 369, 373–74, 378

Exchange rates, flexible a system under which exchange rates are allowed to fluctuate in response to market forces, 373–78

Ex post quantities actual or realized consumption, investment, etc., over a certain period, calculated at the end of the period, 107

Final output goods destined for direct use rather than for further processing, 55

Fine tuning an effort to steer aggregate demand and output toward a target level through monetary and fiscal instruments, 262, 275–76

Fiscal dividend the federal net tax schedule is such that tax receipts rise faster than GNP as the economy grows, 228

Fiscal drag the U.S. net tax schedule brakes economic expansion, as well as recession, 228–29

Fiscal policy use of tax and expenditure changes to influence aggregate demand, 224

Fiscal program a combination of an expenditure level and a net tax schedule, 224

Fixed rule a rule for monetary or fiscal policy, such as constant growth rate of money supply or balanced budget at high employment, which remains unchanged for long periods, 262, 275

Free good a good sufficiently plentiful to satisfy everyone's wants at zero price, 4

Full employment strictly, a situation in which there is no unused production capacity. More commonly, defined as compatible with a specified (small) amount of unused capacity, 104–5

F

Factor price equalization theorem under simplified conditions, trade between two countries with different factor endowments will tend to equalize factor price ratios in the two countries, 349

Factor of production labor, land, and material instruments used in production, 4

Federal debt, net total federal debt minus securities held in federal trust accounts, 234

Federal debt, privately held net federal debt minus securities held by Federal Reserve banks, 234–35

Federal debt, total U.S. government obligations, wherever held, 234

Federal funds market market in which a bank needing additional reserves can borrow deposits at the Fed from a bank with excess reserves, 147–48

Federal funds rate interest rate on loans in the federal funds market, 164

G

Gold exchange standard a system under which international reserves consist of gold plus "key currencies," 370–71

Gold standard a system under which international reserves consist of gold bullion which is transferable among countries, 370–71

Good anything which yields satisfaction to the user, 3–4

Government expenditure government purchases of goods and services, does not include transfer payments, equal to government output, 113

Gross national product, constant dollars national output adjusted for price changes since some base period, 58, 60

Gross national product, current dollars national output valued at prices prevailing during the period in question, 58–60

H

High employment exists when unemployment is at the NAIRU rate, 204–5

High-employment fiscal surplus estimated federal budget surplus (or deficit), under a specified fiscal program, at a specified (high) level of capacity utilization, 225–26

High-employment zone output rates above the NAIRU rate but below maximum capacity, 202, 205

High-powered money bank reserves plus currency in the hands of the public; same as monetary base, 150–52

Human capital productive skills developed through education and job training, 308, 319

I

Import quota a restriction on the quantity of a good which may be imported, *in toto* or from specific countries, 383, 390

Income redistribution, through inflation in an inflationary period some incomes rise faster than others, producing a redistribution of real purchasing power, 216

Income velocity of money number of times per year the average dollar is spent on final goods, 171

Incomes policy efforts to restrain the rate of wage and price increase by some combination of persuasion, incentives, and compulsion, 286, 299, 301–4

Independent variable an economic quantity regarded as causal, as explaining the behavior of some dependent variable, 21

Indexing automatic adjustment of wage rates, interest rates, or other prices to changes in the general price level, 297

Induced change in spending a change in planned spending resulting from a change in income, 101

Induced investment investment induced by increased demand, 245–48

Inflation rise in the average price level, 194

Inflation, anticipated if inflation rate during a period equals the rate expected at the beginning of the period, inflation is fully anticipated, 215

Inflation, cost (or sellers') inflation arising from an effort by sellers (of goods or labor) with market power to increase their share of national income, 195

Inflation, demand inflation arising from pressure of aggregate demand on production capacity, 195

Inflation, unanticipated difference between the inflation rate during a period and the rate expected at the beginning of the period, 215

Inflationary bias tendency for a persistent upward trend in the price level, 195–98

Information lag time required for a change in some economic variable to be measured and reported, 262

Injections into the income stream sources of demand for goods other than U.S. consumer demand; includes investment, government purchases, and net exports, 67

Input labor, capital goods, or materials used to produce an output, 4

Inside lag sum of the information lag, decision lag, and application lag, 263

Interest rate rate paid by a borrower to a lender, 154–59, 163

Intermediate output goods which require further processing before reaching the final user, 155

Intermediate target for monetary policy; rate of money supply growth, or rate of interest, or some combination of these, 265

International reserves a means of payment generally acceptable in settlement of balances among countries; as gold, dollars, pounds, SDRs, 359, 370

Inventory change amount of increase or decrease in business inventories during a specified period, 62

Investment capital formation; construction of a capital good, 62

Investment, desired planned investment at the beginning of a year or other time period; an ex ante quantity, 107–8

Investment, realized investment realized at the end of a time period, including undesired inventory change; an ex post quantity, 107–8

Investment schedule amount of gross investment which would be undertaken at alternative rates of GNP, 100

L

Labor   human effort exerted in production, 4

Labor market policy   attempts to reduce structural unemployment through training and other activities, 286

Lagging series   an economic magnitude which typically turns up or down after a turning point in total output and employment, 255

Leading series   an economic magnitude which typically turns up or down in advance of total output and employment, 254

Leakages from the income stream   income not spent on consumer goods; includes personal saving, business saving, and net tax payments, 67–68

Learning curve   the concept that factor productivity is an increasing function of cumulative past output (or investment), 320

Lending to LDCs, bilateral   government-to-government loans, as from United States to India, 397, 400

Lending to LDCs, "hard" loans   interest rates and repayment terms at levels prevailing in the developed countries, 400

Lending to LDCs, multilateral   loans by international organizations, such as the International Bank for Reconstruction and Development, 397, 401

Lending to LDCs, "soft" loans   interest rates lower and repayment terms easier than those prevailing in the developed countries, 400–402

Leontief paradox   statistical finding that U.S. exports are somewhat more *labor* intensive than U.S. imports, contrary to a priori expectations, 349

Less developed countries (LDCs)   countries with relatively low per capita output; includes almost all countries of Asia, Africa, and Latin America, 380

Life-cycle hypothesis   holds that the percentage of income saved by a family is strongly influenced by age of the family head, 94

Liquidity   the quality of being convertible into money at short notice and without risk of loss, 130

Lower turning point   short period during which a downswing ends and an upswing begins, 242

M

Macroeconomics   analyzes relations among economic aggregates, such as GNP, employment, money supply, and price level, 5–6

Managed float   exchange rates are flexible, but central banks intervene to moderate exchange rate movements, 376

Marginal business saving rate   proportion of an additional dollar of GNP income which goes into gross business saving, 115

Marginal efficiency of investment   a schedule showing the expected rate of return on the "last," or least profitable, unit of investment for alternative amounts of potential investment in a given time period, 176–77

Marginal leakage ratio   difference between a change in income and the resulting change in consumption; includes the personal saving, business saving, and net tax leakages, 119–20

Marginal net tax rate   Proportion of an additional dollar of GNP income which goes into net tax receipts, 115

Marginal   propensity   to   consume, (MPC)   proportion of an additional dollar of disposable income which will be spent on consumption, 88

Marginal   propensity   to   save   (MPS)   1–MPC, 88

Marginal utility   satisfaction yielded by the last unit of a good consumed in a specified time period, 31

Market   an area within which buyers and sellers are in such close communication that price tends to be the same throughout the area, 28–29

Market economy   an economy which is coordinated by a network of markets, 4, 9

Markup pricing   price determined by unit cost of production plus a percentage markup, 199

Microeconomics   analyzes details of the economy, typically behavior in a particular market or set of related markets, 5–6

Monetarist   economist who believes that control of money supply is the main tool for economic stabilization, 170

Monetary base   bank reserves plus currency in the hands of the public, 150–51

Monetary policy use of Federal Reserve instruments to control money supply and interest rates, 150–51

Monetary rule proposal that the Federal Reserve System should increase the money supply at a constant percentage rate, 275

Monetizing the debt an increase in government debt financed by purchases of government securities by commercial or Federal Reserve banks, 233

Money, M1 currency in the hands of the public plus demand deposits, 131

Money, M2 M1 plus savings and small time deposits at commercial banks and thrift institutions, 131

Money, demand for desired money holdings of businesses and households; varies with GNP and the rate of interest, 155, 158–59, 163

Money multiplier change in money supply divided by change in the monetary base, 150–51

Multinational corporation a corporation headquartered in one country but which also operates through subsidiaries in one or more other countries, 402–3

O

Okun's law a change in the rate of full-time unemployment is associated with a percentage change in GNP which is about three times as large, 289

Oligopoly few sellers of a good, 198

Open-market operations purchase or sale of federal securities by the Federal Reserve System, 144

Opportunity cost the opportunity cost of a unit of product A consists of the other products which might have been produced with the same resources, 7

Output gap difference between actual and potential output, 287

Output growth, per capita annual percentage rate of increase in GNP per capita, usually averaged over a period of years, 308

Output growth, total annual percentage rate of increase in GNP, usually averaged over a period of years, 308

Output, potential GNP which could be produced at a specified (high) level of capacity utilization, 288–89

Outside lag time required for a policy action to be reflected in spending decisions; also called "impact lag," 263

N

Near-money assets, such as savings deposits, which are convertible into money with little delay or risk, 130

Net export schedule exports minus imports, at alternative rates of GNP, 115

Net national product gross national product minus capital consumption, 54

Net tax receipts total tax receipts minus transfer payments, 113

Neutrality exists when effects of a monetary or fiscal action are spread evenly over individuals and branches of the economy, 263, 272

Nonmarketed output output not sold at a price, notably government output, 54–55, 73

Normative economics analysis of the welfare consequences of alternative government policies, 3, 23–24

P

Paradox of thrift with no change in planned investment, an effort by individuals to increase their saving will reduce the rate of GNP and leave saving unchanged, 105–6, 110

Permanent income hypothesis holds that a family's consumption expenditure depends mainly on its expected level of permanent income, 94

Personal income total income received by households, including transfer payments, 73

Personal saving disposable personal income minus consumption expenditure, 66

Policy analysis analysis of proposals for government action, involving development of policy alternatives and prediction of their probable effects, 22–23

Policy coordination   need for internal consistency in the mix of monetary and fiscal actions, 273–75

Policy ineffectiveness   predictable actions by government are already incorporated in private plans, so occurrence of such actions will have no further effect, 279

Policy mix   different combinations of monetary and fiscal action may have the same effect on aggregate demand, 273–75

Positive economics   analysis of how the economy operates, by use of economic models, logical predictions, and statistical testing, 3

Price   the amount paid for a specified quantity and quality of any good or service, including factor services, 28–30, 45–46

Price ceiling   government-established maximum price, 47

Price elasticity of demand   for a small change in price, e = percentage change in quantity demanded/percentage change in price, 36–37

Price elasticity of supply   for a small change in price, e = percentage change in quantity supplied/percentage change in price, 36

Price index   a measure of the average change in some type of price (such as farm prices, wholesale prices, consumer prices) relative to a base period, 75

Price-level change   increase or decrease in a price index, 54–56

Price support   government-established minimum price, 46–49

Prime rate   interest rate on loans to a bank's most creditworthy customers; other lending rates vary upward from this, 165

Private enterprise economy   an economy in which most productive resources are owned by private businesses, 4

Production   creation or addition of utility to a good, 4

Production possibilities curve   a locus of all combinations of two products which can be produced with the resources available, 8–11

Public good   a good characterized by nonappropriability, nonrivalness in consumption, or both, 5

Pure competition   many sellers (and buyers) of a standardized product; free entrance, no collusion, 45

Q

Quantity demanded   amount which would be purchased at a particular price, at a moment of time, 30–31

Quantity equation   expresses the necessary identity between money payments in a period and the value of goods exchanged, 170

Quantity supplied   amount which would be supplied at a particular price, at a moment of time, 39–40

Quantity theory   an empirical statement that monetary velocity (V) is relatively stable and that changes in money supply (M) are mainly responsible for fluctuations in the price level (P) and output (T), 170–72

R

Rate of return (on a capital good or other asset)   the rate of interest at which the present value of the income yielded by an asset equals the cost of the asset, 175

Rational expectations   individual and business plans are based on full and correct information, including information on future government actions, 279

Rationing   procedure for allocating a good among buyers in a situation where more is demanded than can be supplied at the established price; usually necessitated by existence of a price ceiling, 45, 47–48

Real national output   gross national output in constant dollars, that is, adjusted for price-level change, 56, 58

Recession   a mild downswing in output and employment, 242

Relative income hypothesis   holds that a family's consumption expenditure depends mainly on its income *relative* to other families, rather than on absolute income level, 94

Reserves, bank checking accounts maintained by a commercial bank at other banks, normally (in the U.S.) a Federal Reserve bank, 133

Reserves, excess actual reserves minus required reserves, 137–39, 150

Reserves, required legally required reserves, specified as a percentage of the bank's deposits, 136–39

Retained corporate profits profit after taxes minus dividend payments, 65

Revaluation upward adjustment in the relative value of a national currency, under a fixed exchange rate system, 369

S

Saving, desired planned saving at the beginning of a year or other time period, 107–8

Saving, realized actual saving during the past year, or other completed period, 107–8

Scarcity a good or a factor of production is scarce if, at a zero price, the quantity demanded would exceed the available supply, 3–4, 6–7

Service an intangible good, 3

Shortage excess of quantity demanded over quantity supplied, indicating that price is below equilibrium, 46

Structural deficit deficit which would still exist at high-employment GNP, 228

Supply a schedule of quantities which would be offered at alternative prices, at a moment of time, 37–40

Supply schedule, of a currency relates the price of a foreign currency in terms of domestic currency to the quantity of that currency which will be supplied, 363

Supply shock disturbance of the U.S. price level by events external to the U.S. economy, such as changes in oil prices, grain prices, and exchange rates, 211–13

Surplus excess of quantity supplied over quantity demanded, indicating that price is above equilibrium, 46

T

Tariff, ad valorem an import tax based on *value* of the imported product, 384

Tariff preferences to LDCs proposal that the developed countries should impose lower rates on manufactured imports from the LDCs than those imposed on comparable imports from developed countries, 400

Tariff, "scientific" argument that it is justifiable to impose a tariff equal to the difference between foreign and domestic production costs, 386

Tariff, specific an import tax based on *quantity* of the imported product, 383–84

Tariffs, infant industry argument for argument that a new industry, if given temporary protection, will be able to reduce production costs by experience and become competitive with foreign producers, 387–88

Tax-based incomes policy uses the tax system to reward compliance with a program of income restraint, 305

Tax friction inconvenience of raising tax revenue to pay interest on federal debt, 236

Tax payments, net tax payments minus government transfer payments to indivduals, 236

Technical assistance expert advisers in technical fields, provided free to a LDC by a developed country or an international organization, 402

Technical progress an increase in the quantity of output which can be produced with a given resource input, 10

Technical progress, disembodied technical progress external to labor and capital inputs, 318

Technical progress, embodied technical progress incorporated in labor or capital inputs, 318–19

Technology total of known methods of production at a particular time, 10

Terms of trade definable in several ways; simplest concept is ratio of prices paid by country A for its imports to prices received for its exports, 341, 345

Time deposit savings account; funds withdrawable after specified notice, 130

Total factor input　combined rates of increase in labor and capital inputs, weighted by the share of each in national income, 314

Total factor productivity　rate of increase in output minus rate of increase in total factor input; also called "the residual," 314

Transactions demand　quantity of money demanded for payment purposes, 155–58

Transfer payments　cash payments by government, exclusive of payments for labor services; counted as a negative tax, 12, 113

Unit labor cost　labor cost per unit of output, for the economy; increases at the rate of wage increase minus the rate of increase in labor productivity, 146, 198–99

Upper turning point　short period during which an upswing ends and a down-swing begins, 242

Upswing　a pervasive upward movement in output and employment, 242

Utility　satisfaction arising from consumption; also, satisfaction or dissatisfaction (disutility) arising from work, 31

U

Underlying rate of inflation　rate which will tend to perpetuate itself in the absence of changes in aggregate demand or external supply shocks; approximates the rate of increase in unit labor cost, 199

Unemployment, demand　an excess of unemployed workers over vacant jobs, arising from low level of aggregate demand, 204–5

Unemployment, frictional　unemployment between jobs, arising from lack of instantaneous adjustment in the labor market, 203

Unemployment, nonaccelerating inflation rate of (NAIRU)　unemployment rate below which the inflation rate will tend to rise, 202

Unemployment rate　workers without jobs and actively seeking work, as percentage of labor force; other measures also possible, 200–202

Unemployment, structural　results from a mismatch between workers' qualifications and job requirements, 293

V–Y

Value added　value of output minus materials purchased from other producers, 65

Vintage capital　a measure of capital stock which assumes that newly produced capital goods are more productive than older ones, 318

Vintage labor　a measure of labor input which takes account of improved quality of the labor force, as measured by educational attainment or occupational mix, 319

Wage-price-wage spiral　tendency for the economy to become locked into a circle of mutually reinforcing wage and price increases, 198–99

Wealth redistribution, through inflation　an inflation which has not been generally anticipated produces a redistribution of real wealth in favor of debtors at the expense of creditors, 216

Yield (of a security)　interest or dividend payment divided by the price of the security, 163

Index

This book has been set CAP, in 10 and 9 point Compano, leaded 2 points. Part numbers are 24 point Helvetica Black and part titles are 30 point Helvetica Regular. Chapter numbers are 36 point Helvetica Black and chapter titles are 24 point Helvetica Regular. The size of the type page is 30 by 48 picas.